Communications in Computer and Information Science   1484

More information about this series at http://www.springer.com/series/7899

Mohammad S. Obaidat · Jalel Ben-Othman (Eds.)

E-Business and Telecommunications

17th International Conference
on E-Business and Telecommunications, ICETE 2020
Online Event, July 8–10, 2020
Revised Selected Papers

 Springer

Editors
Mohammad S. Obaidat
University of Jordan
Amman, Jordan

Nazarbayev University
Nur-Sultan, Kazakhstan

Jalel Ben-Othman
Paris 13 University
Villetaneuse, France

ISSN 1865-0929 ISSN 1865-0937 (electronic)
Communications in Computer and Information Science
ISBN 978-3-030-90427-2 ISBN 978-3-030-90428-9 (eBook)
https://doi.org/10.1007/978-3-030-90428-9

© Springer Nature Switzerland AG 2021
This work is subject to copyright. All rights are reserved by the Publisher, whether the whole or part of the material is concerned, specifically the rights of translation, reprinting, reuse of illustrations, recitation, broadcasting, reproduction on microfilms or in any other physical way, and transmission or information storage and retrieval, electronic adaptation, computer software, or by similar or dissimilar methodology now known or hereafter developed.
The use of general descriptive names, registered names, trademarks, service marks, etc. in this publication does not imply, even in the absence of a specific statement, that such names are exempt from the relevant protective laws and regulations and therefore free for general use.
The publisher, the authors and the editors are safe to assume that the advice and information in this book are believed to be true and accurate at the date of publication. Neither the publisher nor the authors or the editors give a warranty, expressed or implied, with respect to the material contained herein or for any errors or omissions that may have been made. The publisher remains neutral with regard to jurisdictional claims in published maps and institutional affiliations.

This Springer imprint is published by the registered company Springer Nature Switzerland AG
The registered company address is: Gewerbestrasse 11, 6330 Cham, Switzerland

Preface

The present book includes extended and revised versions of a set of selected papers from the 17th International Joint Conference on e-Business and Telecommunications (ICETE 2020), held as an online web-based event, due to the COVID-19 pandemic, during July 8–10, 2020.

ICETE 2020 received 182 paper submissions from authors in 46 countries, of which 5% were included in this book. The papers were selected by the event chairs and their selection was based on a number of criteria including the reviews and suggested comments provided by the Program Committee members, the session chairs' assessments, and also the program chairs' global view of all papers included in the technical program. The authors of selected papers were then invited to submit a revised and extended version of their papers having at least 30% new material.

ICETE 2020 is a joint conference aimed at bringing together researchers, engineers, and practitioners interested in information and communication technologies, including data communication networking, e-business, optical communication systems, security and cryptography, signal processing and multimedia applications, and wireless networks and mobile systems. These are the main knowledge areas that define the six component conferences, namely DCNET, ICE-B, OPTICS, SECRYPT, SIGMAP, and WINSYS, which together form the ICETE joint conference.

The papers selected to be included in this book contribute to the understanding of relevant trends of current research on chained transaction protocol automated verification, RF energy harvesting for IoT, the security and complexity of a new variant of the McEliece cryptosystem, business analyst tasks for requirement elicitation, a bit masking technique to enhance covert channel attacks in everyday IT systems, randomized bit-flipping decoders for the design of LDPC and MDPC code-based cryptosystems, an assurance framework and process for hybrid systems, authentication and key management in decentralized secure email and messaging, secure distributed hash-based encryption suited for big data systems, and efficient attribute-based encryption for compartmented and multilevel access structures.

We would like to thank all the authors for their contributions and also the reviewers who have helped to ensure the quality of this publication. We would also like to thank the staff of INSTICC and staff of Springer for their outstanding support.

July 2020

Mohammad S. Obaidat
Jalel Ben-Othman

Organization

Conference Co-chairs

Mohammad Obaidat   Fordham University, USA
Jalel Ben-Othman   Université Sorbonne Paris Nord, France

Program Co-chairs

DCNET

Christian Callegari   RaSS Lab - CNIT, Italy
Soon Xin Ng   University of Southampton, UK

ICE-B

Marten van Sinderen   University of Twente, The Netherlands

OPTICS

Panagiotis Sarigiannidis   University of Western Macedonia, Greece

SECRYPT

Pierangela Samarati   Università degli Studi di Milano, Italy
Sabrina De Capitani di Vimercati   Università degli Studi di Milano, Italy

SIGMAP

Sebastiano Battiato   University of Catania, Italy
Ángel Serrano Sáanchez de León   Universidad Rey Juan Carlos, Spain

WINSYS

Pascal Lorenz   University of Haute-Alsace, France
Adlen Ksentini   Eurecom, France

DCNET Program Committee

Baber Aslam	National University of Sciences and Technology, Pakistan
Shahram Babaie	Islamic Azad University, Iran
Pablo Belzarena	Universidad de la República, Uruguay
Paolo Castagno	University of Turin, Italy
Markus Fiedler	Blekinge Institute of Technology, Sweden
Hiroaki Fukuda	Shibaura Institute of Technology, Japan
Katja Gilly	Miguel Hernandez University, Spain
Francesco Gringoli	University of Brescia, Italy
Pascal Lorenz	University of Haute-Alsace, France
Eliane Martins	Universidade Estadual de Campinas, Brazil
Matteo Sereno	University of Turin, Italy
Giovanni Stea	University of Pisa, Italy
Tatsuya Suda	University Netgroup Inc., USA
Bernd Wolfinger	University of Hamburg, Germany

DCNET Additional Reviewers

Eduardo Grampin	Universidad de la República, Uruguay
Abdul Rauf	University of Sheffield, UK

ICE-B Program Committee

Andreas Ahrens	Hochschule Wismar, University of Applied Sciences, Technology, Business and Design, Germany
Ana Azevedo	Instituto Politécnico do Porto, Portugal
Efthimios Bothos	Institute of Communication and Computer Systems, Greece
Alexandros Bousdekis	National Technical University of Athens, Greece
Wojciech Cellary	Poznan University of Economics and Business, Poland
Chun-Liang Chen	National Taiwan University of Arts, Taiwan, Republic of China
Dickson Chiu	University of Hong Kong, Hong Kong
Ritesh Chugh	Central Queensland University, Australia
Soon Chun	City University of New York, USA
Pierre Hadaya	University of Quebec at Montreal, Canada
Inma Hernández	Universidad de Sevilla, Spain
Carmen Lam	University of Hong Kong, Hong Kong
Abderrahmane Leshob	University of Quebec at Montreal, Canada
Olga Levina	TH Brandenburg, Germany
Yung-Ming Li	National Chiao Tung University, Taiwan, Republic of China

Rungtai Lin	National Taiwan University of Arts, Taiwan, Republic of China
Peter Loos	German Research Center for Artificial Intelligence, Germany
Samaneh Madanian	Auckland University of Technology, New Zealand
Wai Mok	University of Alabama in Huntsville, USA
Daniel O'Leary	University of Southern California, USA
Wilma Penzo	University of Bologna, Italy
Krassie Petrova	Auckland University of Technology, New Zealand
Charmaine Plessis	University of South Africa, South Africa
Pak-Lok Poon	Central Queensland University, Australia
Ela Pustulka-Hunt	FHNW Olten, Switzerland
Manuel Resinas	Universidad de Sevilla, Spain
Fernando Romero	University of Minho, Portugal
Gustavo Rossi	Lifia, Argentina
Jarogniew Rykowski	Poznan University of Economics and Business, Poland
Hassan Sleiman	Renault Group, France
Agostinho Sousa Pinto	Instituto Politécnico do Porto, Portugal
Vesna Spasojevic Brkic	University of Belgrade, Serbia
Riccardo Spinelli	Università degli Studi di Genova, Italy
Zhaohao Sun	Federation University Australia, Australia, and PNG University of Technology, Papua New Guinea
James Thong	Hong Kong University of Science and Technology, Hong Kong
Ben van Lier	Centric, The Netherlands
Alfredo Vellido	Universitat Politècnica de Catalunya, Spain
Hua Wang	Victoria University, Australia

OPTICS Program Committee

Siti Barirah Ahmad Anas	Universiti Putra Malaysia, Malaysia
Saud Al-Anzi	Kuwait Army, Kuwait
Nicola Andriolli	Scuola Superiore Sant'Anna, Italy
Gaetano Assanto	Università degli Studi Roma Tre, Italy
Luis Cancela	ISCTE-IUL, Portugal
C. Chow	National Chiao Tung University, Taiwan, Republic of China
Fred Daneshgaran	California State University, Los Angeles, USA
Marija Furdek	Chalmers University of Technology, Sweden
Marco Genovese	INRIM, Italy
Luis Gonzalez Guerrero	University College London, UK
Habib Hamam	Université de Moncton, Canada
Sang-Kook Han	Yonsei University, South Korea

Xiaolong Hu	Tianjin University, China
Miroslaw Klinkowski	National Institute of Telecommunications, Poland
Tetsuya Miyazaki	National Institute of Information and Communications, Japan
John Moscholios	University of the Peloponnese, Greece
Masayuki Murata	Osaka University, Japan
Syed Murshid	Florida Institute of Technology, USA
Yasutake Ohishi	Research Center for Advanced Photon Technology, Japan
Satoru Okamoto	Keio University, Japan
Jordi Perelló	Universitat Politècnica de Catalunya, Spain
João Rebola	ISCTE-IUL, Portugal
Dan Sadot	Ben-Gurion University, Israel
Ripalta Stabile	Eindhoven University of Technology, The Netherlands
Michela Svaluto Moreolo	Centre Tecnologic de Telecomunicacions de Catalunya, Spain
Marek Trippenbach	University of Warsaw, Poland
Bal Virdee	London Metropolitan University, UK

SECRYPT Program Committee

Massimiliano Albanese	George Mason University, USA
Cristina Alcaraz	University of Malaga, Spain
Luís Antunes	Universidade do Porto, Portugal
Muhammad Asghar	University of Auckland, New Zealand
Francesco Buccafurri	University of Reggio Calabria, Italy
Frederic Cuppens	TELECOM Bretagne, France
Nora Cuppens	IMT Atlantique, France
Sabrina De Capitani di Vimercati	Università degli Studi di Milano, Italy
Roberto Di Pietro	Hamad Bin Khalifa University, Qatar
Mario Di Raimondo	Università of Catania, Italy
Josep Domingo-Ferrer	Rovira i Virgili University, Spain
Ruggero Donida Labati	Università degli Studi di Milano, Italy
Alberto Ferrante	Università della Svizzera Italiana, Switzerland
Josep-Lluis Ferrer-Gomila	University of the Balearic Islands, Spain
Sara Foresti	Università degli Studi di Milano, Italy
Steven Furnell	University of Nottingham, UK
Joaquin Garcia-Alfaro	Télécom SudParis, France
Angelo Genovese	Università degli Studi di Milano, Italy
Dimitris Gritzalis	Athens University of Economics and Business, Greece
Stefanos Gritzalis	University of Piraeus, Greece
Jinguang Han	Queen's University Belfast, UK
Xinyi Huang	Fujian Normal University, China

SECRYPT Additional Reviewers

Tahir Ahmad	Foundazione Bruno Kessler, Italy
Stefano Berlato	University of Genoa, Italy
Bruhadeshwar Bezawada	Colorado State University, USA
Vasiliki Diamantopoulou	University of the Aegean, Greece
Dimitra Georgiou	Greece
Giacomo Giorgi	IIT-CNR, Italy
Emanuela Marasco	George Mason University, USA
Luca Mariot	University of Milano-Bicocca, Italy
Christina Michailidou	IIT-CNR, Italy
Umberto Morelli	Foundazione Bruno Kessler, Italy
Jianting Ning	Nanyang Technological University, Singapore
Pankaj Pandey	Norwegian University of Science and Technology, Norway
Panagiotis Rizomiliotis	Harokopio University, Greece
Alessandro Tomasi	Fondazione Bruno Kessler, Italy
Theodoros Tzouramanis	University of Thessaly, Greece
Luca Verderame	University of Genova, Italy
Xu Yang	RMIT University, Australia
Yuexin Zhang	Xidian University, China
Fei Zhu	RMIT University, Australia

SIGMAP Program Committee

Harry Agius	Brunel University London, UK
Fadoua Ataa Allah	Royal Institute of Amazigh Culture (IRCAM), Morocco
Adrian Bors	University of York, UK
Wei Cheng	Garena Online Pte. Ltd., Singapore
Kaushik Das Sharma	University of Calcutta, India
Massimo De Santo	Unversità degli Studi di Salerno, Italy
Carl Debono	University of Malta, Malta
Murat Eron	Avionic Instruments, USA
Zongming Fei	University of Kentucky, USA
Markus Fiedler	Blekinge Institute of Technology, Sweden
Borko Furht	Florida Atlantic University, USA
Rosario Garroppo	University of Pisa, Italy
Amarnath Gupta	University of California, San Diego, USA
Rajarshi Gupta	University of Calcutta, India
Emmanuel Ifeachor	Plymouth University, UK
Haci Ilhan	Yildiz Technical University, Turkey
Razib Iqbal	Missouri State University, USA
Li-Wei Kang	National Yunlin University of Science and Technology, Taiwan, Republic of China

Sokratis Katsikas	Norwegian University of Science and Technology, Norway
Konrad Kowalczyk	AGH University of Science and Technology, Poland
Adnane Latif	Cadi Ayyad University, Morocco
Choong-Soo Lee	St. Lawrence University, USA
Chengqing Li	Xiangtan University, China
Vincenzo Lombardo	Università di Torino, Italy
Hong Man	Stevens Institute of Technology, USA
Daniela Moctezuma	CentroGEO, Mexico
Chamin Morikawa	Morpho, Inc., Japan
Alejandro Murua	University of Montreal, Canada
Hiroshi Nagahashi	Japan Women's University, Japan
Alessandro Ortis	University of Catania, Italy
Ioannis Paliokas	Centre for Research and Technology - Hellas, Greece
Peter Quax	Hasselt University, Belgium
Paula Queluz	Instituto Superior Técnico - Instituto de Telecomunicações, Portugal
Simon Romano	University of Napoli, Italy
Simone Santini	Universidad Autónoma de Madrid, Spain
Oscar Siordia	CentroGeo, Mexico
Lauro Snidaro	University of Udine, Italy
Andrew Sung	University of Southern Mississippi, USA
Aristeidis Tsitiridis	Universidad Rey Juan Carlos, Spain
Sanjeewa Witharana	Max Planck Institute for Solar System Research, Germany

WINSYS Program Committee

Andreas Ahrens	Hochschule Wismar, University of Applied Sciences, Technology, Business and Design, Germany
Vicente Alarcon-Aquino	Universidad de las Americas Puebla, Mexico
Jose Barcelo-Ordinas	Universitat Politècnica de Catalunya, Spain
Luis Bernardo	Universidade Nova de Lisboa, Portugal
Llorenç Cerdà-Alabern	Universitat Politècnica de Catalunya, Spain
Ali Chehab	American University of Beirut, Lebanon
Chi Cheung	Hong Kong Polytechnic University, China
Alessandro Cidronali	Università degli Studi di Firenze, Italy
Roberto Corvaja	University of Padova, Italy
Carl Debono	University of Malta, Malta
Panagiotis Fouliras	University of Macedonia, Greece
Janusz Gozdecki	AGH University of Science and Technology, Poland

Fabrizio Granelli	Università degli Studi di Trento, Italy
Aaron Gulliver	University of Victoria, Canada
Brij Gupta	National Institute of Technology, Kurukshetra, India
Athanassios Iossifides	Technological Educational Institute of Thessaloniki, Greece
Georgios Kambourakis	University of the Aegean, Greece
Seong-Cheol Kim	Seoul National University, South Korea
Charalampos Konstantopoulos	University of Piraeus, Greece
Evan Kotsovinos	USA
Gurhan Kucuk	Yeditepe University, Turkey
Jin-Shyan Lee	National Taiwan University of Technology, Taiwan, Republic of China
Wookwon Lee	Gannon University, USA
David Lin	National Chiao Tung University, Taiwan, Republic of China
Koosha Marashi	Romeo Power Technology, USA
Marek Natkaniec	AGH University of Science and Technology, Poland
Amiya Nayak	University of Ottawa, Canada
Cristiano Panazio	Escola Politècnica of São Paulo University, Brazil
Grammati Pantziou	University of West Attica, Greece
Al-Sakib Pathan	IIUM, Malaysia
Jordi Pérez-Romero	Universitat Politècnica de Catalunya, Spain
Jorge Portilla	Universidad Politècnica de Madrid, Spain
Luis Rizo	ITESO University, Mexico
Jörg Roth	University of Applied Sciences Nuremberg, Germany
Farag Sallabi	United Arab Emirates University, UAE
Manuel García Sánchez	Universidade de Vigo, Spain
Christopher Silva	The Aerospace Corporation, USA
Mahmoud Smail	Wayne State University, USA
Alvaro Suárez-Sarmiento	University of Las Palmas de Gran Canaria, Spain
Bert-Jan van Beijnum	University of Twente, The Netherlands
César Vargas Rosales	Tecnológico de Monterrey, Mexico
Rafaela Villalpando-Hernandez	Tecnologico de Monterrey, Mexico
Shibing Zhang	Nantong University, China

Invited Speakers

Henderik Proper	Luxembourg Institute of Science and Technology, Luxembourg
Jaime Lloret Mauri	Universidad Politecnica de Valencia, Spain
Ajith Abraham	Machine Intelligence Research Labs, USA
Moti Yung	Columbia University, USA
Ingemar Johansson Cox	University of Copenhagen, Denmark

Contents

An Improved Bit Masking Technique to Enhance Covert Channel Attacks in Everyday IT Systems

Panagiotis Dedousis[1], George Stergiopoulos[1,2], and Dimitris Gritzalis[1]([✉])

[1] Department of Informatics, Athens University of Economics and Business, Athens, Greece
{dedousisp,dgrit}@aueb.gr
[2] Department of Information and Communication Systems Engineering, University of the Aegean, Samos, Greece
g.stergiopoulos@aegean.gr

Abstract. We present an improved network attack evasion technique that allows malicious two-way communication and bypasses popular host and network intrusion techniques/systems that use deep packet inspection, signature analysis, and traffic behavior. The attack is based on previous research that leverages legitimate network traffic (existing or intuitively generated) from different contexts and reuses it to communicate malicious content. Still, contrary to previous research, the proposed approach: (i) provides increased bandwidth and allows us to exfiltrate large amounts of data with improved execution times while avoiding detection, and (ii) removes the administration privilege constraint that existed in previous implementations. Both novelties now make the attack feasible in real-world scenarios. We present two different attack implementations in different contexts, i.e., scripts/commands two-way communication and large data transfer. We test and validate our two implemented attacks using four popular NIDS, eight of the most popular endpoint protection solutions, and a Data Leakage Prevention System (DLP). Finally, we include a comparison of findings between our implementations of attacks and previous studies.

Keywords: Network security · Intrusion detection · Covert channel · Network traffic generation · Data leakage

1 Introduction

A range of security mechanisms exists to detect and deter malicious activity in modern networks, both to comply with regulatory enforcement and reduce the risk in the event of malicious activity. Intrusion detection systems and prevention systems (IDP/IPS) are used at the host and network level as software applications and/or independent hardware devices. Some systems analyze network links and workstations for breaches, while others try to detect data leakages, such as DLP detection suites [1]. Network-based security mechanisms are still not very efficient in detecting insider attacks and attacks that do not generate significant network traffic [2, 3].

Authors in [4] proposed such an evasion attack methodology called bit-masking. Their approach managed to establish a secure, reverse, and undetected connection to

© Springer Nature Switzerland AG 2021
M. S. Obaidat and J. Ben-Othman (Eds.): ICETE 2020, CCIS 1484, pp. 1–23, 2021.
https://doi.org/10.1007/978-3-030-90428-9_1

transfer malicious data. The main idea is to break any malicious information in a sequence of binary blocks, capture legitimate traffic from the victim's network and try to match the bits inside the payload of captured packets with the binary blocks on the malicious information utilizing a bit-mask (predetermined bit positions). Their proposed implementation transmits matched packets without payload tampering to the listening service of an intruder. Their approach is similar to symmetric key encryption as both parties (server-client) share a bit-mask. Still, the previous methodology suffered from limitations that deem the attack not realistic for real-world scenarios. First, all three presented versions required admin rights to use raw sockets to send malicious commands and data. Another crucial issue is the limited throughput due to performance issues of the proposed matching algorithm.

1.1 Contribution

In this paper, we extend previous work presented in [4]. Our methodology improves upon the first implementation, namely the TCP version, of the evasion attack methodology by eliminating the admin right/administration privilege restriction and increasing the average bandwidth of the attack through a different approach in network filtering and packet crafting. The main differences are that (i) a bit-masked connection uses existing legitimate traffic from the victim to transfer commands and data while, in our approach, we create new white traffic, (ii) we use an improved version of the matching algorithm that maximizes the matched data rate, thus the overall throughput, (iii) we use data compression, during data preparation, in an attempt to minimize the data size, thus reducing matching and transfer times, (iv) we use a new transfer technique that reduces the left footprint of our attacks. Our method can be used to implement various types of attacks, such as a fully functional reverse shell with the ability to hide commands and enable untraced two-way communication between two parties.

To validate our approach, we also utilize network and host security controls such as network and host IDS, endpoint protection solutions, and antivirus programs. The evaluation shows that the presented attack remains undetected as in previous approaches, but with a substantial increase in bandwidth and without the need for administrative privileges. To validate the alleged increase in efficiency, we test the improved matching algorithm against various data sizes from 40 KB to 230 MB files and compare the results with the Standard TCP Version from [4]. Our major contributions are:

1. A novel version of the attack algorithm that utilizes data compression and an improved version of the matching algorithm presented in [4] for faster and more efficient packet detection by combining the bit-masking with parallel programming and data compression.
2. A novel concept able to remove the administration privilege constraint present in all previous implementations by utilizing white/legitimate traffic generation and regular-stream sockets for transferring information.
3. An overall comparison between our implementations and previous research. We access the performance by testing the execution times of our implementations against various sizes payloads and different size bit-masks. Also, we validate their evasion

capabilities against four popular NIDS, eight popular endpoint protection solutions, and a Data Leakage Prevention system.

Someone could argue that the malicious script could simply encrypt its communication, which would still break any payload analysis. Nevertheless, most advanced network intrusion systems often will flag unknown encrypted connections as suspicious. Also, research exists that shows promising results in detecting malicious traffic even when it is encrypted. For example, in [5] and [6], researchers use various packet features to extract information from the physical aspects of the network traffic. While in [7] and [8], authors use malicious HTTPS traffic to train neural networks and sequence classification algorithms to build a system capable of detecting malware traffic over encrypted connections. Our approach can be inhibited by neither of the two.

1.2 Structure

Section 2 presents related work concerning both detection of malicious activity and evasion techniques in both network and host machines. We also argue about the differences with our presented attack. In Sect. 3, we discuss the building blocks of our method, while in Sect. 4, we present the proposed methodology in a series of process steps utilizing a two-way communication model. In Sect. 5, we present two attack implementations, namely Improved Version 1 and Improved Version 2. Section 6 describes experimental results with performance and attack evasion tests. Section 7 concludes and discusses potential solutions.

2 Related Work

Security mechanisms can be divided into two main categories host-based and network-based. Both host and network-based systems use various techniques and methodologies to detect and prevent malicious activities. Research on host-based expands from system call analysis [9] and sandbox virtualization [10, 11] to active mapping/monitoring of the network [12, 13] and automatic policy enforcement [14]. More recent research in host-based systems utilizes machine learning to generate patterns of known attacks [15–18]. In network-based systems, modern network security solutions use session packet heuristic analysis, deep packet inspection, and session patterns along with botnet architectures [19–22]. Others depend on statistical analysis to extract the statistical fingerprint and classify a network flow [23]. More recent solutions use machine learning [7, 8, 16, 24] and deep learning approaches [25–27] to extract knowledge from the various aspects of network traffic.

On the other hand, intruders use evasion techniques to render attacks without raising any alarms or at least minor alerts in the security systems utilized. State-of-the-art evasion methods include fragmentation or splicing of sessions, network traffic flooding, and obfuscation [28–30]. Covert channel techniques similar to steganography can hide information in a carrier. While steganography requires audio, visual, or textual content, covert channels on computer networks require some network protocol as a carrier for hiding information [31]. The number of network protocols suitable as carriers on the web makes covert channel attacks widely available [32]. Covert timing channels use a clock or measurement of time to signal the value being sent over a channel. For example, malicious data can be concealed by utilizing TCP packet headers and exploiting the TCP/IP protocol stack [33, 34]. In contrary to the above approaches, we create distinct TCP connections and send legitimate packets like every other network link, while also preventing security measures detection.

In fragmentation or session splicing evasion techniques packets are fragmented, so that a detector system cannot reassemble them for signature matching [28]. Timeouts, fragment overlap, and overwrite are common methods used by attackers to avoid detection by covering attacks as legitimate traffic [35, 36]. Fragmentation attack replaces/overwrites data in the constituent fragmented packets or overlapping segments with new information to generate a malicious packet [28]. Also, some evasion techniques deliberately manipulate TCP or IP protocols in a way the target machine will process the same data differently from the IDS. If these violations are not handled, the IDS is vulnerable to insertion and evasion techniques similar to those mentioned above [36]. Contrary to the above fragmentation techniques, our approach does not try to exploit limitations of or manipulate the TCP/IP protocol to achieve its goals.

Attackers utilize traffic flooding to mask their malicious activities on the network. These kinds of attacks overwhelm/overpower the detector system with the final goal of causing the control/checking mechanism to fail. Detection systems experience a significant performance drop when trying to find malicious packets in a massive amount of traffic. When the detection system fails, all traffic is allowed [35]. The most common method to create flooding situations is by utilizing the User Datagram Protocol (UDP), or the Internet Control Message Protocol (ICMP), or the Transmission Control Protocol (TCP) packets [37]. Global TCP synchronization offers effective evasion techniques that take advantage of the synchronization of TCP loss between flows when two or more flows experience packet loss in a short period, causing significant performance implications [38, 39]. Denial-of-service attacks aim to overflow the resources of the IDS or create large numbers of false positives to make it difficult to distinguish legitimate and false attacks [40]. In our approach, we generate white traffic to collect data for pattern matching. Our main goal is not to flood the network with traffic or deploy denial-of-service attacks but to gather enough legitimate data to mask the data to transfer.

Some traffic injection attacks involve sending packets that are handled by IDS but not by target machines, generating various session states between IDS and target systems [41]. That is achieved by intentionally fragmenting the attack payload and inserting duplicate segments with different TTL values on the network [30, 42]. Packets with smaller TTL values never reach the end, while the detector system will process all packets without having network topology information [30]. Slow port scans, frequency tests by slowing down packets, matching methods that use alternative HTTP commands to detect CGI scripts, and premature requests that end with malicious data concealed in headers are also commonly carried out against IDS by evasion attacks [43, 44]. In contrast to traffic injection attacks, the transfer data send by our implementation reaches both IDS and target machine. Moreover, we do not interfere in any way in the operation of the IDS.

An attacker can utilize obfuscation or encoding of an attack payload, in a way that the target device can reverse it while an IDS cannot, to exploit the end-host without creating any alerts. Obfuscation techniques conceal an attack by making the transferred message impossible to interpret [45]. This approach packets payloads into entirely different content, while the data still functions in the same way [30, 36]. Altering packet payload makes signature or fingerprint matching obsolete, as the transformed content has a different fingerprint; hence these methods can successfully evade detector systems [29, 30]. Also, obfuscation techniques may utilize any limitations in the signature database and its ability to duplicate the way the computer host examines data [46]. Simple obfuscation attacks use different encoding formats to avoid signature matching [47].

The most common attacks that utilize obfuscation are payload mutations and shellcode attacks [29, 30, 36]. Polymorphic techniques are used to generate dynamically changing signatures for attack instances to evade signature-based IDS. Payload mutation attacks transform malicious packet payloads into semantically equivalent ones. Each time the code is executed, it mutates into a completely different form from what an IPS or a firewall expects, hence results in a completely different signature [36, 48, 49]. In this way, an attacker can successfully evade detection [28, 50]. For example, an attacker can encrypt or compress the shellcode, and prepend a piece of code to decrypt or decompress it successfully, thus evading detection by IDS [28].

Encryption leaves data completely unreadable and irrelevant. If complex encryption methods are used, then the security of the transferred data is significantly high [51]. Attackers employ complex end to end data encryption to escape detection and conceal attacks [30]. For example, an IDS cannot read attacks on encrypted protocols such as HyperText Transfer Protocol Secure (HTTPS) [52]. The IDS cannot match the encrypted traffic to the existing signatures since it cannot interpret the encrypted traffic. Therefore, encrypted traffic makes it difficult for detectors to detect attacks [53]. Besides, encryption and decryption operations are extensive in terms of resources and can affect the performance of a detector system. An attacker may use complex encryption algorithms to exhaust a detector system resources and attempt a denial of service attack [30, 42, 51].

Our approach resembles obfuscation and payload mutation attacks in terms of concealing an attack or data by making the transferred message hard to interpret and utilizing TCP packets payload to transfer data through the network [29, 30, 36, 45, 48, 49]. Nevertheless, in our approach, malicious packets or code are not mutated or converted per se during execution into semantically equivalent, like the previously mentioned attacks. In comparison with attack implementations that employ encryption [30, 42, 51–53], our approach utilizes bit-masking [4], hence does not encrypt data.

In order to address network detection and prevention methods that are based on malicious behavior models [7, 8, 16, 17, 24], our approach utilizes white traffic. In this way, we can escape detection by (i) not having to conceal malicious information and (ii) adding all sorts of payloads into our malicious stream from different legitimate sessions, so data transmitted cannot be identified as malicious. Results show that none of the systems tested could either detect the malicious program and/or characterize as malicious the transmit data and commands over the network.

Our technique uses the structure of an existing layer (i.e., the TCP protocol and transport layer) to transfer information illegally, disguised as a legitimate stream, similar to the work in [54]. However, it differs from other cover storage channel techniques like steganography since it does not directly replace or alter data to hide the malicious payload [31].

3 Building Blocks

3.1 Bit-Masking

A mask is data (bits) that is used for standard binary (bitwise) operations (logical AND, OR, XOR) and defines which part of the information to keep, change, or remove. Masking is the actual act of imposing a mask on a binary value. We define bit-mask as a one-dimensional length μ vector that indicates specific bit locations within valid binary payloads, where μ is the number of bit positions referenced by the bit-mask (i.e., mask length). For example, the bit-mask 4, 3, 7, 6, 9 with length $\mu = 5$, points to the 4th bit, 3rd bit, 7th bit, 6th bit, 9th bit of a payload in binary form (Fig. 1).

Bit Mask

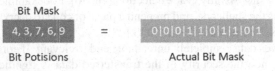

4, 3, 7, 6, 9   =   0|0|0|1|1|0|1|1|0|1

Bit Potisions   Actual Bit Mask

Fig. 1. Bit mask representation in binary form.

As stated in the original paper, "the idea is that the malicious script at the victim's PC will convert malicious data-to-be-sent to binary and break them down into chunks of bits the size of the bit-mask. Then, the algorithm finds legitimate TCP packets that have a payload whose binary form has the same bits as the malicious bit chunk at the positions indicated by the bit-mask. If such a legitimate TCP packet is found, instead of sending a chunk of malicious bits, we send the entire legitimate packet to the attacker" [4]. These bits are then extracted by the attacker and concatenated together with other bits received from similar packets.

The attack needs legitimate packets from white traffic that have the same bits as the data to transfer at the bit positions indicated by the pre-shared bit-mask. The process does not modify any bits on the victim packets to keep existing white traffic patterns and thus break intrusion detection algorithms. White traffic refers to packets or streams of data that are not malicious and originate from legitimate sources (e.g., video, audio Livestream). Figure 2 illustrates the overall process of bit masking.

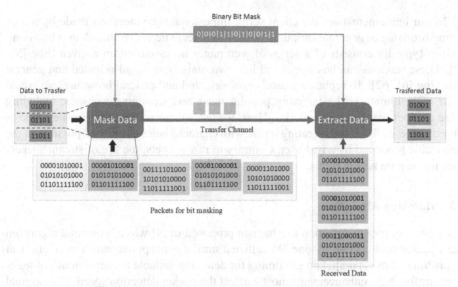

Fig. 2. Graphical representation of bit masking process.

3.2 Acquiring White Traffic

Workstation network traffic consists of OS traffic and user traffic. Based on our measurements, the average OS traffic of typical Windows and Linux workstations (e.g., software updates and OS connections) fluctuates around 0,07 MB per minute (90 MB per day) without any major OS updates. By measuring and analyzing network traffic in four workstations located inside the team's research lab, we estimate around 11 MB per minute of user traffic (e.g., web surfing, music, or video streaming). We should note here that real-world network traffic highly depends on user activity, thus making estimations arbitrary. We consider two ways to acquire white traffic. The first one relies on underlying system network traffic and tries to capture it by sniffing packets. The other way is to try to generate white traffic and utilize the produced data. Both approaches have advantages and disadvantages. Below we discuss each method in detail.

There are broadly two modes in packet sniffing: Promiscuous mode and Monitor mode. Network Interface Controller (NIC) or Wireless NIC in case of Wi-Fi when in Promiscuous mode can capture all network data. In non-promiscuous mode, only the data destined for a particular controller through MAC addresses is sent to CPU, while the rest packets are dropped. In Monitor mode, a user does not need to associate himself with a specific access point [55]. All such sniffing modes require administration rights granted to the sniffer software, a limitation of the previous research approach.

Instead, network traffic generation refers to the creation of network connections in a controlled fashion [56]. Cyber defense tools use network traffic generation to conduct experiments in test environments so that they can distinguish real legitimate traffic from malicious [57]. Network traffic generators can be classified into three major categories: (i) traffic generation based on network traffic model, (ii) traffic generation based on traffic characteristics, (iii) traffic generation based on application protocols [58].

In our implementation, the client script impersonates connections made by a user during browsing to generate various persona-based realistic web traffic. A user browsing session typically consists of a series of web pages accessed within a given time [59, 60]. These sessions can be categorized into two main types: goal-oriented and general browsing [61, 62]. To replicate a user's goal-oriented and general browsing, we create a list of legitimate URLs targeting popular news and streaming websites, including some random search engine queries. Next, we use stream sockets to generate requests targeting these URLs, thus creating traffic with characteristics as close as possible to the web traffic produced by a real user. Contrary to raw sockets, the use of stream sockets does not require admin rights.

3.3 Matching Algorithm

The matching packet detection mechanism proposed in [4] was a sequential algorithm that checked packers one-by-one. We utilize a similar concept to create a more efficient algorithm that uses parallel programming for detecting suitable packets/chunks of legitimate traffic. New enhancements mostly affect the packet detection speed. The original complex problem of detecting packet payloads whose binaries match malicious data binaries was divided into smaller algorithms, which can then be solved at the same time, thus improving execution time and general efficiency [63]. We identified that the part of checking a data block against the acquired legitimate TCP/IP traffic packets is the most computationally intensive, so we assigned it to a task to be computed in parallel. Detailed steps of the improved algorithm are described below:

1. Convert data to transfer D into binary and break them down to k blocks of bits of length μ, $D = k * \mu$
2. Capture legitimate TCP/IP traffic, and convert packet payloads to binary
3. For each of the k blocks of data to transfer start a new TASK to be computed in parallel
4. In each TASK iterate over the acquired packets to detect packets that have the same bits as the bits with the provide k_i block, at positions indicated by the bit-mask

   (a) If a suitable payload is found, replace the corresponding block of data to transfer with the packet,
   (b) Else mark the corresponding block of data to transfer as NOT MATCHED

5. When all tasks are finished check the block of data to transfer list for NOT MATCHED items
6. If there are NOT MATCHED items go to STEP 2,
7. Else all data to transfer are replaced with captured legitimate packets

4 Methodology

Each step of the presented methodology utilizes a set of algorithms, where each one step provides the necessary outputs to be used as input in the step to follow. The main

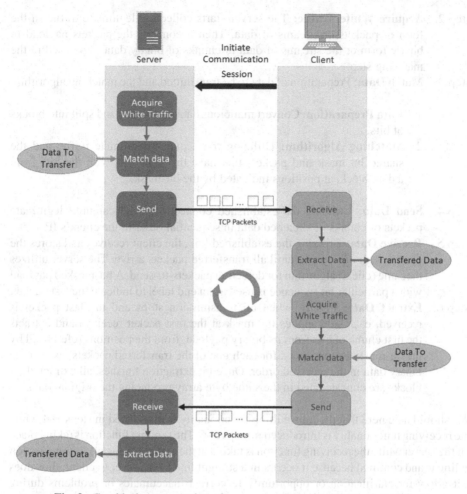

Fig. 3. Graphical representation of two-way communication attack model.

component of the proposed approach is a Client-Server architecture where both client(s) and server communicate over a computer network on separate hardware. The client initiates communication sessions with the server, which awaits incoming requests. The server starts collecting white traffic/legitimate packets to match the data to transfer based on the known bit-mask. The algorithm then sends legitimate packets to the client in sequential order. Once the client receives all the transmitted packets, he (the client) reconstructs the original data by extracting and concatenating the bit content indicated by the bit-mask. This approach allows for one-way communication between client and server.

Below we discuss in detail each step of the proposed approach.

Step 1. **Initiate Communication Session:** The client establishes a connection to the server and initiate a three-way handshake.

Step 2. **Acquire White Traffic:** The server starts collecting legitimate traffic in the form of packets or streams of data. Then it converts the packets payload in binary form or the streams of data in chunks of binary data to be used in the matching step.

Step 3. **Match Data:** Preparation of data to be transmitted and the matching algorithm.

1. **Data Preparation:** Convert malicious data into binary and split into blocks of bits.
2. **Matching Algorithm:** Utilizing the acquired legitimate traffic and the shared bit mask find packets that have the same bits with the bits from a data block, at positions indicated by the bit-mask.

Step 4. **Send Data:** Utilizing the established connection, send captured legitimate packets or chunks of streamed data in sequential order to the client's IP.

Step 5. **Receive Data:** Utilizing the established link, the client receives and stores the packets sent one by one until all transferred packets arrive. The server utilizes the same (client) algorithm for detecting packets-to-send. A bit-masked payload with a particular bit sequence is used as an end label to indicate the last packet.

Step 6. **Extract Data:** Finally, when all transmission stops and the last packet is received, each side applies the mask at the first packet received and extracts the first chunk of bits from its binary payload, from the positions referenced by the bit-mask. Respectively, for each one of the transferred packets, extract the binary data in the received order. Once bit extraction finishes, all extracted bit blocks are concatenated in the same byte array producing the original data.

We should note here that the transmitting functionality is introduced in steps 1–4 while the receiving functionality is introduced in steps 5–6. The sending function is taking place on the server while the receiving function is taking at the client. One-way communication is linear and confined because it occurs in a straight line from server to client, thus does not allow for clarification or opportunity to correct inaccuracies or problems during the timeframe of an attack. The one-way communication approach is more suitable for hit-and-run attack types. To allow both parties to communicate, we provide both server and client with sending and receiving functionality (Fig. 3). Two-way communication always includes feedback from the receiver to the sender and ensures reliable messaging. The two-way communication approach creates a bi-directional path where both server and client can listen to each other, which provides constant reporting about the status of the attack. Two-way communication approaches allow for more complex monitored-controlled attacks.

5 Attack Implementations

We developed two attack implementations that are based on and improve the TCP version presented in [7]. Both versions address performance issues by processing legitimate traffic faster and more efficiently, and eliminate the restriction of administrator privilege. The first version utilizes sniffing for capturing legitimate traffic depending on network traffic availability. In contrast, the second version drops the constraint of the network traffic availability found both in the first version and in all implementations presented in [7]. The proposed implementations are essentially modified reverse shell attacks with the use of the bit-masking logic. In both cases, based on the proposed methodology, a two-way communication channel is established where the server executes the attacker's script, and the client executes the victim's one. We should note here that both of our implementations use full TCP handshakes to deal with the loss of synchronization (e.g., due to packet drops) between client and server. The client needs to run the victim's code, which is less than 2KB in size. In Sects. 5.1 and 5.2, we present in detail the proposed attack implementations.

5.1 Improved Version 1

For our first implementation, we utilize data compression and the improved matching algorithm presented in Sect. 3.2 as the base components to extent the TCP version. Starting from the data to be transferred we utilize the python zlib data compression library to minimize their size. If the compressed size is smaller than the original then we continue with the matching algorithm, otherwise, we use the original data. This addresses a limitation where any lossless data compression algorithm that compresses some files smaller must necessarily compress some files larger [64, 65]. Data compression proved to be rather efficient when the data to transfer has a large size but useless when the payload was under 8 bytes (single commands). The zlib algorithm adds a two-byte header and four-byte trailer around the raw compressed data. The minimum size of a zlib output is eight bytes; in the case of an empty string, the raw compressed data is two bytes. For example, eight repeated input bytes can result in raw compressed data as short as four bytes, so the minimum zlib output result is ten bytes.

Once the compression stage is complete, we start collecting legitimate traffic. We utilize raw sockets for sniffing packets from the network. We collect a sufficient amount, around 2000 packets, and stop. Using the improved matching algorithm presented in Sect. 3.2, the collected packets, and the shared bit-mask, we try to match and mask all the data to transfer. The code checks each packet, until either mask all the data or the unchecked packets finish. In that case, we return and sniff legitimate packets again. We filter packets with the proto label in the IP header because the sniffing for IPPROTO TCP is not permitted. Since we access low-level by utilizing raw sockets, admin rights are needed both for the attacker and the victim during the sniffing stage.

Once all the data to transfer are masked, we start the transmission stage by utilizing stream sockets. Since TCP operates on streams of data and does not use fixed framing of messages on its own, we need to ensure that the client receives intact and distinct masked packets. For this reason, we created new connections for every masked packet sent by the attacker to the victim's machine. To achieve that, we exploited a socket feature that blocks the socket until a packet is received. This way, we do not send an END signal, and TCP employs a timeout after the last transferred packet. In this way, we accomplish that all the packets are transmitted successfully.

The receiver must obtain the transferred packets in the correct order to extract the original data. To that end, we extend the utilized bit-mask by 2 bits and use them as a packet sequence number. During the data preparation stage, we split the data to transfer in chunks of length μ-2, where μ the length of the bit-mask in binary form, and use the last two bits as an incremental sequence number that resets and continues. Furthermore, we can deal with possible packet loss during transmission. In the case of an erroneous sequence, we stop processing and notify the sender to retransmit the same packet again (using the two-way communication channel). In the unlikely scenario where four packets are lost (the sequence number will be correct without noticing data loss), the attack will fail, although this never happened during experiments.

When the packet transmission finishes, the receiver acquires the original data by concatenating the extracted bits indicated by the bit-mask (in binary form) for each received packet.

5.2 Improved Version 2

In our implementation, we opt to generate legitimate traffic instead of sniffing existing, since capturing traffic generated by our process does not require administrative privileges. That is a major difference from previous research. Previous implementations required administrative privileges to sniff traffic from the victim's PC. Attacks that require administrator privileges to execute are often considered unrealistic for real-world scenarios. To this end, the second part of our experiments focused on alleviating this restriction from the previous research.

For legitimate traffic generation, we utilize a list of legitimate URL that consist mostly of (i) popular news websites, (ii) video and music services, and (iii) random web searches utilizing popular web search engines. For each of those URL we create a request generating a web session, utilizing sockets. We store the responses in binary form in chunks length μ where μ the size of the bit-mask for further processing. Once we collect a sufficient amount of data, around 2000 chunks of data, we stop. Similar to the first implementation, we utilize data compression to minimize the size of the initial data. We should note here that for the receiver to acquire the original data, he must split the payload of the received packet stream in chunks μ where μ the size of the bit-mask and then extract the bits indicated by the bit-mask (in binary form).

For data transmission, we use stream sockets, which are Connection-oriented and typically implemented using TCP, which is on top of IP and Ethernet. Contrary to raw sockets that provide access to un-extracted packets, the use of stream sockets does not require to administrate privileges for execution as it does not directly access lower-level protocols. We create and bound a stream socket to an attacker's client with a particular IP address and port number. Since the data to transfer is serialized into a single byte stream, we require only one TCP connection to transmit them. Again, we use a known TCP port to draw less attention. Once we create an initial connection between the victim and attacker, the transmission starts and finishes when all data are transmitted.

6 Experiments and Results

We execute the experiments on an Intel Core-i7 with 16 GB RAM and an SSD. We use Python version 3.7.2 to develop both of our attack implementations code. The executed experiments can be classified into two main categories: (i) performance tests (ii) attack evasion tests. During performance tests, we assess and compare our implementations utilizing the improved matching algorithm against various sizes payloads and different size bit-masks with the standard version present in [7]. During the attack evasion tests, we assess the ability of our attack implementations to evade network intrusion detection systems (NIDS), host intrusion detection systems (HIDS), antivirus software's and data leakage systems (DLPs). Sections 6.1 and 6.2 below discuss results for performance and attack evasion tests, respectively.

6.1 Performance Tests

We ran tests for various data sizes and different size bit-masks to access our implementations' overall performance and efficiency. Furthermore, we compare the final results with the standard TCP version, as presented in [4]. The most critical part of the proposed methodology is to find legitimate traffic payloads that have specific bits at the specified points referenced by the shared bit-mask. Thus, the implementation and performance of the matching algorithm are of major importance. Three variables affect the processing time of the matching algorithm: (i) the length of the bit-mask in binary form, (ii) the amount of legitimate traffic present, and (iii) the amount of data to transfer.

In Fig. 4, we illustrate the comparison results of our experiments using various sizes of payloads. We used different size bit-masks to access the performance of our implementation but focused on presenting results for bit-masks of length 4, 8, and 10 bits. Experiments suggest that by using the improved version of the matching algorithm, we achieved a 65–70% reduction in execution times for matching patterns, when compared to the standard version for all bit-mask lengths. Graph functions below depict execution times (Fig. 4). The horizontal axis depicts different data sizes (40 KB, 400 KB, 800 KB, 8 MB, and 230 MB files) that we paired with predefined bit-mask of fixed size (Fig. 4a, Fig. 4b, Fig. 4c). Each size has a column that depicts the time needed (in seconds) to complete the aforementioned malicious data size attack. Also, performance tests show that, for matching larger files (230 MB), the improved matching algorithm needed approximately 9 min to complete its task with an 8-bit mask.

As we notice from charts in Fig. 4, even though the improved matching algorithm reduced execution times for packet matching, the selected bit-mask plays a significant role in the matching algorithm's performance. Based on the results, if we choose a small bit-mask, the execution is faster independently from data size. Our goal is to transmit undetected a large amount of data in the shortest time possible. If we use a small size bit-mask matching execution times are reduced, but the number of masked packets increases. Since the number of created connections depends on the number of masked packets to be transferred, we risk detection (higher number of TCP connections equals higher detection risk). Therefore, when choosing the size of the utilized bit-mask, there is a tradeoff and a balance to kept. As mention in [4], binary bit-masks of length 8 seem to provide the best overall efficiency. In Fig. 4, it is clear that both 4-bit and 8-bit masks reduce the matching execution time by two thirds for larger files. At the same time, the difference between an 8-bit and a 10-bit mask is almost non-existent for files smaller than 8000 KB. For larger files (>8000 KB), the 10-bit mask is by far the worst, proving that the algorithm finds matches more difficult for larger bit-masks.

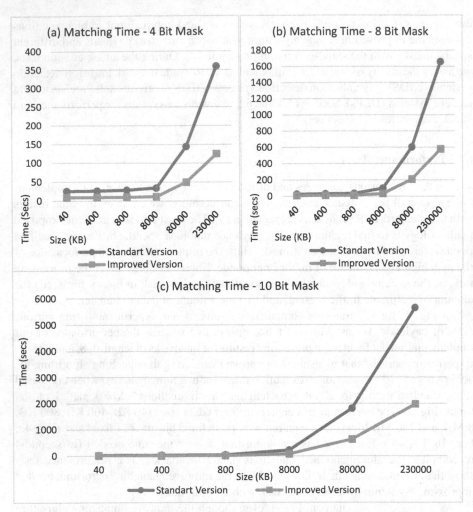

Fig. 4. Matching algorithm execution times utilized in standard and improved attack implementations for different sizes of mask and data.

In Table 1, we present the total execution times for standard and improved attacks. As we notice, execution times are significantly lower for implementations that use the improved matching algorithm since less time is spent in the sniffing process, collecting legitimate traffic. Improved Version 2 substantially reduces the amount of time spent acquiring packets since it does not rely on existing network traffic. For both Improved Version 1 and Standard, the available network traffic severely affects the attack's performance. Even though the generated network traffic of our test environment was constant and sufficient (approx. 11 MB/min), OS/programs and user-generated network traffic varies considerably in the real world, thus creating a disparity in performance results.

We observed a higher reduction in total execution times between our implementations and the standard version for larger sizes. Data compression resulted in smaller data sizes

Table 1. Total Execution Times for standard and improved attack implementations for different sizes of mask and data.

Size (KB)	Standard version			Improved version 1			Improved version 2		
	4-bit	8-bit	10-bit	4-bit	8-bit	10-bit	4-bit	8-bit	10-bit
40	69.51	70.41	162.33	17.37	17.05	40.58	9.18	9.41	9.49
400	70.6	75.64	177.85	17.65	18.91	44.25	9.82	11.54	12.95
800	71.74	78.50	187.56	17.35	19.65	46.89	10.47	12.56	16.41
8000	86.44	139.00	346.50	21.5	34.75	86.65	11.66	15.46	28.27
80000	221.23	659.00	1923.97	28.75	64.75	115.25	12.22	17.59	49.83
230000	483.66	1781.90	5708.40	35.91	75.47	225.15	15.72	37.85	98.9

for processing by the matching algorithm, thus improving the overall performance. Data-file types and actual content utilized in the experiment allowed for optimal data compression. Depending on the type of malicious data, actual execution times may vary. Still, execution times improved both for smaller and larger sizes of malicious data, allowing for better control and monitoring of an attack. Related results can be seen in Table 1 above.

We conclude that the selection of the bit-mask length plays a critical role in execution times. Our tests show that the number of active bits inside the mask and the mask length significantly affect the total execution times; thus, the time needed to deploy an attack. Also, based on the performed experiments in which we used different bit-masks both in size and content, the position of the selected active bits does not appear to affect execution times.

6.2   Attack Evasion Tests

For accessing the evasion capabilities of our attack implementations, we set up a network using Oracle's VirtualBox 6.1.16, as depicted in Fig. 5. Virtual machines formed a network where one Kali Linux machine represented the attacker (server-side), and an MS Windows machine represented the victim (client-side) with Windows 10 64-bit system running different security suites.

For testing purposes, we configured 4 NIDS (Table 2). We also tested 8 of the most popular host endpoint protection solutions (Table 4) and two Data Leakage Prevention systems (DLPs) against our enhanced bit-masking attack. Attack content data included several shell commands, scripts, and data transfers of various sizes (from 4 KB up to 230 MB) on both our implementations.

Network Intrusion Evasion Tests. We opted to use the Security onion [66] distribution for accessing the attack's network evasion capabilities. Security Onion offers common implementations for several IDS. We utilized the Snort VRT rule set for the Snort setup, default rules for Bro, and JA3 rules for Suricata. The network intrusion detection and monitoring systems tested are presented in Table 2. By utilizing the proposed internal

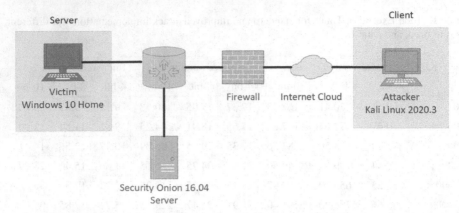

Fig. 5. Visual representation of the test environment's network topology.

network topology (Fig. 5), virtual machines can only see each other, which provides impartial network traffic.

Table 2. Utilized network intrusion detection systems.

IDS	Description
Suricata	A free open-source network threat detection engine capable of network intrusion detection, inline intrusion prevention, network security monitoring and offline pcap processing (https://suricata-ids.org/)
Snort	An open-source, free and lightweight network intrusion detection system (NIDS) for both Linux and Windows (https://www.snort.org/)
Zeek (Bro)	A flexible, open source system powered by defenders that sits on a "sensor", hardware, software, virtual, or cloud platform and quietly and unobtrusively observes network traffic (https://zeek.org/)
Ossec	A multi-platform, open source, host-based Intrusion Detection System (HIDS) (https://www.ossec.net/)

Both of our implementations create similar results as the standard TCP version regarding Bro IDS (Table 3). To an extent, we expected this since all attack methods share a similar transmission mechanism and do not access raw packets header to spoof source and destination address. For Improved Version 1, some detection mechanisms created "suspicious traffic" warnings for our connection, similar to the older Standard TCP version. That is occurred due to the large number of TCP connections established during the transmission stage, not necessarily a worrying sign. However, for commands that need many packets (e.g., "dir"), the attack probably will have been detected by an experienced security officer.

Table 3. Network intrusion detection systems results.

NIDS	Improved version 1	Improved version 2	Standard TCP Version
Snort	Warning	Pass	Warning
Bro	Logged (no warning)	Logged (no warning)	Logged (no warning)
Suricata	Warning (unknown)	Pass	Warning (unknown)
OSSEC	Pass	Pass	Pass

Improved version 1 triggers similar warning messages for both Snort and Suricata. That alone does not mean that our attack will be discovered, although multiple and repeated warnings on the same IP will be enough to alert a security expert and prompt an investigation. We should mention here that real traffic (e.g., SSH connections) can often cause similar warning messages concerning the TCP segment threshold, connection reset packet, and PAWS window. Nevertheless, the observed warning messages are strongly related to the mechanism in both Improved Version 1 and Standard Version, which allows us to send packets in the correct order. To achieve that, we create new connections for every packet sent by the attacker to the victim's machine by exploiting a socket feature that blocks the socket until a packet is received. We never send an END signal, and we must trigger a timeout after the last packet is sent, thus generating the warnings mentioned above. While at Improved Version 2, by creating a single TCP connection and properly ending the communication, we do not cause such warning messages.

Endpoint Security Evasion Tests. In this experiment, we tested our attack implementations against various host IDS and business antivirus suites (free and commercial) and compared the results for assessing evasion performance. We selected them based on several internet rankings from the press [67, 68]. Detection results for our attack implementations against endpoint security solutions are present in Table 4 below.

Our implementations passed all installed security systems. Improved Version 1 passed the entire test even though it created new TCP packets each time and established numerous connections to send or receive packets. Regarding firewall systems, most companies install flexible rules instead of blocking all incoming connections by default, allowing our attacks to pass without any problems. Even the Zone Alarm PRO firewall, which utilizes a strict whitelisting policy, did not detect our attacks. This high rate of success is because we do not change or alter the headers of the legitimate TCP packets. Besides, in Improved Version 2, we do not access low-level network protocol layers at all. Still, in a real-world scenario, advanced endpoint solutions and SOCs would probably raise some warning flags since the attacker's IP is not concealed, and all those multiple reconnections would be suspicious. We could argue here that, by utilizing Improved Version 2, we create a single connection to transmit all malicious data, drastically decreasing the possibility of detection in real-world conditions.

Data Leakage Evasion Tests. In this experiment we tested both of our implementations against MyDLP (http://www.mydlp.com/). MyDLP is a popular data leakage prevention

Table 4. Endpoint security systems attack experiment results.

Security system	Improved version 1	Improved version 2	TCP
Windows Defender	Pass	Pass	Pass
McAfee AntiVirus Plus	Pass	Pass	Pass
McAfee Total Protection	Pass	Pass	Pass
Symantec Norton Security Premium	Pass	Pass	Pass
Kaspersky Internet Security	Pass	Pass	Pass
Eset Nod32 Antivirus	Pass	Pass	Pass
Trend Micro Internet Security	Pass	Pass	Pass
ZoneAlarm PRO Antivirus + Firewall	Pass	Pass	Pass

system. MyDLP monitors the network traffic to detect data leakage using content-based techniques. Also, it regulates data usage by controlling input/output interfaces of end-host machines. We use it to assess the capability of our attacks when exfiltrating victim files such as PDFs and documents. Moreover, we set MyDLP up on an Ubuntu Server 18.04 VM and used it as a proxy through Squid, a caching and forwarding HTTP web proxy, to monitor network traffic of the test VM (Fig. 6). For testing, we used a DOCX file with personal and financial data, and we tried to upload it to various servers (i.e., Smash, Dropbox, OneDrive).

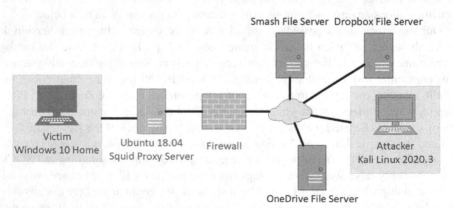

Fig. 6. Visual representation of network topology utilized for data leakage tests.

To set a baseline, we upload the file containing the sensitive data to each of the file servers (i.e., Smash, Dropbox, OneDrive). As expected, MyDLP recognized the transmission of sensitive data and logged the activity in all cases. Next, and by utilizing our implementations, we transfer the file from the victim to the attacker VM. The application did not log any suspicious activity on the network, which means that it did not recognize the patterns used to leak personal and financial data. Compared with uploading the file directly to the specified file servers, the overall time required transferring the file between the victim and attacker's VM, and by utilizing both our implementations was higher.

7 Conclusion

In this paper, we introduce two network evasion attack enhancements that build upon previous work and address implementation limitations and performance bottlenecks. Both our implementations were able to avoid different network and host intrusion detection systems and data leakage prevention frameworks while achieving better execution times and by utilizing captured traffic compared to previous implementations. We improve the matching algorithm and utilize data compression. Also, we remove the administrator privilege constraint using stream sockets for creating white traffic instead of sniffing existing traffic on the victim's machine. Preliminary tests showed that, in workstations with less than 12 MB/h of traffic (i.e., idle PCs), previous attacks would take an estimate of four times more than our enhanced version. Data compression proved to be efficient when exfiltrating large chunks of data but provided no edge for relatively small amounts of data.

In our first implementation, the attacker needs to create multiple connections by creating new TCP connections and embed previous, valid payloads within new packets to transmit all the necessary data. Using this approach generates warning messages regarding TCP misuse but provides packet sequence validity. In our second implementation, we address the warnings issue by concatenating masked data into a single object, serialize it and transmit it utilizing only one connection. This technique managed to avoid checks from intrusion detection systems, as compared to the first approach and leaves a minimal footprint of "connection logged" as a simple informational checkpoint.

Whitelisting outgoing connections and testing the validity of software connecting to external addresses is the most powerful and potentially the most straightforward solution to the proposed attacks. Future work should aim at recognizing the relevance in a sequence of packets. Also, we should test machine-learning detection techniques against the presented attacks and identify their detection rates.

Acknowledgment. This work was supported, in part, by the Ministry of Digital Governance, Greece, through a research grant offered to the Research Centre of Athens University of Economics & Business (RC/AUEB). The research grant aims at, mainly, developing innovative methodologies for implementing the National Cybersecurity Strategy of Greece (2020-25).

References

1. Marpaung, J., Sain, M., Lee, H.-J.: Survey on malware evasion techniques: state of the art and challenges. In: 2012 14th International Conference on Advanced Communication Technology (ICACT), pp. 744–749 (2012)
2. Khraisat, A., Gondal, I., Vamplew, P., Kamruzzaman, J.: Survey of intrusion detection systems: techniques, datasets and challenges. Cybersecurity 2(1), 1–22 (2019). https://doi.org/10.1186/s42400-019-0038-7
3. Zanero, S.: Flaws and frauds in the evaluation of IDS/IPS technologies. In: Proceedings of FIRST. Citeseer (2007)
4. Stergiopoulos, G., Lygerou, E., Tsalis, N., Tomaras, D., Gritzalis, D.: Avoiding network and host detection using packet bit-masking: In: Proceedings of the 17th International Joint Conference on e-Business and Telecommunications, pp. 52–63. SCITEPRESS - Science and Technology Publications, Lieusaint, Paris, France (2020)
5. Yetiser, T.: Mutation Engine Report. VIRUS-L Digest. 5 (1992)
6. Lakhina, A., Papagiannaki, K., Crovella, M., Diot, C., Kolaczyk, E.D., Taft, N.: Structural analysis of network traffic flows. In: Proceedings of the Joint International Conference on Measurement and Modeling of Computer Systems - SIGMETRICS 2004/PERFORMANCE 2004. p. 61. ACM Press, New York (2004)
7. Stergiopoulos, G., Talavari, A., Bitsikas, E., Gritzalis, D.: Automatic detection of various malicious traffic using side channel features on TCP packets. In: Lopez, J., Zhou, J., Soriano, M. (eds.) ESORICS 2018. LNCS, vol. 11098, pp. 346–362. Springer, Cham (2018). https://doi.org/10.1007/978-3-319-99073-6_17
8. Prasse, P., Machlica, L., Pevný, T., Havelka, J., Scheffer, T.: Malware detection by analysing network traffic with neural networks. In: 2017 IEEE Security and Privacy Workshops (SPW), pp. 205–210 (2017)
9. Marteau, P.: Sequence covering for efficient host-based intrusion detection. IEEE Trans. Inf. Forensics Secur. 14, 994–1006 (2019). https://doi.org/10.1109/TIFS.2018.2868614
10. Maass, M.: A theory and tools for applying sandboxes effectively. 1904944 Bytes (2018). https://doi.org/10.1184/R1/6714425.V1
11. Vokorokos, L.: Application security through sandbox virtualization. APH 12 (2014). https://doi.org/10.12700/APH.12.1.2015.1.6
12. Jaber, A.N., Zolkipli, M.F., Shakir, H.A., Jassim, M.R.: Host based intrusion detection and prevention model against DDoS attack in cloud computing. In: Xhafa, F., Caballé, S., Barolli, L. (eds.) 3PGCIC 2017. LNDECT, vol. 13, pp. 241–252. Springer, Cham (2018). https://doi.org/10.1007/978-3-319-69835-9_23
13. Qin, T., Chen, R., Wang, L., He, C.: LMHADC: lightweight method for host based anomaly detection in cloud using mobile agents. In: 2018 IEEE Conference on Communications and Network Security (CNS), pp. 1–8 (2018)
14. Adi, K., Hamza, L., Pene, L.: Automatic security policy enforcement in computer systems. Comput. Secur. 73, 156–171 (2018). https://doi.org/10.1016/j.cose.2017.10.012
15. Ashfaq, R.A.R., Wang, X.-Z., Huang, J.Z., Abbas, H., He, Y.-L.: Fuzziness based semi-supervised learning approach for intrusion detection system. Inf. Sci. 378, 484–497 (2017). https://doi.org/10.1016/j.ins.2016.04.019
16. Besharati, E., Naderan, M., Namjoo, E.: LR-HIDS: logistic regression host-based intrusion detection system for cloud environments. J. Ambient. Intell. Humaniz. Comput. 10(9), 3669–3692 (2018). https://doi.org/10.1007/s12652-018-1093-8
17. Chawla, A., Lee, B., Fallon, S., Jacob, P.: Host based intrusion detection system with combined CNN/RNN model. In: Alzate, C., et al. (eds.) ECML PKDD 2018. LNCS (LNAI), vol. 11329, pp. 149–158. Springer, Cham (2019). https://doi.org/10.1007/978-3-030-13453-2_12

18. Nobakht, M., Sivaraman, V., Boreli, R.: A host-based intrusion detection and mitigation framework for smart home IoT using OpenFlow. In: 2016 11th International Conference on Availability, Reliability and Security (ARES), Salzburg, Austria. pp. 147–156. IEEE (2016)

19. Binkley, J.R., Singh, S.: An algorithm for anomaly-based botnet detection. In: Proceedings of the 2nd Conference on Steps to Reducing Unwanted Traffic on the Internet, USA, vol. 2, p. 7. USENIX Association (2006)

20. Meidan, Y., et al.: Network-based detection of IoT botnet attacks using deep autoencoders. IEEE Pervasive Comput. **17**, 12–22 (2018). https://doi.org/10.1109/MPRV.2018.03367731

21. Sun, R., Shi, L., Yin, C., Wang, J.: An improved method in deep packet inspection based on regular expression. J. Supercomput. **75**(6), 3317–3333 (2018). https://doi.org/10.1007/s11 227-018-2517-0

22. Umbarkar, S., Shukla, S.: Analysis of heuristic based feature reduction method in intrusion detection system. In: 2018 5th International Conference on Signal Processing and Integrated Networks (SPIN), pp. 717–720 (2018)

23. Boero, L., Cello, M., Marchese, M., Mariconti, E., Naqash, T., Zappatore, S.: Statistical fingerprint-based intrusion detection system (SF-IDS). Int. J. Commun. Syst. **30**, e3225 (2017). https://doi.org/10.1002/dac.3225

24. Abubakar, A., Pranggono, B.: Machine learning based intrusion detection system for software defined networks. In: 2017 Seventh International Conference on Emerging Security Technologies (EST), Canterbury, pp. 138–143. IEEE (2017)

25. Al-Qatf, M., Lasheng, Y., Al-Habib, M., Al-Sabahi, K.: Deep learning approach combining sparse autoencoder with SVM for network intrusion detection. IEEE Access. **6**, 52843–52856 (2018). https://doi.org/10.1109/ACCESS.2018.2869577

26. Liu, Z., et al.: Deep learning approach for IDS: using DNN for network anomaly detection. In: Yang, X.-S., Sherratt, S., Dey, N., Joshi, A. (eds.) Fourth International Congress on Information and Communication Technology, pp. 471–479. Springer, Singapore (2020)

27. Papamartzivanos, D., Mármol, F.G., Kambourakis, G.: Introducing deep learning self-adaptive misuse network intrusion detection systems. IEEE Access **7**, 13546–13560 (2019). https://doi.org/10.1109/ACCESS.2019.2893871

28. Cheng, T.-H., Lin, Y.-D., Lai, Y.-C., Lin, P.-C.: Evasion techniques: sneaking through your intrusion detection/prevention systems. IEEE Commun. Surv. Tutorials. **14**, 1011–1020 (2012). https://doi.org/10.1109/SURV.2011.092311.00082

29. Dyrmose, M.: Beating the IPS. SANS Institute (2013)

30. Särelä, M., Kyöstilä, T., Kiravuo, T., Manner, J.: Evaluating intrusion prevention systems with evasions: evaluating intrusion prevention systems with evasions. Int. J. Commun. Syst. **30**, e3339 (2017). https://doi.org/10.1002/dac.3339

31. March, M.O., Gsec, G.: A Discussion of Covert Channels and Steganography. Presented at the (2002)

32. Zander, S., Armitage, G., Branch, P.: A survey of covert channels and countermeasures in computer network protocols. IEEE Commun. Surv. Tutor. **9**, 44–57 (2007). https://doi.org/10.1109/COMST.2007.4317620

33. Mileva, A., Panajotov, B.: Covert channels in TCP/IP protocol stack - extended version. Centr. Eur. J. Comput. Sci. **4**(2), 45–66 (2014). https://doi.org/10.2478/s13537-014-0205-6

34. Rowland, C.H.: Covert channels in the TCP/IP protocol suite. FM. (1997). https://doi.org/10.5210/fm.v2i5.528

35. Kolias, C., Kambourakis, G., Stavrou, A., Gritzalis, S.: Intrusion detection in 802.11 networks: empirical evaluation of threats and a public dataset. IEEE Commun. Surv. Tutor. **18**, 184–208 (2016). https://doi.org/10.1109/COMST.2015.2402161

36. Ptacek, T.H., Newsham, T.N.: Insertion, evasion, and denial of service: eluding network intrusion detection. Secure Networks Inc Calgary Alberta (1998)

37. Kunhare, N., Tiwari, R., Dhar, J.: Network packet analysis in real time traffic and study of snort IDS during the variants of DoS attacks. In: Abraham, A., Shandilya, S.K., Garcia-Hernandez, L., Varela, M.L. (eds.) HIS 2019. AISC, vol. 1179, pp. 362–375. Springer, Cham (2021). https://doi.org/10.1007/978-3-030-49336-3_36

38. Cui, C., Xue, L., Chiu, C., Kondikoppa, P., Park, S.: DMCTCP: desynchronized multi-channel TCP for high speed access networks with tiny buffers. In: 2014 23rd International Conference on Computer Communication and Networks (ICCCN), pp. 1–8 (2014)

39. Joncheray, L.: A simple active attack against TCP. In: Proceedings of the 5th Conference on USENIX UNIX Security Symposium, USA, vol. 5, p. 2. USENIX Association (1995)

40. Tjhai, G.C., Papadaki, M., Furnell, S.M., Clarke, N.L.: Investigating the problem of IDS false alarms: an experimental study using Snort. In: Jajodia, S., Samarati, P., Cimato, S. (eds.) SEC 2008. ITIFIP, vol. 278, pp. 253–267. Springer, Boston, MA (2008). https://doi.org/10.1007/978-0-387-09699-5_17

41. El-Hajj, W., Al-Tamimi, M., Aloul, F.: Real traffic logs creation for testing intrusion detection systems: real traffic logs creation for testing intrusion detection systems. Wirel. Commun. Mob. Comput. 15, 1851–1864 (2015). https://doi.org/10.1002/wcm.2471

42. Gibbs, P.: Intrusion Detection Evasion Techniques and Case Studies. SANS Institute (2017)

43. Martin, S.: Anti-IDS Tools and Tactics. SANS Institute (2001)

44. Ring, M., Landes, D., Hotho, A.: Detection of slow port scans in flow-based network traffic. PLoS ONE 13, e0204507 (2018). https://doi.org/10.1371/journal.pone.0204507

45. Kim, D., et al.: DynODet: detecting dynamic obfuscation in malware. In: Polychronakis, M., Meier, M. (eds.) DIMVA 2017. LNCS, vol. 10327, pp. 97–118. Springer, Cham (2017). https://doi.org/10.1007/978-3-319-60876-1_5

46. Alazab, A., Khresiat, A.: New strategy for mitigating of SQL injection attack. IJCA 154, 1 (2016). https://doi.org/10.5120/ijca2016911974

47. Cova, M., Kruegel, C., Vigna, G.: Detection and analysis of drive-by-download attacks and malicious JavaScript code. In: Proceedings of the 19th International Conference on World Wide Web - WWW 2010, Raleigh, North Carolina, USA, p. 281. ACM Press (2010)

48. Fogla, P., Sharif, M., Perdisci, R., Kolesnikov, O., Lee, W.: Polymorphic blending attacks. In: Proceedings of the 15th Conference on USENIX Security Symposium, USA, vol. 15. USENIX Association (2006)

49. Fogla, P., Lee, W.: Evading network anomaly detection systems: formal reasoning and practical techniques. In: Proceedings of the 13th ACM conference on Computer and communications security - CCS 2006, Alexandria, Virginia, USA, pp. 59–68. ACM Press (2006)

50. Valenza, A., Demetrio, L., Costa, G., Lagorio, G.: WAF-A-MoLE: an adversarial tool for assessing ML-based WAFs. SoftwareX. 11, 100367 (2020). https://doi.org/10.1016/j.softx.2019.100367

51. Banescu, S., Pretschner, A.: A Tutorial on software obfuscation. In: Advances in Computers, pp. 283–353. Elsevier, Amsterdam (2018)

52. Metke, A.R., Ekl, R.L.: Security technology for smart grid networks. IEEE Trans. Smart Grid 1, 99–107 (2010). https://doi.org/10.1109/TSG.2010.2046347

53. Butun, I., Morgera, S.D., Sankar, R.: A survey of intrusion detection systems in wireless sensor networks. IEEE Commun. Surv. Tutor. 16, 266–282 (2014). https://doi.org/10.1109/SURV.2013.050113.00191

54. Handel, T.G., Sandford, M.T.: Hiding data in the OSI network model. In: Anderson, R. (ed.) IH 1996. LNCS, vol. 1174, pp. 23–38. Springer, Heidelberg (1996). https://doi.org/10.1007/3-540-61996-8_29

55. Goyal, P., Goyal, A.: Comparative study of two most popular packet sniffing tools-Tcpdump and Wireshark. In: 2017 9th International Conference on Computational Intelligence and Communication Networks (CICN), Girne, pp. 77–81. IEEE (2017)

56. Botta, A., Dainotti, A., Pescape, A.: Do you trust your software-based traffic generator? IEEE Commun. Mag. **48**, 158–165 (2010). https://doi.org/10.1109/MCOM.2010.5560600
57. Javali, C., Revadigar, G.: Network web traffic generator for cyber range exercises. In: 2019 IEEE 44th Conference on Local Computer Networks (LCN), Osnabrueck, Germany, pp. 308–315. IEEE (2019)
58. Ouyang, W., Zhang, X., Wang, D., Zhang, J., Tang, J.: A survey of network traffic generation. In: Third International Conference on Cyberspace Technology (CCT 2015), Beijing, China, p. 6. Institution of Engineering and Technology (2015)
59. Benson, A.R., Kumar, R., Tomkins, A.: Modeling user consumption sequences. In: Proceedings of the 25th International Conference on World Wide Web - WWW 2016, Montral, Qubec, Canada. pp. 519–529. ACM Press (2016)
60. Lo, C., Frankowski, D., Leskovec, J.: Understanding behaviors that lead to purchasing: a case study of pinterest. In: Proceedings of the 22nd ACM SIGKDD International Conference on Knowledge Discovery and Data Mining, San Francisco, California, USA, pp. 531–540. ACM (2016)
61. Cheng, J., Lo, C., Leskovec, J.: Predicting intent using activity logs: how goal specificity and temporal range affect user behavior. In: Proceedings of the 26th International Conference on World Wide Web Companion - WWW 2017 Companion, Perth, Australia, pp. 593–601. ACM Press (2017)
62. Dupret, G.E., Piwowarski, B.: A user browsing model to predict search engine click data from past observations. In: Proceedings of the 31st Annual International ACM SIGIR Conference on Research and Development in Information Retrieval - SIGIR 2008, Singapore, Singapore, p. 331. ACM Press (2008)
63. Roosta, S.H.: Parallel Processing and Parallel Algorithms. Springer, New York (2000). https://doi.org/10.1007/978-1-4612-1220-1
64. Mittal, S., Vetter, J.: A survey of architectural approaches for data compression in cache and main memory systems. IEEE Trans. Parallel Distrib. Syst. **27**, 1524–1536 (2016). https://doi.org/10.1109/TPDS.2015.2435788
65. Shannon, C.E.: A mathematical theory of communication. Bell Syst. Tech. J. **27**, 379–423 (1948). https://doi.org/10.1002/j.1538-7305.1948.tb01338.x
66. Burks, D.: Security onion. Securityonion. blogspot.com (2012)
67. Wagenseil, P.: Best antivirus 2020: free antivirus and paid software (2020). https://www.tom sguide.com/us/best-antivirus,review-2588.html
68. Williams, M.: The best antivirus software for 2020 (2020). https://www.techradar.com/best/best-antivirus

Security and Complexity of a New Variant of the McEliece Cryptosystem Using Non-linear Convolutional Codes

Michael Ekonde Sone$^{(\boxtimes)}$

College of Technology, University of Buea, Buea, Cameroon
michael.sone@ubuea.cm

Abstract. The McEliece public-key cryptography (PKC) has fewer encryption/decryption operations compared to other PKC schemes such as RSA, ECC, and ElGamal. The use of Goppa codes in its implementation ensures the hardness of the decoding problem. Conversely, the original McEliece PKC has a low encryption rate and large key size. In this paper, a new variant of the McEliece cryptosystem is presented based on non-linear convolutional codes. Cascaded convolutional codes are used to be part of the public key with each stage of the cascade separated by a product cipher to increase the security level. Convolutional codes are used as an alternative to Goppa codes since the Viterbi decoding algorithm is suitable for high data-rate applications by providing maximum-likelihood solutions. The convolutional code used in the implementation increases both security and throughput due to its high error-correcting capacity. It is shown that the new variant has small key sizes with enhanced security-complexity trade-off. Cryptanalysis of the new version of the McEliece cryptosystem is performed using existing attacks of the classical cryptosystem to demonstrate the difficulties in breaking the new cryptosystem. Also, it is shown that security levels comparable to the original McEliece cryptosystem could be obtained by using smaller public key sizes of the new version if multiple stages of the generator matrix are employed. This aspect makes the new version of the McEliece cryptosystem attractive in mobile wireless networks since it could be ported onto a single Field Programmable Gate Array (FPGA).

Keywords: McEliece cryptosystem · Non-linear convolutional code · Product cipher · Generator matrix

1 Introduction

Major research efforts are currently targeting the McEliece public-key cryptography (PKC) since it is an attractive option for post-quantum PKC. Original McEliece cryptosystem [1] based on Goppa codes remains unbroken for appropriate system parameters. However, the large key sizes used in the original McEliece cryptosystem led Niederreiter in 1986 [2] to propose a different scheme based on GRS codes. Niederreiter variant employs smaller key sizes compared to the original McEliece version but encountered

© Springer Nature Switzerland AG 2021
M. S. Obaidat and J. Ben-Othman (Eds.): ICETE 2020, CCIS 1484, pp. 24–50, 2021.
https://doi.org/10.1007/978-3-030-90428-9_2

limited interest in practical applications. Several other proposals were made to modify the original McEliece's scheme by replacing the Goppa codes with other codes [3–5]. However, most of the versions based on coding theory turned out to be insecure or inefficient compared to the original McEliece cryptosystem. Of recent, there have been several attempts to build other cryptographic schemes based on error-correcting codes [6, 7]. In some of these schemes, convolutional codes have been used as an alternative in the implementation of the McEliece cryptosystem since the Viterbi decoding algorithm is suitable for high data-rate applications by providing maximum-likelihood solutions. However, existing McEliece cryptosystem variants based on convolutional codes turned out to be insecure [8]. Most security experts believe that convolutional code-based cryptosystems are vulnerable to attacks if enough input/output data is used and preamble data is provided. It is in this light that the security level of the cryptographic algorithm based on convolutional codes could be enhanced by introducing a non-linear cryptosystem [9, 10]. The efficient attack reported in [8] could be circumvented if the non-linear convolutional cryptosystem is used to implement the McEliece cryptosystem. However, the non-linear convolutional code in [9, 10] is a globally invertible (k,k,m) code with limited error-correcting capability.

In this paper, the implementation of a new variant of the McEliece cryptosystem using non-linear convolutional codes is presented. The codes used in the implementation have good error protection properties as highlighted in [11–13]. Hence, a (3,1,3) non-linear convolutional code with an error-correcting capacity of $t = 20$ errors will be used to implement the new variant of the McEliece cryptosystem. The number of operations required to effectively determine the states of the convolutional code, the transition functions used to switch from one state to another and the combinations in the product cipher in the new variant of the McEliece cryptosystem will be used to establish bounds for the key size. The generator matrix, G like the existing convolutional codes used in the McEliece cryptosystem, the difference in this new method is that the generator matrices are implemented in stages interspaced with product ciphers. The complexity to decode the ciphertext which increases with the number of stages will be analyzed and compared to existing schemes. To determine the security level of the new variant of the McEliece cryptosystem, cryptanalysis is performed using existing attacks of the classical cryptosystem to demonstrate the difficulties in breaking the new cryptosystem. Also, it is shown that security levels comparable to the original McEliece cryptosystem could be obtained by using smaller public key sizes of the new version if multiple stages of the same generator matrix are employed. The aspect of small key sizes makes the new version of the McEliece cryptosystem attractive in mobile wireless networks since it could be ported into a single FPGA. Future research will involve the application of this novel version of the McEliece cryptosystem to wireless cooperative networks.

The complete outline of the paper is as follows. In the next section, a new algorithm for encoding/decoding using the non-linear convolutional cryptosystem will be presented. The (3,1,3) code which has a high error-correcting capacity [13] will be used to illustrate the new algorithm. The non-linear convolutional coding is implemented by inserting product ciphers between conventional convolutional coding blocks. The classical McEliece PKC and the new variant of the McEliece PKC based on the non-linear convolutional codes are presented in Sect. 3 [14]. Section 4 presents two important cryptographic algorithm metrics, namely key size, and complexity. The key size analysis of the new variant is based on the number of operations required to determine the states of the convolutional code, the transition functions, and the combinations in the product cipher. The complexity to decode the ciphertext in the new variant is analyzed based on the Viterbi algorithm. Section 5 presents the cryptanalysis of the novel McEliece cryptosystem to determine the security level. The cryptanalysis is based on assessing the number of operations required to curb security attacks. Results and discussion are presented in Sect. 6. The section presents a comparative study of existing McEliece cryptosystems and the new variant of the McEliece cryptosystem concerning the key size, complexity, and security level. Finally, the conclusion and future work are presented in Sect. 7.

2   A New Non-linear Convolutional Encoding/Decoding Algorithm

This section presents the basic parameters of a non-linear convolutional cryptosystem such as the states, transition functions, and combinations of the product cipher. It also presents the new encoding/decoding algorithm based on the non-linear convolutional cryptosystem with the (3,1,3) used in the illustration of the new algorithm.

2.1   Non-linear Convolutional Cryptosystem

A convolutional cryptosystem is characterized by its different states and transition functions used to switch from one state to another. The transition compares the input data and the present state and decides the next state. This change of state due to input data makes convolutional cryptosystem to be dynamic since configuration can change at runtime. The transition functions, the meta S-boxes, the sets of permutations, the states of each convolutional code of the cascade are private. The specifications of the private keys for the non-linear convolutional cryptosystem assuming 2-bit input/output and three states are as follows:

- States of the convolutional code: the states are given by the connections of the input data register and the $L = 2$ memory registers to the modulo-2 adder. The contents in the state matrices indicate the connections between the registers and the mod-2 adder. A '1' in the state matrix indicates that the corresponding shift register is connected to the modulo-2 adder and a '0' in a given position indicates that no connection exists between that shift register and the modulo-2 adder.
- Transition functions: The transition function, f gives a set of transition conditions for switching from one state to another. For example, a possible transition table for a 2-bit input/output and three states convolutional cryptosystem is shown in Table 1.

   In Table 1, the function, f for example compares the inputs [0 0] to the present state, S1, and switches to the next state S2.

- S-box shuffling: They are used to shuffle the outputs of a preceding convolutional code stage before being fed to the input of the P-box.

Table 1. Transition table.

F	[0 0]	[0 1]	[1 0]	[1 1]
S1	S2	S3	S3	S1
S2	S3	S1	S2	S3
S3	S3	S2	S1	S2

- P-box permutations: They are used to permute the outputs of the S-box before being fed to the input of the next convolutional stage.

In this paper, (3,1,3) non-linear convolutional code will be analyzed. Figure 1 shows two possible states for the code.

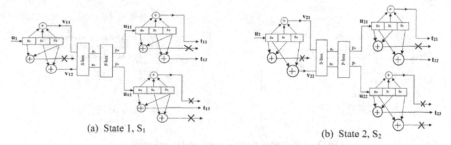

(a) State 1, S_1 (b) State 2, S_2

Fig. 1. 2 Possible states for the (3,1,3) non-linear convolutional code.

The transition table, S-box combinations, and P-box permutations are shown in Table 2.

Table 2. Possible S-box, P-box, Transition table for (3,1,3) non-linear convolutional code.

Input	00	01	10	11
Output	01	11	00	10

S-box

Input	1	2
Output	2	1

P-box

f	[00]	[01]	[10]	[11]
S_1	S_2	S_2	S_1	S_2
S_2	S_1	S_1	S_2	S_1

Transition Table

2.2 New Encoding/Decoding Algorithm Using Non-linear Convolutional Code

For an (n,k,m) convolutional code, the algorithm to encode/decode a bitstream, x(n) of N bits is as follows:

1. Pad the bitstream, x(n) with zeros so that it is of length N + L bits where L = constraint length = k(m − 1)
2. x(n) is partitioned into non-overlapping segments of length m bits

3. Encode each m + L bits where the L bits added to the segment corresponding to the number of L bits to the right of the segment.

   As shown in Fig. 2, overlapping is used in the encoding process, that is, the least significant L bits of the preceding segment will become the Most Significant Bits (MSB) of the next segment.

4. Encode each segment using a clearly defined state of the encoder which is determined by the transition table. To determine the encoder state, the L bits in the transition functions which correspond to the most significant L bits in each segment are used.

5. Encode next segment using next state of the encoder which is determined using the most significant L bits of the preceding segment

6. Decode the outputs of each segment using the Viterbi algorithm and discard the least significant L bits of each decoded segment

7. Obtain the original bitstream by concatenating the retained decoded bits from the segment.

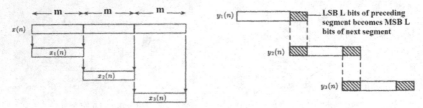

Fig. 2. Bitstream partitioning and overlapping.

Example: Encoding/decoding the bitstream x(n) = 100101 using the (3,1,3) non-linear convolutional code.

   Transition tables for the (3,1,3) convolutional code shown in the appendix are used to encode the message, M = 110101.

- The constraint length, L = k(m − 1) this gives L = 1(3 − 1) = 2
- Modified codeword, M' = 11010100
- The segments derived from the modified codeword are as follows: $u_1 = 1101$ $u_2 = 0101$ $u_3 = 0100$
- Using step 3 of the algorithm, the overlapping of the segments is as follows:

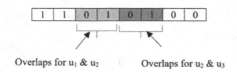

Overlaps for u_1 & u_2 Overlaps for u_2 & u_3

– Encoding Process

- The segment, $u_1 = 1101$: The encoding of segment u_1 is summarized in Table 3.

Table 3. Encoding table for segment u_1.

STAGE 1, STATE 1				S-box outputs	P-box outputs	STAGE 2, STATE 1		
Input bits	Input state	Output state	Output bits			Input state	Output state	Output bits
u_1	s_1 s_2	s_1 s_2	v_{11} v_{12}	a_1 a_2	p_1 p_2	$s_1 s_2 s_1 s_2$	$s_1 s_2 s_1 s_2$	t_{11} t_{12} t_{13}
1	0 0	1 0	1 0	0 0	0 0	0 0 0 0	0 0 0 0	0 0 0
1	1 0	1 1	0 1	1 1	1 1	0 0 0 0	1 0 1 0	1 0 1
0	1 1	0 1	0 0	0 1	1 0	1 0 1 0	1 1 0 1	0 1 0
1	0 1	1 0	0 1	1 1	1 1	1 1 0 1	1 1 1 0	1 0 0

From Table 3, the encoded codeword segment is given as $T_1 = 000\ 101\ 010\ 100$

- The segment, $u_2 = 0101$: Present state is state 1, S_1 and MSB L bits of the preceding vector is $u_1[11]$, hence from transition table, the encoder switches to state 2, S_2. The encoding of segment u_1 is summarized in Table 4.

Table 4. Encoding table for segment u_2.

STAGE 1, STATE 2				S-box outputs	P-box outputs	STAGE 2, STATE 2		
Input bits	Input state	Output state	Output bits			Input state	Output state	Output bits
u_2	s_1 s_2	s_1 s_2	v_{11} v_{12}	a_1 a_2	p_1 p_2	$s_1 s_2 s_1 s_2$	$s_1 s_2 s_1 s_2$	t_{21} t_{22} t_{23}
0	0 0	0 0	0 0	0 1	1 0	0 0 0 0	1 0 0 0	1 1 0
1	0 0	1 0	1 1	1 0	0 1	1 0 0 0	0 1 1 0	1 0 1
0	1 0	0 1	1 0	0 0	0 0	1 0 1 0	0 1 0 1	1 0 1
1	0 1	1 0	0 0	0 1	1 0	1 1 0 1	1 1 0 0	1 0 0

From Table 4, the encoded codeword segment is given as $T_2 = 110\ 101\ 101\ 100$

- The segment, $u_3 = 0100$: Present state is state 2, S_2 and MSB L bits of the preceding vector is $u_2[01]$, hence from transition table, the encoder switches to state 1, S_1. The encoding of segment u_1 is summarized in Table 5.

From Table 5, the encoded codeword segment is given as $T_3 = 100\ 110\ 111\ 001$

Table 5. Encoding table for segment u_3.

STAGE 1, STATE 1				S-box outputs	P-box outputs	STAGE 2, STATE 1		
Input bits	Input state	Output state	Output bits	outputs	outputs	Input state	Output state	Output bits
u_3	$s_1\ s_2$	$s_1\ s_2$	$u_{11}\ u_{12}$	$a_1\ a_2$	$p_1\ p_2$	$s_1\ s_2\ s_1\ s_2$	$s_1\ s_2\ s_1\ s_2$	$t_{11}\ t_{12}\ t_{13}$
0	0 0	0 0	0 0	0 1	1 0	0 0 0 0	1 0 0 0	1 0 0
1	0 0	1 0	1 0	0 0	0 0	1 0 0 0	0 1 0 0	1 1 0
0	1 0	0 1	1 1	1 0	0 1	0 1 0 0	0 0 1 0	1 1 1
0	0 1	0 0	1 1	1 0	0 1	0 0 1 0	0 0 1 1	0 0 1

– **Decoding Process**
The entire process is reversed compared to the encoding process, namely, the transmitted segment is the first process in the second stage through the P-box and later S-box and finally the first stage to retrieve the original segment.

• The decoding of the transmitted segment, $T_1 = 000\ 101\ 010\ 100$ is summarized in Fig. 3.

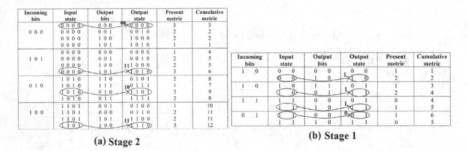

(a) Stage 2   (b) Stage 1

Fig. 3. Viterbi algorithm to decode $T_1 = 000\ 101\ 010\ 100$.

The output of Stage 2, $R_1 = 00\ 11\ 10\ 11$ is fed to the P-box. The output of the P-box, $P = 00\ 11\ 01\ 11$ is fed to the S-box. Finally, the output of the S-box, $S = 10\ 01\ 11\ 01$ is fed to Stage 1. From Fig. 3, the output of the first stage which is the retrieved segment is given as $V_1 = 1110$. From step 6 of the algorithm, discard least significant L bits which correspond to $V_1[2\ 3] = 10$. The final retrieved message which will be concatenated to the other retrieved vectors is $V_1[0\ 1] = 11$.

• The decoding of the transmitted segment, $T_2 = 110\ 101\ 101\ 100$ is summarized in Fig. 4.

(a) Stage 2

Incoming bits	Input state	Output bits	Output state	Present metric	Cumulative metric
1 1 0	0 0 0 0	0 0 0	0 0 0 0	1	1
	0 0 0 0	0 0 1	100 0 1 0	0	0
	0 0 0 0	1 1 0	1 0 0	3	3
	0 0 0 0	1 1 1	1 0 1 0	2	2
1 0 1	1 0 0 0	1 0 0	010 1 0 0	2	5
	1 0 0 0	1 0 1	0 1 1 0	3	6
	1 0 0 0	1 1 0	1 1 0 0	0	3
	1 0 0 0	0 1 1	1 1 1 0	1	4
1 0 1	0 1 1 0	1 1 1	0 0 0 1	2	8
	0 1 1 0	1 1 0	100 0 1 1	1	7
	0 1 1 0	0 0 1	1 0 0	2	8
	0 1 1 0	0 0 0	1 0 1 1	1	7
1 0 0	0 0 0 1	0 0 0	0 0 0 0	2	10
	0 0 0 1	0 0 1	0 0 1 0	1	9
	0 0 0 1	1 1 0	1 0 0 0	1	9
	0 0 0 1	1 1 1	001 0 1 0	1	9
	1 0 0 1	1 0 0	0 1 0 0	3	11
	1 0 0 1	1 0 1	0 1 1 0	2	10
	1 0 0 1	0 1 0	1 1 0 0	1	9
	1 0 0 1	0 1 1	1 1 1 0	0	8

(b) Stage 1

Incoming bits	Input state	Output bits	Output state	Present metric	Cumulative metric
0 0	0 0	0 0	0 0	2	2
	0 0	0 0	1 0	0	0
1 1	0 0	0 0	0 0	0	2
	0 0	0 0	1 0	2	4
0 0	1 0	1 0	0 1	1	5
	1 0	0 1	1 0	1	5
	0 1	1 1	0 0	1	6
1 0	0 1	0 0	1 0	1	6
	1 1	0 1	0 1	0	5
	0 1	1 0	1 0	2	7

Fig. 4. Viterbi algorithm to decode $T_2 = 110\ 101\ 101\ 100$.

$V_1[0\ 1] = 11$ is used to determine the state of the decoder. The present state is state 1, S_1, hence from the transition table, the decoder switches to state 2, S_2

The output of Stage 2, $R_2 = 10\ 01\ 10\ 00$ is fed to the P-box. The output of the P-box, $P = 01\ 10\ 01\ 00$ is fed to the S-box. Finally, the output of the S-box, $S = 00\ 11\ 00\ 10$ is fed to Stage 1. From Fig. 4, the output of the first stage which is the retrieved segment is given as $V_2 = 0111$. From step 6 of the algorithm, discard least significant L bits which correspond to $V_2[2\ 3] = 11$. The final retrieved message which will be concatenated to the other retrieved vectors is $V_2[0\ 1] = 01$.

- The decoding of the transmitted segment, $T_3 = 100\ 110\ 111\ 001$ is summarized in Fig. 5.

(a) Stage 2

Incoming bits	Input state	Output bits	Output state	Present metric	Cumulative metric
1 0 0	0 0 0 0	0 0 0	0 0 0 0	2	2
	0 0 0 0	0 0 1	100 0 1 0	1	1
	0 0 0 0	1 0 0	1 0 0	3	3
	0 0 0 0	1 0 1	00 1 0 1 0	2	2
1 1 0	0 0 0 0	1 1 0	1 0 0	3	6
	1 0 0 0	1 1 1	0 1 1 0	2	5
	1 0 0 0	0 1 0	1 1 0 0	2	5
	1 0 0 0	0 1 1	1 1 1 0	1	4
1 1 1	0 1 0 0	1 1 0	010 0 0 0	2	8
	0 1 0 0	1 1 1	0 0 1 0	3	9
	0 1 0 0	0 1 0	1 0 0 0	1	7
	0 1 0 0	0 1 1	1 0 1 0	2	8
0 1 1	0 0 1 0	0 0 0	01 0 0 0 1	1	10
	0 0 1 0	0 0 1	0 0 1 1	2	11
	0 0 1 0	1 0 0	1 0 0 1	0	9
	0 0 1 0	1 0 1	1 0 1 1	1	10

(b) Stage 1

Incoming bits	Input state	Output bits	Output state	Present metric	Cumulative metric
0 0	0 0	0 0	0 0	2	2
	0 0	0 0	1 0	1	1
1 0	0 0	0 0	0 0	2	3
	0 0	0 1	1 0	2	4
1 1	1 0	1 0	0 0	2	6
	1 0	0 1	0 0	1	5
1 1	0 1	0 0	1 0	2	8
	0 1	0 0	1 0	2	6

Fig. 5. Viterbi algorithm to decode $T_3 = 100\ 110\ 111\ 001$.

$V_2[0\ 1] = 01$ is used to determine the state of the decoder. The present state is state 2, S_2, hence from the transition table, the decoder switches to state 1, S_1

The output of Stage 2, $R_3 = 10\ 00\ 01\ 01$ is fed to the P-box. The output of the P-box, $P = 01\ 00\ 10\ 10$ is fed to the S-box. Finally, the output of the S-box, $S = 00\ 10\ 11\ 11$ is fed to Stage 1. From Fig. 5, the output of the first stage which is the retrieved segment is given as $V_3 = 0100$. From step 6 of the algorithm, discard least significant L bits which correspond to $V_3[2\ 3] = 00$. The final retrieved message which will be concatenated to the other retrieved vectors is $V_3[0\ 1] = 01$.

The final retrieved message, $V = V_1[0\ 1]\|V_2[0\ 1]\|V_3[0\ 1] = 110101$

Hence, the final retrieved message, V is identical to the original message, M = 110101

3   A New Variant of the Mceliece Cryptosystem

This section explains the implementation of the new variant of the McEliece cryptosystem using the non-linear convolutional code in combination with a scrambled invertible matrix and a permutation matrix [14].

3.1   The Classical McEliece Cryptosystem

- Key generation

  - Pick a random [n, k, 2t + 1] linear code, C where n is the number of bits for codeword; k is the number of message bits an t is the number of errors the code can correct
  - Compute a k x n generator matrix, G for C
  - Generate a random k x k binary non-singular (invertible) matrix S
  - Generate a random n x n permutation matrix P
  - Compute k x n matrix $G' = SGP$
  - Public key is (G', t)
  - The private key is (S, G, P, D) where D is the efficient decoding algorithm

- Encryption

  - Message, $m \in \{0, 1\}^k$
  - Random vector, $e \in \{0, 1\}^n$
  - Ciphertext, $c = mG' + e$

- Decryption

  - Ciphertext, $c \in \{0, 1\}^n$
  - Compute $CP^{-1} = (mS)G + eP^{-1}$

    Since $(mS)G$ is a valid codeword for the chosen linear code and eP^{-1} has weight t, the decoding algorithm, D can be applied to CP^{-1} to obtain $c' = mS$

  - Compute $m = c'S^{-1}$.

The difficulty of decoding a random encoder, known to be an NP-hard problem underscores the security of McEliece cryptosystem. This is possible for high order block codes such as 1024-bit code.

3.2 The New Variant of the McEliece Cryptosystem [14]

In the new variant of the McEliece cryptosystem proposed in this research, the key parameters are as follows:

- Public key: (G', t);
- Private key: $(S, G, s_{box}, p_{box}, P, D)$ where s_{box} and p_{box} are the additional keys from the product cipher.

G' corresponds to a k x n non-linear convolutional code that is permutation-equivalent to the chosen secret key such that P permutes the columns of the non-linear convolutional code, G and S switches to a different basis of the same code.

In Sect. 2, aspects of the private key such as the encoding/decoding, D; states and transition functions of generator matrix, G; keys for the product cipher s_{box}, p_{box} were presented.

The permutation matrix, P used in this research is matrix $P(D,D-1) \in \mathbb{F}^{nxn}$ developed in [15].

Meanwhile, in classical McEliece cryptosystem, $c' = mS$ is synonymous with scrambling data m to obtain c' where $m = c'S - 1$ is equivalent to descrambling. The scrambling method will be used for the implementation of the invertible matrix, S in this research since it involves shift registers that is easy to implement in an FPGA.

A simple scrambler and descrambler in Fig. 6 will be used to explain the proposed invertible matrix, S [16].

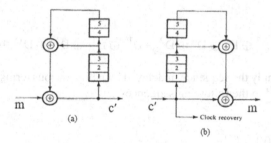

Fig. 6. (a) Scrambler and (b) descrambler.

The scrambler consists of a feedback shift register and the matching descrambler has a feedforward shift register. If m is the input sequence to the scrambler, then

$$m \oplus D^3 c' \oplus D^5 c' = c'$$

where D represents the delay operator, that is $D^n c'$ is the sequence c' delayed by n units. Adding $(D^3 \oplus D^5) c'$ to both sides of the equation gives

$$m = c' \oplus \left(D^3 \oplus D^5\right) c' = \left[1 \oplus \left(D^3 \oplus D^5\right)\right] c' = (1 \oplus F) c'$$

where $F = D^3 \oplus D^5$.

To design the descrambler at the receiver, we start with c' and perform the equation

$$m = c' \oplus F c' = c' \oplus \left(D^3 \oplus D^5\right)c'$$

Let message, m = 1010101 be fed into the scrambler.

Initially $c' = m$, and the sequence m enters the register and is returned as $(D^3 \oplus D^5)m = Fm$ through the feedback path. This new sequence Fm enters the register and is returned as F^2m, and so on. Hence

$$c' = m \oplus Fm \oplus F^2m \oplus F^3m \oplus \ldots$$

Recognizing that

$$F = D^3 \oplus D^5$$

we have

$$F^2 = \left(D^3 \oplus D^5\right) \cdot \left(D^3 \oplus D^5\right) = D^6 \oplus D^{10} \oplus D^8 \oplus D^8 = D^6 \oplus D^{10}.$$

Since $D^8 \oplus D^8 = 0$
Similarly,

$$F^3 = \left(D^6 \oplus D^{10}\right) \cdot \left(D^3 \oplus D^5\right) = D^9 \oplus D^{11} \oplus D^{13} \oplus D^{15}$$

and so on.
Hence

$$c' = \left(1 \oplus D^3 \oplus D^5 \oplus D^6 \oplus D^9 \oplus D^{10} \oplus D^{11} \oplus D^{13} \oplus D^{15} \oplus \ldots\right)m.$$

Because D^nm is simply the sequence m delayed by n bits, various terms in the preceding equation correspond to the following sequences:

$m = 1 0 1 0 1 0 1$
$D^3m = 0 0 0 1 0 1 0 1 0 1$
$D^5m = 0 0 0 0 0 1 0 1 0 1 0 1$
$D^6m = 0 0 0 0 0 0 1 0 1 0 1 0 1$
$D^9m = \underline{0 0 0 0 0 0 0 0 1 0 1 0 1}$
$c' = 1 0 1 1 1 0 0$

It is worth noting that, the string c' is calculated vertically using mod-2 arithmetic and input sequence, m has 7 digits hence only 7 digits of the scrambler output are retained.

When sequence c' is applied to the input of the descrambler, the output is the original sequence, m

$m = (1 \oplus D^3 \oplus D^5) c'$
$c' = 1 0 1 1 1 0 0$
$D^3c' = 0 0 0 1 0 1 1 1 0 0$

$D^5 c' = 0\,0\,0\,0\,0\,1\,0\,1\,1\,1\,0\,0$

mod-2 arithmetic gives the 7-bit sequence 1010101 which is identical to the input sequence m = 1010101.

Based on the afore-mentioned analysis, a k x k invertible matrix, S, and the scrambled message c′ could be deduced from a k-bit message fed into the scrambler as follows:

- Each row of the k × k matrix, S contains elements of the shifted message, m deduced from the scrambler
- Each bit of the scrambled message, c′ is computed from the sum of each column of the k × k matrix.

Hence the k × k matrix, S of the scrambler in Fig. 6 is given as

$$S = \begin{pmatrix} D^0 m(0) & D^0 m(1) & D^0 m(2) & D^0 m(3) & D^0 m(4) & D^0 m(5) & D^0 m(6) & D^0 m(7) & D^0 m(k) \\ D^3 m(0) & D^3 m(1) & D^3 m(2) & D^3 m(3) & D^3 m(4) & D^3 m(5) & D^3 m(6) & D^3 m(7) & D^3 m(k) \\ D^5 m(0) & D^5 m(1) & D^5 m(2) & D^5 m(3) & D^5 m(4) & D^5 m(5) & D^5 m(6) & D^5 m(7) & \cdots D^5 m(k) \\ D^6 m(0) & D^6 m(1) & D^6 m(2) & D^6 m(3) & D^6 m(4) & D^6 m(5) & D^6 m(6) & D^6 m(7) & D^6 m(k) \\ D^9 m(0) & D^9 m(1) & D^9 m(2) & D^9 m(3) & D^9 m(4) & D^9 m(5) & D^9 m(6) & D^9 m(7) & D^9 m(k) \\ D^{10} m(0) & D^{10} m(1) & D^{10} m(2) & D^{10} m(3) & D^{10} m(4) & D^{10} m(5) & D^{10} m(6) & D^{10} m(7) & D^{10} m(k) \\ D^{11} m(0) & D^{11} m(1) & D^{11} m(2) & D^{11} m(3) & D^{11} m(4) & D^{11} m(5) & D^{11} m(6) & D^{11} m(7) & \cdots D^{11} m(k) \\ D^{13} m(0) & D^{13} m(1) & D^{13} m(2) & D^{13} m(3) & D^{11} m(4) & D^{13} m(5) & D^{13} m(6) & D^{13} m(7) & D^{13} m(k) \end{pmatrix} \qquad (1)$$

Similarly, for the descrambler, the matrix S^{-1}, and the original message, m are obtained as follows:

- Each row of the matrix, S^{-1} contains elements of the shifted scrambled message, c′ deduced from the descrambler
- Each bit of the message, m is computed from the sum of each column of the matrix, S^{-1}

Hence the matrix, S^{-1} of the descrambler in Fig. 4 is given as

$$S^{-1} = \begin{pmatrix} D^0 c'(0) & D^0 c'(1) & D^0 c'(2) & D^0 c'(3) & D^0 c'(4) & D^0 c'(5) & D^0 c'(6) & D^0 c'(7) & \dots & D^0 c'(k) \\ D^3 c'(0) & D^3 c'(1) & D^3 c'(2) & D^3 c'(3) & D^3 c'(4) & D^3 c'(5) & D^3 c'(6) & D^3 c'(7) & \dots & D^3 c'(k) \\ D^5 c'(0) & D^5 c'(1) & D^3 c'(2) & D^5 c'(3) & D^5 c'(4) & D^5 c'(5) & D^5 c'(6) & D^5 c'(7) & \dots & D^5 c'(k) \end{pmatrix} \qquad (2)$$

4 Cryptographic Algorithm Metrics

This section presents two important cryptographic algorithm metrics, namely key size, and complexity. The key size analysis of the new variant is based on the number of operations required to determine the states of the convolutional code, the transition functions, and the combinations in the product cipher. The complexity to decode the ciphertext in the new variant is analyzed based on the Viterbi algorithm. Both metrics will be analyzed based on the (3,1,3) non-linear convolutional cryptosystem.

4.1 Key Size Analysis

The size of the keyspace required to reveal the following parameters will be evaluated:

- Number of states
- Number of transition functions
- Number of operations for S-box
- Number of operations for P-box

Keys Required for the Number of States
The state is represented by the contents of the memory, that is, for an (n,k,m) convolutional code, it corresponds to the $k(m - 1)$ previous bits, namely, the $k(m - 1)$ bits contained in the first $k(m - 1)$ stages of the shift register. Hence for static connections to fixed mod-2 adders, the number of states, q required is given as

- No. of states, $q = 2^{k(m-1)}$
- No of bits required, $N_1 = k(m - 1)$

  – For (3,1,3) convolutional code:

- No. of states, $q = 2^2 = 4$
- No of bits required $= k(m - 1) = 2$ bits

For n output bits or n mod-2 adders, the different connections of the different states to the mod-2 adders are as follows:

- Total No. of states, $q_T = nq$
- Total No. of bits required, $N_2 = \lceil \log_2 q_T \rceil$

  Hence, using the parameters of (3,1,3) code, $q_T = 3 \times 4 = 12$ and $N_2 = 4$ bits

  $\Rightarrow$ keys required to reveal all the states $= 2^4$ keys.

Keys Required for Transition Functions
For constraint length, L No. of transition functions $= 2^L$ and the No. of bits, $N_3 = L$ bits

- For a (3,1,3) code, No. of bits, $N_3 = 2$ and the number of keys required to reveal all the transition functions is 2^2 keys.

Keys Required for S-box Shuffling Operations
For n-bit shuffled boxes, Number of operations, $N_{TS} = (2^n - 1) \cdot 2^{n+1}$.
    The number of bits required to establish key size, $N_4 = \lceil \log_2 N_{TS} \rceil$

- For 2-bit shuffling; $N_{TS} = 3 \times 8 = 24$ and $N_4 = 5$ bits and the number of keys required to reveal all the S-box combinations is 2^5 keys.

Keys Required for P-box Permutation Operations
For n-bit output, Number of operations, $N_{TP} = n!$
    Number of bits required to establish key size, $N_5 = \lceil log_2 N_{TP} \rceil$

- For 2-bit output, $N_{TP} = 2$ operations and $N_5 = 2$ bits and the number of keys required to reveal all the P-box permutations are 2^2 keys.

Total number of bits, N_T required to reveal the states, transition functions, S-boxes, and P-boxes for an (n,k,m) convolutional code with n-bit shuffling S-box and n-bit output P-box is given as

$$N_T = log_2 n \cdot 2^{k(m-1)} + L + log_2(2^n - 1) \cdot 2^{n+1} + \lceil log_2 n! \rceil \qquad (3)$$

4.2 Complexity Analysis

The basis of the complexity measure is the number of binary operations performed by encryption and decryption per information bit. The analysis will commence with the decryption process and later deduce the number of operations for the encryption process.

Number of Operations Required for the Decryption Process. Complexity analysis for the decryption process for the new variant will be based on three complexity measures as follows:

- Trellis module complexity is derived from the Viterbi algorithm for the first and second stages.
- Product cipher complexity is derived from the arithmetic operations in the S-boxes and the P-boxes.
- Transition function complexity is derived from the dynamic selection of a state using the transition table to decode the next segment.

Trellis Module Complexity Measure (C_{TR})
Decoding operation at each trellis has three components:

- Hamming distance calculation (HDC);
- Add-compare-select (ACS);
- Traceback

    In the new variant, encoding/decoding is performed in segments of input bitstream, hence the traceback operation which does not require arithmetic operations could be performed in negligible time.

Therefore, to estimate the complexity measure, C(M) of the new variant only HDC and ACS will be considered. Hence, C(M) could be stated as follows

$$C(M) = \alpha S + \beta C_b + \sigma C_i \tag{4}$$

where S = summations; C_b = bit comparisons; C_i = integer comparisons and the constants α, β and σ refer to the number of operations S, C_b, and C_i.

The following properties of the trellis will be exploited to establish the complexity measure, C(M) in (1):

- The output bits in a section constitutes an 'Edge' with each edge labeled as O_t bits. It should be noted that O_t is the same for all bit comparisons.
- Results of bit comparisons are added using $O_t - 1$ sum operations. It should be noted that the incoming bits and output bits are compared and added to obtain the present metric.
- For an (n,k,m) convolutional code, the number of states, N_{states}, and number of edges, N_{edges} in a section is given as

$$N_{edges} = 2^{\lambda_t+k} \text{ and } N_{states} = 2^{\lambda_t} \tag{5}$$

where $\lambda_t = 0, 1, ..., 2^m$.

The above-mentioned properties of the trellis will be used to establish expressions to determine the constants α, β and σ.

The number of operations required for HDC, N_t^{HDC} for the section of the trellis is given as

$$N_t^{HDC} = (O_t - 1)2^{\lambda_t+k}(S) + O_t 2^{\lambda_t+k}(C_b) \tag{6}$$

The number of operations required for ACS, N_t^{ACS} for section, t of the trellis could be established using the following steps:

- The number of sum operations required to perform cumulative metric is the same as the number of edges, $N_{edges} = 2^{\lambda_t+k}$
- Number of states for section t + 1 = $2^{\lambda_{t+1}}$
- The number of edges/state is given as $\frac{2^{\lambda_t+k}}{2^{\lambda_{t+1}}}$
- The number of comparison operations/state is given as $\frac{2^{\lambda_t+k}}{2^{\lambda_{t+1}}} - 1$
- Total number of comparison operations for a section = $2^{\lambda_t+k} - 2^{\lambda_{t+1}}$

Using the above steps, the number of operations required for ACS, N_t^{ACS} for section, t of the trellis is given as

$$N_t^{ACS} = 2^{\lambda_t+k}(S) + \left[2^{\lambda_t+k} - 2^{\lambda_{t+1}}\right](C_i) \tag{7}$$

Using (6) and (7), the total number of operations per information bit is given as

$$C_{TR}(M) = \frac{1}{k}\sum_{t=0}^{n'-1}\left(N_t^{HDC} + N_t^{ACS}\right) \tag{8}$$

where n' is the number of steps which corresponds to the number of transmitted bits per segment.

Replacing N_t^{HDC} and N_t^{ACS} with corresponding expressions in (6) and (7) we have

$$C_{TR}(M) = \frac{1}{k} \sum_{t=0}^{n'-1} O_t 2^{t+k}(C_b + S) + \left(2^{t+k} - 2^{\lambda_{t+1}}\right)(C_i) \qquad (9)$$

Product Cipher Complexity Measure (C_{PC})
No arithmetic operation is required with the P-box since it involves mapping of input bits to output bits. Meanwhile, S-box which involves bit shuffling has the arithmetic operations of summation, S, bit comparisons, C_b, and integer comparisons, C_i. A mapping which does not involve any arithmetic operation is finally used to link the input to the appropriate shuffled output.

For an n-bit S-box, the complexity measure (C_{PC}) is given as

$$C_{PC}(M) = \left[2^n C_b + nS + \left(2^{n+1} - 2^{n-1}\right)C_i\right] \qquad (10)$$

Transition Function Complexity Measure (C_{TF})
The transition table which ensures the selection of the next state for the next bitstream segment has the arithmetic operations of summation, S, bit comparisons, C_b, and integer comparisons, C_i. A mapping that does not involve any arithmetic operation is finally used to link the next state to the appropriate present state and the input bitstream.

For an (n,k,m) convolutional code with L bits constraint length, the complexity measure (C_{TF}) is given as

$$C_{TF}(M) = \left[2^L C_b + LS + \left(2^{L+1} - 2^{L-1}\right)C_i\right] \qquad (11)$$

To establish the total complexity measure, C(M) of the new variant of the McEliece cryptosystem based on non-linear convolutional codes, a detailed block diagram of the scheme is shown in Fig. 7.

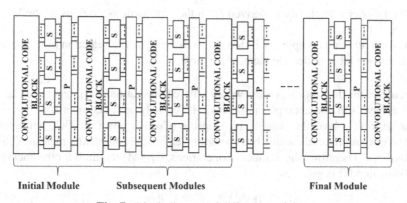

Fig. 7. Block diagram of different modules.

A Module comprises sections and sections have edges which are the different output bits. A section is used to retrieve the original message bits after traceback.

From Fig. 7, the initial module is identical to the final module with two convolutional code blocks used for the basic Viterbi algorithm and one product cipher. Meanwhile, subsequent modules in the multi-stage non-linear convolutional code comprise of two convolutional code blocks and two product ciphers.

Hence, the complexity measure, which gives the total number of arithmetic operations required to transmit n' bits in a bitstream segment for the initial and final modules is computed as follows

$$C_{initial}(M) = C_{final}(M) = 2\,C_{TR} + C_{PC} \tag{12}$$

Meanwhile, the complexity measure, which gives the total number of arithmetic operations required to transmit n' bits in a bitstream segment for the subsequent modules is computed as follows

$$C_{subsequant}(M) = 2\,C_{TR} + 2\,C_{PC} \tag{13}$$

It is worth noting that, for a transmitted bitstream with nT bits, the encoding/decoding is performed in ns segments with each segment having n' bits. Hence, $n_T = n' \cdot n_s$.

The complexity measure, $C_T(M)$ which gives the total number of arithmetic operations required to transmit n_T bits in a bitstream is computed from (12) and (13) as follows

$$C_T(M) = \sum_{t=1}^{n_s} 2\bigl(2C_{TR,t} + C_{PC}\bigr) + 2\bigl(C_{TR,t} + C_{PC}\bigr) + (n_s - 1)C_{TF} \tag{14}$$

Regrouping like terms, (14) becomes

$$C_T(M) = \sum_{t=1}^{n_s} 6C_{TR,t} + 4C_{PC} + (n_s - 1)C_{TF} \tag{15}$$

Number of Operations Required for the Encryption Process. Complexity analysis for the encryption process for the new variant will be based on two complexity measures as follows:

- Product cipher complexity is derived from the arithmetic operations in the S-boxes and the P-boxes.
- Transition function complexity is derived from the dynamic selection of a state using the transition table to decode the next segment.

Hence, unlike the decryption process which is based on summation, integer comparison, and bit comparison, the encryption process is based only on bit comparison.

For an n-bit S-box, the complexity measure (C_{PC}) is given as $2^n C_b$ while for an (n,k,m) convolutional code with L bits constraint length, the complexity measure (C_{TF}) is given as $2^L C_b$. Therefore, the number of operations, $C_{TE}(M)$ required for the encryption per information bit is given as

$$C_{TE}(M) = (2^n + 2^L)C_b \tag{16}$$

5 Cryptanalysis

The security of the cryptosystem is based on two computationally hard problems namely, an exhaustive search of the keyspace and maximum-likelihood decoding (syndrome decoding). Therefore, the two types of attacks, which are principally structural and decoding, will be the basis of the cryptanalysis of the new variant of the McEliece cryptosystem. In this section, cryptanalysis will explore the additional security due to the non-linear convolutional cryptosystem and not the entire new variant which also involves the invertible matrix, S and the permutation matrix, P. Hence, the cryptanalysis will establish baseline values for the key sizes for the new variant of the McEliece cryptosystem [14].

5.1 Structural Attack [14]

Structural attacks against the McEliece cryptosystem involve recovering the secret key from the public key, G' to determine an equivalent code from c generated by G. It is worth noting that, in classical convolutional codes, G is a generator matrix characterized by the states of the mod-2 adders and the transition functions, whereas, in the new variant of the McEliece cryptosystem, G is a generator matrix that is coupled to the product cipher. Hence, in addition to the states and transition functions of the generator matrix, the combinations in the S-boxes and P-boxes must be considered.

Therefore, a successful structural attack on the new variant of the McEliece cryptosystem should require a minimum number of plaintext – ciphertext pairs to reveal the following parameters:

- States and transition functions of the generator matrix.
- Bit shuffling and permutation combinations of the S-box and P-box.

States and Transition Functions of the Generator Matrix. In [14], the number of operations required to reveal all the states and transition functions of the generator matrix was obtained using state matrices which constituted the generator matrix and Gaussian elimination. The generator matrix for a (k,k,m) convolutional code using state matrices is given as

$$
g_{kp}(u) = \begin{bmatrix} g_0^0 & g_1^1 & \cdots & g_m^m & & & \\ & g_0^1 & \cdots & g_{m-1}^m & g_m^{m+1} & & \\ & & \ddots & & & \ddots & \\ & & & \ddots & g_0^{p-1} & \cdots & \cdots & g_m^{m+p-1} \end{bmatrix} \tag{17}
$$

where g_m^{m+p+1} are the different m state matrices and p is the number of blocks of k-bit input data. The same result for the number of operations to reveal all the states and the transition functions can be obtained by using the transition function table, the state matrices, and the mod-2 addition. This method which is presented in Sect. 4.1 will be adopted in this research.

Number of Operations to Reveal All States. The state is represented by the contents of the memory, that is, for an (n,k,m) convolutional code, it corresponds to the $k(m-1)$ previous bits, namely, the $k(m-1)$ bits contained in the first $k(m-1)$ stages of the shift register. Hence for static connections to fixed mod-2 adders, the number of states, q required is given as $q = 2^{k(m-1)}$.

For n output bits or n mod-2 adders, the different connections of the different states to the mod-2 adders is given as $q_T = nq$.

Hence the number of operations required to reveal all the states is given as

$$N_1 = n \cdot 2^{k(m-1)} \tag{18}$$

Number of Operations to Reveal All Transition Functions. From steps 5 and 6 in the proposed new algorithm, encoding the next segment using the next state of the encoder is determined using the most significant L bits of the preceding segment. Hence the number of operations required to reveal all the transition functions is given as

$$N_2 = 2^L \tag{19}$$

Bit Shuffling and Permutation Combinations. To analyze all the permutations, the minimum number of operations required to reveal all the permutations for an (n,k,m) code is given as

$$N_3 = n! \tag{20}$$

Also, to analyze all the different n-bit combinations in the s-boxes, the minimum number of operations required to reveal the shuffling combinations is given as

$$N_4 = (2^n - 1) \cdot 2^{n+1} \tag{21}$$

Hence, for a successful structural attack for either

- one stage or
- multiple stages with the same generator matrix and product cipher

of the new non-linear convolutional code, G the total number of representation code which the attacker must compare to ciphertext c' generated by G' has to be N_T for an (n,k,m) code with q states and is given as

$$N_T = n \cdot n! 2^{k(m-1)+L+(n+1)} \cdot (2^n - 1) \tag{22}$$

For μ stages and p blocks of k-bit input bitstream of the new variant of the McEliece cryptosystem using stages with different states, the total number of representation code which the attacker has to compare to ciphertext c' generated by G' has to be N_{Total} for an (n,k,m) code with q states and is given as

$$N_{Total} = [p \cdot n \cdot n! 2^{k(m-1)+L+(n+1)} \cdot (2^n - 1)]^{\mu} \tag{23}$$

5.2 Decoding Attack [14]

A decoding attack consists of decoding the intercepted ciphertext. The cost of the attack depends on the parameters of c' namely, length, dimension, and error-correcting capability since the underlying code and c' are equivalent.

If a message of length n bits is received, then the possible number of codewords is 2^n. For an (n,k,m) convolutional code, only 2^{kL} codewords are valid of the possible 2^n. The Viterbi algorithm applies the maximum-likelihood principles to limit the comparison to 2^{kL} surviving paths instead of checking all the paths where $L = $ constraint length $= k(m - 1)$ with p blocks of k-bit input bitstream. For μ stages of the new variant of the McEliece cryptosystem using non-linear convolutional codes, the total number of operations the attacker must perform to decode the ciphertext has to be N_{Tot} for an (n,k,m) code with q states and is given as

$$N_{Tot} = [pk! \cdot (2^k - 1) \cdot 2^{k+1} \cdot 2^{kL}]^\mu \qquad (24)$$

Note that, in establishing (24) the product cipher was used in conjunction with the Viterbi algorithm.

6 Results and Discussion

The structural and decoding attacks will be used to determine the number of stages, μ, and size of the block, p of k-bit bitstream of the new variant which gives the same security level as the original McEliece cryptosystem. The values of μ and p will be used to establish key sizes and complexity measure of the new variant and compared to the existing schemes.

6.1 Structural Attack

For the original McEliece parameters with a codeword, $n = 1024$, message bits, $k = 512$, and error-correcting capability, $t = 50$, this mounts up to roughly 2^{461} total number of representation code which the attacker has to compare to ciphertext c' generated by G' [17]. (23) is used to compute either the number of stages, μ, or the number of blocks, p of L-bit input bitstream. It is advisable in terms of implementation to have a fixed value for the number of stages and compute the number of blocks, p. For $\mu = 19$, (23) gives the number of blocks, p as follows

$$N_{Total} = [p \cdot n \cdot n! 2^{k(m-1)+L+(n+1)} \cdot (2^n - 1)]^\mu$$

For the (3,1,3) non-linear convolutional code, (23) becomes

$$N_{Total} = [p \cdot 18.256.7]^{19} = 2^{461} \Rightarrow p \cong 641 \text{ blocks.}$$

Hence, the input bitstream required to achieve the security level equivalent to the original McEliece cryptosystem is $N = 641 \times k$ bits $= 641 \times 1$ bits $= 641$ bits for a 19-stage non-linear convolutional cryptosystem. A complete table is shown in Sect. 6.3.

6.2 Decoding Attack

A decoding attack consists of decoding the intercepted ciphertext. Since the underlying code and c' are equivalent, they have the same error-correcting capability. Thus, the cost of the attack depends only on the parameters of c'– its length, dimension, and error-correcting capability. When the length is n = 1024, the dimension is k = 512 and the error-correcting capability is t = 50, decoding one word requires 2^{64} binary operations [17]. Similarly, (24) is used to compute either the number of stages, μ, or the number of blocks, p of k-bit input bitstream. For $\mu = 10$, (24) gives the number of blocks, p as follows

$$N_{Tot} = [pk! \cdot (2^k - 1) \cdot 2^{k+1} \cdot 2^{kL}]^\mu.$$

For the (3,1,3) non-linear convolutional code, (23) becomes

$$N_{Tot} = [p \cdot 16]^{10} = 2^{64} \Rightarrow p \cong 5 \text{ blocks.}$$

Hence, the input bitstream required to achieve the security level equivalent to the original McEliece cryptosystem is N = 5 × k bits = 5 × 1 bits = 5 bits for a 10-stage non-linear convolutional cryptosystem.

Less complex new variant of the McEliece cryptosystem could be used for curbing decoding attacks, for example, a 4-stage non-linear convolutional cryptosystem with block size of p = 3514 k-bit blocks = 3514 bits could be used.

6.3 Comparison with Existing McEliece Cryptosystems

In this research, we shall consider the baseline parameters n = 1024, k = 524, t = 50 as the basis for comparison with the new variant of the McEliece cryptosystem. It is worth noting that, the expressions deduced in Sect. 5 for N_{Total} and N_{Tot} are the baseline number of operations required for the structural and decoding attacks since only the non-linear convolutional code, G was considered instead of the entire public key $G' = SGP$. Hence, the values for the number of stages, μ and the bitstream blocks, p could be smaller resulting in less complex schemes for the new variant. The values for μ and p computed from the structural and decoding attacks will be used to establish values for the key size and complexity measure for the new variant. The established values will be compared with those of existing schemes.

Key Size Values for the New Variant. Using (3) in Sect. 4.1, the key size for the (3,1,3) non-linear convolutional code with 2-bit S-boxes and 2-bit output P-boxes could be computed as follows:

$$N_T = log_2 n . 2^{k(m-1)} + L + log_2(2^n - 1).2^{n+1} + \left[log_2 n!\right]$$

$$N_T = log_2 3 . 2^{1(3-1)} + 2 + log_2\left(2^3 - 1\right).2^{3+1} + \left[log_2 3!\right] = 16 \text{ bits.}$$

Key size, K = 2^{16} = 65536 bits = 8192 bytes.

Complexity Measure for the New Variant. Using (15) in Sect. 4.2, the complexity measure for the (3,1,3) non-linear convolutional code with 2-bit S-boxes and 2-bit P-boxes could be computed as follows:

Segment 1, SEG1 ≡ 1110

OPERATIONS ON Fig. 6(a)					
Section	k	λ_t	O_t	N_t^{HDC}	N_t^{ACS}
000	2	0	3	8S+12C_b	4S+3C_i
101	2	0	3	8S+12C_b	4S+3C_i
010	2	0	3	8S+12C_b	4S+3C_i
100	2	0	3	8S+12C_b	4S+3C_i
OPERATIONS ON Fig. 6(b)					
10	1	0	2	2S+4C_b	2S+C_i
10	1	0	2	2S+4C_b	2S+C_i
11	1	0	2	2S+4C_b	2S+C_i
01	1	0	2	2S+4C_b	2S+C_i
				40S+64C_b	24S+16C_i
$C_{TR,1}(M)$				64S+64C_b+16C_i	

Segment 2, SEG2 ≡ 0111

OPERATIONS ON Fig. 7(a)					
Section	k	λ_t	O_t	N_t^{HDC}	N_t^{ACS}
110	2	0	3	8S+12C_b	4S+3C_i
101	2	0	3	8S+12C_b	4S+3C_i
101	2	0	3	8S+12C_b	4S+2C_i
100	2	1	3	16S+24C_b	8S+7C_i
OPERATIONS ON Fig. 7(b)					
10	1	0	2	2S+4C_b	2S+C_i
10	1	0	2	2S+4C_b	2S+C_i
11	1	0	2	2S+4C_b	2S+C_i
01	1	0	2	2S+4C_b	2S+C_i
				48S+76C_b	28S+19C_i
$C_{TR,2}(M)$				76S+76C_b+19C_i	

Segment 3, SEG3 ≡ 0100

OPERATIONS ON Fig. 8(a)					
Section	k	λ_t	O_t	N_t^{HDC}	N_t^{ACS}
000	2	0	3	8S+12C_b	4S+3C_i
101	2	0	3	8S+12C_b	4S+3C_i
010	2	0	3	8S+12C_b	4S+3C_i
100	2	0	3	8S+12C_b	4S+3C_i
OPERATIONS ON Fig. 8(b)					
10	1	0	2	2S+4C_b	2S+C_i
10	1	0	2	2S+4C_b	2S+C_i
11	1	0	2	2S+4C_b	2S+C_i
01	1	0	2	2S+4C_b	2S+C_i
				40S+64C_b	24S+16C_i
$C_{TR,3}(M)$				64S+64C_b+16C_i	

The product cipher complexity measure, $C_{PC}(M)$ is computed as follows

$$C_{PC}(M) = 2^2 C_b + 2S + (2^3 - 2^2)C_i = 4C_b + 2S + 4C_i.$$

The transition function complexity measure, $C_{TF}(M)$ is computed as follows

$$C_{TF}(M) = 2^2 C_b + 2S + (2^3 - 2^2)C_i = 4C_b + 2S + 4C_i.$$

For the (3,1,3) non-linear convolutional code analyzed in the tables above, on the initial and final modules are involved, for simplicity in terms of manual calculations, subsequent modules were not included. Hence, the total complexity measure, $C_{TD}(M)$ is computed as follows

$$C_{TD}(M) = \sum_{t=1}^{n_s=3} 2(2C_{TR,t} + C_{PC}) + (n_s - 1)C_{TF}$$

Hence, using the complexity measures computed above we have

$$C_{TD}(M) = 2(2C_{TR,1} + C_{PC}) + 2(2C_{TR,2} + C_{PC}) + 2(2C_{TR,3} + C_{PC}) + (3-1)C_{TF}$$

$$= 4(C_{TR,1} + C_{TR,2} + C_{TR,3}) + 6C_{PC} + 2C_{TF}$$

$$= 4(64S + 64C_b + 16C_i + 76S + 76C_b + 19C_i + 64S + 64C_b + 16C_i)$$

$$+6(2S + 4C_b + 4C_i) + 2(2S + 4C_b + 4C_i)$$

$$= 832S + 848C_b + 128C_i$$

Hence to completely decode the message, $M = 6$ bits, 1808 operations are required to perform summations, bit comparisons and integer comparisons. Therefore, the number of binary operations performed by the decryption per information bit is 302 operations. The number of operations, therefore, depends on the length of the bitstream, p and the number of stages, μ in the non-linear convolutional code.

Assuming an identical number of states, λ_t in a trellis module for the different stages, the total complexity measure, $C_{TD}(M)$ for the number of stages, μ, and the bitstream blocks, p could be computed as follows:

$$C_{TD}(M) = \sum_{t=1}^{n_s=p/4} \mu(2C_{TR,t} + C_{PC}) + (n_s - 1)C_{TF}$$

Using (16), the complexity measure for the encryption process, $C_{TE}(M)$ for the number of stages, μ, and the bitstream blocks, p could be computed as follows:

$$C_{TE}(M) = \mu\left(2^n + \frac{p}{4}2^L\right)C_b$$

Comparison Tables for Key Size and Complexity Measure
Table 6 displays key size for the new variant of the McEliece cryptosystem compared to existing public key ciphers

Table 6. Public-key size for public-key ciphers.

	New variant of McEliece cryptosystem based on non-linear convolutional code	McEliece [1024,524,101] binary code	Niederreiter [1024.524,101] binary code	RSA 1024-bit modulus Public exponent = 17
Public-key size	8,192 bytes	67,071 bytes	32,750 bytes	256 bytes

Using (23) and (24) in Sect. 5.1, appropriate values for the structural attack and decoding attack for the number of stages, μ and block size, p used for the computation of the complexity measure are shown in Tables 7 and 8 respectively.

Table 7. Appropriate μ and p values for structural attack.

μ	17	18	19	20	21	22	23	24	25	26	27	28
p (bits)	4654	1635	641	277	128	64	34	19	12	6	4	2

Table 8. Appropriate μ and p values for decodingl attack.

μ	4	5	6	7	8	9	10
p (bits	3514	394	92	32	15	8	5

For structural attack, for values of the number of stages, μ less than 17, the block size, p is very large rendering implementation cumbersome while for values of μ greater than 28 the block size, p is infeasible that is, less than 1 bit. The same applies to the decoding attack for μ ≤ 4 and μ > 10.

Hence, to compute the complexity measures $C_{TD}(M)$ and $C_{TE}(M)$ for the structural attack, the values $20 \leq \mu \leq 25$ will be used while for decoding attack, the values $5 \leq \mu \leq 10$. For simplicity in the computation, we assume the operations in the different bit segments are identical to the first three segments analyzed in Sect. 6.3.

$C_{TD}(M)$ for the number of stages, μ and block size, p could be computed as follows:

$$C_{TD}(M) = \sum_{t=1}^{n_s=p/4} \mu(2C_{TR,t} + C_{PC}) + (n_s - 1)C_{TF}$$

$$C_{TD}(M) = (p \cdot \mu/6) \cdot (C_{TR,1} + C_{TR,2} + C_{TR,3}) + (p \cdot \mu/12) \cdot C_{PC} + (p/4 - 1) \cdot C_{TF}$$

$$C_{TE}(M) = \mu \cdot (8 + 2p).$$

The number of binary operations performed by the encryption/decryption per information bit is deduced by dividing $C_{TD}(M)$ and $C_{TE}(M)$ by the block size, p

The results for the structural and decoding attacks are displayed in Tables 9 and 10 respectively.

Table 11 displays complexity measure for existing McEliece cryptosystems which will be compared to the complexity measure of the new variant displayed in Tables 9 and 10.

Table 9. Number of binary operations for structural attack.

Structural attack	μ = 20 p = 277	μ = 21 p = 128	μ = 22 p = 64	μ = 23 p = 34	μ = 24 p = 19	μ = 25 p = 12
Number of binary operations performed by the encryption per information bit	41	43	47	51	58	67
Number of binary operations performed by the decryption per information bit	1585	1665	1746	1818	1903	1980

Table 10. Number of binary operations for decoding attack.

Decoding attack	$\mu = 5$ $p = 394$	$\mu = 6$ $p = 92$	$\mu = 7$ $p = 32$	$\mu = 8$ $p = 15$	$\mu = 9$ $p = 8$	$\mu = 10$ $p = 5$
Number of binary operations performed by the encryption per information bit	10	13	16	20	27	36
Number of binary operations performed by the decryption per information bit	397	477	551	635	714	761

Table 11. Complexity measure of existing McEliece Cryptosystems.

	McEliece [1024,524,101] binary code	Niederreiter [1024.524,101] binary code
Number of binary operations performed by the encryption per information bit	514	50
Number of binary operations performed by the decryption per information bit	5,140	7,863

The results in Tables 9, 10, and 11 points out that, the new variant of the McEliece cryptosystem using non-linear convolutional codes could be implemented using smaller key sizes and is less complex compared to the existing McEliece cryptosystem.

It is worth noting that, the values computed for complexity measure are the baseline number of operations required for the structural and decoding attacks since only the non-linear convolutional code, G was considered instead of the entire public key $G' = SGP$.

7 Conclusion

In this paper, a new variant of the McEliece cryptosystem using non-linear convolutional codes is proposed. The rationale in designing the new variant is to establish key sizes that could enable the implementation of the McEliece cryptosystem in a single FPGA device with ultimate application in mobile wireless communication. The new variant of the McEliece cryptosystem is implemented using non-linear convolutional codes, a scrambled matrix, and a permutation matrix. The non-linear convolutional code is a combination of the conventional convolutional code and product ciphers. It is shown that the new variant has small key sizes with enhanced security-complexity trade-off. Also, it is shown that security levels comparable to the original McEliece cryptosystem could be obtained by using smaller public key sizes of the new version if multiple stages of the generator matrix are employed.

Appendix

Transition Tables

STAGE 1, State 1

Input Bits	Input State		Output Bits		Output State	
u_1	s_1	s_2	v_{11}	v_{12}	s_1	s_2
0	0	0	0	0	0	0
1	0	0	1	0	1	0
0	0	1	1	1	0	0
1	0	1	0	1	1	0
0	1	0	1	1	0	1
1	1	0	0	1	1	1
0	1	1	0	0	0	1
1	1	1	1	0	1	1

STAGE 1, State 2

Input Bits	Input State		Output Bits		Output State	
u_2	s_1	s_2	v_{21}	v_{22}	s_1	s_2
0	0	0	0	0	0	0
1	0	0	1	1	1	0
0	0	1	1	1	0	0
1	0	1	0	0	1	0
0	1	0	1	0	0	1
1	1	0	0	1	1	1
0	1	1	0	1	0	1
1	1	1	1	0	1	1

Stage 2, State 1

Input Bits	Input State				Output Bits			Output State			
u_{11} u_{12}	s_1	s_2	s_1	s_2	t_{11}	t_{12}	t_{13}	s_1	s_2	s_1	s_2
0 0	0	0	0	0	0	0	0	0	0	0	0
0 1	0	0	0	0	0	0	1	0	0	1	0
1 0	0	0	0	0	1	0	0	1	0	0	0
1 1	0	0	0	0	1	0	1	1	0	1	0
0 0	0	0	0	1	0	0	1	0	0	0	0
0 1	0	0	0	1	0	0	0	0	0	1	0
1 0	0	0	0	1	1	0	1	1	0	0	0
1 1	0	0	0	1	1	0	0	1	0	1	0
0 0	0	0	1	0	0	0	0	0	0	0	1
0 1	0	0	1	0	0	0	1	0	0	1	1
1 0	0	0	1	0	1	0	0	1	0	0	1
1 1	0	0	1	0	1	0	1	1	0	1	1
0 0	0	0	1	1	0	0	1	0	0	0	1
0 1	0	0	1	1	0	0	0	0	0	1	1
1 0	0	0	1	1	1	0	1	1	0	0	1
1 1	0	0	1	1	1	0	0	1	0	1	1
0 0	0	1	0	0	1	1	0	0	0	0	0
0 1	0	1	0	0	1	1	1	0	0	1	0
1 0	0	1	0	0	0	1	0	1	0	0	0
1 1	0	1	0	0	0	1	1	1	0	1	0
0 0	0	1	0	1	1	1	1	0	0	0	0
0 1	0	1	0	1	1	1	0	0	0	1	0
1 0	0	1	0	1	0	1	1	1	0	0	0
1 1	0	1	0	1	0	1	0	1	0	1	0
0 0	0	1	1	0	1	1	0	0	0	0	1
0 1	0	1	1	0	1	1	1	0	0	1	1
1 0	0	1	1	0	0	1	0	1	0	0	1
1 1	0	1	1	0	0	1	1	1	0	1	1
0 0	0	1	1	1	1	1	1	0	0	0	1
0 1	0	1	1	1	1	1	0	0	0	1	1
1 0	0	1	1	1	0	1	1	1	0	0	1
1 1	0	1	1	1	0	1	0	1	0	1	1
0 0	1	0	0	0	1	1	0	0	1	0	0
0 1	1	0	0	0	1	1	1	0	1	1	0
1 0	1	0	0	0	0	1	0	1	1	0	0
1 1	1	0	0	0	0	1	1	1	1	1	0
0 0	1	0	0	1	1	1	1	0	1	0	0
0 1	1	0	0	1	1	1	0	0	1	1	0
1 0	1	0	0	1	0	1	1	1	1	0	0
1 1	1	0	0	1	0	1	0	1	1	1	0
0 0	1	0	1	0	1	1	0	0	1	0	1
0 1	1	0	1	0	1	1	1	0	1	1	1
1 0	1	0	1	0	0	1	0	1	1	0	1
1 1	1	0	1	0	0	1	1	1	1	1	1
0 0	1	0	1	1	1	1	1	0	1	0	1
0 1	1	0	1	1	1	1	0	0	1	1	1
1 0	1	0	1	1	0	1	1	1	1	0	1
1 1	1	0	1	1	0	1	0	1	1	1	1
0 0	1	1	0	0	0	0	0	0	1	0	0
0 1	1	1	0	0	0	0	1	0	1	1	0
1 0	1	1	0	0	1	0	0	1	1	0	0
1 1	1	1	0	0	1	0	1	1	1	1	0
0 0	1	1	0	1	0	0	1	0	1	0	0
0 1	1	1	0	1	0	0	0	0	1	1	0
1 0	1	1	0	1	1	0	1	1	1	0	0
1 1	1	1	0	1	1	0	0	1	1	1	0
0 0	1	1	1	0	0	0	0	0	1	0	1
0 1	1	1	1	0	0	0	1	0	1	1	1
1 0	1	1	1	0	1	0	0	1	1	0	1
1 1	1	1	1	0	1	0	1	1	1	1	1
0 0	1	1	1	1	0	0	1	0	1	0	1
0 1	1	1	1	1	0	0	0	0	1	1	1
1 0	1	1	1	1	1	0	1	1	1	0	1
1 1	1	1	1	1	1	0	0	1	1	1	1

Stage 2, State 2

Input Bits	Input State				Output Bits			Output State			
u_{21} u_{22}	s_1	s_2	s_1	s_2	t_{21}	t_{22}	t_{23}	s_1	s_2	s_1	s_2
0 0	0	0	0	0	0	0	0	0	0	0	0
0 1	0	0	0	0	0	0	1	0	0	1	0
1 0	0	0	0	0	1	1	0	1	0	0	0
1 1	0	0	0	0	1	1	1	1	0	1	0
0 0	0	0	0	1	0	0	1	0	0	0	0
0 1	0	0	0	1	0	0	0	0	0	1	0
1 0	0	0	0	1	1	1	1	1	0	0	0
1 1	0	0	0	1	1	1	0	1	0	1	0
0 0	0	0	1	0	0	0	0	0	0	0	1
0 1	0	0	1	0	0	0	1	0	0	1	1
1 0	0	0	1	0	1	1	0	1	0	0	1
1 1	0	0	1	0	1	1	1	1	0	1	1
0 0	0	0	1	1	0	0	1	0	0	0	1
0 1	0	0	1	1	0	0	0	0	0	1	1
1 0	0	0	1	1	1	1	1	1	0	0	1
1 1	0	0	1	1	1	1	0	1	0	1	1
0 0	0	1	0	0	1	1	0	0	0	0	0
0 1	0	1	0	0	1	1	1	0	0	1	0
1 0	0	1	0	0	0	0	0	1	0	0	0
1 1	0	1	0	0	0	0	1	1	0	1	0
0 0	0	1	0	1	1	1	1	0	0	0	0
0 1	0	1	0	1	1	1	0	0	0	1	0
1 0	0	1	0	1	0	0	1	1	0	0	0
1 1	0	1	0	1	0	0	0	1	0	1	0
0 0	0	1	1	0	1	1	0	0	0	0	1
0 1	0	1	1	0	1	1	1	0	0	1	1
1 0	0	1	1	0	0	0	0	1	0	0	1
1 1	0	1	1	0	0	0	1	1	0	1	1
0 0	0	1	1	1	1	1	1	0	0	0	1
0 1	0	1	1	1	1	1	0	0	0	1	1
1 0	0	1	1	1	0	0	1	1	0	0	1
1 1	0	1	1	1	0	0	0	1	0	1	1
0 0	1	0	0	0	1	0	0	0	1	0	0
0 1	1	0	0	0	1	0	1	0	1	1	0
1 0	1	0	0	0	0	1	0	1	1	0	0
1 1	1	0	0	0	0	1	1	1	1	1	0
0 0	1	0	0	1	1	0	1	0	1	0	0
0 1	1	0	0	1	1	0	0	0	1	1	0
1 0	1	0	0	1	0	1	1	1	1	0	0
1 1	1	0	0	1	0	1	0	1	1	1	0
0 0	1	0	1	0	1	0	0	0	1	0	1
0 1	1	0	1	0	1	0	1	0	1	1	1
1 0	1	0	1	0	0	1	0	1	1	0	1
1 1	1	0	1	0	0	1	1	1	1	1	1
0 0	1	0	1	1	1	0	1	0	1	0	1
0 1	1	0	1	1	1	0	0	0	1	1	1
1 0	1	0	1	1	0	1	1	1	1	0	1
1 1	1	0	1	1	0	1	0	1	1	1	1
0 0	1	1	0	0	0	1	0	0	1	0	0
0 1	1	1	0	0	0	1	1	0	1	1	0
1 0	1	1	0	0	1	0	0	1	1	0	0
1 1	1	1	0	0	1	0	1	1	1	1	0
0 0	1	1	0	1	0	1	1	0	1	0	0
0 1	1	1	0	1	0	1	0	0	1	1	0
1 0	1	1	0	1	1	0	1	1	1	0	0
1 1	1	1	0	1	1	0	0	1	1	1	0
0 0	1	1	1	0	0	1	0	0	1	0	1
0 1	1	1	1	0	0	1	1	0	1	1	1
1 0	1	1	1	0	1	0	0	1	1	0	1
1 1	1	1	1	0	1	0	1	1	1	1	1
0 0	1	1	1	1	0	1	1	0	1	0	1
0 1	1	1	1	1	0	1	0	0	1	1	1
1 0	1	1	1	1	1	0	1	1	1	0	1
1 1	1	1	1	1	1	0	0	1	1	1	1

References

1. McEliece, R.J.: A public-key cryptosystem based on algebraic coding theory. In: DSN Progress Report, pp. 114–116 (1978)
2. Niederreiter, H.: Knapsack-type cryptosystems and algebraic coding theory. Probl. Contr. Inform. Theory **15**, 159–166 (1986)

3. Gabidulin, E.M., Ourivski, A.V., Honary, B., Ammar, B.: Reducible rank codes and their applications to cryptography. IEEE Trans. Inf. Theory **49**, 3289–3293 (2003)
4. Gaborit, P.: Shorter keys for code-based cryptography. In: Proceedings of WCC, pp. 81–90 (2005)
5. Sidelnikov, V.M.: A public-key cryptosystem based on binary Reed-Muller codes. Discrete Math. Appl. **4** (1994)
6. Baldi, M., Bianchi, M., Chiaraluce, F.: Security and complexity of the McEliece cryptosystem based on quasi-cyclic low-density parity-check codes. IET Inf. Secur. **7**(3), 212–220 (2013)
7. Moufek, H., Guenda, K.: A new variant of the mceliece cryptosystem based on the smith form of convolutional codes. Cryptologia **42**(3), 227–239 (2018)
8. Landais, G., Tillich, J.-P.: An efficient attack of a McEliece cryptosystem variant based on convolutional codes. In: Gaborit, P. (ed.) PQCrypto 2013. LNCS, vol. 7932, pp. 102–117. Springer, Heidelberg (2013). https://doi.org/10.1007/978-3-642-38616-9_7
9. Trinca, D.: Sequential and parallel cascaded convolutional encryption with local propagation: toward future directions in symmetric cryptography. In: 3rd International Conference on Information Technology, USA, pp. 464–469 (2006)
10. Sone, M.E.: Efficient key management scheme to enhance security-throughput trade-off performance in wireless networks. In: Proceedings of the Science and Information Conference (SAI), London, UK, pp. 1249–1256 (2015)
11. Peterson, W.W., Weldon, E.J.: Error Correcting Codes, 2nd edn. MIT Press, Cambridge (1972)
12. Kumari, D., Saini, M.L.: Design and performance analysis of convolutional encoder and viterbi decoder for various generator polynomials. Int. J. Eng. Res. Appl. **6**(5), 67–71 (2016)
13. Moufek, H., Guenda, K.: McEliece cryptosystem based on punctured convolutional codes and the pseudo-random generators. In: ACM Communications in Computer Algebra, vol. 49, No. 1 (2015)
14. Sone, M.: FPGA-based McEliece cryptosystem using non-linear convolutional codes. In: Proceeding of the 17th International Joint Conference on e-Business and Telecommunications (ICETE 2020) – SECRYPT, pp. 64–75 (2020)
15. Almeida, P., Napp, D., Pinto, R.: A new class of superregular matrices and MDP convolutional codes. Linear Algebra Appl. **439**(7), 2145–2157 (2013)
16. Lathi, B.P.: Modern Digital and Analog Communication Systems, 3rd edn. Oxford University Press, Oxford (1998)
17. Loidreau, P., Sendrier, N.: Weak keys in the McEliece public-key cryptosystem. IEEE Trans. Inf. Theory **47**(3), 1207–1211 (2001)

A Secure Distributed Hash-Based Encryption Mode of Operation Suited for Big Data Systems

Oussama Trabelsi[1]([✉]) [ID], Lilia Sfaxi[1,2] [ID], and Riadh Robbana[1,2]

[1] Faculty of Science of Tunis, Tunis el Manar University, Tunis, Tunisia
Oussama.Trabelsi@insat.u-carthage.tn
[2] INSAT, University of Carthage, Tunis, Tunisia

Abstract. Big Data systems are now present in almost all mature organizations and not just IT focused ones. From luxury hotels to health care organizations, data storage and processing is witnessing a huge technological improvement thanks to the extensive research that is being conducted to improve these two areas. However, there is a lack of adaptability when it comes to security and more importantly encryption, as traditional security solutions are still being used today without any changes that can adapt them to Big Data environments. In this article, we are interested in working on data at rest encryption in a big data environment. In particular we pay special attention to distributed storing as well as large volumes of data. We base our work of a very known encryption mode of operation called CBC which is heavily used for data at rest encryption, but suffers from the high cost of running sequential encryption over the entire plaintext. Our solution offers an alternative that guarantees the same properties as CBC, and even enhances some of them (namely the diffusion property), while offering the possibility for parallel encryption which makes it more efficient especially in distributed environments. These claims will be proved using a set of theoretical equations that will be detailed in the article.

Keywords: Cryptography · Modes of operation · CBC · Parallel encryption · Hash-based encryption · Big data security

1 Introduction

Data is considered to have states. It is either, in motion, at rest, or in use. Handling data encryption in use refers to encrypting data in a way that keeps it obfuscated, even from the machine processing it, while allowing changes in the ciphertext to be mapped to changes in the plaintext. This is a relatively new problematic, especially with the rise of cloud computing, and mainly relies on multiple approaches to homomorphic encryption.

Data in transit encryption refers to encrypting data to secure it while it passes through one or several networks [12]. For this use case encryption performance is of high importance as it affects directly the user's experience. It also mainly aims to protect against eavesdroppers by obfuscating the plaintext which is why they are rarely used in systems where strong cryptographic security is required [16].

© Springer Nature Switzerland AG 2021
M. S. Obaidat and J. Ben-Othman (Eds.): ICETE 2020, CCIS 1484, pp. 51–78, 2021.
https://doi.org/10.1007/978-3-030-90428-9_3

Data at rest encryption refers to encrypting data to secure it while it resides statically on disk. Even though it might seem counter intuitive, protecting data at rest can be more crucial than protecting it in transit. Even thought data is more exposed in transit, the attackers are limited especially by the available targets (people on the same network and probably same physical space). However, when a data breach occurs, entire databases fall victim to attackers allowing them to steel huge amounts of data that are only limited by the total amount of information stored on the server. Thus, when securing data at rest, it can be acceptable to partially sacrifice performance in favor of more security properties being verified.

Moreover, when it comes to large or even medium volumes of data, symmetric encryption is usually preferred due to it's performance compared to asymmetric encryption. However, block ciphers, which are the most commonly used for symmetric encryption, are limited by the number of bits they can encrypt at once. For example, the Advanced Encryption Standard (AES) can only encrypt 128 bits (or 256 bits depending on the version used) at once. To solve this issue, multiple encryption modes of operation where introduced to define how encrypting multiple blocks of data can be orchestrated. These modes of operation can be divided into two groups. The first group keeps some level of diffusion, which we will talk about in more details later, that is originally offered by the underlying block cipher. The second group, uses the block cipher to generate keys that are later used to encrypt the plaintext bit by bit, thus effectively creating a stream cipher out of the original block cipher. The most used encryption modes of operation for these groups are respectively Chained Block Cipher (CBC) and Counter (CTR).

The Chained Block Cipher (CBC) mode was suggested to offer some level of diffusion by chaining the different blocks of data [6].

This ended up offering multiple security features such as *Semantic Security* [10], while requiring a sequential execution of the encryption operation as well as an overhead in the ciphertext's size because of the need to save an extra block containing an *Initialization Vector (IV)* used by this mode to ensure semantic security.

Even though CBC seems to respect the requirement for securing data in storage by offering the diffusion property as defined in [8], it doesn't quite take advantage of the large computational resources that are usually offered by big data systems as the encryption process is sequential and therefore uses only a single CPU.

On the other hand, the Counter mode (CTR) opted for using the underlying Block Cipher as a key generator for a stream cipher. Unlike block ciphers that encrypt the message one block at a time, stream ciphers encrypt it bit by bit until the full message is encrypted. In these modes of operation this is ensured thanks to the One Time Pad (OTP) that relies on the XOR operation to encrypt the plaintext using a secret key that is only used once per message.

For our purposes, the main advantage of CTR is the possibility for parallel encryption as well as parallel decryption. CBC however, only offers parallel decryption while encryption can only be executed sequentially. When it comes to security and more precisely the diffusion property, CBC has the advantage over CTR (as it suffers from malleability [9]). The ideas of diffusion and confusion were introduced by Shannon as two properties of a secure cipher. Confusion will not be covered in this article as it is ensured by the underlying block cipher encryption function and is therefore independent of the mode of operation used. When it comes to diffusion, it is defined as the ability of the encryption function to translate a change in a plaintext bit, into a change of statistically half the ciphertext bits. Even though CBC doesn't completely fulfill this ideal condition, it offers some level of diffusion that varies according to the position of the plaintext bit that was modified. CTR however, doesn't offer any level of diffusion.

In this article, we are interested in data at rest encryption, therefore diffusion is an important property that must be ensured. However, as we mentioned earlier, CBC requires sequential encryption, therefore it is not practical to run CBC encryption on large volumes of data or more importantly huge volumes of data such as in the case of big data systems which happen to be part of our work's focus as well. Some big data solutions, such as Hadoop, get around this problem by dividing the large data file into chunks which will, each, be encrypted using CBC separately. Even though this solution provides parallel execution between the different chunks, the diffusion rate is only limited to a single chunk. This means that if a chunk is modified, some bits inside that chunk will change, since diffusion is ensured internally thanks to CBC, but the remaining chunks will never be affected by that change. So, in Big Data solutions, we currently have to choose between diffusion and acceptable performance.

Moreover, there have been some attempts to provide parallelizable implementations derived from CBC, either by chaining only a subset of blocks at a time such as with Interleaved Chained Block Cipher (ICBC) [5], or by using a hash-based solution to offer a link between the plaintext blocks instead of CBC's chaining [11]. In both these cases, some weaknesses, that we will detail in Sect. 2, were introduced in order to allow for parallel execution. For this reason, we looked for a solution that can provide a reasonable trade-off between the chaining level and performance while keeping the mode's security intact.

In this paper, we will suggest a hash-based solution that offers a parallelizable encryption and decryption process while keeping some level of chaining between the different blocks of the plaintext. First we describe the suggested solution along with the encryption and decryption processes associated to it. Next, we cover some security aspects of the solution and how it behaves in cases where appending or editing data is necessary. Then, we estimate a theoretical cost of running the proposed mode and compare it to the cost of running CBC in multiple scenarios. Following that, we calculate a theoretical diffusion rate that allows us to compare our solution's security to CBC's. Finally, we present in more depth other works that are related to this subject and compare them to the results we found for our proposed mode and proceed to a conclusion and some perspectives.

2   Related Work

Some attempts have been made to reduce the cost of encrypting data through parallelism while keeping some level of chaining between the different blocks.

For instance, the works presented by [5] and [4] use Interleaved Cipher Block Chaining (ICBC) to parallelize the encryption process and enhance its performance.

ICBC consists on running N independent CBC operations with a randomly generated IV for each one.

In each operation, the chaining will occur on blocks with a step of N blocks. So, the first CBC encryption will run with blocks 0, N, 2N, 3N, ..., the second one on blocks 1, N+1, 2N+1, 3N+1, ... and so on. Using ICBC, the more we parallelize the encryption (the bigger N is), the less chained blocks we get. This means that there is a strict trade-off between performance and diffusion.

By comparison, our proposed solution presents a middle ground between performance and diffusion, as chaining is preserved for the whole plaintext no matter how parallelized the encryption gets, but in return, an added cost is present because of the hashing operation.

Other attempts tried to ensure parallelism and diffusion using hash-based solutions, such as the work presented by [11], where the full plaintext is hashed, then the hash (H(P)) is used along with the IV and the encryption key K to generate a new key that will be used to encrypt the plaintext block P_i: $Y_i = E(P_i, IV \oplus K \oplus H(P))$

However, this solution presents multiple issues:

Appending Data: Just like in CBC, it is not possible to append data directly to the ciphertext. Any append operation would require the full decryption and re-encryption of the whole plaintext. In comparison, in the worst case scenario, our proposed solution only requires the decryption and re-encryption of the last chunk as well as the encryption of the appended data.

Hashing Cost: Even though the hash operation would take considerably less time than the encryption, running the hash function on the plaintext can prove to be very costly for very large files. In this aspect, our solution presents the advantage of parallelizing the hashing operation as well and not just the encryption.

CPA Security: The presented mode does not offer security against chosen plaintext attacks, since all message blocks P_i are encrypted using the same key and with no IV. A simple game scenario to show this is as follows: An attacker sends a message $M1$ composed of two identical blocks ($M1_0 = M1_1$) and a message $M2$ made of two distinct blocks ($M2_0 \neq M2_1$). In the resulting Cipher returned by the encryption oracle, if $C_0 = C_1$ then output 0, else output 1. This results in an advantage equal to 1 for the adversary, which means that the attacker can tell which of the two messages $M1$ and $M2$ was encrypted by the oracle, thus, making the discussed solution vulnerable to CPA.

On the other hand, we claim that our proposed solution is CPA secure thanks to the use of unpredictable IVs for the different CBC encryption operations running on the different chunks as explained previously.

3   Proposed Solution

In this paper, we propose a partially parallelizable encryption mode based on CBC and the use of hash functions, which we will be referring to as *Distributed Cipher Block Chaining* or *DCBC*. Before we proceed to describing our proposed solution, we first need to fully understand how *Cipher Block Chaining* (*CBC*) works.

3.1 Distributed Cipher Block Chaining: DCBC

DCBC will operate on multiple chunks of data in a parallel manner, while using a chaining layer to allow for some level of diffusion between them. Up until now, we have only discussed the plaintext as the concatenation of blocks of data. *Blocks* of data are a subset of the plaintext for which the size is determined by the underlying Block Cipher. For instance, when using the Advanced Encryption Standard (AES) a block of data would refer to 16 bytes of data, however with the Data Encryption Standard (DES) a block refers to 8 bytes of data. When it comes to DCBC, we will be introducing what we refer to as a *Chunk* of data, which is a subset of the plaintext of a size determined by the user. Each of these chunks will be seperately encrypted using CBC, so it is recommended to choose a chunk size that is a multiple of the block size used by the underlying Block Cipher, in order to avoid unnecessary padding with each chunk's CBC encryption. As shown in Fig. 1, the full plaintext message is made of multiple chunks, which in turn can be considered as a series of blocks for which the size is predetermined by the Block Cipher.

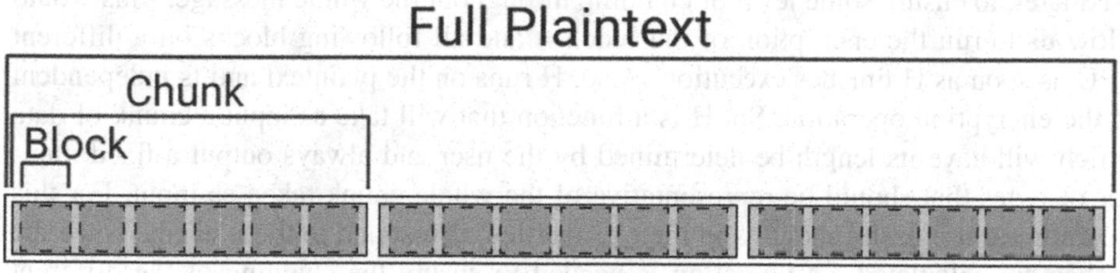

Fig. 1. The adapted plaintext subsets [14].

In the subsequent sections we will be using the following notations: M_i, H_i and C_i, respectively, denote the plaintext and ciphertext and Hash relative to the chunk of index i. IV_i represents the calculated Initialization Vector used to encrypt M_i and IV is the Initialization Vector supplied by the user to DCBC. The operations we will be using are: the hash function H, the CBC encryption and decryption functions E_{CBC} and D_{CBC}, the IV generation function G and finally the encryption using a block cipher for the IV Generation E_G.

In order for DCBC to be a usable mode of operation, it must satisfy some requirements that cover both its security and its performance which we will define in the next section.

3.2 Target Criteria

Our work on DCBC, will focus on four axes.

1. *Semantic Security under Chosen Plaintext Attack*: In a perfect system, the ciphertext should not reveal any information about the plaintext. This concept has been introduced as *Perfect Secrecy* by [3]. *Semantic Security under Chosen-Plaintext Attack* is a looser and more applicable version of *Perfect Secrecy* as it refers to preventing an attacker from being able to extract any information about the plaintext using only

the ciphertext in a polynomial time [10]. To achieve this level of security, an attacker must be unable to link different messages to their respective ciphertexts. As CBC is secure against Chosen Plaintext Attacks (CPA), as proved by [2], DCBC must keep that property intact.

2. *Diffusion*: DCBC should provide some level of chaining to ensure that a slight difference in the input will affect all following blocks in the output.
3. *Parallelizability*: DCBC must be parallelizable to allow for the full use of available resources (CPUs, Cores or Machines).
4. *Secure Append Operations*: DCBC must allow for appending data securely without having to decrypt and re-encrypt the full plaintext.

3.3 How Does DCBC Work?

A message M is divided into multiple chunks of a fixed size. Each chunk can be encrypted using CBC independently from the encryption of all other chunks, while using a function H to provide a "summary" of the corresponding chunk, which will be used later, to ensure some level of chaining throughout the whole message. This would allow us to run the encryption of the block n and all following blocks on a different CPU as soon as H finishes execution. Also, H runs on the plaintext and is independent of the encryption operation. So, H is a function that will take as input a chunk of data which will have its length be determined by the user and always output a fixed number of bytes that should be representative of the whole chunk taken as input. For this we chose to use hash functions as their properties correspond to these needs. Once the hashes are calculated, an operation is needed to ensure the chaining of the different blocks. We will be referring to it in this article as the **IV Generator**, since its output will be used as an IV for the CBC encryption of the chunk. The properties of this IV generator and the reasons behind them will be discussed in Sect. 3.5, but for now all we need to know is that it takes as input the output of H when ran on the current chunk, as well as the IV of the previous chunk.

To sum up, the mode we are proposing can be viewed as the combination of three layers of processing, two of which are the most costly ones but are fully parallelizable and one is sequential but of very low cost.

The first layer is a hashing operation (**H**), where each chunk will be hashed independently from all previous chunks. The second layer is an IV generation layer (**G**), which generates a pseudo-random IV from the hash of the current layer and the IV generated by the previous layer, thus guaranteeing that any IV depends on all previous chunks. Moreover, the generated IV must be pseudo-random to ensure some security properties that we will discuss later in this article. The third layer is a regular CBC encryption layer ($\mathbf{E_{CBC}}$), in which every chunk is encrypted independently from all other chunks' encryption results, making it parallelizable.

3.4 Encryption and Decryption in DCBC

In this section we will be presenting the encryption and decryption operations at a chunk level as well as at a block level.

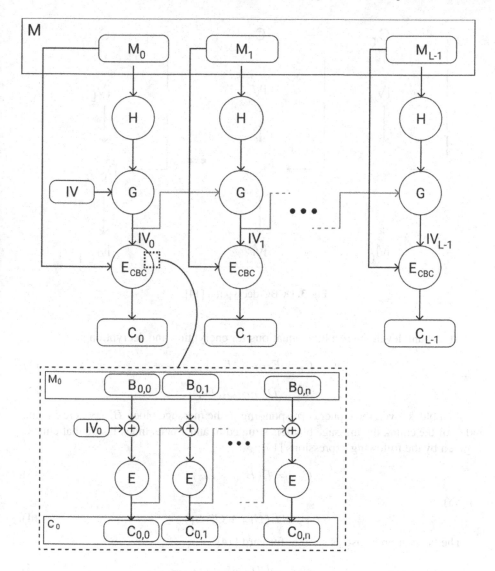

Fig. 2. DCBC encryption [14].

We denote by encryption at a chunk level, the expression of the encryption operation as a function using full chunks of plaintext as opposed to the encryption at a block level, where the operation is expressed as a function using single blocks of plaintext.

Figure 2 illustrates how the previously mentioned operations (E_{CBC}, H and G) interact and depend on each other for encrypting a message M.

The decryption process, as shown in Fig. 3, is fully parallel, as each chunk's ciphertext is decrypted independently from all others, using its corresponding IV which was generated and stored in the encryption phase.

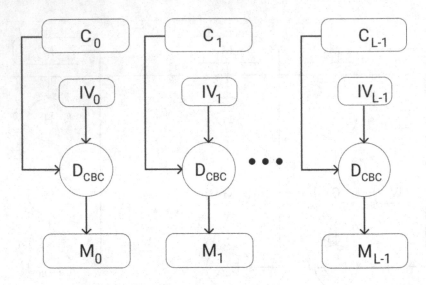

Fig. 3. DCBC decryption [14].

At a chunk level, the resulting equations for encryption and decryption are:

$$C_i = E_{CBC}(M_i, IV_i) \tag{1}$$

$$M_i = D_{CBC}(C_i, IV_i) \tag{2}$$

At a block level, the cipher corresponding to the message block $B_{i,j}$, where i is the index of the chunk the message block is situated in and j is its index inside that chunk, is given by the following expressions [14]:

$$C_{i,0} = E(B_{i,0} \oplus IV_i) \tag{3}$$

$\forall j > 0$:

$$C_{i,j} = E(B_{i,j} \oplus C_{i,j-1}) \tag{4}$$

The decryption is also as straight forward [14]:

$$B_{i,0} = D(C_{i,0}) \oplus IV_i \tag{5}$$

$\forall j > 0$:

$$B_{i,j} = D(C_{i,j}) \oplus C_{i,j-1} \tag{6}$$

In both these cases IV_i is generated as follows [14]:

$$IV_0 = G(H_0, IV) \tag{7}$$

$\forall i > 0$:

$$IV_i = G(H_i, IV_{i-1}) \tag{8}$$

where **G** is an *IV Generator* respecting the properties we will be detailing in the following section.

3.5   IV Generator

Even though the efficiency of this approach depends heavily on the Block Cipher and the hashing function used for encryption and hashing, its security relies mainly on the security of the IV generation algorithm which is why we propose three main conditions that must be met by any function in order for it to be usable as an IV generator for this mode.

1. The IV of a chunk i must depend on the IV of its previous chunk $i - 1$, in order to ensure some level of chaining between the different chunks. The first chunk is the only exception to this rule, for which an Initialisation Vector (IV) is used.
2. The IV of chunk i must depend on the chunk's hash, to make sure the IV is updated for every update on the chunk, and thus avoid having a predictable/known IV when modifying the contents of existing chunks.
3. The IV generator must be CPA secure to keep the CPA security of CBC intact. This will be detailed further in Sect. 4.1.

For the purposes of this paper, we will be using the following function G [14]:

$$G(H_i, IV_{i-1}) = E_G(H_i \oplus IV_{i-1})$$

Each of the components of the proposed IV Generation function verifies one of the three conditions we just mentioned:

1. H_i: Since each Initialisation Vector IV_i depends on the hash of M_i (H_i), this would ensure the existence of a link between the plaintext and the initialisation vector. One advantage to having this link is that, when M_i is updated, so is IV_i.
2. IV_{i-1}: By using IV_{i-1} in the expression of IV_i, the latter would depend on all previous Initialisation Vectors and therefore on all previous plaintext chunks, since each Initialisation vector depends on the plaintext chunk associated to it thanks to the use of H_i. This ensures the existence of some level of chaining between the different chunks.
3. E_G: Using a Block Cipher, the Initialisation Vector generated will be unpredictable, even when H_i and IV_{i-1} are known to potential attackers, which is very important to the security of DCBC. The use of this property will be further detailed in Sect. 4.2.

Notice that this suggestion is not a universal solution. It is designed for a particular case where the output of the hashing operation H is of equal size to the input of the Block Cipher used for CBC encryption. Similarly, we assumed that the Block Cipher used in the IV generation algorithm has an input of the same size as the one used in the CBC encryption. If this is not the case, a slightly more complex IV generation algorithm might be required.

Many of the choices mentioned in this section are adopted to ensure some security properties for our proposed solution. In the next section, we define these properties and explain how they are ensured by DCBC.

4 Security Properties

4.1 CPA Security

CBC's CPA security was proved by [2], under the condition that the IV is not predictable [13]. In its essence, the proposed mode is formed by multiple CBC encryption operations using calculated IVs instead of randomly generated ones. In this section we will demonstrate that the CPA security of the *IV Generator G* is a necessary condition for the CPA security of DCBC. In order to do this, we will show that if G is not CPA secure, then DCBC is not CPA secure either. Consider the following cryptographic game:

- The Attacker **A** sends two different messages M_0 and M_1 to the Challenger.
- The Challenger **C** chooses a message b randomly and return $C_b = E_{DCBC}(M_b)$, where the first blocks of C_b are the IVs used for the encryption.
- The Attacker inspects C_b and outputs $b' \in 0, 1$.

The advantage of **A** is defined as [14]:

$$Adv_{CPA}(A) = |Pr[b = b'] - Pr[b \neq b']|$$

If the *IV Generator* is not CPA secure, **A** can use the blocks containing the IVs, to figure out which of the messages M_0 or M_1 has been used to generate them and then conclude which message the cipher represents. This would give **A** an advantage of $Adv_{CPA}(A) = 1$ and DCBC would not be CPA secure.

Therefore, the CPA security of the *IV Generator* is a necessary condition for the CPA security of *DCBC*.

4.2 Blockwise Adaptive Chosen Plaintext Attack Security

Even though CPA security ensures Semantic Security, it is limited to messages that are presented as an atomic unit, meaning that a message is fully received, fully encrypted and only then is the full cipher returned to the user or potential attacker. Blockwise Adaptive Chosen Plaintext Attack (BACPA), as described by [7], removes this constraint and handles non atomic messages. This includes cases where the plaintext message is either sent one or a few blocks at a time, or is appended to old, already encrypted data using the existing cipher's last block as IV for the newly received blocks' encryption.

Attacks against BACPA-vulnerable implementations have already been proved feasible, for instance they have been used to attack some old implementations of SSL as described in [1].

BACPA is a threat in two cases:

1. *Editing existing data*: The plaintext is modified but the old IV is preserved for the new encryption.
2. *Appending new data*: New blocks are encrypted using CBC's logic (C_{i-1} serves as IV for the encryption of C_i) and appended to the existing cipher.

Editing Existing Data. When it comes to modifying existing data, if CBC is used, it is mandatory that the whole message gets decrypted, modified then re-encrypted with a new IV.

This is due to the fact that if we only edit the concerned blocks then re-encrypt them using their respective previous cipher blocks as IVs, we would be vulnerable to attacks that abuse predictable IVs.

Using our proposed mode, re-encrypting the whole message is recommended but not mandatory.

Since the IV of a chunk depends on the hash of the chunk itself, once a chunk is updated, its IV is also modified in an unpredictable manner thanks to the use of a Block Cipher. For this reason, it is possible to update only the concerned chunk and the ones following it without having to deal with all previous chunks, while keeping the mode's semantic security intact. However, doing things this way allows attackers to detect the first chunk where changes took place. In case this information is critical to the security of the encrypted data, it is recommended to re-encrypt the full plaintext.

Appending New Data. Chaining the chunks as described in this paper offers security against Adaptive Chosen Plaintext Attacks at a chunk level, meaning that it's possible to append new chunks to the existing data securely without having to interact with any of the old chunks. This is due to the fact that the IV used in each chunk is not deducible from any previously calculated values, including previous IVs, ciphers, hashes, etc. ...

In general, an append operation will go through the following steps:
If the size of the last chunk is less than the predefined *Chunk Size*:

1. Decrypt the final chunk. We will consider n to be its index.
2. Append the new blocks to the plaintext of the final chunk.
3. Encrypt the resulting chunk/chunks using the proposed method and by providing the IV of the chunk $n - 1$ to the initial IV Generator.

Otherwise, we get a simple one step process:

1. Encrypt the new chunk/chunks using the proposed method and by providing the IV of the last chunk (chunk n) to the initial IV Generator.

Using these steps to append data, the operation is secure and costs at most one extra decryption operation over a single chunk while retaining the chaining between old and newly added data.

5 Theoretical Performance Cost

In this section we will be running a theoretical performance comparison between the respective costs of using DCBC and CBC to encrypt some plaintext message M.

5.1 Assumptions

In this section we make the following assumptions:

- The time threads take to hash different chunks ($h(CS)$) is only function of the chunk's size.
- The time threads take to encrypt different chunks ($e(CS)$) is only function of the chunk's size.
- The time threads take to generate the IV for chunks of the same size (g) is constant.
- The whole encryption process of a chunk takes place on the same CPU.
- At the start of the operation all CPUs are free.

5.2 Cost Function C

We aim to calculate a theoretical approximation for the cost of encrypting some plain text M that will be divided into L chunks and encrypted using N CPUs/Cores.

First, we will define $C(i)$ as a combination of two different expressions over two disjoint intervals:

1. $0 \leq i < N$: We will be referring to it as *the first iteration*, during which the first batch of chunks will be encrypted.
2. $i \geq N$, which represents all following iterations.

Then, we will look to provide a unified expression for the cost function over both of these intervals.

First Iteration: $0 \leq i < N$ During the first iteration of encryption operations, all CPUs are free. So, the encryption of a chunk i starts as soon as the chunk $(i - 1)$ finishes the IV Generation step (except, of course, for the initial chunk). So, we define $C(i)$ as follows [14]:

$$C(i) = \begin{cases} h(CS) + g + e(CS), \text{ if } i = 0 \\ C(i-1) + g, \text{ if } i \geq 1 \end{cases}$$

We can proceed by induction to show that the previous expression is equivalent to:

$$C(i) = h(CS) + i \times g + g + e(CS), \forall i \in [0, N[\tag{9}$$

where $i \times g$ represents how long it takes for the previous IV to be calculated using the function G. <u>Base case</u>($i = 0$): By definition:

$$C(0) = h(CS) + g + e(CS)$$
$$\Longleftrightarrow C(0) = h(CS) + 0 \times g + g + e(CS)$$

So C(0) is correct.

<u>Induction Hypothesis</u>: Suppose that there exists $i < N$ such that: $\forall k \leq i, C(k) = h(CS) + k \times g + g + e(CS)$

<u>Induction step</u>: We need to prove that:

$$C(i+1) = h(CS) + (i+1) \times g + g + e(CS)$$

We know that $i \geq 0$, so $i + 1 \geq 1$ which gives the following expression of $C(i+1)$:

$$
\begin{aligned}
C(i+1) &= C(i+1-1) + g \\
&= C(i) + g \\
&= h(CS) + i \times g + g + e(CS) + g \\
&= h(CS) + (i+1) \times g + g + e(CS)
\end{aligned}
$$

Therefore, $\forall i \in [0, N[$, Eq. 9 is correct.

Following Iterations: $N \leq i < L$ In general, $C(i)$ can be expressed as the sum of: the duration it took for the current chunk to get on the CPU (which is the same as calculating the cost of encrypting the chunk $i - N$), the hashing duration, the encryption duration, the IV generation duration and, possibly, a waiting duration where the thread is blocked until the previous IV is generated.

This translates into the following formula:

$$C(i) = C(i - N) + h(CS) + wd(i) + g + e(CS) \tag{10}$$

For all iterations except the first one, the waiting duration for chunk i is the difference between the point in time where the previous IV is calculated, which is expressed by $(C(i-1) - e(CS))$, and the one where the hashing operation for chunk i finishes execution, denoted by $(C(i - N) + h(CS))$:

$$(C(i-1) - e(CS)) - (C(i - N) + h(CS))$$

The waiting duration is either a positive value or 0, so instead we define the waiting duration $wd(i)$ as:

$$max(0, [C(i-1) - e(CS)] - [C(i - N) + h(CS)])$$

Since the expression of $wd(i)$ depends on the sign of $(C(i-1) - e(CS)) - (C(i - N) + h(CS))$, then so does the expression of $C(i)$.

When replacing $wd(i)$ by its expression we get:

Case 1: $wd(i) = 0$

$$C(i) = C(i - N) + h(CS) + g + e(CS) \tag{11}$$

Case 2: $wd(i) > 0$

$$C(i) = C(i - 1) + g \tag{12}$$

Figure 4, helps visualize the execution scenario of DCBC's threads on each CPU for both cases 1 and 2. * **Case 1:** $wd(i) = 0$

Our goal is to prove that Eq. (11) is equivalent to:

$$C(i) = (div(i, N) + 1) \times (h(CS) + e(CS) + g) + mod(i, N) \times g \tag{13}$$

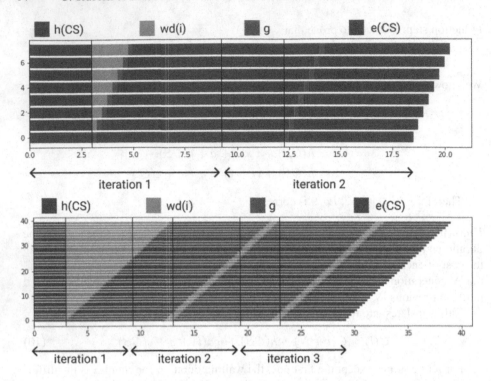

Fig. 4. DCBC's execution scenario according to Cases 1 and 2 [14].

To prove this, we will proceed by induction:

<u>Base case:</u> $i = N$

$$C(N) = C(0) + h(CS) + g + e(CS)$$
$$= 2 \times (h(CS) + g + e(CS))$$

So C(N) is correct.

<u>Induction Hypothesis:</u> Suppose that there exists an i such that $\forall k \leq i$:

$$C(k) = (div(k, N) + 1) \times (h(CS) + e(CS) + g) + mod(k, N) \times g$$

<u>Induction step:</u> We need to prove that $\forall i \geq N$:

$$C(i+1) = ((div(i+1), N) + 1) \times (h(CS) + e(CS) + g) + mod(i+1, N) \times g$$

According to Eq. (11):

$$C(i+1) = C(i+1-N) + h(CS) + g + e(CS)$$

So, we need to distinguish between two cases:
$i + 1 - N < N$ and $i + 1 - N \geq N$.

*If $i + 1 - N < N$, we can apply Eq. (9):

$$C(i+1) = h(CS) + (i + 1 - N + 1) \times g + e(CS) + h(CS)$$
$$+ g + e(CS)$$
$$= 2 \times (h(CS) + g + e(CS)) + (i + 1 - N) \times g$$

However, $0 < i + 1 - N < N$
$\Longleftrightarrow N < i + 1 < 2N$
$\Longleftrightarrow div(i + 1, N) = 1$
$\Rightarrow mod(i + 1, N) = (i + 1) - div(i + 1, N) \times N$
$\Rightarrow mod(i + 1, N) = i + 1 - N$

$$\Rightarrow C(i+1) = 2 \times (h(CS) + e(CS) + g) + (i - N + 1) \times g$$
$$= (div(i+1, N) + 1) \times (h(CS) + e(CS) + g)$$
$$+ mod(i+1, N) \times g$$

So, Eq. (13) is correct for $i + 1$ if $i + 1 - N < N$.
*If $i + 1 - N \geq N$: According to Eq. (11):

$$C(i+1) = C(i + 1 - N) + h(CS) + g + e(CS)$$

Since $N \geq 1$ then, $i + 1 - N \leq i$, therefore the induction hypothesis is applicable to $i + 1 - N$, which gives us:

$$C(i+1) = (div(i + 1 - N, N) + 1) \times (h(CS) + e(CS) + g)$$
$$+ mod(i + 1 - N, N) \times g + h(CS) + g + e(CS)$$
$$= (div(i+1, N) - 1 + 1) \times (h(CS) + e(CS) + g)$$
$$+ mod(i+1, N) \times g + (h(CS) + g + e(CS))$$
$$= (div(i+1, N)) \times (h(CS) + e(CS) + g)$$
$$+ (h(CS) + g + e(CS)) + mod(i+1, N) \times g$$
$$= (div(i+1, N) + 1) \times (h(CS) + e(CS) + g)$$
$$+ mod(i+1, N) \times g$$

So, Eq. (13) is correct for $i + 1$ if $i + 1 - N \geq N$.
By induction, we conclude that, $\forall i \geq N$, Eq. (13) is correct.

* Case 2: $wd(i) > 0$
In this Case, we will be considering the expression of $C(i)$ as given by Eq. (12).
We notice that in this case $C(i)$ is just an extension of the expression we calculated for the first iteration over the interval $[N, L[$. In conclusion, $\forall i \in [N, L[$:

$$C(i) = h(CS) + (i + 1) \times g + e(CS)$$

General Formula. In this section, we will calculate an expression for $C(i)$, $\forall i \in [0, L[$. For the first case: $wd(i) = 0$, we notice that if we apply the expression of $C(i)$, as defined by Eq. (13), for $i < N$ we get:

$$
\begin{aligned}
C(i) &= (div(i, N) + 1) \times (h(CS) + e(CS) + g) \\
&\quad + mod(i, N) \times g \\
&= (0 + 1) \times (h(CS) + e(CS) + g) + i \times g \\
&= h(CS) + (i + 1) \times g + e(CS)
\end{aligned}
$$

So, for $i < N$, both Eqs. (13) and (9) are equivalent and we can use Eq. (13) as a general expression for $C(i)$, $\forall i \in [0, L[$, as long as $wd(i) = 0$.

For the other case, where $wd(i) > 0$, $C(i)$ has the same expression for all iterations. So Eq. (9) will be the general expression of $C(i)$ under that condition.

In conclusion, we can express $C(i)$ as: $\forall i \in [0, L[$,
if $wd(i) = 0$: $C(i) = (div(i, N) + 1) \times (h(CS) + e(CS) + g) + mod(i, N) \times g$
otherwise:

$$
C(i) = h(CS) + (i + 1) \times g + e(CS)
$$

Now that the expression of $C(i)$ is determined, we need to simplify the conditional expression $wd(i) > 0$, to have it use initial parameters only.

If we consider $wd(i) > 0$, then in this case:

$$
wd(i) = C(i - 1) - e(CS) - C(i - N) - h(CS) \tag{14}
$$

We will be proceeding by induction to prove that:

$$
wd(i) = (N - 1) \times g - (e(CS) + h(CS)) \tag{15}
$$

<u>Base case:</u> $i = N$

$$
\begin{aligned}
wd(N) &= C(N - 1) - e(CS) - C(0) - h(CS) \\
&= C(N - 1) - C(0) - (e(CS) + h(CS))
\end{aligned}
$$

Using the expression of $C(i)$ in Eq. (9), we get:

$$
wd(N) = (N - 1) \times g - (e(CS) + h(CS))
$$

Which means that, $wd(N)$ is correct.

<u>Induction Hypothesis:</u>

$$
\forall k \le i, wd(k) = (N - 1) \times g - (e(CS) + h(CS))
$$

<u>Induction step:</u> We need to prove that:

$$
wd(i + 1) = (N - 1) \times g - (e(CS) + h(CS)), i \ge N
$$

$wd(i) > 0$, then according to Eq. (12):

$$
C(i) = C(i - 1) + g
$$

$$\Rightarrow wd(i+1) = C(i) - e(CS) - C(i+1-N) - h(CS)$$
$$= C(i-1) + g - e(CS) - (C(i-N) + g) - h(CS)$$
$$= C(i-1) - e(CS) - C(i-N) - h(CS)$$
$$= wd(i) = (N-1) \times g - (e(CS) + h(CS))$$

So, Eq. (15) is correct for $i + 1$.

By induction, we conclude that if $wd(i) > 0$, then Eq. (15) is correct $\forall i \in [N, L[$. In conclusion, $\forall i \geq N$:

$$wd(i) > 0 \iff (N-1) \times g > e(CS) + h(CS)$$

$\forall i \in [0, L[$, the final expression of $C(i)$ is:

Case 1: $(N-1) \times g \leq (e(CS) + h(CS))$:
$C(i) = (div(i,N) + 1) \times (h(CS) + e(CS) + g) + mod(i,N) \times g$
Case 2: $(N-1) \times g > (e(CS) + h(CS))$
$C(i) = h(CS) + (i+1) \times g + e(CS)$

5.3 Theoretical Performance Comparison

In this section, our goal is to compare the theoretical cost of running DCBC to that of running CBC in different scenarios.

To do so, we will be using the cost function C which represents the cost of computing the encryption of a given chunk starting from the origin, which we define as the point in time when the encryption of the first chunk started. We will denote by i, the index of the chunk we are interested in, so: $i \in [0, L]$.

The expression of $C(i)$ is, $\forall i \in [0, L[$:

Case 1: $(N-1) \times g \leq e(CS) + h(CS)$:

$$C(i) = (div(i,N) + 1) \times (h(CS) + e(CS) + g) + mod(i,N) \times g$$

Case 2: $(N-1) \times g > e(CS) + h(CS)$

$$C(i) = h(CS) + (i+1) \times g + e(CS)$$

The proof behind the equations defining the function C is provided in Sect. 5.2.

In order to compare the function C to the cost of running plain CBC, we respectively vary the *file size* **S**, the *chunk size* **CS** then the *number of CPUs* **N**. For the fixed variables, we will work with empirically estimated values which requires us to specify the algorithms used for each step of DCBC's execution as well as the definition of a method that allows for a fair estimate of the needed values.

In this section, we will use **MD5** for **H**, **AES** [3] for **E** and **E$_G$**. As for **G** we will use: $G(H_i, IV_{i-1}) = E_G(H_i \oplus IV_{i-1})$.

When it comes to estimating a value empirically, we will use the following method:

1. The operation for which we wish to estimate the cost, is executed 100 times and the duration of each iteration's execution is saved.

2. The mean value is calculated over all recorded values.
3. Outliers are detected using simple conditions and replaced with the calculated mean value: We consider a value to be an outlier if the distance between it and the mean value is higher then 3 times the standard deviation.
4. If any outliers have been found, go to step 2. Otherwise exit and use the calculated mean value as the cost of that operation.

The results shown in Table 1, will be used to calculate the theoretical performance of DCBC in different scenarios in order to compare it to the performance of CBC. When it comes to the IV generation, its cost is a constant value since it is independent of the size of the plaintext.

Table 1. Empiric cost for AES_CBC and MD5 [14].

Size (MB)	E (ms)	H (ms)	S (ms)
128	607.169	196.278	0.004
256	1209.63	386.864	
384	1807.156	558.95	
512	2410.118	771.739	
640	3007.476	930.84	
768	3612.55	1117.435	
896	4219.523	1301.641	
1024	4825.55	1542.107	

As we mentioned earlier, in order to estimate the total cost of running DCBC we will resort to the expression of $C(i)$ which, at the beginning of the section, we defined as the duration it takes to encrypt the chunk of index i since the start of the encryption of first chunk (chunk 0). This means that the cost of encrypting the whole plaintext is equal to the cost of encrypting the last chunk (chunk $L-1$). So, from this point on, we will be using the expression of $C(L-1)$ as the cost of encrypting the whole plaintext. Also, as you may notice, the value of g is negligible compared to that of $e(x) + h(x)$, where x represents values from the size column in Table 1. This means that for realistic values of N, we will always verify: $(N-1) \times g \leq e(CS) + h(CS)$ which in turn means that we only need to consider the expression of $C(i)$ according to **Case 1**. We conclude that the cost of running DCBC over the whole plaintext is:

$$C(L-1) = (div(L-1, N) + 1) \times (h(CS) + e(CS) + g) + mod(L-1, N) \times g$$

Which is equivalent to:

$$C(L-1) = (div(L-1, N)+1) \times (h(CS)+e(CS)) + (div(L-1, N)+1+mod(L-1, N)) \times g$$

However, we will need to use the chunk size CS as a parameter instead of the number of chunks L.

So, for all following sections, instead of using the number of chunks as a constant L, we will be calculating it by ceiling the result of dividing the full plaintext's size by the size of a single chunk: $L = ceil(\frac{S}{CS})$

Scenario 1: Varying the Plaintext Size. For this case, we will be using a function $f_1(x)$ to refer to the cost of encrypting a file of size x using DCBC, where x is expressed in *MB*. The expression of f_1 will be:

$$f_1(x) = (div(ceil(\frac{x}{CS}) - 1, N) + 1) \times (e(CS) + h(CS)) + (div(ceil(\frac{x}{CS}) - 1, N) + 1 + mod(ceil(\frac{x}{CS}) - 1, N)) \times g, \forall x > 0$$

Our goal is to compare the cost of running CBC (represented by the function $e(x)$, where x is the size of the plaintext), and DCBC for various file sizes while fixing all other parameters: $N = 4$ and $CS = 128$ MB. To do this we start by plotting $f_1(x)$ and $e(x)$, for $x \in \{128, 256, 512, 513, 1024\}$. First, we use the empirically estimated values taken by $e(x)$ listed in Table 1. Then, to get the values taken by $f_1(x)$, we use the value of $e(128)$ we got from the previous step as well as the approximation of $h(128)$.

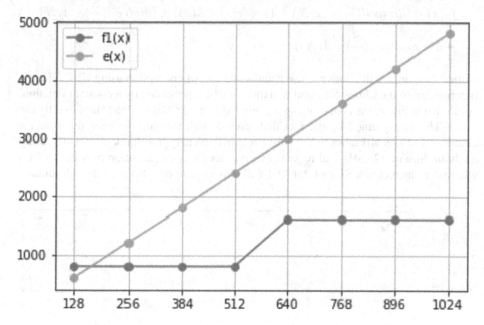

Fig. 5. Performance comparison for various values of S [14].

The results shown in Fig. 5, present some interesting findings: when running the encryption on a plaintext of size 128 MB, DCBC shows a slightly worse performance compared to CBC. This is to be expected since with 128 MB of data and a *Chunk Size* of 128 MB as well, DCBC will be using a single chunk and will therefore, not only run in a sequential manner over the whole plaintext, but also suffer from the added weight of the extra hashing operation compared to CBC.

We also notice that f_1 is constant for the interval $[128, 512]$ and is doubled for $x \in\,]512, 1024]$. This is due to the fact that, in the example we considered, we are using $N = 4$ and $CS = 128$, therefore, for a plaintext of size $x \leq 512$, we will be running a single iteration of encryption. However, for any value of x such that $x \in\,]512, 1024]$, two iterations are required, which explains why the cost doubles.

When running the encryption on a plaintext of 256 MB of data or more, we notice that, the larger the plaintext, the higher the difference between the cost of running CBC and that of running DCBC, except for the points where transitions from using n iterations to $n + 1$ iterations take place ($x \in]512, 640]$ in our case), where this difference in performance gets slightly reduced especially for much bigger plaintexts.

In conclusion, DCBC presents a much bigger advantage in performance as the plaintext gets bigger in size, but it is not recommended for cases where the plaintext is of almost equal size to the *Chunk Size* chosen by the user. This leads us to watch how various values for the *Chunk Size* can affect the performance of DCBC.

Scenario 2: Varying the Chunk Size. We will be using a function f_2 to represent the cost of encrypting a plaintext of a known size S (1024) with 4 CPUs using DCBC with various values for CS:

$$f_2(x) = (div(ceil(\frac{S}{x}) - 1, N) + 1) \times (e(x) + h(x)) + (div(ceil(\frac{S}{x}) - 1, N)$$
$$+ 1 + mod(ceil(\frac{S}{x}) - 1, N)) \times g, \forall x > 0$$

Notice that, since CBC does not use chunks, the cost of encryption using CBC, $e(x)$, is independent of the Chunk Size and will therefore be represented by a constant function. As shown in Fig. 6, the cost of using a *Chunk Size* of 128 MB or 256 MB is exactly the same. This is explained by the fact that, even though running the encryption over a chunk of size 128 MB takes half the time required to encrypt a chunk of 256 MB, using a Chunk Size of 128 MB will require two full iterations of execution over all 4 CPUs whereas using a chunk Size of 256 MB will only require one. So even though running

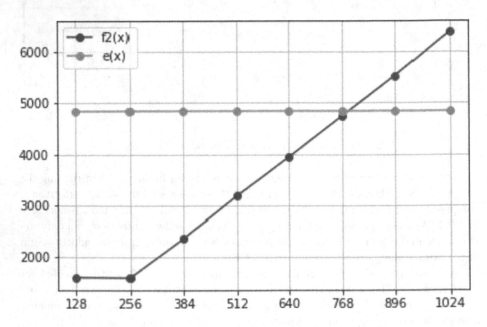

Fig. 6. Performance comparison for various values of CS [14].

DCBC with a Chunk Size of 128 MB will take only half the time to encrypt a single chunk when compared to using a Chunk Size of 256 MB, it would in return need to run twice as many times as in the latter case, which would eventually even out the results.

When CS is set to a value of 512 MB, we notice that the cost of running DCBC doubles.

Intuitively, this is to be expected since $S = 1024$, therefore the plaintext will be split into only two chunks, which means that only 2 of the 4 CPUs will be used for the encryption as opposed to using all 4 CPUs when $CS \leq 256$. More generally, if the *Chunk Size* is higher then 256 MB, only a subset of 4 available CPUs will be used. Also, encryption and hashing over a single chunk will cost more time the higher the *Chunk Size* is. These two factors add up to an overall higher cost when running DCBC with $CS \geq 256$.

Finally, we notice that at a certain point, DCBC presents a worse performance in comparison to CBC, as the cost of the added hashing over a relatively large chunk will surpass the benefit of running the encryption in parallel. In conclusion, the choice of the chunk size is important to the performance of DCBC, and even though it seems that, in theory, the smaller the *Chunk Size* is, the better the performance gets, this has to be verified in practice, as many other factors may interfere. We also have to keep in mind that we are working on cases where $(div(ceil(\frac{S}{CS}) - 1, N) + 1 + mod(ceil(\frac{S}{CS}) - 1, N)) \times g$ happens to be of negligible effect over the results. If this constraint is negated by the use of a very small *Chunk Size* compared to the *full plaintext size*, the value of $\frac{S}{CS}$ might get big enough for the previous expression to have an important impact on the results, even though $g \approx 0.004$.

Scenario 3: Varying the Number of CPUs. We will be using a function f_3 to represent the cost of encrypting a plaintext of a known size $S = 1024$ MB and a fixed Chunk Size $CS = 128$ MB using DCBC with various values for the *Number of CPUs N*:

$$f_3(x) = (div(ceil(\frac{S}{CS}) - 1, x) + 1) \times (e(CS) + h(CS)) + (div(ceil(\frac{S}{CS}) - 1, x)$$
$$+ 1 + mod(ceil(\frac{S}{CS}) - 1, x)) \times g, \forall x > 0$$

Notice that the cost of running CBC encryption ($e(x)$) is independent of the Number of CPUs used, since it is a sequential process that, in theory, runs on a single process. Therefore e presents a constant function in this case. As Fig. 7 shows, when $N = 1$, DCBC presents a much worse performance compared to CBC, as it will be running sequentially with the added weight of using the hash function H.

For $N = 2$, since $S = 1024$ and $CS = 128$ we will be encrypting $L = 8$ chunks of data. Each of the 2 CPUs will be responsible for encrypting 4 of these chunks, which is equivalent to encrypting and hashing 128 MB of data 4 times. However, using CBC, the encryption will be sequential over a single CPU for the full 1024 MB of data which results in a relatively high difference in performance as the overhead of hashing 128 MB of data 4 times is less significant than the difference in time between running CBC over a full 1024 MB of data and only 128 MB of data 4 times. This result is confirmed by the distance between $f_3(2)$ and $e(2)$, in Fig. 7.

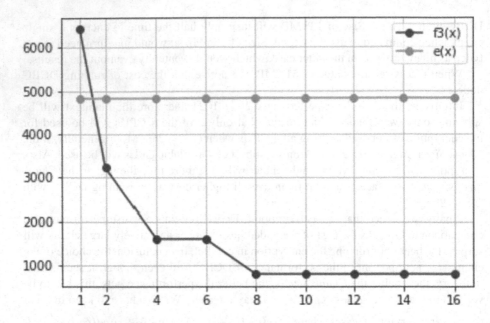

Fig. 7. Performance comparison for various values of N [14].

For $N = 4$, the cost is reduced by half compared to using only 2 CPUs. However, using 6 CPUs instead of 4 doesn't affect at all the performance of DCBC, this is because in both cases we will have to run a total of 2 iterations.

For $N \geq 8$, we notice that the cost of running DCBC becomes constant. This is due to the fact that at this point we are only running a single iteration of encryption which gives the lowest cost possible, so all extra CPUs are not being used.

Even though these results make perfect sense in theory, in practice there can be a slightly different behaviour.

In a modern system, multiple other processes might be running alongside the DCBC encryption operation. This can cause a slightly higher cost than the theoretical values calculated above. It can also result in a slight improvement of performance when using 6 CPUs compared to the actual cost of using 4 CPUs and further increasing the number of CPUs will help us approach this theoretical value.

In conclusion, the performance of DCBC depends, not only on the computational resources available, but also on the chunk size chosen by the user and the size of the file they look to encrypt.

6   Theoretical Diffusion

In this section, we aim to find a function that allows us to estimate the diffusion rates of CBC and DCBC in order for us to plot them in different scenarios and compare the results.

6.1   The Probability of a Bit Flipping

In this subsection we look to calculate the probability of a bit flipping, depending on its position, when another bit flips at a given position in the plaintext.

Bit Flip in Same Block. In this subsection we will calculate the probability of a bit flipping in the ciphertext if it is affected by changes in the plaintext.

Assume bit b is affected[1] by changes to plaintext, b can either flip or keep its old value. Let F_b be the event of b flipping ($F_b = 1$ if bit b flips and 0 otherwise).

Using a secure block cypher encryption such as AES gives a result that is indistinguishable from a random string. Therefore, having a bit b in any two ciphertexts with a value of 0 or 1 can happen with a probability of 0.5 no matter how similar or different the plaintexts are.

For our purposes, we will refer to the value of a bit b in the original ciphertext as V_b and the value of bit b of the ciphertext associated to the modified plaintext as V_b'.

We will continue working on the assumption that bit b is affected by the changes in the plaintext.

The probability of bit b flipping ($F_b = 1$) is the same as the probability of ($V_b = 0$ AND $V_b' = 1$) OR ($V_b = 1$ AND $V_b' = 0$):

$$P(F_b = 1) = P((V_b = 0 \cap V_b' = 1) \cup (V_b = 1 \cap V_b' = 0)).$$

Since, as we mentioned, the ciphertext represents a random string, the current and possible future values of b are independent, so:

$$P(F_b = 1) = P(V_b = 0) \times P(V_b' = 1) + P(V_b = 1) \times P(V_b' = 0)$$
$$= 0.5 \times 0.5 + 0.5 \times 0.5 = 0.5$$

Bit Flip in a Following Block. In case bit b is not affected by the changes in plaintext, it will keep its value, therefore $P(F_b = 1) = 0$.

In CBC, this case can occur if the modification in the plaintext took place in a bit k that can be located on any block that comes after the one where bit b is located ($k \; div \; 128 > (b \; div \; 128)$, 128 being the size of the block in AES).

Bit Flip in a Previous Block. We know from Sect. 6.1 that each bit in the block where the change (a bit **k** being flipped) took place, can flip with a probability of 0.5. First we start by calculating the probability of at least one bit flipping in the ciphertext of the block containing **k**.

Let p_n be the probability of at least one bit flipping among n bits, each having a probability to flip of 0.5.

---

[1] Affected: has a chance to change; as opposed to unaffected bits which are guaranteed to keep same value.

Having at least one bit out of n flipping means that:

- bit n flips and none of the other bits do
- bit n flips and at least one more out of the remaining bits flips
- bit n doesn't flip and at least one of the remaining bits flips

$$p_n = P(F_n = 1) \times p_{n-1} + P(F_n = 0) \times p_{n-1} + P(F_n = 1) \times \prod_{i=1}^{n-1} P(F_i = 0)$$

$$= 0.5 \times p_{n-1} + 0.5 \times p_{n-1} + 0.5 \times (0.5)^{n-1}$$

$$= p_{n-1} + (0.5)^n$$

$$\Rightarrow p_n = \sum_{i=1}^{n} \frac{1}{2^i}$$

In our scenario, a block is made up of 128 bits. Moreover, if any bit of the block's plaintext flips, every bit in the block's ciphertext has a chance to flip of 0.5 (as shown in Sect. 6.1). Therefore, Eq. 6.1 can be applied and the probability of at least one bit flipping out of 128 is:

$$p_{128} \approx 1$$

Thus, if a bit changes in a block, the block's ciphertext is guaranteed to have at least one bit in it flipping. Going back to our original context, if a bit **k** is flipped in the block that is right before bit b's block, we can guarantee that at least one bit of that block's ciphertext will flip. Since CBC applies a XOR between each plaintext block and the previous block's ciphertext, then the bit sequence that is passed to AES is guaranteed to have changed by at least one bit compared to its value before flipping bit **k**. This puts us back to the situation discussed in Sect. 6.1, since a bit flipped in the same block as bit b, then:

$$P(F_b = 1) = 0.5$$

Conclusion. By applying the results we reached in this section, we can conclude that, if a bit flips in the plaintext, bits from the same block as well as all following blocks in the ciphertext have, each, a chance of 0.5 to flip and the bits in all previous blocks are guaranteed to keep their values.

6.2 Probability of at Least M Bits Flipping

Now that we have established that when a bit **b** is flipped, all future bits have a probability of 0.5 to flip, we will be calculating the probability of at least m bits flipping out of the affected bits, which we will later refer to as *candidates*.

First, let's calculate the general formula for at least m bits flipping out of n candidates. We will refer to this probability as $p(m, n)$.

If $n < m$:

$p(m, n) = 0$, since we don't have enough candidate bits to flip.

If $n > m$:

Since bit flips are completely independent events or experiences, each with a probability of 0.5, then having m out of n bits flipped in the ciphertext represents a binomial trial [17] (it can be thought of as a series of coin flips, where getting heads represents that the bit flipped and tails that it didn't):

$$
\begin{aligned}
p(n, m) &= \frac{n!}{m! \times (n-m)!} \times (0.5)^n \times (0.5)^{n-m} \\
&= \frac{n!}{m! \times (n-m)!} \times (0.5)^n
\end{aligned}
\tag{16}
$$

This formula can be applied to CBC after having determined n, the number of candidate bits that have a chance to flip.

In CBC, if bit b is flipped, all bits of b's block as well as bits from all next blocks have a chance to flip, therefore $n = (N - b) + b\%128$, where N is the full plaintext size.

Hence, for each bit b, if it gets flipped in the plaintext, the probability of m bits flipping is: $p(m, N - b + b\%128)$.

When it comes to DCBC, the same logic can be applied since changes in the plaintext are propagated, but with a difference in scope, as changes in a chunk (for which the size can be much larger than that of an AES block) are propagated to all following bits as well as previous bits from the same chunk. This is ensured by the fact that the entire chunk is hashed to generate the IV, which propagates the change in a single bit to the ciphertext of the entire chunk.

This means that the only difference between CBC and DCBC is the number of candidate bits n, which, for DCBC is $n = (N - b + b\%CS)$, where CS is the chunk size.

Hence, the probability of m bits flipping when bit b flips is $p(m, N - b + b\%CS)$.

To compare CBC and DCBC when it comes to diffusion we will look for the value m such that: $p(m, n) \geq 0.9999$, for different values of b. We will also consider the chunk size to be 128 bytes ($CS = 128 \times 8bits$) and the file size to be 1Kb ($N = 1024 \times 8bits$)

This will allow us to calculate a theoretical estimation of the number of bits that are almost guaranteed to flip when the plaintext is modified in various positions. The results of this estimation are shown in Fig. 8.

This representation shows that DCBC has larger intervals where the diffusion rate is constant, which is to be expected since DCBC's chunk size is larger than AES's 128 bit block size. This leads to an overall greater mean diffusion rate for DCBC which can be confirmed by calculating:

$$
md = \sum_{i=1}^{N} d_i \times \frac{1}{N}
\tag{17}
$$

where md is the mean diffusion (average number of bits that flipped when flipping bits of the plaintext at indices starting from 1 up to N), and d_i is the number of bits that flip in the ciphertext when plaintext bit i is flipped. So,

$$
md_{cbc} = 1965.59
$$

$$
md_{dcbc} = 2181.87
$$

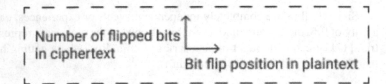

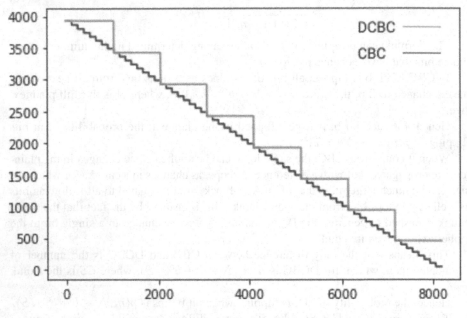

Fig. 8. DCBC and CBC diffusion.

This proves that DCBC would have an 11% advantage in terms of mean diffusion rate. It is important to note that we used very small values for the chunk and full plaintext sizes, in order to have a reasonable calculation time for the diffusion rates on the equipment we have available for us. However, with larger chunk sizes, the advantage CBC offers in terms of diffusion will grow and will be more clear and more interesting (especially if we use chunk sizes in the order of Mega Bytes, while AES blocks are in the order of bits).

To sum up, CBC offers a higher diffusion rate than regular CBC, which can be further enhanced by using larger chunk sizes, however, using very large chunk sizes (for examples dividing the entire plaintext into only two chunks), will slow down the performance as we have less room for parallel encryption (in the example we just mentioned we will only be able to encrypt using two parallel processes even though we could have an 8 core machine or even an 8 node cluster). Thus, choosing the right chunk size depending on the available resources and the needs of the user is essential.

7   Conclusion and Future Work

The main idea behind DCBC is running multiple independent CBC encryption operations in order to enhance performance, especially for large volumes of data, while keeping a relatively light-weight chaining layer. This chaining layer relies on hashing for local change propagation in the different chunks, as well as XORing with the previous chunk's hash in order to ensure change propagation in all future chunks. We also cover some conditions that need to be met in order to ensure DCBC's encryption security, as it inherits some of CBC's properties. This has lead us, for example, to encrypting the chunk's hash after having XORed it with the previous IV, in order to generate a unique and pseudo-random IV for each chunk. The generated chunk IVs can even be used, in a later stage, to ensure message integrity by hashing the result of chunk decryption and comparing it to the chunk's hash that was used during encryption.

Even though integrity verification is a very important aspect of data security, the most important feature that DCBC is designed for, is offering a configurable trade-off between parallelizability (therefore performance) and diffusion. Calibrating DCBC to favor one property over the other simply comes down to the choice of the *Chunk Size*, which makes DCBC very easy to use without the need for knowing how it works internally.

In this article we also provide theoretical performance cost, as well as theoretical diffusion rate, estimations. Both of them aim to study the viability of our solution compared to traditional CBC. We found that DCBC offers an advantage in both performance and diffusion which get even more interesting the bigger the data gets.

We intend in our ongoing work to validate these theoretical results by some empirical tests that will also target both performance and diffusion. These tests will be run for a parallel version of DCBC that runs locally on a single machine using threads, as well as in a distributed environment containing multiple nodes.

Later, we will study the possibility of integrating DCBC in existing Big Data solutions such as Hadoop, by implementing our encryption logic in a resource manager such as YARN [15].

Finally, we will look into generalizing the idea used to create DCBC to produce a higher level of abstraction that allows it to be used with any underlying mode of operation and not just CBC. To do that, we won't only have to ensure that our solution still provides a higher diffusion rate and a better or at least comparable performance, but also to respect all security settings required by the remaining modes of operation, during the IV generation phase.

References

1. Bard, G.V.: A challenging but feasible blockwise-adaptive chosen-plaintext attack on SSL. In: SECRYPT 2006 - International Conference on Security and Cryptography, Proceedings, pp. 99–109 (2006)
2. Bellare, M., Desai, A., Jokipii, E., Rogaway, P.: Concrete security treatment of symmetric encryption. In: Annual Symposium on Foundations of Computer Science - Proceedings, pp. 394–403 (1997)
3. Daemen, J., Rijmen, V.: AES proposal: Rijndael (1999)

4. Desai, A., Ankalgi, K., Yamanur, H., Navalgund, S.S.: Parallelization of AES algorithm for disk encryption using CBC and ICBC modes. In: 2013 4th International Conference on Computing, Communications and Networking Technologies, ICCCNT 2013, November 2001
5. Duţă, C.L., Michiu, G., Stoica, S., Gheorghe, L.: Accelerating encryption algorithms using parallelism. In: Proceedings - 19th International Conference on Control Systems and Computer Science, CSCS 2013, pp. 549–554 (2013)
6. Dworkin, M.: Recommendation for Block Cipher Modes of Operation. National Institute of Standards and Technology Special Publication 800–38A 2001 ED, X(December), pp. 1–23 (2005)
7. Joux, A., Martinet, G., Valette, F.: Blockwise-adaptive attackers revisiting the (in)security of some provably secure encryption modes: CBC, GEM, IACBC. In: Yung, M. (ed.) CRYPTO 2002. LNCS, vol. 2442, pp. 17–30. Springer, Heidelberg (2002). https://doi.org/10.1007/3-540-45708-9_2
8. Katos, V.: A randomness test for block ciphers. Appl. Math. Comput. **162**(1), 29–35 (2005)
9. McGrew, D.A.: Counter Mode Security: Analysis and Recommendations, pp. 1–8 (2002)
10. Phan, D.H., Pointcheval, D.: About the security of ciphers (semantic security and pseudorandom permutations). In: Handschuh, H., Hasan, M.A. (eds.) SAC 2004. LNCS, vol. 3357, pp. 182–197. Springer, Heidelberg (2004). https://doi.org/10.1007/978-3-540-30564-4_13
11. Sahi, A., Lai, D., Li, Y.: An efficient hash based parallel block cipher mode of operation. In: 2018 3rd International Conference on Computer and Communication Systems, ICCCS 2018, vol. 4, pp. 212–216 (2018)
12. Shetty, M.M., Manjaiah, D.H.: Data security in Hadoop distributed file system. In: Proceedings of IEEE International Conference on Emerging Technological Trends in Computing, Communications and Electrical Engineering, ICETT 2016, pp. 10–14 (2017)
13. Stallings, W.: NIST block cipher modes of operation for confidentiality. Cryptologia **34**(2), 163–175 (2010)
14. Trabelsi, O., Sfaxi, L., Robbana, R.: DCBC: A Distributed High-performance Block-Cipher Mode of Operation, pp. 86–97 (2020)
15. Vavilapalli, V.K., et al.: Apache Hadoop YARN: yet another resource negotiator. In: Proceedings of the 4th Annual Symposium on Cloud Computing, SoCC 2013 (2013)
16. Verdult, R.: Introduction to Cryptanalysis: Attacking Stream Ciphers, pp. 1–22 (2001)
17. Viti, A., Terzi, A., Bertolaccini, L.: A practical overview on probability distributions. J. Thoracic Dis. **7**(3), E7–E10 (2015). PMID: 25922757

An Assurance Framework and Process for Hybrid Systems

Marco Anisetti[✉][iD], Claudio A. Ardagna[✉][iD], Nicola Bena[✉][iD],
and Ernesto Damiani[✉][iD]

Dipartimento di Informatica, Università degli Studi di Milano, Milan, Italy
{marco.anisetti,claudio.ardagna,nicola.bena,
ernesto.damiani}@unimi.it

Abstract. Security assurance is a discipline aiming to demonstrate that a target system holds some non-functional properties and behaves as expected. These techniques have been recently applied to the cloud, facing some critical issues especially when integrated within existing security processes and executed in a programmatic way. Furthermore, they pose significant costs when hybrid systems, mixing public and private infrastructures, are considered. In this paper, we a present an assurance framework that implements an assurance process evaluating the trustworthiness of hybrid systems. The framework builds on a standard API-based interface supporting full and programmatic access to the functionalities of the framework. The process provides a transparent, non-invasive and automatic solution that does not interfere with the working of the target system. It builds on a Virtual Private Network (VPN)-based solution, to provide a smooth integration with target systems, in particular those mixing public and private clouds and corporate networks. A detailed walkthrough of the process along with a performance evaluation of the framework in a simulated scenario are presented.

Keywords: Assurance · Hybrid system · Security · Virtual private network

1 Introduction

In today digital and connected society, users and enterprises interact with smart services and devices to carry out day-to-day activities and business processes. Distributed systems are rapidly and continuously evolving, from service-based systems to cloud and microservices-based architectures and, more recently, towards Internet of Things (IoT) and edge infrastructures. At the same time, traditional private infrastructures are still widely used, resulting in hybrid systems mixing public and private endpoints and introducing new concerns undermining the users' perceived trust (e.g., [25]).

In the last couple of decades, the research community has extensively produced new solutions to increase the trustworthiness of such systems. Security verification and protection have been increasingly important, and should be fully integrated within systems'

Research supported, in parts, by EC H2020 Project CONCORDIA GA 830927 and Università degli Studi di Milano under the program "Piano sostegno alla ricerca".

M. S. Obaidat and J. Ben-Othman (Eds.): ICETE 2020, CCIS 1484, pp. 79–101, 2021.
https://doi.org/10.1007/978-3-030-90428-9_4

lifecycle and executed in a automated way. Security assurance, defined as a way to gain justifiable confidence that IT systems will consistently demonstrate a (set of) security property and operationally behave as expected [6], is gaining the momentum. Assurance solutions in fact have been applied to service-based systems, cloud, and IoT [7,9], addressing novel and peculiar requirements such as multi-layer evaluation and continuous monitoring, as well as evidence-based verification. Notwithstanding their huge benefits, little focus has been put in defining assurance frameworks that can be easily integrated into existing hybrid systems, complementing other security processes and providing a programmatic way to execute assurance evaluations. Many of the existing assurance techniques and frameworks (e.g., [10,14]) are ad hoc and cannot handle a modern IT system as a whole. They require some effort for being integrated with the target system, interfering with its normal operation (e.g., performance) and introducing not-negligible (monetary and business) costs. Also, they fall short in providing some form of automation.

In this paper, we extend our assurance framework in [4] enabling a centralized security assurance, complementing existing security processes and systems, and providing automation of assurance activities. The framework implements an API-based approach facilitating integration and automation, and relies on Virtual Private Networks (VPNs) to target both public and private infrastructures. Our contribution is threefold. We first define the requirements a security assurance framework and corresponding process have to fulfill in our hybrid scenario (Sect. 2). We then propose a novel API-based assurance framework addressing these requirements and targeting hybrid systems (Sect. 3). To this aim, the assurance process implemented by the framework relies on an enhanced REST interface (Sect. 4) and on several modifications to a standard VPN configuration (Sect. 5). We finally present a detailed walkthrough of such a process (Sect. 6.1), an experimental evaluation of the framework performance (Sect. 6.2), and a comparison with the state of the art according to the identified requirements (Sect. 7).

2   Assurance Requirements

The advent and success of cloud computing and Internet of Things (IoT) are radically changing the shape of distributed systems. Hybrid systems, building on both private and public technologies, introduce new requirements and challenges on security assurance techniques, which must take a step forward for being applicable to modern architectures. In particular, the definition of new assurance processes is crucial to fill in the *lack of trustworthiness* that is one of the main hurdles against the widespread diffusion of such systems.

Despite targeting complex systems, a security assurance process should be lightweight and not interfere with the normal operation of the system under verification. The need of a lightweight process is strictly connected to its *psychological acceptability* [22], meaning that final users are more willing to *accept* to perform assurance activities that preserve the behavior of the system and do not increase overall costs. In fact, although the undebatable advantages given by a continuous evaluation of system security, users are recalcitrant with respect to a process perceived as heavy and costly [27].

Cost management and optimization are the foundation of assurance adoption. Costs refer to *monetary costs* in terms of additional human and IT resources, as well as *performance and business costs* in terms of overhead, latency, and reliability. *Monetary costs* include the need of highly specialized personnel, on one side, and resources allocated and paid on demand on the other side, which are spent to manage non-functional aspects of the system often considered as superfluous. *Performance costs* include the need of continuously verifying the security status of a system. They intrinsically introduce a not-negligible overhead and latency, an assurance process has to cope with. Assessment activities are only viable if they take resource demands under control, avoiding scenarios where they become a source of attack. *Business costs* are partially overlapped with performance costs and model how much assurance activities interfere with the normal operations of a business process. On one side, the changes required to connect an assurance process to the system under evaluation should be reduced to the minimum, and mostly work at the interface level. On the other side, an assurance process cannot threat itself the system. For example, run-time verification of a system security status cannot increase the risk of system unavailability by performing penetration testing on the production system. A good balance between active and passive testing/monitoring should be provided. Finally, security assurance is just one of the security activities that should be performed. An assurance process must complement and integrate with traditional detection and prevention security, by means of an assurance framework implementing a (semi-)automatic process that is easy to integrate with existing security solutions.

We identify the main requirements an *assurance process* has to satisfy (MUST/ SHOULD) to address the peculiarities of modern systems, as follows.

Transparency: it MUST not interfere with the normal operation of the business process, being transparent to the final user of the system where the assurance process is performed.

Non-invasivess: it MUST require the least possible set of changes to the target system.

Safety: it MUST not introduce (or at least minimize) new risks on the target system.

Continuity: it SHOULD provide a continuous process, verifying the status of security while the system is operating and evolving.

Lightness: it SHOULD be lightweight and cope with systems having limited resources.

Adaptivity: it SHOULD be dynamic and incremental to adapt to changes in the system under verification and its environment.

Complementarity: it SHOULD complement and integrate with existing security processes.

Such requirements should be supported by a centralized framework tuning each aspect of the assurance evaluation. The *framework* itself has its own requirements [5], which are summarized in the following.

Evidence-Based Verification: it SHOULD implement a verification built on evidence collected on the target system, to get the real picture of its security status.

Extensibility: it MUST inspect hybrid targets, from traditional private networks to public clouds, as well as hybrid clouds and IoT.

Multi-layer: it SHOULD assess system security at different layers, from network protocols to application-level services.

Scalability: it SHOULD support a scalable process, able to manage an increasing number of assurance processes and evaluations.

Automation: it SHOULD be an automatic or semi-automatic process, whose actions can be triggered either manually or by external events.

Generally speaking, an assurance framework MUST *at least* implement a process that has the lowest possible impact on the target resources and normal system activities (*transparency*), do not modify the current ICT infrastructure or at least require very few modifications (*non-invasiveness*), do not affect security by introducing new risks (*safety*) or hindering existing security processes (*complementarity*), while being generic enough to address peculiarities of hybrid systems (*extensibility*).

3   Assurance Framework

We present a framework that provides a lightweight assurance solution addressing the peculiarities of modern distributed systems, mixing public endpoints on the cloud, microservices, and *private* deployments not directly reachable from the outside (e.g., *traditional* private corporate networks and private clouds). The framework has been first defined in [4] and here extended to address requirements *complementarity* and *automation*. The original framework in [4], offering only a graphical dashboard, constrained the ability to integrate framework's functionalities with existing security processes, and to trigger such functionalities in a automated way. To address all requirements in Sect. 2, it adopts a layer-3 VPN that connects the framework with the private deployments under verification (i.e., the *target networks*), and offers a REST API providing full and programmatic access to framework's functionalities.

The architecture of the assurance framework is presented in Fig. 1 and aims to address two main scenarios: *i)* support from programmatic integration of the framework within existing (possibly legacy) systems, *ii)* support for the verification of modern systems mixing public and private endpoints. Concerning scenario *i)*, the framework can be used either *manually* by users interacting with the dashboard, or *programmatically*, by exploiting standard *REST APIs*, thus satisfying requirements *complementarity* and *automation*. Concerning scenario *ii)*, the framework implements a VPN-based approach to seamlessly integrate with and verify private corporate networks and private clouds, thus satisfying requirements *transparency*, *non-invasiveness*, and *extensibility*. To this aim, different *VPN Servers* are installed within the framework, each one responsible to handle isolated VPN tunnels with client devices placed in the target networks. A single VPN connection consists of a *VPN Client* directly connected to the target network, and a *VPN Server* installed in the framework.

The framework manages an assurance process (Sect. 5) that consists of a (set of) evaluation rule (evaluation in the following). Each evaluation is a Boolean expression of test cases, which are evaluated on the basis of the evidence collected by *probes* and *meta-probes*. *Probes* are self-contained test scripts that assess the status of the given target by collecting relevant evidence on its behavior. They return as output a Boolean result modeling the success or failure of the test case. *Meta probes* are defined as *probes* collecting *meta-information*, such as the response time of a service. The framework components are summarized in the following.

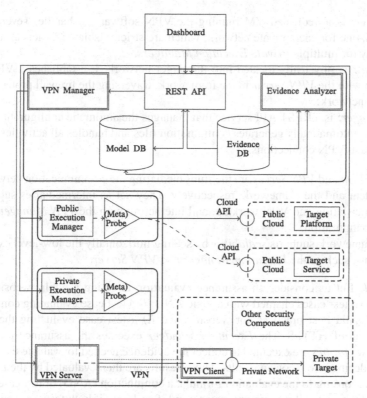

Fig. 1. Our framework architecture. Double line rectangles highlight new components.

Dashboard: is the graphical user interface used to configure new evaluations and access their results. It works by connecting to the APIs provided by component *REST API*.

REST API: manages the overall assurance process by the means of a REST interface. Upon receiving an evaluation request, either from the *Dashboard* or directly from the APIs, it creates the necessary objects in the database and orchestrates their execution.

Execution Manager: is in charge of the evaluation process. It selects and executes the relevant *probes*. There are two types of *Execution Managers*: one targeting public clouds (*Public Execution Manager*), and one targeting private deployments (*Private Execution Manager*). The only difference between them is the way in which traffic is routed to the destination.

Model Database: is the main database. It stores most of the information needed by the framework, including evaluation configurations and target details.

Evidence Analyzer: produces the overall result of an evaluation by collecting the results of the single test cases and validating them against the Boolean expression of the evaluation.

Evidence Database: stores the results of *probe* execution, including both the collected evidence and the Boolean results.

VPN Server: is a dedicated VM running the VPN software. It handles several VPN tunnels, one for each private network, which are strictly isolated. It acts as a default gateway for multiple *Private Execution Managers.*

VPN Client: is physically located into the target network. It establishes a VPN connection with the *VPN Server* in the framework, traversing the firewall protecting the private network.

VPN Manager: is a REST API service that manages the automatic configuration of the VPN. It automatically generates configuration files and handles all activities needed to manage VPN connections.

VPN Client and *VPN Server* are the stubs mediating the communication between the target system and the framework, respectively. They act as intermediaries supporting protocol translation and VPN working, and interacting with the *VPN Manager* for the channel configuration.

The framework supports *scalability* by scaling horizontally the low-level execution components, such as the *Execution Manager* and *VPN Server.*

Example 1. Let us consider an assurance evaluation targeting a public website composed of two test cases chained with a logic AND: *i)* a test case evaluating compliance against Mozilla best practices for websites and *ii)* a test case evaluating the proper configuration of HTTPS. The *Execution Manager* executes the assurance process as follows. Two *probes* are executed to collect the evidence needed to evaluate the two test cases, producing two Boolean results. Those results are then evaluated by the *Evidence Analyzer* according to the evaluation formula, a conjunction (AND) of test cases *i)* and *ii).* As such, the overall evaluation is successful if and only if both test cases succeed.

4   REST Interface

REST is a popular paradigm for developing backend applications, which is based on the concepts of *resources* and *operations* performed on such resources, in terms of HTTP paths (resources) and HTTP methods (operations). A REST interface can be described by using the *OpenAPI* standard, the standard for documenting REST applications [19]. The standard itself is referred to as the *OpenAPI specification*, and defines the format of the application's documentation, which is referred to as *OpenAPI document*. A valid OpenAPI document is a JSON object and can be represented either in JSON or YAML.

Our assurance framework builds on an API-based approach, where component *REST API* provides a REST interface complemented by an OpenAPI document. Together, they facilitate the integration of assurance activities with existing security solutions, addressing requirement *complementarity*, and the automation of such activities, addressing requirement *automation*.

4.1   OpenAPI Document

An OpenAPI document is composed of different parts describing all the aspects of a REST service: resources, operations on such resources, valid requests and responses, possibly with examples, as well as non-functional aspects, such as how authentication is handled. They are briefly described in the following, along with short excerpts of the OpenAPI document of our component *REST API*.

Metadata: is the header of the document and specifies, among the others, the version of the specification the document adheres to, a high-level description of the APIs, and the version of the APIs the document refers to.

```
openapi: 3.0.1
info:
  contact:
    email: info@moon-cloud.eu
  description: Moon Cloud REST API are the most important component of Moon
  ↪  Cloud, governing the overall framework.
  license:
    name: BSD License
  termsOfService: https://www.moon-cloud.eu/policies/terms/
  title: Moon Cloud API
  version: v1.9.9-alpha
```

The *metadata* excerpt shows section metadata of our framework. For instance, it shows that the version of the APIs is v1.9.9-alpha.

Paths: defines the available resources; for each resource, it specifies the HTTP URL and the possible operations, in terms of HTTP methods, that can be performed on it. Each operation contains, among the others, a mnemonic name, valid requests, and corresponding responses.

```
paths:
  /abstract-evaluation-rules/:
    summary: The possible evaluations a user can execute.
    description: This resource represents an evaluation a user can execute,
    ↪  possibly by composing it with other Abstract Evaluation Rule.
    get:
      operationId: abstract-evaluation-rules_list
      summary: List all the existing Abstract Evaluation Rule.
```

The *paths* excerpt shows the resource abstract-evaluation-rules and one of the possible operations, identified by the HTTP method GET. Such an operation lists all the resources of that type.

Request: defines a valid request for an operation. It contains the schema detailing the format of such a request.

```
  /evaluation-rules/:
    post:
      operationId: evaluation-rules_create
      summary: Creates a new User Evaluation Rule
      description: Creates a new User Evaluation Rule by composing together one
      ↪  or more Abstract Evaluation Rule.
      requestBody:
        content:
          application/json:
            schema:
              $ref: '#/components/schemas/EvaluationRule'
        required: true
```

The *request* excerpt shows a POST operation creating a new resource (evaluation-rules). It provides a short and long description, and the request format.

Responses: defines the possible responses that can be returned upon an operation on a resource. Different responses are identified by different HTTP status codes (e.g., 200 success, 400 bad request). Each response contains the schema detailing the format of such a response.

```
responses:
  "201":
    description: User Evaluation Rule created and started successfully.
    content:
      application/json:
        schema:
          $ref: '#/components/schemas/EvaluationRule'
```

The *response* excerpt shows the response returned upon a successful creation of a resource of type evaluation-rule. It is identified by the status code 201 and contains the format of the response.

Components: is a top-level section including the definition of resources, requests, and responses. This way, they are defined only once and referred to in other parts of the document using a specific syntax and increasing reuse along the document.

```
components:
  schemas:
    EvaluationRule:
      type: object
      properties:
        id:
          readOnly: true
          title: ID
          type: integer
        name:
          maxLength: 50
          minLength: 1
          title: Name
          type: string
```

The *components* excerpt shows a portion of the schema of a resource of type EvaluationRule.

4.2   Component *REST API*

The component *REST API* contains the framework main business logic and offers a REST interface to use the framework functionalities. The exposed resources can be divided in two main categories: *i) asset management*, allowing users to manage the assets (i.e., targets) registered within the framework, *ii) evaluation management*, allowing users to schedule evaluations and view their results. This interface is used by the *Dashboard*, which is the web-based graphical interface the users interact with. Recalling Sect. 2, an assurance process should be integrated with existing (security) solutions and processes (*complementarity*), as well as provide some form of *automation*. Both requirements are achieved by means of the exposed REST APIs, and facilitated by the corresponding OpenAPI document. The OpenAPI document is automatically generated from the application code, and served at a REST endpoint itself.

   In general, an OpenAPI document serves for three main purposes: *i)* model-driven engineering (MDE), *ii)* documentation, *iii)* analysis.

Model-Driven Engineering: consists of a development process centered around the business models. An OpenAPI-based model-driven engineering defines the first steps of the development process. The OpenAPI document describes the interface the application exposes and then develops the application by adhering to such a document. The coding phase can be partially automated by using code generation tools that, based on the OpenAPI document, generate most of the code boilerplate. Code generation can be also used to generate client libraries interacting with a REST server. These libraries are provided at a higher level of abstraction than plain HTTP calls. In our case, the OpenAPI document is used to generate several clients, supporting the use of our framework through a command-line interface (CLI) and in a continuous integration/continuous delivery (CI/CD) pipeline.

Documentation: is another important use case for OpenAPI documents. Being a standard format, applications wishing to consume an API can exploit its OpenAPI document to get a detailed view of how such a service works. Parts of the application can be realized by code generation tools. Furthermore, developers can leverage visual tools, such as *ReDoc*, which display graphically an OpenAPI document. In our case, the OpenAPI document is served at a public endpoint, providing a comprehensive documentation of the framework REST interface, including several examples.

Analysis: of an OpenAPI document is a research line that focuses on service validation by automatically generating test cases [18], transformations to other models (e.g., UML [13]), extensions to the specification to improve code generation [23]. In our case, the OpenAPI document is used to automatically generate several test cases, making it easier to perform functional and non-functional testing.

Our framework supports the complementarity and automation of assurance activities bypassing the graphical user interface and making use of the programmatic interface, namely the APIs offered by component *REST API*. These APIs can be, in fact, invoked within automatic or semi-automatic processes, for instance by triggering an evaluation when other events occur. Furthermore, libraries interacting with the framework can be automatically generated by exploiting the published OpenAPI document.

5 Assurance Process

The assurance process implemented by the framework in Fig. 1 must assess both public and private targets. To address both scenarios, the framework builds on Virtual Private Network (VPN), addressing the must-have requirements *transparency*, *non-invasiveness*, *safety*, and *extensibility* in Sect. 2. The goal is to implement an assurance process that can be smoothly integrated with any kind of private target system, by means of a Site-to-Site VPN between the framework and the private targets the framework has to assess.

5.1 Building Blocks

Virtual Private Network (VPN) stands for a set of technologies used to build overlay networks over the public network. It provides hosts with remote access to a corporate

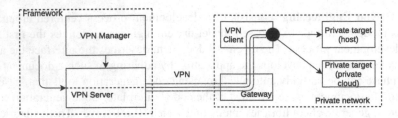

Fig. 2. Architecture of VPN-based solution [4].

network, or connects several geographically-distributed networks as if they are separated by one router [3].

In this paper, we focus on *Site-to-Site VPN*, where several networks are connected using the VPN. In each network connected to the VPN, there is a host acting as a *VPN gateway*, mediating traffic between internal hosts within its network and *other networks*. It routes traffic coming from internal hosts to the other *VPN gateways* and back. *VPN gateways* are called either *VPN clients* or *VPN servers*, where servers can handle connections to multiple clients, while a client establishes a single tunnel with a server.

VPNs usually combine a *virtual network interface card* (virtual NIC) and a socket-like connection. A virtual NIC is a NIC that has no physical correspondence, and is associated with a userspace process – in this case the VPN software. Packets *sent* by such process to its virtual NIC are *received* by the Operating System (OS), and further processed just like a real network packet. At the same time, the OS can *send* packets to it, and the VPN software, through its NIC, acts as the receiver. The socket-like connection is used to transmit packets between *VPN gateways* using a cryptographic protocol. The virtual NIC is used to send and receive packets coming from and whose destination is the host's network.

Virtual NICs of the same VPN have IP addresses belonging to the same subnet, called *VPN subnet*. When the operating system of the *VPN gateway* handles a packet whose destination is a host in the *VPN subnet*, it sends the packet to the local virtual NIC, like a normal routing operation. Two sets of routing rules have to be defined: *i)* on each network, a rule on the default gateway that specifies to route traffic for *other networks* to the local *VPN gateway*; *ii)* on each *VPN gateway*, a rule that specifies to route traffic for *other networks* to the local virtual NIC.

However, a traditional VPN implementation does not permit to address many of the requirements in Sect. 2. The aforementioned routing rules, in fact, must be installed on both sides of the communication. Setting up these routes on the targets' default gateways requires access to the devices to alter their configurations. This violates properties *non-invasiveness*, *transparency*, and *safety*. We therefore propose a VPN-based approach at the basis of our assurance process that addresses the requirements, by adding several configurations on top of a standard VPN setup. The three logical building blocks of our VPN approach are: *VPN Client*, *VPN Server* and *Conflict-Resolution Protocol* (Fig. 2).

VPN Client. *VPN Client* establishes a VPN connection with the server, exposing its network to the framework. It realizes a *Client-side NAT* that avoids setting up routing rules on the target network. The issue is that packets generated by the framework and injected by the *VPN Client* into the target network have a source IP address belonging to the framework network. As such, responses to such packets would be routed to the target network default gateway (because they appertain to a different network than the current one) instead of the *VPN Client*. To address this, we propose a lightweight app-roach based on network address translation (*NAT*), which does not require to configure default gateways. Once packets are received by the *VPN Client* from the framework through the VPN, it translates their source IP address in the *VPN Client* IP address. Since this belongs to the same subnet of the target hosts, no routes need to be config-ured. Responses can directly reach the *VPN Client*, where the destination IP address of the packets is translated back. We implemented this address translation with *nftables*, available in Linux-based operating systems.

VPN Server. *VPN Server* handles VPN tunnels with several clients; each tunnel is iso-lated to each other. It implements a *Server-side NAT*, to provide higher dynamics. There are two problems behind *Server-side NAT*, both involving routing configuration. On one side, *VPN Clients* need to know the network IP address of the framework (Sect. 5.1); on the other side, these routes must be known a priori, an assumption not trivial in our scenario. The network IP address of the framework, in fact, can change, for example, if the framework moves to a different cloud provider or for security reasons. We address the aforementioned problems by setting up different NAT rules on the *VPN Server*. They modify packets coming from the framework just before being received by the virtual NIC of the VPN software. These rules change the source IP address of packets by replacing it with the virtual NIC IP address of the server. Thus, packets received by a *VPN Client* have a source IP address belonging to the current *VPN subnet*. Then, corresponding responses generated by the target hosts, after the application of *Client-side NAT*, have a destination IP address appertaining to the *VPN subnet*. Recalling that a *VPN Client* knows how to handle packets generated – or appearing to be generated – directly from the *VPN subnet*, the *VPN Client* OS can route those packets to the local virtual NIC, without additional configurations. They are then received by the VPN soft-ware and finally sent to the server. *Server-side NAT* is implemented as a set of *nftables* rules.

Conflict-Resolution Protocol. A mandatory requirement for a Site-to-Site VPN is that each participating network must have a non-conflicting net ID. Guaranteeing this assumption is necessary to allow a single VPN server to connect multiple networks together – in our case to allow a single *VPN Server* to handle several target networks. In corporate VPNs, it is trivial to assert this property, since the networks are under the control of the same organization. This assumption is not valid in our scenario, where two target networks could have the same network IP address, or a target network could conflict with the framework network. We propose an approach called *IP Mapping* to solve this issue.

INPUT
$s \in S$: VPN Server
n_O: network to *map*

OUTPUT
n_M: mapped version of n_O

MAP_NET
available_nets ← **db_query_select**(s);
if length(*available_nets*) != 0 **then**
  pair ← ⟨*available_nets[0]*, n_O⟩;
  db_query_insert(*pair*);
else Error();
return *pair*;

INPUT
$n_O.j$: j-th IP address ∈ network n_O

OUTPUT
$n_M.j$: j-th corresponding
    IP address ∈ network n_M

MAP_IP
n_O ← **net_id**($n_O.j$);
host_id ← **host_id**($n_O, n_O.j$);
n_M ← **get_corresponding_net**(n_O);
$n_M.j$ ← **build_address**(n_M, *host_id*);
return $n_M.j$;

INPUT
$n_M.k$: k-th IP address ∈ network n_M

OUTPUT
$n_O.k$: k-th corresponding
    IP address ∈ network n_O

REMAP_IP
n_M ← **net_id**($n_M.k$);
host_id ← **host_id**($n_M, n_M.k$);
n_O ← **get_corresponding_net**(n_M);
$n_O.k$ ← **build_address**(n_O, *host_id*);
return $n_O.k$;

Fig. 3. IP Mapping: pseudocode [4].

IP Mapping is based on the concept of *mapping* the *original* network to a new one, called *mapped* network and guaranteed to be unique. Each IP address of the *original* network is translated into a new one, belonging to the corresponding *mapped* network. This translation is reversible, and the *mapped* address is specified by the framework as the target when executing a new evaluation. *IP Mapping* is realized through 3 functions whose pseudocode is described in Fig. 3. The overall protocol, which is completely transparent to the final user, works as follows.

First, when a new target network is being registered, the function *map_net* is invoked by the framework, to obtain a non-conflicting version of the *original* target network. The pair ⟨*original, mapped*⟩ is saved into the database. Function *map_net* is offered by *VPN Manager* as a REST API.

When a user issues a new evaluation, she enters the *original* target IP address. The framework calls *map_ip* to obtain its *mapped* version, and builds the corresponding test case using this IP address as destination. The test packets are then sent through the VPN. Function *map_ip* is offered by *VPN Manager* as a REST API.

The *VPN Client* receives the packets and calls *remap_ip* to get the *original* version of the destination IP address of the packets. This address is then set as the destination address: packets can now be sent to the target.

When corresponding responses reach back the *VPN Client*, the latter invokes *map_ip* to obtain the *mapped* version of the current IP source address; the result is set as the new IP source address. This second translation is issued to re-apply *IP Mapping* and let packets becoming correct responses to the ones generated by the framework. Finally, they are sent along the VPN and reach the framework.

Functions *map_ip* and *remap_ip* are implemented by a set of NAT rules using *nftables*.

The soundness of the overall VPN setup passes from *IP Mapping*, which, using the terminology in Fig. 3, must support the following properties.

1. *Mapping uniqueness*: let $A \subseteq n_M \times S$; $\forall a_i, a_j \in A$, $(a_i.s = a_j.s \land a_i \neq a_j) \Rightarrow (a_i.n \neq a_j.n)$

Table 1. Comparison of a standard layer-3 VPN and a layer-3 VPN with our modifications on top [4].

	Standard layer-3 VPN	Our approach
Client-side requiring configuration	Yes	No (*Client-side NAT*)
Server network known a priori	Yes	No (*Server-side NAT*)
Conflicting networks	Not allowed	Allowed (*IP Mapping*)
Address conflict resolution	Manual	Automatic (*VPN Manager*)
Plug-and-play integration	No	Yes

2. *Mapping correctness*: $\forall\ n_O\ \forall$ address $\in\ n_O\ remap\_ip(map\_ip(address)) = map\_ip(address)^{-1}$
3. *Implementation correspondence*: $\forall\ n_O,\ \forall$ address $\in\ n_O,\ map\_ip'(address) = map\_ip''(address)$

The first property expresses that no conflicts can happen, that is, two *mapped* networks with the same network IP address attached to the same *VPN Server* cannot exist. The second property expresses the reversibility of the translation process. It guarantees that a response to *mapped* packets generated by the framework is correct, that is, the source IP address of a response is equal to the destination IP address of a request. The third property expresses the need of having two implementations of *map_ip* (as a REST API or NAT rule) with the same behavior. We note that the pseudocode in Fig. 3 is a possible implementation of the three functions.

Table 1 summarizes the differences between a standard VPN and the one described in this paper. Our solution does not require any configurations on the target network, thanks to *Client-side NAT*; it also does not require to know the network IP address of the framework, thanks to *Server-side NAT*. Moreover, the networks participating in the VPN can have conflicting IP addresses, which are automatically disambiguated by *IP Mapping* and *VPN Manager*. To conclude, our solution allows a plug-and-play integration between the framework and the target network.

5.2 Assurance Process

The assurance process implemented by our framework is first configured with the registration of a private network and the creation of the *VPN Client*. We note that all actions involving interactions with our framework can be performed either manually by using the *Dashboard* or automatically by using the *REST API*. It then starts its activities with an evaluation request, where the user specifies the (set of) evaluation she wants to execute and the corresponding configurations. *REST API* orchestrates the process by creating the necessary objects within the database (*Model Database*) and by selecting the *Execution Manager* that executes the evaluation. In case of a private target, a *Private Execution Manager* connected to a *VPN Server* is selected. Also, *REST API* transparently obtains the *mapped* version of the target IP address, by invoking REST function *map_ip* exposed by *VPN Manager*.

The (set of) test case, derived from the requested (set of) evaluation, is sent to the selected *Execution Manager*, which executes the necessary (set of) *probe*. In case of a public target, test packets generated by the *probe* are sent directly to the target, and responses reach back the *probe* without involving the VPN. Otherwise, they are sent to the *VPN Server* that applies *Server-side NAT*, and then, passing through the VPN, reach the *VPN Client*. At this point, it applies *i) remap_ip* changing the destination IP address of the packets and *ii) Client-side NAT* changing the source IP address of the packets. Thanks to the last modification, responses to such packets flow back to the *VPN Client*, applying the converse of the previous steps: *i)* the reverse of *Client-side NAT* and *ii)* the reverse of *remap_ip*, that is, *map_ip*. When those packets are received by *VPN Server*, it applies the converse of *Server-side NAT*, by first forwarding them to the *probe* and then to the *Execution Manager*.

The *probe* produces the Boolean result of the test case and stores it into the *Evidence Database*. The overall result of the evaluation is determined by the *Evidence Analyzer*, which evaluates the evaluation's Boolean formula against the Boolean result(s) of the execution.

A concrete example of the process is described in Sect. 6.

6   Walkthrough and Experiments

We present a walkthrough of our assurance process and its experimental evaluation.

6.1   Process in Execution

Our framework supports the composition of multiple evaluations, tailoring framework's functionalities to match user needs. In the following, for simplicity but no lack of generality, we consider a singleton evaluation, named *Observatory-Compliance*, which checks whether a website has implemented common best practices, such as HTTPS redirection and cross-site-scripting countermeasures. In particular, we present the detailed working of an assurance process whose target is located into a private network, thus involving the use of our VPN-based solution (Sect. 5). We note that our VPN-based approach is transparent to the users, introducing no differences between private and public targets, except for the *VPN Client*.

The parameters describing this process are the following: framework net ID 192.168.1.0/24, target net ID 192.168.50.0/24, mapped target net ID 192.168.200.0/24, and VPN subnet net ID 10.7.0.0/24.

Preparation. A prerequisite for the working of a VPN-based process is to register the private network within the framework. When the user inserts a new net ID (192.168.50.0/24 in our example), the component *REST API* calls the *map_net* API exposed by *VPN Manager*, obtaining the *mapped* version of the input network (192.168.200.0/24). As described in Sect. 5.1, this mapping is stored in the framework database and triggers the creation of a new *VPN Client*. *VPN Manager* also configures *VPN Server* to support connections from the client. The client device is then moved into the correct location and connected to the server, establishing a VPN tunnel whose net ID (VPN subnet) is 10.7.0.0/24.

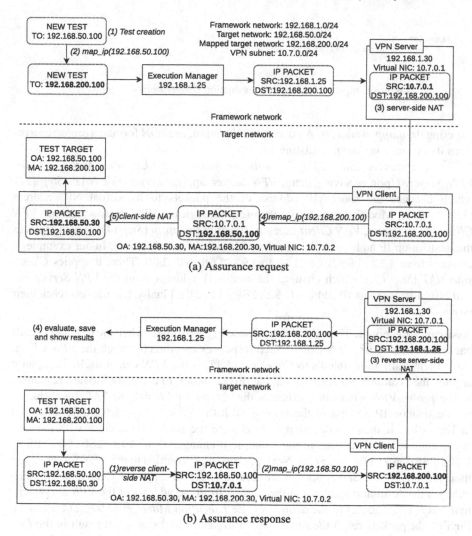

Fig. 4. Packet flow: (a) assurance request, (b) assurance response [4].

Assurance Request. The assurance request in Fig. 4(a) starts with the framework receiving an evaluation request (*Step (1)* in Fig. 4(a)), in this case for evaluation *Observatory-Compliance*. Such request contains, among the others, the IP address of the target (192.168.50.100 in our example). Component *REST API* orchestrates the process as follows. First, it creates the necessary objects, for instance, a test case, in the database to manage the evaluation. Being a private target, it calls the *map_ip* API exposed by *VPN Manager*, obtaining the *mapped* version of the target address (192.168.200.100) (*Step (2)*). Next, it chooses the *Execution Manager* that is in charge of the evaluation. For the aforementioned reason, a *Private Execution Manager* is selected. Such *Execution Manager* executes the *probe* as specified by *REST API*,

```
{
    "config": {
        "url": "http://192.168.200.100"
    }
}
```

Listing 1. Input of the *probe* for evaluation *Observatory-Compliance*.

targeting the *mapped* address. An excerpt of the input, in JSON format, a *probe* receives from its executor is shown in Listing 1.

The test packets generated by the *probe* are routed by the *Execution Manager* to the *VPN Server*. Upon receiving them, *VPN Server* applies *Server-side NAT (Step (3))*, which changes the source IP address of the packets to its virtual NIC address (10.7.0.1). Modified packets are then sent through the VPN, finally reaching *VPN Client*. At this point, *VPN Client* executes function *remap_ip (Step (4))*, which replaces the destination IP address of the packets with their *original* version. In our example, it changes from 192.168.200.100 to 192.168.50.100. Then, it applies *Client-side NAT (Step (5))*, which changes the source IP address from the *VPN Server* virtual NIC address to its IP address (192.168.50.30). Finally, test packets reach their target.

Assurance Response. The assurance response Fig. 4(b) starts when the test target sends back responses to the *VPN Client*. Such responses can directly reach the *VPN Client*, since their destination, thanks to *Client-side NAT*, is the *VPN Client* itself. This phase applies the assurance request steps in the reverse order, to correctly forward responses to the *probe*. *VPN Client* first executes the reverse of *Client-side NAT*, by replacing the destination IP address of the packets with the *VPN Server* virtual NIC (*Step (1)* in Fig. 4(b)). It then applies *map_ip* to change the source IP address with the corresponding *mapped* version, in our example it changes from 192.168.50.100 to 192.168.200.100 (*Step (2)*). Next, packets are forwarded to the *VPN Server*. Upon their reception, *VPN Server* applies the reverse of *Server-side NAT (Step (3))*. This step changes the destination address of the packets from the address of the *VPN Server* virtual NIC (10.7.0.1) to the address of the *Execution Manager* (192.168.1.25). Finally, the packets reach the *probe*, which evaluates and stores test result in the *Evidence Database (Step (4))*. In parallel and asynchronously, the component *Evidence Analyzer* produces the evaluation result, by collecting the Boolean results of the test cases forming the evaluation and evaluating them against the formula. In our example, this step is trivial since it involves evaluating a formula composed of either TRUE or FALSE. The result is finally written in the main database (*Model Database*) and can be accessed by the user.

An excerpt of the evaluation output is shown in Listing 2, showing that two best practices, x-content-type-options and x-frame-options, have been effectively implemented. As such, the evaluation result is TRUE.

6.2 Experiments

Our framework has been implemented as a set of microservices written in Python. Our VPN-based solution has been realized on top of *OpenVPN*, a flexible and open-source

```
{
    "status": true,
    "data": {
        "grade": "A",
        "x-frame-options": {
            "expectation": "x-frame-options-sameorigin-or-deny",
            "result": "x-frame-options-sameorigin-or-deny",
            "description": "X-Frame-Options (XFO) header set to SAMEORIGIN or
            ↪   DENY",
            "link": "https://infosec.mozilla.org/guidelines/web_security#x-frame-⌐
            ↪   options",
            "hint": "X-Frame-Options controls whether your site can be framed,
            ↪   protecting against clickjacking attacks. It has been superseded
            ↪   by Content Security Policy's <code>frame-ancestors</code>
            ↪   directive, but should still be used for now."
        },
        "x-xss-protection": {
            "expectation": "x-xss-protection-1-mode-block",
            "result": "x-xss-protection-enabled-mode-block",
            "description": "X-XSS-Protection header set to \"1; mode=block\"",
            "link": "https://infosec.mozilla.org/guidelines/web_security#x-xss-pr⌐
            ↪   otection",
            "hint": "X-XSS-Protection protects against reflected cross-site
            ↪   scripting (XSS) attacks in IE and Chrome, but has been superseded
            ↪   by Content Security Policy. It can still be used to protect users
            ↪   of older web browsers."
        }
    }
}
```

Listing 2. Sample output of the *probe* for evaluation *Observatory-Compliance*.

VPN solution that permits to tune every aspect of a VPN tunnel. In particular, we configured a layer-3 VPN using TCP as the encapsulating protocol, to maximize the probability of traversing firewalls in the path from the framework to the target system. *Client-side NAT*, *Server-side NAT*, and *IP Mapping* have been implemented as NAT rules with *nftables*.

Framework components have been packaged as *Docker containers* executed within Virtual Machines, all using operating system *CentOS 7 x64*. The following components run on single-container dedicated VMs: *REST API* (2 vCPUs, 4 GBs of RAM) *Execution Manager* (6 vCPUs, 4 GBs of RAM), *VPN Server* (1 vCPU, 4 GBs of RAM), running *OpenVPN* version *2.4.6* and *nftables* version *0.8*. All VMs have been deployed on a Dell PowerEdge M360 physical host that features 16 CPUs Intel® Xeon® CPU E5-2620 v4 @ 2.10 GHz and 191 GBs of RAM.

The target system has been deployed on AWS EC2 and was composed of two virtual machines *t2.micro*, both with 1 vCPU and 1 GB of RAM. The first one, *VPN Client*, with operating system *Ubuntu 18.04 x64*, *OpenVPN* version *2.4.7*, and *nftables* version *0.8*. The second one, test target, with operating system *Ubuntu 16.04 x64* offering *WordPress* version *5.2.2*.

We finally setup two experiments with the goal of computing the difference between two possible deployments: *i) public deployment* exposing the target on the public network, *ii) private deployment* using the approach in Sect. 5. The difference between the two deployments has been expressed in terms of the overhead that the private deployment adds on top of the public deployment, according to the following evaluations.

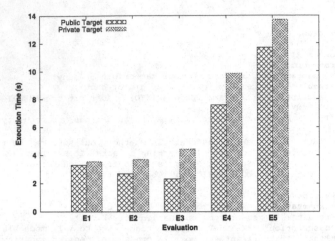

Fig. 5. Execution times of evaluations E1 – *Infowebsite*, E2 – *Observatory-Compliance*, E3 – *SSH-Compliance*, E4 – *TLS-strength*, E5 – *WordPress-scan* [4].

- *Infowebsite* that extracts as much information as possible from a target website. It is denoted as E1 in Fig. 5.
- *Observatory-Compliance* that checks whether a website has implemented common best practices, such as HTTPS redirection and cross-site-scripting countermeasures. It is denoted as E2 in Fig. 5.
- *SSH-Compliance* that checks the compliance of a SSH configuration against Mozilla SSH guidelines. It is denoted as E3 in Fig. 5.
- *TLS-strength* that evaluates whether the TLS channel has been properly configured, such as avoiding weak ciphers and older versions of the protocol. It is denoted as E4 in Fig. 5.
- *WordPress-scan* that scans the target *WordPress*-based website looking for *WordPress*-specific vulnerabilities. It is denoted as E5 in Fig. 5.

We chose these evaluations to maximize test coverage and diversity, from the evaluation of web resources (*Infowebsite*, *Observatory-Compliance*), to the evaluation of protocol configurations (*SSH-Compliance*, *TLS-strength*) and specific applications (*WordPress-scan*). Each evaluation was executed 10 times and the average time was computed. In particular, the execution time measurement started when the *Execution Manager* received the evaluation request, and finished when the executed *probe* terminated.

Performance and Discussion. Figure 5 presents the average execution time of evaluations E1–E5. It shows that, as expected, the execution time in the private scenario is higher than the same in the public scenario, with an overhead varying between ≈0.3 s and 2 s.

More in detail, evaluation E1 (*Infowebsite*) experienced a very low overhead, less than a second. Evaluation E2 (*Observatory-Compliance*) experienced an overhead of approximately 1 s. Evaluations E3, E4 and E5 (*SSH-Compliance*, *TLS-strength*, *Word-Press-scan*, resp.) experienced a higher overhead, approximately 2 s, increasing execution time from ≈2 s to ≈4 s for E3, from ≈8 s to ≈10 s for E4 and from ≈12 s to ≈14 s. Overall, the increase in the execution time was globally under control, never exceeding 2 s. This overhead can be tolerated in all scenarios supporting requirements in Sect. 2.

To conclude, there is a subtlety to consider when an assurance process for hybrid systems is concerned: the accuracy of the retrieved results. There could be some cases in which the evidence collected by a *probe* on a public endpoint is different from the one collected by the same *probe* on a private endpoint. For instance, evaluation E1 (*Infowebsite*), in the private scenario, failed to discover the version of the target *WordPress* website. This was due to a partial incompatibility between the *probe* implementation and our VPN-based solution. Being our approach *probe*-independent, this issue can be solved by refining the *probe* associated with *Infowebsite*. In our experiments, evaluation E1 was the only experiencing such problem, while the other evaluations were able to collect the same evidence in both private and public deployments.

7 Comparison with Existing Solutions

Many security assurance approaches have been presented in literature, targeting software-based systems [16] and service-based environments [7], and providing certification, compliance, and audit solutions based on testing and monitoring. We analyzed the main assurance frameworks and processes, which can be classified according to the following categories: *monitoring-based*, *test-based* and *domain-specific*. Table 2 provides a comparison of these frameworks, including the one in this paper, with respect to requirements in Sect. 2.

Monitoring-Based Frameworks. Aceto et al. [1] provided a comprehensive survey of assurance solutions based on monitoring. They first considered requirement *intrusiveness*, which is similar to our requirements *transparency* and *non-invasiveness*, and found that many commercial monitoring tools do not address such requirement. They then considered requirement *lightness*, because monitoring tends to be expensive in term of resource consumption. Two monitoring frameworks have been presented in [2,12], both building on monitoring tool *Nagios*, thus satisfying, partially, *complementarity* and *automation*. Due to the intrinsic nature of monitoring, these frameworks can easily satisfy the requirement *continuity*. Moreover, the work in [2] can achieve a very good *adaptivity* and offers a monitoring platform both for cloud providers and users. Nevertheless, they require a significant effort in terms of setting up the monitoring infrastructure and resources for maintaining it, thus violating requirements *non-invasiveness* and *lightness*. Framework in [12] has also proven to suffer of *extensibility* and *scalability* issues [24]. [21] described a monitoring framework called *DARGOS*, built with scalability and flexibility in mind. Being fully distributed, it supports *scalability* and can be enriched with more sensors. However, being specifically tailored for the cloud, it cannot be easily adapted to other scenarios. Ciuffoletti [11] presented a novel approach, where a simple, cloud-independent API-based solution has been used to configure monitoring activities. Being based on APIs, it easily satisfies requirements *com-*

Table 2. Comparison of state-of-the-art frameworks with the one in this paper [4].

References	Transparency	Non Invasiveness	Safety	Continuity	Lightness	Adaptivity	Complementarity
[2]	✓	~	~	✓	✗	✓	~
[8]	✓	✗	~	~	~	~	~
[10]	~	✗	~	✗	✗	✗	~
[11]	✓	~	✓	✓	✓	~	✓
[12]	~	~	✓	✓	✗	~	~
[26]	~	~	✓	~	~	~	✗
[14]	~	✓	~	✓	✗	~	✓
[17]	✗	✗	~	✓	✗	✓	✗
[20]	✗	✗	✗	✓	✗	✗	✗
[21]	✓	~	✗	~	~	✗	✓
[28]	✗	✗	✗	✗	✓	✓	✗
[4]	✓	✓	~	✓	~	✓	✗
This paper	✓	✓	~	✓	~	✓	✓

(a) Process requirements

Reference	Evidence-based verification	Extensibility	Multi-layer	Scalability	Automation
[2]	~	✗	✓	~	~
[8]	~	✗	~	~	~
[10]	✓	✗	~	✗	✗
[11]	~	✗	~	✓	✓
[12]	~	~	~	~	~
[26]	~	✗	✗	~	✗
[14]	~	✗	~	✓	✓
[17]	✗	✗	✗	✗	✓
[20]	✗	~	~	~	~
[21]	~	✗	✓	✓	✓
[28]	✗	~	~	✗	✗
[4]	✓	~	✓	~	~
This paper	✓	~	✓	✓	✓

(b) Framework requirements

plementarity and *automation*. Its cloud-agnosticism is realized through an OCCI (*Open Cloud Computing Interface*) extension, designed towards *Monitoring-as-a-Service*.

Test-Based Frameworks. Wu and Marotta [28] presented a work-in-progress testing-based framework that instruments client binaries to perform cloud testing. The main issue is that binaries instrumentation may not be always feasible, and might also introduce undesired behavior in modified programs. As such, the framework fails to satisfy requirements *transparency*, *non-invasiveness*, and *safety*. Ouedraogo et al. [20] presented a framework that uses agents to perform security assurance, although agents themselves need to be properly secured. Greenberg et al. [15] claimed that, to protect hosts from agent misuse or attacks, several techniques need to be properly employed. Agents also pose a maintenance problem: they have to be kept updated and things can only become worse as the number of agents increases. Also, they introduce substantial costs since they need to be physically installed on each host/device to be assessed and coordinated, introducing not-negligible network traffic. For these reasons, the agent-based framework in [20] does not satisfy requirements *transparency*, *non-invasiveness* and *safety*. Jahan et al. [17] discussed *MAPE-SAC*, a conceptual approach for security assurance of self-adaptive systems, where the system itself changes, and security requirements must adapt to these changes. While it is not possible to completely evaluate our requirements due to the lack of a real, implemented framework, *MAPE-SAC* fulfills requirements *adaptivity*, *continuity* and *automation*. A different solution has been given in our work in [4], which has served as the basis for the framework described in Sect. 3. As already discussed, the proposed approach is based on *probes* and *meta-probes*, and fails to address mainly requirements *complementarity* and, partially, *automation*. Also, it addresses only partially requirements *safety, lightness, extensibility* and *scalability*.

Domain-Specific Frameworks. Aslam et al. [8] focused on the assurance of fog computing, discussing a framework based on TPM (Trusted Platform Module) for node audit. By relying on TPMs, it does not satisfy requirement *non-invasiveness*. De la Vara et al. [26] presented an assurance framework targeting cyber-physical systems. Their approach provides several tools supporting the certification process. However, being tailored for model-driven engineering, it requires significant effort and fails to address many of our framework requirements, such as *multi-layer* and *automation*. Elsayed and Zulkernine [14] described a distributed framework for monitoring cloud analytics applications, based on analyzing logs produced by such applications. The proposed approach requires very few configurations at the cloud side, and can be offered through the *Security-as-a-Service* paradigm. Cheah et al. [10] considered the automotive world, where cases are generated after evaluating the severity of threats. Threats are found through threat modeling and confirmed with a penetration testing. The usage of penetration testing violates requirement *non-invasiveness* and, requiring human intervention, requirement *automation*. Often, being tailored for a specific domain, solutions in this category cannot claim requirement *extensibility*.

To conclude, the comparison in Table 2 shows that the existing frameworks (and corresponding processes) do not even come close to addressing the requirements in Sect. 2. In general, existing solutions mainly target *continuous evaluation* and *multi-layer* infrastructures, as well as *transparency* and *adaptivity*, failing to achieve *non-invasiveness, safety, lightness*, and *extensibility*. The framework in this paper, instead, provides a first boost in this direction addressing, at least partially, all requirements in Table 2. Following the comparison therein, this paper leaves space for future work. We will first aim to extend our framework towards Big Data and IoT environments, further improving *extensibility, lightness*, and *scalability*. We will also focus on strengthening the *safety* of the framework and its components, for example the *Execution Manager* that can easily become a single point of failure/attack.

8   Conclusions

Security assurance solutions verify whether a distributed system holds some security properties and behaves as expected, usually complementing traditional security approaches. Existing assurance frameworks and processes however are limited in impact by the fact that they often lack extensibility and interfere with the functioning of the system under verification. In this paper, we extended the VPN-based assurance framework in [4] to provide an assurance process for hybrid systems, from private networks to public clouds, that addresses properties *automation* and *complementarity*. The proposed assurance process has limited impact and costs on the target system, while providing a safe and scalable approach that integrates with existing security solutions and support automatic configuration of assurance activities.

References

1. Aceto, G., Botta, A., de Donato, W., Pescapè, A.: Cloud monitoring: a survey. Comput. Netw. **57**(9), 2093–2115 (2013). https://doi.org/10.1016/j.comnet.2013.04.001
2. Alcaraz Calero, J.M., Aguado, J.G.: MonPaaS: an adaptive monitoring platform as a service for cloud computing infrastructures and services. IEEE TSC **8**(1), 65–78 (2015). https://doi.org/10.1109/TSC.2014.2302810
3. Alshalan, A., Pisharody, S., Huang, D.: A survey of mobile VPN technologies. IEEE COMST **18**(2), 1177–1196 (2016). https://doi.org/10.1109/COMST.2015.2496624
4. Anisetti, M., Ardagna, C.A., Bena, N., Damiani, E.: Stay thrifty, stay secure: a VPN-based assurance framework for hybrid systems. In: Proceedings of SECRYPT 2020, Paris, France (Virtual), July 2020
5. Anisetti, M., Ardagna, C.A., Damiani, E., Gaudenzi, F.: A certification framework for cloud-based services. In: Proceedings of ACM SAC 2016, Pisa, Italy, April 2016
6. Anisetti, M., Ardagna, C.A., Damiani, E., Gaudenzi, F.: A semi-automatic and trustworthy scheme for continuous cloud service certification. IEEE TSC **13**, 30–43 (2017)
7. Ardagna, C., Asal, R., Damiani, E., Vu, Q.: From security to assurance in the cloud: a survey. ACM CSUR **48**(1), 2:1-2:50 (2015)
8. Aslam, M., Mohsin, B., Nasir, A., Raza, S.: FoNAC - an automated fog node audit and certification scheme. Comput. Secur. **93**, 101759 (2020)
9. Baldini, G., Skarmeta, A., Fourneret, E., Neisse, R., Legeard, B., Le Gall, F.: Security certification and labelling in Internet of Things. In: Proceedings of IEEE WF-IoT 2016, Reston, VA, USA, December 2016
10. Cheah, M., Shaikh, S.A., Bryans, J., Wooderson, P.: Building an automotive security assurance case using systematic security evaluations. COSE **77**, 360–379 (2018)
11. Ciuffoletti, A.: Application level interface for a cloud monitoring service. CS&I **46**, 15–22 (2016)
12. De Chaves, S.A., Uriarte, R.B., Westphall, C.B.: Toward an architecture for monitoring private clouds. IEEE Commun. Mag. **49**(12), 130–137 (2011). https://doi.org/10.1109/MCOM.2011.6094017
13. Ed-douibi, H., Cánovas Izquierdo, J.L., Cabot, J.: OpenAPItoUML: a tool to generate UML models from OpenAPI definitions. In: Mikkonen, T., Klamma, R., Hernández, J. (eds.) ICWE 2018. LNCS, vol. 10845, pp. 487–491. Springer, Cham (2018). https://doi.org/10.1007/978-3-319-91662-0_41
14. Elsayed, M., Zulkernine, M.: Towards security monitoring for cloud analytic applications. In: Proceedings of IEEE BigDataSecurity/HPSC/IDS 2018, Omaha, NE, USA, May 2018. https://doi.org/10.1109/BDS/HPSC/IDS18.2018.00028
15. Greenberg, M.S., Byington, J.C., Harper, D.G.: Mobile agents and security. IEEE Commun. Mag. **36**(7), 76–85 (1998). https://doi.org/10.1109/35.689634
16. Herrmann, D.: Using the Common Criteria for IT Security Evaluation. Auerbach Publications, Boca Raton (2002)
17. Jahan, S., Pasco, M., Gamble, R., McKinley, P., Cheng, B.: MAPE-SAC: a framework to dynamically manage security assurance cases. In: Proceedings of IEEE FAS*W 2019, Umea, Sweden, June 2019. https://doi.org/10.1109/FAS-W.2019.00045

18. Karlsson, S., Čaušević, A., Sundmark, D.: QuickREST: property-based test generation of OpenAPI-described RESTful APIs. In: Proceedings of IEEE ICST 2020, Porto, Portugal, March 2020
19. OpenAPI Initiative: OpenAPI Specification (2018). http://spec.openapis.org/oas/v3.0.2
20. Ouedraogo, M., Mouratidis, H., Khadraoui, D., Dubois, E.: An agent-based system to support assurance of security requirements. In: Proceedings of SSIRI 2010, Singapore, June 2010. https://doi.org/10.1109/SSIRI.2010.32
21. Povedano-Molina, J., Lopez-Vega, J.M., Lopez-Soler, J.M., Corradi, A., Foschini, L.: DAR-GOS: a highly adaptable and scalable monitoring architecture for multi-tenant Clouds. FGCS 29(8), 2041–2056 (2013). https://doi.org/10.1016/j.future.2013.04.022
22. Saltzer, J.H., Schroeder, M.D.: The protection of information in computer systems. Proc. IEEE 63(9), 1278–1308 (1975). https://doi.org/10.1109/PROC.1975.9939
23. Sferruzza, D.: Top-down model-driven engineering of web services from extended OpenAPI models. In: Proceedings of IEEE/ACM ASE 2018, Montpellier, France, September 2018
24. Taherizadeh, S., Jones, A.C., Taylor, I., Zhao, Z., Stankovski, V.: Monitoring self-adaptive applications within edge computing frameworks: a state-of-the-art review. JSS 136, 19–38 (2018). https://doi.org/10.1016/j.jss.2017.10.033
25. Teigeler, H., Lins, S., Sunyaev, A.: Chicken and egg problem: what drives cloud service providers and certification authorities to adopt continuous service certification? In: Proceedings of WISP 2017, Seoul, South Korea, December 2017
26. de la Vara, J.L., et al.: The AMASS approach for assurance and certification of critical systems. In: Proceedings of Embedded World 2019, Norimberg, Germany, February 2019
27. West, R.: The psychology of security. Commun. ACM 51(4), 34–40 (2008). https://doi.org/10.1145/1330311.1330320
28. Wu, C., Marotta, S.: Framework for assessing cloud trustworthiness. In: Proceedings of IEEE CLOUD 2013, Santa Clara, CA, USA, June–July 2013 (2013). https://doi.org/10.1109/CLOUD.2013.76

PakeMail: Authentication and Key Management in Decentralized Secure Email and Messaging via PAKE

Itzel Vazquez Sandoval[1]([✉]), Arash Atashpendar[1,2], Gabriele Lenzini[1], and Peter Y. A. Ryan[1]

[1] SnT, University of Luxembourg, Esch-sur-Alzette, Luxembourg
{itzel.vazquezsandoval,gabriele.lenzini,peter.ryan}@uni.lu
[2] itrust consulting s.á r.l., Niederanven, Luxembourg
atashpendar@itrust.lu

Abstract. We propose the use of password-authenticated key exchange (PAKE) for achieving and enhancing entity authentication (EA) and key management (KM) in the context of decentralized end-to-end encrypted email and secure messaging, i.e., without a public key infrastructure or a trusted third party. This not only simplifies the EA process by requiring users to share only a low-entropy secret such as a memorable word, but it also allows us to establish a high-entropy secret key. This approach enables a series of cryptographic enhancements and security properties, which are hard to achieve using out-of-band (OOB) authentication. We first study a few vulnerabilities in voice-based OOB authentication, in particular a combinatorial attack against lazy users, which we analyze in the context of a secure email solution. We then propose tackling public key authentication by solving the problem of *secure equality test* using PAKE and discuss various protocols and their properties. This method enables the automation of important KM tasks such as key renewal and future key pair authentications, reduces the impact of human errors and lends itself to the asynchronous nature of email and modern messaging. It also provides cryptographic enhancements including multi-device synchronization, and secure secret storage/retrieval, and paves the path for forward secrecy, deniability and post-quantum security. We also discuss the use of auditable PAKEs for mitigating a class of online guess and abort attacks in authentication protocols. We present an implementation of our proposal, called PakeMail, to demonstrate the feasibility of the core idea and discuss some of its cryptographic details, implemented features and efficiency aspects. We conclude with some design and security considerations, followed by future lines of work.

Keywords: Password-authenticated key exchange · Public key authentication · Key management · Secure email · Secure messaging · Implementation · Decentralized trust model

1 Introduction

Largely owing to cryptography, modern messaging tools (e.g., Signal) have reached a considerable degree of sophistication, balancing advanced security features, ranging from end-to-end encryption to forward secrecy and deniability, with high usability.

© Springer Nature Switzerland AG 2021
M. S. Obaidat and J. Ben-Othman (Eds.): ICETE 2020, CCIS 1484, pp. 102–128, 2021.
https://doi.org/10.1007/978-3-030-90428-9_5

However, this has not been the case for email, even though it has a long history and remains the most pervasive and interoperable form of digital communication, with billions of emails exchanged on a daily basis [15]. Yet, secure messaging and email share two long-standing challenges, namely entity authentication and key management.

The primary concern is entity authentication, which invariably involves a mechanism that associates some cryptographic material with an identity, e.g., public key authentication. Key management, affecting email more acutely, is intertwined with authentication and the need for automating it has been known for a long time, e.g., see [39].

Over the years, several methods have been established for accomplishing key authentication, and indirectly key management: manual validation of key fingerprints, web of trust, public key infrastructure (PKI) and hierarchical validation, public key directories as well as server-derived public keys such as identity-based encryption (IBE).

The set of viable techniques becomes much smaller once we consider a decentralized setting, i.e., without a PKI or a trusted third party (TTP). In this context, approaches based on the use of out-of-band (OOB) channels and short authentication string (SAS) comparisons (see Sect. 1.3) have received a great deal of attention from the research community. Due to the required user interaction in these approaches—e.g., manually verifying public key fingerprints—usability plays a key role in achieving authentication. Therefore, reducing the gap between security and usability by finding optimal trade-offs has been a central theme of research for decades, with a plethora of long-standing open problems [15,46].

In an attempt to improve usability in the entity authentication process, Alexander and Goldberg [3] proposed a modified solution to the socialist millionaires' problem (SMP) by Boudot et al. [14], also known as secure equality test, for authentication in the off-the-record messaging (OTR) protocol [13]. To the best of our knowledge, this is the only work that proposes an approach for key validation, mainly suitable for online (synchronous) settings, that relies on users pre-sharing a low-entropy secret.

Here we revisit the problem of public key authentication in a decentralized setting to propose a user-friendly and robust approach based on password-authenticated key exchange (PAKE) for solving SMP via low-entropy secrets. These secrets are not expected to be sampled from a large, uniformly distributed space, but rather from a small set of values, e.g., typical human-memorable passwords or pin numbers. The task of SMP boils down to two parties verifying equality of their inputs $\pi_{\mathcal{A}}$ and $\pi_{\mathcal{B}}$ in a zero-knowledge manner such that by the end they learn nothing but the boolean result of the test.

Apart from offering improved usability properties and eliminating a host of vulnerabilities present in OOB-based protocols, as discussed in Sect. 3, we show how the PAKE-generated secret key can be used to pave the path towards providing a series of cryptographic enhancements in secure email and messaging. These include automation in key management and key renewal, forward secrecy in a symmetric-key setting, deniability, post-quantum security, secure secret retrieval and storage, and auditability for mitigating a certain class of online guess and abort attacks in authentication protocols.

To demonstrate the feasibility of the proposed approach, we provide a complete implementation of the core ideas. This also shows how the suggested approach would not only work naturally in the context of secure messaging, but also in the inherently asynchronous setting of email.

By applying PAKE to this problem, we advance the state-of-the-art in the use of shared low-entropy secrets for entity authentication, an idea considered only in [3]. Moreover, while SMP is a subproblem solved naturally by PAKE, the latter has not been applied to tackle the problem of authenticating public keys in decentralized settings.

1.1 Motivation

Despite its crucial importance, secure email and messaging solutions tend to brush aside the entity authentication step and as such, this feature often tends to go unnoticed,[1] which contributes to users neglecting the process. Solutions that do consider the entity authentication problem in decentralized non-PKI environments, typically rely on users correctly executing a manual comparison, which has been repeatedly shown to be error-prone and inconvenient for users (e.g. [26]). Our incentive for replacing OOB authentication with a cryptographic protocol lies in the significant impact of failures occurring in methods highly-dependent on user behavior, which could completely jeopardize security.

Our motivation for using PAKE—a method that does not seem to have enjoyed enough recognition due to a lack of mature implementations, reluctance towards client side cryptography, patent-encumbered designs and perhaps even unawareness of its usefulness—is grounded not only in its independence from a PKI or a TTP, but also in its provision of a zero-knowledge (ZK) solution for the secure equality test problem using a low number of rounds, which makes it compatible with asynchronous settings, and in the fact that it enables additional cryptographic enhancements.

Additionally, the need for addressing common challenges such as key management automation and device synchronization spurred us on. By implementing our PAKE-based solution for entity authentication, we address two open problems in secure email and messaging [15,46]: bridging the gap between known theoretical results and real-world solutions, and the need for more robust authentication methods that also improve the trade-off between security and usability in secure solutions.

1.2 Contributions and Structure

A brief review of the state-of-the-art is covered in Sect. 1.3, followed by an overview of background concepts in Sect. 2. In Sect. 3, we discuss a few vulnerabilities in the use of OOB channels for authentication, including a partial preimage attack targeting lazy users, which we analyze in the context of the p ≡ p [34] secure email solution.

Next, in Sect. 4 we describe how solving the *secure equality test* using PAKE leads not only to entity authentication but also to the establishment of a shared high-entropy secret key that can be used to achieve additional cryptographic tasks and properties. We provide a concrete illustrative scheme along with an analysis of various PAKE constructions and properties relevant for our work, and briefly analyze network transport mechanisms and security.

---

[1] For example, in order to access the authentication menu in Signal or WhatsApp, users need to (1) select a chat (2) click on the contact's name (3) select "View safety number/Encryption".

In Sect. 5, we elaborate on the said cryptographic enhancements, such as inattentive user resistance, automated key renewal, automated future key pair authentication and multi-device synchronization, along with security properties such as deniability, forward secrecy, post-quantum security, auditability for detecting guess and abort attacks, and secure secret storage and retrieval with applications in email and secure messaging.

Extended Version. The main contributions of this work, which is an extended version of our previous paper [48], are as follows:

- PAKE-based Public Key Authentication and Key Exchange over Email (PakeMail): in Sect. 6, we present a complete implementation of the main idea for a PAKE-based authentication and key management approach in the context of decentralized secure email, serving as a proof of feasibility. The source code, along with the corresponding documentation, can be found at [4].
- In Sects. 2 and 4 we provide more theoretical details on PAKE protocols and cryptographic elements relevant for a concrete implementation.
- We provide an analysis in Sect. 5.4, comparing our proposal with state-of-the-art trust establishment approaches.
- We extend and improve our descriptions of the cryptographic enhancements in Sect. 5, including the notion of secure secret storage and retrieval, a variant of which has been recently implemented for the Signal messaging system, but using a combination of different cryptographic constructions.

In Sect. 7 we review the main security properties of our solution and elaborate on a few methods for low-entropy secret agreement and improving usability. We conclude in Sect. 8 with a more detailed outline of future directions and open questions.

1.3 Related Work

Unger et al. [46] and Clark et al. [15] provide extensive systematic surveys covering numerous aspects of secure messaging and email. We limit ourselves to the decentralized setting without elaborating on the drawbacks of web of trust approaches covered in the above mentioned works.

The literature contains a sizeable body of work on OOB-based approaches, considered first by Rivest [36], many of which are inspired by the original work of Vaudenay [47] based on SAS comparisons, e.g., [26,27,32,45], to name a few. This area has also been investigated by the formal methods community, see e.g. [18] for a recent formal analysis of SAS-based schemes in the symbolic model.

As for low-entropy secret-based authentication, to the best of our knowledge, the only work in the literature is by Alexander and Goldberg [3] using a modified version of the SMP protocol by Boudot et al. [14] for improving the OOB-based authentication process in off-the-record messaging (OTR) [13]. OTR is a cryptographic protocol originally designed by Borisov and Goldberg, aimed at enabling encrypted, authenticated and deniable instant messaging conversations with forward secrecy; this protocol was proposed as an alternative to PGP for "casual" conversations.

The variant proposed by Alexander and Goldberg sacrifices the fairness property of [14] for efficiency and the authentication process requires $\mathcal{A}$ and $\mathcal{B}$ to be both online when entering their secret and for the subsequent exchange of messages.

2 Framework and Preliminaries

We use $\mathcal{A}$ and $\mathcal{B}$ to refer to honest parties Alice and Bob, and $\mathcal{M}$ for the adversary, Mallory. We use $\leftarrow\!\!$$ to denote an element sampled uniformly at random, and $\|$ to denote concatenation. We denote low-entropy secrets provided by users with π.

Security Model. We consider the standard Dolev-Yao model [21]. We do not assume any additional trusted infrastructure. In one of our proposed methods for transport protocol, we assume the existence of untrusted buffer/relay servers, somewhat akin to the ones used in the design of Signal or OTR4 (see Sect. 4.4). Regarding PAKEs, we will consider several constructions in Sect. 4, largely proven secure in the so-called BPR model [8] under various hardness assumptions.

System Requirements. Our proposal does not require any format modifications and preserves compatibility between existing email clients and servers; therefore, we assume standard requirements for email transfer. As for secure messaging, we do not introduce any extra trust assumptions and no additional infrastructure requirements. Any exchanges relayed or buffered by intermediate servers can be done by untrusted ones.

Cryptographic Notions. Due to space limitations, we assume familiarity with common cryptographic concepts, in particular with Diffie-Hellman (DH)-based computational hardness assumptions.

We discuss schemes based on the Ring Learning With Errors (RLWE) problem, a special case of the Learning With Errors (LWE) problem whose security may be reducible to the hardness of solving the Shortest Vector Problem (SVP) in lattices, for which no efficient quantum algorithms are known, thus conjectured to be quantum-secure. Post-quantum (PQ) cryptography encompasses schemes that are considered to be safe against adversaries equipped with scalable, cryptographically relevant quantum computers.

We use $KDF(s)$ to denote a key derivation function that takes a source s of keying material, typically with a fair amount of entropy but not uniformly distributed, and produces one or more cryptographically strong secret keys, see [29] for details. We denote with $MAC(k, m)$ a keyed message authentication code scheme that computes a tag on m under key k. We use "Curve25519" to refer to the underlying elliptic curve used in the elliptic-curve-Diffie-Hellman function by Bernstein [10].

Socialist Millionaires' Problem. In the realm of secure multi-party computation (MPC), Yao's millionaires' problem [50] is a famous example in which two parties want to find out whose input is greater without revealing any more information on the actual value. SMP is a variant of this and a ZK proof of knowledge protocol, with the difference that the parties only wish to know if their inputs are equal.

A series of works has been dedicated to solving SMP, including a well-known solution by Boudot et al. [14] that provides a fair and efficient protocol, where fairness roughly means that no party can evaluate the function and walk away with the result without the other party learning the output.

Garay et al. [23] showed that the fairness and the security definition of [14] are not compatible with the simulation paradigm and that their solution would not be secure when composed concurrently; they present a construction that can be composed arbitrarily, with similar complexity results.

PAKE. Password-authenticated key exchange (PAKE) protocols enable the establishment of secure channels without the need for a PKI, TTP or empirical OOB channels. In essence, they address a secure two-party computation problem and allow two parties $\mathcal{A}$ and $\mathcal{B}$ who share only a low-entropy secret/password $\pi \in \mathcal{D}$, with $\mathcal{D}$ being some relatively small dictionary, to agree on a high-entropy cryptographic secret key k, using π for authentication. Since the seminal work of Bellovin and Merritt [9], numerous PAKE protocols have been proposed, which largely fall into the two categories of balanced (symmetric) and augmented (or asymmetric), referred to as aPAKE. The latter stores one-way mappings of passwords on the server side in client-server settings.

Intuitively, a core property of PAKE is that a run of the protocol should not leak any information about the password. Moreover, apart from protection against man-in-the-middle (MITM) attacks and variants thereof such as replay/reuse and mixing attacks, they should also provide security against offline dictionary attacks by passive and active adversaries. While due to the use of low-entropy passwords, any PAKE protocol is vulnerable to an online guessing attack, the goal is to ensure that at most one test per run constitutes the optimal attack strategy for an active $\mathcal{M}$ interacting with a party. Similar to SMP, $\mathcal{M}$ can mask failed guessing attempts as network failures, thus allowing numerous attempts without raising suspicion. This is in general unavoidable, however, we will see in Sect. 4 how a recent work by Roscoe and Ryan [38] can mitigate this.

Most well-known PAKE protocols rely on different variants of the Diffie-Hellman Problem (DHP), which means that their security is ultimately reduced to that of the Discrete Logarithm Problem (DLP). These typically make use of a cyclic group $\mathbb{G}$ of prime order p, generated by $g \in \mathbb{G}$, along with a hash function H, modelled as a random oracle, plus a few other public parameters, e.g., $M, N \in \mathbb{G}$ in the case of SPAKE2, as shown in Fig. 1. Moreover, the passwords are viewed as elements of $\mathbb{Z}_p$ (obtained by hashing user passwords to some $\pi \in \mathbb{Z}_p$), which are used to blind the DH terms by multiplying these terms by randomly chosen elements of $\mathbb{G}$ raised to π, e.g., $g^x \cdot M^\pi$, where $x \leftarrow_{\$} \mathbb{Z}_p$. The final session key is then derived by computing a hash of the entire transcript T_P of a run of protocol P, which includes all of the parties' public and private values, the user identities, the DH terms and the password, i.e., $k = H(\pi, id_{\mathcal{A}}, id_{\mathcal{B}}, T_P)$.

Often, how passwords are agreed upon and the actual details pertaining to the exchange of user identities are left out, i.e., deferred to higher-level applications implementing the protocol. It is typically required for a higher-level application to be able to refer to a session using a globally unique identifier, a channel binding often also called a session ID, which for technical reasons rooted in composability should be computed as a function of user instance roles and information exchanged over the network during the execution of the protocol, e.g., user IDs and public randomness. The session identification (ID) is usually defined as the transcript T_P of the communication/conversation between $\mathcal{A}$ and $\mathcal{B}$, which can also be viewed as a random variable, being a function of the random values generated by $\mathcal{A}$ and $\mathcal{B}$. These, among other things, protect against MITM, unknown key share attacks and replay attacks.

3   Pitfalls in Out-of-Band Authentication

In OOB authentication, users typically compare some representation of a cryptographic hash (fingerprint) of their partners' public keys via a separate authenticated channel. This representation is usually in the form of a list of words, numbers or images.

Strong security properties can be achieved if users execute the manual verification correctly. Yet, the difficulty of having users do the corresponding tasks correctly while finding the right balance between usability and security is the root cause of security drawbacks, which have been amply discussed by research on fingerprint and SAS comparison via OOB channels (e.g., [26,27,45]). Naturally, usability studies encourage the replacement of manual comparisons by automated software whenever possible [45]. Some of the problems rooted in OOB authentication are as follows.

Selection of an Adequate OOB Channel. In practice, the theoretical and strong authentication requirements of OOB methods are not easy to satisfy. While face-to-face conversations provide a strong authenticated channel [32], they are often not viable. It is usually assumed that an OOB channel cannot be forged, but it can be blocked, overheard, delayed or replayed. Typical instantiations are done via voice-based channels, e.g., a phone call. However, some already consider voice-based SAS comparison to be obsolete from a security perspective [46] as nowadays messages can be forged by voice synthesizers with a small sample of the victim's voice. Indeed, a voice impersonation attack on users comparing PGP words [41] reported the fake voice to be indistinguishable in about 50% of the cases.

Social Engineering Attacks. Although there are multiple options for users to interact via OOB, little effort has been gone into designing precise protocols for humans to carry out the authentication process in a privacy-preserving and fair manner. This leads to various attack vectors based on misleading users as opposed to finding technical vulnerabilities. For instance, without knowing the authentication value, M can fool A into trusting her key by pretending to be B, asking A to read her fingerprint representation first, and then simply confirming that the fingerprints match.

3.1   Inattentive Users and Partial Preimage Attacks

Inattentive and Lazy Users. Here we consider users misreading words (inattentive) or comparing only subsets of them (lazy). A recent paper by Naor et al. [31] analyzes approaches based on SAS authentication that are vulnerable to MITM attacks w.r.t. lazy users. For instance, the approach in WhatsApp and Signal would be flawed if users compared only either the first or the second half of the value, since it would amount to verifying only one peer's fingerprint. To fix this, the authors propose an influence spreading technique in which every bit of the value to be authenticated influences the generation of each element of the OOB representation.

Partial Preimage Attack. Dechand et al. [17] study an attack aimed at finding a partial preimage for a fingerprint verified by lazy users; specifically, they assume that users check subsets of bits at the boundaries and in the middle.

We now give a more detailed description of their analysis. Let p denote the probability of finding a partial preimage for a given fingerprint f and q its complementary event. To calculate $p = 1 - q$, we work out q (i.e., the absence of partial preimages for a specific bit permutation). Let b be the length of the fingerprint f and assuming that r consecutive boundary bits are fixed (checked by the user), in this case, the leftmost and rightmost bits of f, we let ℓ denote the number of remaining bits in the middle from which a possible variation of u bits could be fixed, i.e., checked by the user.

Thus, we have $2 \cdot r + u$ fixed bits that the adversary cannot invert without the user noticing. Valid preimages can thus be obtained by flipping up to $t = \ell - u$ bits within the middle bits; by removing these from the total space of size 2^b, we obtain the number of invalid ones. With k denoting a given number of positions to modify, the valid strings are then given by $\binom{\ell}{k}$ choices of positions to flip. Thus, q is given by

$$q = \frac{2^b - \sum_{k=1}^{t} \binom{\ell}{k}}{2^b}. \tag{1}$$

Expressing p as a function of the computational effort in terms of e brute-force attempts, we have $p = 1 - q^e$. To estimate the number of steps needed for finding partial preimages with a success probability $\geq p$, we simply compute $e = \log_q(1 - p)$. Expressing e in base 2 gives results comparable to [17].

3.2   Case Study

Pretty Easy Privacy ($p \equiv p$) is a software aimed at providing usable privacy-by-default in email via end-to-end opportunistic encryption. The tool largely automates key management tasks. The public key of a user is attached to outgoing emails when a key of the recipient has not been stored. Received keys are automatically stored for future use (*trust-on-first-use*) and outgoing emails are automatically encrypted when a public key of the intended receiver is available. This approach requires neither a PKI nor a TTP.

Similar to the PGP word list, $p \equiv p$ *trustwords* [12] are natural language words that two users compare via a low-bandwidth OOB authenticated channel to prevent MITM attacks. The trustwords generation algorithm $\mathrm{tws}(\cdot)$ is a deterministic algorithm that runs locally taking as input the public key of the peer obtained by email and the user's own public key. Informally, $\mathrm{tws}(\cdot)$ performs an XOR over the fingerprints of each of the input arguments, and then maps each block of 16 bits from the resulting 160-bit long string to a word in a predefined dictionary of size 2^{16}, thus yielding a list of ten words.

To encourage users to perform the OOB authentication, by default $p \equiv p$ shows only five words; this means that the peers compare the first 80 out of the 160 bits of a PGP fingerprint, assuming that they check all the words. Since an "influence spreading" property, similar to Naor et al.'s, is already present, the best adversarial strategy is a brute-force attack over the public key space requiring $O(2^{80})$ steps to find a key k such that the first 80 bits of $\mathrm{fpr}(k)$ are equal to those of $\mathrm{fpr}(pk_B)$, with pk_B being the public key of $\mathcal{B}$.

We consider lazy users and compute estimates for partial preimage attacks similar to the one presented above. We consider the two cases where, out of five words, the user verifies (*i*) the first and last words as well as two from the middle (*ii*) the first and last words, along with one of the three in the middle. Let $b = 80$, $\ell = 48$ and for (*i*) we have $u = 32$ and we get $e \approx 2^{38}$; for (*ii*), with $u = 16$, we get $e \approx 2^{32}$. These results show that $\mathcal{M}$ would succeed with costs equal to and lower than the computational power estimated for an average adversary [17].

Clearly the decision to show five words instead of ten by default needs to be reconsidered. Users might feel less annoyed by having to compare fewer words, however, its adverse effect on security is considerable as it practically renders brute-force attacks viable.

4   Authentication in Secure Email and Messaging via PAKE

We now show how PAKE can be used to perform a secure equality test and thereby authentication, yielding a more efficient solution, compared to OOB methods and the OTR approach, with better security guarantees and further cryptographic features.

Trust Establishment using Low-entropy Secrets. For now, we assume that $\mathcal{A}$ and $\mathcal{B}$ share a low-entropy secret—e.g., a short password—either agreed upon beforehand or decided by posing and answering a question at the beginning of the mutual authentication.

Intuitively, the goal is for $\mathcal{A}$ and $\mathcal{B}$ to authenticate their public keys via a secure equality test of their respective secrets π_A and π_B, without revealing any information about the latter; hence the need for a zero-knowledge protocol guaranteeing that upon termination of the protocol, the resulting transcript of the exchanges does not leak any information on π_A and π_B, allowing $\mathcal{A}$ and $\mathcal{B}$ to learn only whether or not their respective secrets were equal. In addition, it should not be possible for $\mathcal{M}$ to brute-force the password via offline dictionary attacks. Thus, $\mathcal{M}$'s only strategy would amount to making online attempts.

4.1   Public Key Authentication via PAKE

To determine at the end of a PAKE run whether the user secrets π_A and π_B are equal, without revealing anything else, we enforce explicit authentication using a key confirmation (KC) step after the key establishment phase. While this step may be optional in the general case for PAKE protocols, here it would be necessary in order to bind the cryptographic material with an identity. The information that $\mathcal{A}$ and $\mathcal{B}$ wish to authenticate—e.g., public key fingerprints for email addresses or phone numbers in Signal—can be incorporated either into the KC phase or into the initial user secrets.

Next, we delve into the details of how this can be achieved using a concrete PAKE protocol. The literature contains several well-studied instances of PAKE, therefore, we first pick a candidate to demonstrate how it can be used to validate public keys, and then compare a few prominent schemes according to specific properties of interest. For the moment, we do not focus on engineering aspects related to (a)synchronicity and message transport mechanisms, but we will come back to these in Sects. 4.4 and 6.

4.2   An Instantiation Based on SPAKE2

For illustration, in Fig. 1 we propose an extension of SPAKE2, a one-round protocol, with a KC step to achieve explicit authentication, thus binding a public key to an entity. This yields a 2-round scheme, the minimum when KC is enforced; see [28] for optimal-round PAKEs. For KC we can use the generic refresh-then-MAC transformation. Despite its long history, this transform was only recently proved secure [22].

With $\mathbb{G}$ being a finite cyclic group of prime order p, generated by an element $g \in \mathbb{G}$, let $\mathbb{G}, g, p, M \leftarrow_\$ \mathbb{G}, N \leftarrow_\$ \mathbb{G}$ and hash function $H(\cdot)$ denote public parameters and $\pi \in \mathbb{Z}_p$ the private low-entropy secret, with the user password assumed to be appropriately mapped to an element in $\mathbb{Z}_p$. The parties perform the key exchange phase, as shown in Fig. 1, which concludes with the generation of a symmetric key. Upon termination of the key establishment, $\mathcal{A}$ and $\mathcal{B}$ each use the symmetric key to carry out a key-refreshing step via a key derivation function in order to generate fresh MAC keys (for both parties), along with a new session key, K, which will be the final shared secret key. Next, under the freshly generated keys, they each compute a MAC on the fingerprints of both parties' public keys. The authentication now amounts to exchanging and verifying the obtained tags τ^a and τ^b, i.e., to see if the received tag and its locally computed counterpart match.

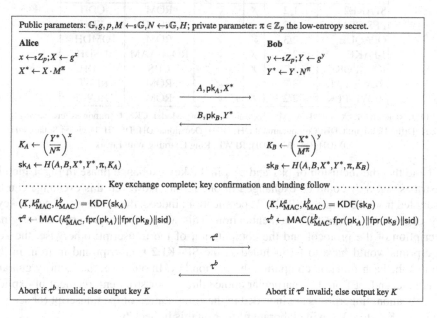

Fig. 1. pk authentication using SPAKE2 with refresh-then-MAC key confirmation for entity binding. (Originally presented as such in our previous work [48]).

The addition of the KC step increases the number of rounds and flows to 2 and 4, respectively. Note that this is merely an illustrative example and as already mentioned, other possibilities for KC do exist, some of which offer additional properties. For instance, in [7] the authors showed that a modified version of SPAKE2, called PFS-SPAKE2, coupled with a KC step can achieve perfect forward secrecy (PFS) at the cost of increasing the number of rounds from 1 to 3. More recently, Abdalla et al. [1]

showed that SPAKE2 does indeed satisfy PFS even without KC under a different hardness assumption. They also prove a version with a KC step (yielding a better bound) almost identical to the one given in Fig. 1, except that the protocol has one less flow.

Alternatively, the public key fingerprints can be embedded in the secret π, but note that even in that case, the KC step cannot be skipped as an explicit authentication of the public keys would be still needed. More precisely, we would let $\pi = \pi' \| \mathsf{fpr}(\mathsf{pk}_{\mathcal{A}}) \| \mathsf{fpr}(\mathsf{pk}_{\mathcal{B}})$, where π' denotes the original user provided secrets, and we would compute the tags as $\tau^a \leftarrow \mathsf{MAC}(k_{\mathsf{MAC}}^a, \mathsf{sid})$, where the session identifier sid is defined as the transcript of conversation between $\mathcal{A}$ and $\mathcal{B}$, with τ^b computed similarly. The IETF documents for SPAKE2[2] and J-PAKE[3] provide similar one round KC methods.

Table 1. Comparison of PAKE protocols. (Originally presented in [48].)

Protocol	Rounds/ Flows	KC	Forward secrecy	Security model	Hardness assumption
SPAKE2	1/2	✗	✓	ROM	CDH
PFS-SPAKE2	3/3	✓	✓	ROM	CDH
OPAQUE	2/3	✓	✓	ROM	OMDH
J-PAKE	2/4	✗	✓	ROM-AAM	DSDH
KV-SPOKE	1/2	✗	-	CRS	DDH
RLWE-PAK	3/3	✓	✓	ROM	RLWE
RLWE-PPK	2/2	✗	✓	ROM	RLWE

ROM: Random Oracle Model; AAM: Algebraic Adversary Model; CRS: Common Reference String
DH: Diffie-Hellman; CDH: Computational DH; DDH: Decisional DH; DSDH: Decision Square DH;
OMDH: One-More DH; RLWE: Ring Learning With Errors

Note that the inclusion of pk_A and pk_B in the key exchange phase in Fig. 1 merely illustrates that they could be exchanged in one round. However, this exchange can be decoupled from the original SPAKE2 specification; indeed, the exchange of public keys may occur long before their authentication. This allows us to preserve the original description of the protocol and the computation of the transcript; otherwise, the key fingerprints would have to be included in the SPAKE2 transcript and in turn, in the input of the hash function computing the session key. In our case, the security guarantee is independent from this particular choice due to our strict enforcement of explicit authentication: fingerprints are included in the computation of the transcript (or session ID) in the KC step. We will elaborate further on this in Sect. 6.

---

[2] https://tools.ietf.org/id/draft-irtf-cfrg-spake2-08.html.
[3] https://tools.ietf.org/html/rfc8236.

4.3 Selecting a PAKE Protocol

We consider a number of representative PAKE protocols and analyze their properties w.r.t. our use case: SPAKE2 [2], OPAQUE [25], PFS-SPAKE2 [7], J-PAKE [24], KV-SPOKE [28], RLWE-PAK and PPK [20]. PAKEs are typically evaluated according to the security model in which they are proven secure, support for forward secrecy, the number of rounds, along with their communication and computational complexity. The complexity related aspects become more relevant in a client-server setting wherein a server has to process a high number of requests and sessions in a short time span. In a decentralized peer-to-peer setting, such properties no longer play a major role.

In Table 1, we present some relevant properties of the said constructions. Except for RLWE-PAK and RLWE-PPK that make use of lattice-based cryptography, all other schemes are Diffie-Hellman-based. In terms of PQ security, this implies that the latter cases would not be quantum-safe, whereas the first two would provide conjectured quantum-security due to the underlying RLWE problem.

Minimizing the number of rounds is more important for secure email than it is for messaging, especially if the transport mechanism is based on attachments or hidden emails (see Sect. 4.4). As for secure messaging, this may be equally relevant for solutions that do not operate in a purely decentralized and peer-to-peer setting in which one may wish to reduce the load on relay or buffer servers, e.g., Signal or OTR4, but the number of rounds would in general be arguably less of a concern. Note that KC can be added to schemes that do not have it by default at the cost of an extra round.

Intuitively, the notion of forward secrecy (FS) captures the requirement that a long-term secret compromise should not result in prior session keys getting compromised and consequently the corresponding exchanges. Weak FS (wFS) refers to those schemes satisfying FS against passive adversaries who did not interfere in the previous sessions and perfect FS to those achieving the same against active adversaries. We will come back to this in Sect. 5.2.

We limit the discussion on security models to practical considerations. In the random oracle model (ROM), an ideal truly random function being accessible to the parties through oracle calls is typically instantiated using cryptographic hash functions, and the common reference string (CRS) model implies the accessibility of a random string to all parties, generated in a trusted way. The latter may be less obvious to implement in the case of email due to the constraints of decentralization given that the generation of the CRS would be typically done by a trusted party or via a secure MPC protocol, e.g., the decentralized CRS generation shown in [40]. Finally, regarding the RLWE-based schemes, their proofs are unfortunately in the ROM, as opposed to the quantum ROM (QROM), which would allow adversaries to query the random oracle in superposition.

4.4 Transport Mechanism

Email-Based Approach. Given the small number of rounds required by PAKE protocols, in the case of email we can afford to use standard email attachments or specially formatted hidden emails as message carriers, processed in the background by the email client. Since we primarily deal with authentication, these exchanges would have minimal impact in terms of communication and computational complexity as the protocol would have to take place only once per peer.

For the case of attachments, a PAKE-based implementation could give $\mathcal{A}$ the option to enter her secret $\pi_{\mathcal{A}}$ upon sending her first email to $\mathcal{B}$, thus allowing the first flow of the protocol to occur via an attachment; the initial PAKE round would be completed when $\mathcal{B}$ replies after entering his secret $\pi_{\mathcal{B}}$. The subsequent exchange for the KC step can be done automatically.

Alternatively, the implementations could encapsulate cryptographic messages in specially crafted emails, kept hidden from the user (e.g., archived separately) and processed automatically—as p ≡ p does for multi-device key synchronization.

Untrusted Server Approach. Although early instant messaging (IM) tools were entirely online services that maintained an active session for each conversation, modern IM tools follow an asynchronous model similar to that of email. For instance, both Signal and the latest version of OTR [33] achieve offline messaging by using "buffer servers" for hosting pre-key bundles that can be fetched without the other party being online.

We can use a similar mechanism to overcome transport engineering obstacles in email more elegantly, since all aspects related to the exchange of emails remain unchanged and thus interoperable. In fact, the use of an intermediate server would not introduce additional trust assumptions as the transcript of a PAKE protocol does not leak useful information to the adversary; such a server would be untrusted and any entity would be able to set up their own instance.

5   Enhancements to Secure Email and Messaging by PAKE

Our PAKE-based approach for authentication satisfies and improves a number of key properties related to security and usability that have been identified in the literature [46]. We first discuss how these properties are satisfied and then introduce novel uses of PAKE in secure email and messaging. Note that once a PAKE-generated symmetric key is established, subsequent PAKE instances can be run automatically via a chaining self-sustaining mechanism; moreover, while we primarily focus on enhancements for existing paradigms that depend on public keys—e.g. PGP-based or OTR-inspired systems such as Signal—one could also consider the benefits of transitioning to symmetric-key constructions, e.g., MAC-based authentication and symmetric-key encryption schemes.

5.1   Key Management and Authentication Improvements

The improvements presented here mainly deal with key management automation and error resilience.

Automation of Future Key Pair Authentications. Once authentication between $\mathcal{A}$ and $\mathcal{B}$ is bootstrapped from an initial PAKE, the authentication of new key pairs belonging to either $\mathcal{A}$ or $\mathcal{B}$ can be automated by using the PAKE-generated key as input, without prompting the users to yet again enter new secrets. Authentication of new keys is needed for instance when keys expire, when a new key pair needs to be associated with an existing identity, or when new email addresses need to be associated with key pairs. These can be automatically authenticated by running a PAKE with the stored shared symmetric key as input. Note that each execution of a PAKE refreshes the stored PAKE-generated symmetric keys. Automating the authentication of future keys enables the achievement of the other properties in this category.

Immediate Enrolment. This property holds if when a user reinitializes their keys, other parties can verify and use them immediately. The PAKE-generated key allows to automate the new key exchange and the corresponding authentication as explained above.

Alert-Less Key Renewal. Complementing the previous property, this one refers to users not receiving alerts or warnings prompting them to take action when other parties renew their public keys. This would be automated similarly to immediate enrolment.

Low Key Maintenance. This property refers to minimizing users efforts related to key management tasks, such as signing keys or renewing expired keys. By achieving immediate enrolment and alert-less key renewal as explained above, the PAKE-based approach improves key maintenance too.

Inattentive User Resistance. As discussed earlier, manual OOB key/fingerprint verification methods are susceptible to human error and inattentiveness. In the PAKE-based approach, even if users enter the wrong password, the result would not be as catastrophic as trusting a key prepared by the adversary. At worst, it would be inconvenient as the authentication would fail, prompting the user to eventually repeat the process.

5.2 Cryptographic Properties Enabled by PAKE

Symmetric Key Cryptography. An immediate and rather evident advantage of using a PAKE protocol in this context is that the resulting cryptographic secret key can be already used for performing cryptographic tasks, whereas in a general PKI setting, upon authenticating the public keys, one would then typically make use of a Key Encapsulation Mechanism (KEM) in order to establish a symmetric key.

Perfect Forward Secrecy (PFS). Once, more popular in the context of secure messaging (e.g., Signal and OTR), PFS is now a requirement for cipher suites supported in TLS 1.3. PFS means that in the event of a password disclosure, previously derived session keys remain secure. To minimize the impact of a long-term key disclosure, one could implement a PAKE-chaining mechanism that automatically performs key rotations and periodically refreshes the symmetric key; this would provide limited windows of opportunity for M to compromise the channel, past which point, the fresh key would be secure again. If there is evidence that M has corrupted the channel, the cryptographic key would have to be discarded and replaced by a new PAKE execution. This refreshing paradigm might be expensive, however it would be relevant when PAKE-based approaches are used for synchronization purposes, either device-to-device or device-to-server, where PAKE can be used to both authenticate and establish a secure channel, thus providing PFS for the session keys used for syncing.

Several PAKE constructions provide PFS by default, some of which are listed in Table 1; moreover, PFS can be obtained by adding explicit authentication via a KC step to constructions that do not have this property [8]. Alternatively, to improve efficiency we could resort to symmetric-key schemes that provide PFS, e.g., SAKE [5]. In this case, a PAKE can be used once to bootstrap authentication via a low-entropy secret and to generate the initial symmetric master key required by SAKE.

The use of PAKEs could for instance improve the approach based on regular sub-key rotations, adopted by the Sequoia-PGP project for adding FS to OpenPGP-based solutions; a PAKE-based solution could automate authentication in case the master key, certifying the short-term sub-keys, needs to be refreshed. For additional security, with slightly hampered usability, a separation of storage can be enforced by for example storing such PAKE long-term keys in dedicated hardware, e.g., hardware security modules or smart key storage devices such as YubiKey or Nitrokey, to protect against a device compromise; see Sect. 5.3 for more details on this.

Deniability. This is another subtle and fundamental property that has been of particular interest in recent secure messaging systems such as Signal and OTR. Deniable exchange, applied to tasks ranging from authentication to encryption, has a long and somewhat controversial history due to the subtleties in various existing security definitions. We limit ourselves to the case of key exchange and the seminal framework of Di Raimondo et al. [19], which provides security definitions in the simulation paradigm for deniable key exchange and authentication, where both message and participation repudiation are considered as requirements.

Assuming that the secret keys cannot be traced back to identities, we conjecture that sender/receiver-only deniability for symmetric PAKE would satisfy the said definition of deniability in the symmetric-key setting: in a two-party setup, a malicious accusing party $\mathcal{M}$ would not be able to produce binding cryptographic proofs from communication transcripts, associating another party with a particular exchange, as all messages could have been simulated by the accusing party $\mathcal{M}$. More specifically, in terms of distribution indistinguishability, a simulator in the said framework [19] can be constructed given that π is the only private input, symmetrically shared by both parties, and all other parameters are public and drawn at random. Indeed, this may not be surprising as Di Raimondo et al. [19] consider deniability in the symmetric key setting to be trivially satisfied.

Finally, assuming composability, using the PAKE-generated key with symmetric ciphers and MAC-based authentication would preserve deniability. Clearly, this and other forms of deniability for PAKE need to be studied rigorously in future work.

As a side note, deniability of messages and FS were among OTR's original goals, however, such features are independent from their SMP solution for authentication; they are implemented separately, e.g., by using MAC-based authentication and revealing keys. In the case of PAKE, these properties are rather built into the scheme.

Post-Quantum Security. As pointed out in Sect. 4.3, in the event that secure messaging and email tools transition to post-quantum cryptography, there are already candidate PAKE constructions that provide conjectured PQ security (e.g. see Table 1). Moreover, the recent symmetric-key authenticated key exchange (SAKE) by Avoine et al. [5] is conjectured to be PQ-secure due to its use of symmetric-key primitives. Thus, a quantum-resistant PAKE can be combined with SAKE, to obtain a low cost and efficient PQ-AKE with PFS suitable for settings with limited computational power, e.g., the IoT.

5.3   Cryptographic Enhancements to Email and Messaging

The uses of PAKEs for securing email and messaging go beyond entity authentication and KM. Here, we discuss some areas that could benefit from the use of these schemes.

Multi-device Synchronization. A quite natural application of PAKE is in the realm of device pairing and secure multi-device synchronization, where the goal is to create an authenticated and private channel between devices, usually by the same user. Most solutions typically rely on a human interactive security protocol (HISP) and OOB channels, thus requiring manual intervention, which can give rise to new and subtle attacks. The application of PAKEs for device pairing in other contexts has been considered before [30]; it is thus natural to consider its use in multi-device syncing of secure email and messaging systems, for instance, to synchronize a user's keys for encryption and keys of trusted contacts.

A secure email solution can display a screen in each of $\mathcal{A}$'s devices that are to be paired, D_1 and D_2, so that after $\mathcal{A}$ enters a password in both, a PAKE protocol is triggered. Alternatively, this process can even be done asynchronously, i.e., without the two devices being online: D_1 pushes its state (e.g., key store, chat or email archive) to a server in encrypted form and later D_2 retrieves the secrets stored on the server in an oblivious manner w.r.t. the server. We discuss this further in the following part regarding secure secret retrieval.

For instance, the current implementation of p $\equiv$ p resorts to an ad-hoc pairing technique for key synchronization based on OOB comparison of SAS. Instead, it could benefit from such a PAKE-based solution. The established channel could be used not only for sharing key material but also contact lists, calendars, etc.

Secure Secret Sharing and Retrieval. This feature is inspired by the notion of password-protected secret sharing (PPSS) schemes formalized by Bagherzandi et al. [6], which are (t, n)-threshold constructions wherein security is preserved against an adversary controlling up to t servers out of n. A problem that PPSS addresses is protecting $\mathcal{A}$'s secret data d (e.g., a secret key used for decryption, authentication credentials, crypto-currency wallet key, etc.) in the event of a device compromise or failure.

An implementation of PPSS would secret-share d among a set of n entities so that only a collusion of more than t corrupt ones would compromise the data. A password-based mechanism would allow the authentication of the owner of d to the secret-share holders in order to trigger a reconstruction protocol and then retrieve the secret. The private storage of d can be shared among n external network entities; alternatively, if $\mathcal{A}$ does not trust external entities, her device can instead partake in the secret-sharing by storing multiple shares, thus preventing online dictionary attacks by a network attacker and not allowing $\mathcal{M}$ to learn anything about the secret without corrupting $\mathcal{A}$'s device.

Secret retrieval would have several use cases in secure messaging. For instance, a general anonymity/privacy related criticism directed at messaging services has to do with the identification of users via their phone numbers. This can be dealt with by securely storing long-term identities in encrypted form on the server, accessible only to the users. Servers could also store per user lists of contacts in encrypted form; this would enable asynchronous syncing of contacts across multiple devices without the service provider learning the content.

Another use case would be to secret-share user data among several of their own devices, e.g., smartphone, laptop and tablet, so that a device compromise would not provide any useful information to an attacker; this can also be used for performing key synchronization among multiple devices. All these mechanisms would work in a similar manner from the user's point of view, i.e., simply by providing a password.

Recently, the Signal messaging system was enhanced with a functionality referred to as "Secure Value Recovery" [42], which aims at storing encrypted backups of user's data that can be recovered using a PIN. Among other things, the design involves a key stretching of the user's PIN along with a master key derivation from the stretched key and a piece of server-side stored randomness. The same core functionality can be achieved with the use of either PPSS or PAKE constructions such as OPAQUE, a recent aPAKE construction that, among other things, offers a secure secret retrieval mechanism based on oblivious pseudo-random functions, to fetch a secret stored in encrypted form on a server, using only a low-entropy password. It also offers protection against breaches and server password file compromises.

Signal's developers also mention secret sharing and oblivious pseudo-random functions as future possibilities [43], both of which could be achieved using existing cryptographic primitives, as explained above.

Auditable PAKEs for Thwarting Online Guessing Attacks. As is the case for SMP in OTR, online guessing attacks are unavoidable in PAKEs. This is usually dealt with by fixing a limit on the number of failed attempts that can be tolerated before invalidating a password.

However, in certain cases, another subtle adversarial strategy aimed at sidestepping the (at most) one online test per run would be to resort to a class of guess and abort attacks in which $\mathcal{M}$ intercepts a message in a given session (or initiates a session of her own) at a crucial step of a protocol run, verifies her guess at the password and in case of an incorrect guess, drops the said message to disguise her attempt as a network communication failure.

This can be done in both directions to double the chance of discovering the password, or in parallel against many network nodes depending on the setting. Such an attack can be carried out repeatedly without raising an alarm as the honest parties may simply view this as a network failure.

We identify a similar vulnerability in the use of a modified version of SMP in OTR: just before the last phase where the parties perform their secure equality test, when $\mathcal{A}$ and $\mathcal{M}$ exchange their blinded DH terms incorporating the low-entropy password in the exponent, i.e., $(g_3^a, g_1^a g_2^{\pi_{\mathcal{A}}})$, $\mathcal{M}$ could make a guessing attempt at $\pi_{\mathcal{A}}$ and in case of obtaining 0 (not equal), drop the message and force an abort, see Sects. 4.2 and 4.3 in [3]. Note that the non-interactive zero-knowledge (NIZK) proofs that are attached to the messages at every exchange are not meant to protect against this type of attack.

In a relatively recent work, Roscoe and Ryan [38] apply a mechanism based on commitment schemes and delay functions (e.g., timed-release encryption), originally developed by Roscoe [37] for protecting against online attacks in HISPs that use SAS, to the setting of PAKEs in order to make them auditable by achieving *stochastic fair exchange*.

Roughly speaking, this is achieved by a transformation for PAKEs at the level of KC using a combination of blinding, randomization, commitments and delay functions such that a series of messages consisting of fake ones and the real intended message are exchanged and the parties will only get to know which is the *right* one until their exchange is complete. In a follow-up work, Couteau et al. [16] generalize this result to achieve ε-fair exchange using oblivious transfer and timed-release encryption.

This transformation can be used to enhance any PAKE with auditability, thus lending itself quite naturally to the authentication method suggested in this work. An important limitation here is that, due to the highly interactive design of the solution, it would be more suitable to the setting of secure messaging than email, unless a given email solution were to opt for untrusted buffer servers for transport, see Sect. 4.4.

Table 2. Comparison of trust establishment approaches. (Partial modifications to the original presented in [48]).

Paradigm	Example	Security									Usability									Adoption		
		Network MitM Prevented	Operator MitM Prevented	Operator MitM Detected	Operator Accountability	Key Revocation Possible	Privacy Preserving	Deniability Facilitated	Forward Secrecy Facilitated	Post-quantum Security	Automatic Key Initialization	Low Key Maintenance	Easy Key Discovery	Easy Key Recovery	In-Band	No Shared Secrets	Alert-less Key Renewal	Immediate Enrollment	Inattentive User Resistant	No Service Provider	Asynchronous	Multiple Key Support
Web of Trust	PGP	●	●	●	◐	◐	✗	✗	-	✗	✗	✗	◐	◐	✗	✗	✗	✗	✗	●	●	●
KD + SaL	CONIKS	●	✗	◐	●	●	●	✗	-	✗	●	●	●	●	●	●	●	●	●	●	●	●
OE + TOFU	TextSecure	◐	◐	◐	◐	✗	●	-	-	-	●	●	●	●	●	●	✗	●	✗	●	●	✗
OE + TOFU + OOB	p≡p	◐	◐	◐	◐	◐	●	-	-	-	●	◐	●	◐	✗	●	✗	✗	✗	●	✗	✗
OE + SMP	OTR	◐	◐	◐	◐	●	●	-	-	✗	✗	●	✗	✗	◐	◐	✗	●	✗	●	✗	●
OE + PAKE	PakeMail	◐	◐	⊛	⊛	◐	●	⊛	⊛	⊛	●	●	●	●	●	✗	●	●	●	●	●	●
KFV: OOB	SilentText	●	●	●	●	◐	●	-	-	-	✗	✗	✗	✗	✗	●	✗	✗	✗	●	✗	✗
KFV: SMP	OTR	●	●	●	●	◐	●	-	-	✗	✗	✗	✗	✗	●	✗	✗	✗	✗	●	✗	✗
KFV: PAKE	PakeMail	●	●	●	●	◐	◐	●	●	⊛	●	●	●	●	●	✗	●	●	●	●	●	●

The property is: ● = satisfied; ◐ = partially satisfied; ✗ = not satisfied; ⊛ = implementation dependent; - = N/A
KD = Key directory; KFV = Key fingerprint verification; OE = Opportunistic encryption; SaL = Self-auditable logs; TOFU = Trust-on-first-use

Finally, note that some of the ideas in this transformation, specifically those related to enforcing fairness, have common elements with the original SMP [14] solution aimed at providing fairness, a property that was removed from the modified version of SMP used in OTR [3] on account of achieving efficiency.

5.4 Comparison

Table 2 shows a comparison of our proposal with a select set of approaches for trust establishment extracted from a relatively recent survey by Unger et al. on secure messaging [46]. We limit our analysis to the most relevant aspects with respect to our proposal and refer the reader to the cited source for a more detailed explanation of the approaches and their properties. If the reason behind a given evaluation is not specified in [46], we provide our own interpretation and evaluate our approach accordingly.

Most of the properties have self-explanatory names, except perhaps operator accountability, which is considered to be satisfied if the paradigm provides support for verifying the correct behavior of service providers during the trust establishment process, when a centralized infrastructure is required. The network and operator attackers considered for MITM refer respectively to adversaries controlling large segments of the internet and infrastructure operators (service providers).

PAKE-based approaches satisfy privacy preservation as the transcript of a PAKE execution does not leak information. *Deniability facilitated, FS facilitated* and post-quantum security are subject to the selection and exact usage of the PAKE scheme.

Approaches built upon opportunistic encryption (OE) partially provide MITM prevention because an attack can be successful during the initial communication round, before a key is authenticated. When combined with SMP, operator accountability and MITM detection are also partially satisfied given that if the execution of the SMP protocol fails, the users do not learn whether this was due to mismatching passwords or an adversarial attempt at compromising the channel. However, when it comes to our PAKE-based approach, these last two properties could be potentially satisfied with the use of auditable PAKEs (see Sect. 5.3), mainly in the context of messaging.

It is somewhat ambiguous as to why the authors of [46] consider key revocation—users being able to revoke and renew keys—to be fully satisfied for SMP applied to OE. While revocation is possible, the process would still suffer from the known limitations of a truly decentralized setting, e.g., informing all users of an expired key. The latter is indeed stated to be the reason for considering that KFV approaches only partially satisfy this property. Therefore, PAKE applied to OE would also partially satisfy key revocation. Thanks to the derived cryptographic key, the main advantages of OE with PAKE can be observed at the level of usability related properties, e.g., automation of tasks.

In key fingerprint verification (KFV) approaches, the verification is considered to occur before using the public keys, which leads to achieving most of the security properties. The evaluations for the OOB approach assume that the manual comparison is executed correctly; this assumption is not needed for SMP or PAKE. As we can observe, PAKE-based KFV significantly improves usability compared to OOB and SMP fingerprint verification.

Key directory combined with self-auditable logs (KD+SaL) is arguably the most promising approach identified by Unger et al. due to the wide range of properties that it provides. It allows users to efficiently verify the consistency of their own entry in a central key directory and therefore to detect and expose misbehavior by a third party.

The set of properties that KD+SaL and KFV:PAKE can achieve is similar, yet, the latter has the advantage of enhancing security with the properties discussed in Sect. 5.2.

Overall, PAKE-based key fingerprint verification offers the most complete set of properties with reasonable trade-offs between security and usability in a purely decentralized setting.

Clark et al. [15] present a similar table evaluating primitives used to enhance email security. Considering end-to-end encryption as a baseline, PAKE-based key verification/management would perform as shared secret key verification (R14 in [15]), except that, additionally, our PAKE-based approach partially satisfies the property that refers to providing support for server-side content processing (P12) as this can be enabled without exposing the encrypted content, e.g., via secure secret retrieval (see Sect. 5.3).

6   Implementation: PakeMail

Here we present PakeMail, an implementation of the core set of features of our proposal, mainly aimed at demonstrating the feasibility of the key ideas presented in this work. The source code and related documentation are available at [4].

PakeMail is a complete implementation of the main functionalities, namely, carrying out a PAKE protocol in a decentralized setting to authenticate public keys and establish a shared symmetric cryptographic key, using standard email and attachments as transport mechanism for networking, while preserving interoperability and without introducing any extra trust assumptions. However, this implementation should be rather viewed as a proof of concept given that a full-fledged version would not only require additional design and security considerations, but it would also provide support for the other remaining features that we have discussed in Sect. 5.

Our solution is implemented in Python 3, specifically targeted at version 3.6, with minimal dependencies, largely using standard Python libraries for tasks such as email formatting (MIME), encoding and exchange (IMAP, SMTP, TLS) as well as networking and file system operations. In terms of design, we have mainly adopted an object-oriented programming paradigm, enabling well-established properties such as a modular implementation with better separation of concerns via encapsulation, extensibility and re-usability. The current implementation is geared towards Unix-like operating systems, but it can be easily ported to other platforms.

6.1   Cryptographic Details

PakeMail makes use of the SPAKE2 library developed by Warner [49], which by default uses "Curve25519"[4] for the underlying elliptic curve, offering 128 bits of security. It is however possible to switch to 1024/2048/3072-bit integer groups as well. For the key confirmation phase described in Fig. 1, we use HKDF (HMAC-based Extract-and-Expand Key Derivation Function)[5] by H. Krawczyk for implementing the key derivation function, and HMAC[6] keyed-hashing for message authentication to derive the authentication tags. Finally, we use the PyNaCl library, which is a wrapper for the

---

[4] https://mailarchive.ietf.org/arch/msg/cfrg/-9LEdnzVrE5RORux3Oo_oDDRksU/.

[5] https://tools.ietf.org/html/rfc5869.html.

[6] https://tools.ietf.org/html/rfc2104.html.

well-known NaCl library, for performing cryptographic tasks such as encryption using 256-bit PAKE-derived secret keys.

PAKE messages and passwords are stored and transferred as byte strings. While an encoding at the application layer can be applied, ultimately, the underlying SPAKE2 Application Programming Interface (API) requires byte strings, thus leaving such choices to the users of the library. Moreover, due to the inherently asymmetric design of the SPAKE2 implementation, we assign distinct roles to PAKE instances, which in our implementation are referred to as "initiator" and "responder". Also, among other things, to prevent message reuse in different contexts and in line with the original protocol description [2] and the SPAKE2 library, we also enforce identities—again as byte strings—at the level of PAKE instances, which can refer to a username, user ID or server names, to name a few. As detailed in Sect. 4.2, the public key fingerprints could be included in the transcript and thus in the input of the hash function computing the intermediate shared key before KC, however the SPAKE2 API accepts only the user IDs and the weak password. We deal with this using the KC step and the inclusion of the public key fingerprints as associated data into the HMAC-authenticated message.

For further information on the details of the underlying SPAKE2 implementation, we refer the reader to the corresponding documentation by Warner [49].

6.2 PAKE Protocol Carried Out over Email

We have implemented the email-based approach suggested in Sect. 4.4, mainly because it corresponds to the solution that preservers compatibility and interoperability without imposing any additional requirements on standard email exchange solutions. PakeMail essentially makes use of email messages and attachments as transport mechanism for exchanging cryptographic messages and key confirmation tags belonging to PAKE protocol sessions as well as other data such as public keys that are to be authenticated by PAKE messages, effectively implementing the communication channel via mailboxes. In the case of secure messaging, the networking would be rather trivial given that most current solutions make use of intermediary servers, which in our case can be untrusted.

6.3 Implemented Scenarios

The solution provides PAKE clients and email services designed to deal with the requirements of PAKE exchanges and state maintenance in a decentralized and distributed computing setting. The PAKE clients have been implemented such that they take on either the role of an "initiator" or that of a "responder", consistent with the original SPAKE2 protocol design and the requirements of the SPAKE2 Python API.

Moreover, we provide a module containing easy to use executable implementations of the following scenarios: (i) a local execution of two independent threads of PAKE clients running a PAKE session with key confirmation, followed by some cryptographic tasks using the established key; (ii) an online execution of two clients (an initiator and a responder instance) running on the same hardware but routing their messages via email exchanges and attachments, currently implemented to work with Gmail but adapting it to other services would simply amount to providing the appropriate access data, e.g., the corresponding mail server credentials and port numbers; (iii) and (iv) provide the execution of initiator and responder instances, respectively, on two different machines, again using email as transport mechanism.

6.4 Performance

In terms of performance, the main scenario of interest, namely that of running two separate instances of PakeMail on two different machines, carrying out a PAKE protocol with explicit key confirmation over Gmail, requires $\approx 3 \cdot 10^{-3}$ s, averaged over 10 runs. The results were obtained from executions on two laptops running at 1.6 GHz (Dual-Core Intel Core i5) with 8 GB of RAM, 256 KB and 4 MB of L2 and L3 cache, respectively.

Given the setting for which this approach is designed, i.e., distributed peer-to-peer connections between entities running point-to-point PAKE sessions, we consider the current overall execution time to be fast enough for all practical purposes. Table 3 provides a concise comparison of execution times for pure SPAKE2 sessions with its PakeMail counterpart, providing some information on the overall overhead added by our email-based networking and other non-PAKE computations.

Note that once both parties have entered their passwords, the added networking overhead due to email exchanges triggered by PakeMail will arguably not be perceptible by users given the inherent delay in email exchanges.

Table 3. Execution time comparison averaged over 10 runs.

Group	Pure SPAKE2	Local PakeMail	PakeMail via Gmail
Curve25519	26 ms	50 ms	350 ms

Finally, in terms of the underlying SPAKE2 library's performance on the same hardware, the average execution times using Curve25519 and 1024/2048/3072-bit integer groups are 26 ms, 9 ms, 42.1 ms and 82.6 ms, respectively. The delta would simply contribute additively to the PakeMail executions as the additional overhead incurred by switching to different representations is independent from the details of PakeMail.

6.5 Further Design and Security Considerations

Due to the nature of the current proof of concept implementation, certain design decisions have been made simply to ensure the implementation of a functional tool capable of demonstrating the feasibility, usability and efficiency of the proposed approach. However, a mature and robust implementation would have to account for a number of nuances. For instance, for the purpose of our proof of concept, we simply use universally unique identifier (UUID) numbers along with other user identifiers, which are stored in the email subject, to synchronize and map initiator and responder messages belonging to the same session to one another, coupled with a persistent per client session history to track and resolve sessions. A robust networking component capable of addressing distributed systems corner cases such as deadlocks and race conditions remains to be done.

Regarding the cryptographic details of the implementation, it should be pointed out that a secure and scalable industrial implementation would have to at the very least rely on a constant-time implementation of the PAKE library as the currently used SPAKE2 library is by no means constant-time and is thus vulnerable to timing attacks.

Finally, note that dedicated optimization efforts remain to be done as future work. Clearly, the alternative transport mechanism based on intermediary servers, enabling more natural communication channels and networking, would lead to far lower communication overhead, albeit at the cost of somewhat hampering interoperability and compatibility, unless projects such as Matrix[7] and MLS[8] gain widespread adoption.

7 Security and Low-Entropy Secrets

The schemes considered thus far come with proofs of security, see Table 1 for the corresponding models and assumptions. The security guarantees can be traced back to the core properties of PAKEs: they can in effect fulfill the role of ZK proof of knowledge schemes such that a run of the protocol does not leak any information on the password and upon termination only reveals whether the secrets were equal; they resist offline dictionary attacks against passive and active adversaries, and online guessing attacks by limiting adversarial tests to one password per run; compromised session keys do not compromise the security of other established session keys; depending on the choice of PAKE, FS would ensure that session keys remain secure in case of password disclosure.

The only way for $\mathcal{M}$ to gain knowledge about the secret would be via active online guessing attempts, typically dealt with by fixing a limit on the number of failed attempts, e.g., SMP in OTR. As we previously discussed, the possibility of making PAKEs auditable can be used to mitigate this class of attacks by distinguishing between failed adversarial attempts and network failures to minimize the adversary's tries to one, under the assumption of correct input entry by honest users.

Low-Entropy Secret Agreement. Our proposal does come with a caveat, namely the need for either presharing or agreeing on a low-entropy secret in-band. As already discussed in [3], users can either share a secret over a secure channel, e.g. OOB, or agree on one via an in-band solution without revealing sensitive information about the secret itself, e.g., $\mathcal{A}$ asking $\mathcal{B}$ to use the name of their favorite restaurant. The user interface of a tool implementing this could warn users not to include the secret itself, similar to standard email warnings reminding users to attach documents in case they have mentioned it in the body of the message.

Assuming already bootstrapped authentication to avoid circularity, another possibility would be to use another already authenticated and secure channel to agree on a secret. For instance, given the widespread use of tools such as Signal, parties could simply use it to agree on a secret for a one-time entity authentication of their secure email solution. While it may not be appealing from a theoretical point of view, due to

---

[7] https://matrix.org/docs/spec/.
[8] https://messaginglayersecurity.rocks/.

the assumption of there being an already authenticated and secure channel, practically speaking, this approach would in fact provide a realistic and usable solution.

Usability Aspects. Particular attention must be paid to the implementation of an adequate interface for entering the low-entropy secret, along with the corresponding documentation and manuals with simple explanations for users. A lesson learned from a usability study on the OTR/SMP tool [44] stresses the need for further research on how to guide users towards establishing a secure shared human-memorable secret.

For instance, adding a list pre-populated with questions might serve to reduce user effort by allowing them to choose one from the list, or as a guide for users to generate similar questions. The questions should not lead to evident answers or to answers belonging to very small known sets, such as "yes/no" or colors, as such cases increase the successful guessing probability of the adversary. Another measure for dealing with disparities due to letter cases would be to for example simply convert the secret to upper-case, at the cost of reducing entropy.

8   Further Directions

A clear and promising line of future work consists of improving the current implementation and adding the various enhancements discussed here.

Producing secure implementations of cryptographic primitives and protocols is a notoriously difficult task. Consequently, over the past decades, a considerable amount of research in formal verification has focused on developing techniques for ensuring that security software preserves the security guarantees of the underlying cryptographic constructions. Although our solution builds on provably secure cryptographic constructions, the actual implementation makes use of cryptographic software that has not been proven secure. Therefore, pursuing the development of a verified implementation of a PAKE protocol would be another promising research direction. This could be achieved using dedicated languages such as F* [35], which has been used, among other things, to produce a verified reference implementation of the TLS (1.2) protocol [11].

Alternatively, a robust PAKE implementation in a language designed for performance and safety such as RUST would be yet another viable path. An initial rough implementation of SPAKE2 in RUST is already available and subject to ongoing work.[9]

Follow-up theoretical work on all the suggested cryptographic enhancements and implementations thereof represents another line of research. In particular, given the fact that mature PAKE implementations are quite rare, we consider further theoretical work on the design and analysis of a quantum-secure PAKE, proven secure in the QROM, accompanied by an actual implementation to be worth pursuing. Similarly, to the best of our knowledge, an implementation, let alone practical and efficient, of the secure secret storage and retrieval tasks (e.g., using PPSS or OPAQUE) represents yet another promising line of work.

Moreover, research on effective and usable methods for assisting users in agreeing on low-entropy secrets while reducing the mental effort and the likelihood of mistakes, is also encouraged. Other interesting directions include the application of

---

[9] https://github.com/RustCrypto/PAKEs.

PAKE to authentication for encrypted mailing lists, and studying the possibility of sharing/synchronizing existing trust assignments for contacts across different services—e.g., from Signal to p ≡ p or vice versa. In this case, once an entity is trusted in one application, other applications that recognize this entity could inherit the trust stored in the user's device; clearly, it is vital to do this in a secure and privacy-preserving manner.

References

1. Abdalla, M., Barbosa, M.: Perfect forward security of SPAKE2. Cryptology ePrint Archive, Report 2019/1194 (2019). https://eprint.iacr.org/2019/1194
2. Abdalla, M., Pointcheval, D.: Simple password-based encrypted key exchange protocols. In: Menezes, A. (ed.) CT-RSA 2005. LNCS, vol. 3376, pp. 191–208. Springer, Heidelberg (2005). https://doi.org/10.1007/978-3-540-30574-3_14
3. Alexander, C., Goldberg, I.: Improved user authentication in off-the-record messaging. In: Proceedings of the 2007 ACM Workshop on Privacy in Electronic Society. ACM (2007)
4. Atashpendar, A., Vazquez Sandoval, I.: PakeMail (2020). https://github.com/CryptographySandbox/PakeMail
5. Avoine, G., Canard, S., Ferreira, L.: Symmetric-Key Authenticated Key Exchange (SAKE) with perfect forward secrecy. In: Jarecki, S. (ed.) CT-RSA 2020. LNCS, vol. 12006, pp. 199–224. Springer, Cham (2020). https://doi.org/10.1007/978-3-030-40186-3_10
6. Bagherzandi, A., Jarecki, S., Saxena, N., Lu, Y.: Password-protected secret sharing. In: Proceedings of the 18th ACM Conference on Computer and Communications Security, pp. 433–444 (2011)
7. Becerra, J., Ostrev, D., Škrobot, M.: Forward secrecy of SPAKE2. In: Baek, J., Susilo, W., Kim, J. (eds.) ProvSec 2018. LNCS, vol. 11192, pp. 366–384. Springer, Cham (2018). https://doi.org/10.1007/978-3-030-01446-9_21
8. Bellare, M., Pointcheval, D., Rogaway, P.: Authenticated key exchange secure against dictionary attacks. In: Preneel, B. (ed.) EUROCRYPT 2000. LNCS, vol. 1807, pp. 139–155. Springer, Heidelberg (2000). https://doi.org/10.1007/3-540-45539-6_11
9. Bellovin, S.M., Merritt, M.: Encrypted key exchange: password-based protocols secure against dictionary attacks. In: 1992 IEEE Computer Society Symposium on Research in Security and Privacy, pp. 72–84. IEEE Computer Society (1992)
10. Bernstein, D.J.: Curve25519: new Diffie-Hellman speed records. In: Yung, M., Dodis, Y., Kiayias, A., Malkin, T. (eds.) PKC 2006. LNCS, vol. 3958, pp. 207–228. Springer, Heidelberg (2006). https://doi.org/10.1007/11745853_14
11. Bhargavan, K., Fournet, C., Kohlweiss, M., Pironti, A., Strub, P.Y.: Implementing TLS with verified cryptographic security. In: 2013 IEEE Symposium on Security and Privacy, pp. 445–459. IEEE (2013)
12. Birk, V., Marques, H., Hoeneisen, B.: pEp Foundation: IANA registration of trustword lists (2019). https://tools.ietf.org/html/draft-birk-pep-trustwords-03
13. Borisov, N., Goldberg, I., Brewer, E.: Off-the-record communication, or, why not to use PGP. In: Proceedings of the 2004 ACM Workshop on Privacy in the Electronic Society (2004)
14. Boudot, F., Schoenmakers, B., Traore, J.: A fair and efficient solution to the socialist millionaires' problem. Discrete Appl. Math. **111**, 23–36 (2001)
15. Clark, J., van Oorschot, P.C., Ruoti, S., Seamons, K., Zappala, D.: Securing email. arXiv preprint arXiv:1804.07706 (2018)
16. Couteau, G., Roscoe, A.W., Ryan, P.Y.A.: Partially-fair computation from timed-release encryption and oblivious transfer. Cryptology ePrint Archive, Report 2019/1281 (2019). https://eprint.iacr.org/2019/1281

17. Dechand, S., Schürmann, D., Busse, K., Acar, Y., Fahl, S., Smith, M.: An empirical study of textual key-fingerprint representations. In: 25th {USENIX} Security Symposium, pp. 193–208 (2016)
18. Delaune, S., Kremer, S., Robin, L.: Formal verification of protocols based on short authenticated strings. In: 2017 IEEE 30th Computer Security Foundations Symposium (CSF), pp. 130–143. IEEE (2017)
19. Di Raimondo, M., Gennaro, R., Krawczyk, H.: Deniable authentication and key exchange. In: Proceedings of the 13th ACM Conference on Computer and Communications Security, pp. 400–409 (2006)
20. Ding, J., Alsayigh, S., Lancrenon, J., RV, S., Snook, M.: Provably secure password authenticated key exchange based on RLWE for the post-quantum world. In: Handschuh, H. (ed.) CT-RSA 2017. LNCS, vol. 10159, pp. 183–204. Springer, Cham (2017). https://doi.org/10.1007/978-3-319-52153-4_11
21. Dolev, D., Yao, A.C.: On the security of public key protocols. In: Proceedings of the 22Nd Annual Symposium on Foundations of Computer Science, SFCS 1981, pp. 350–357. IEEE Computer Society (1981)
22. Fischlin, M., Günther, F., Schmidt, B., Warinschi, B.: Key confirmation in key exchange: a formal treatment and implications for TLS 1.3. In: 2016 IEEE Symposium on Security and Privacy (SP). IEEE (2016)
23. Garay, J.A., MacKenzie, P.D., Yang, K.: Efficient and secure multi-party computation with faulty majority and complete fairness. IACR Cryptol. ePrint Arch. **2004**, 9 (2004)
24. Hao, F., Ryan, P.: J-PAKE: authenticated key exchange without PKI. In: Gavrilova, M.L., Tan, C.J.K., Moreno, E.D. (eds.) Transactions on Computational Science XI. LNCS, vol. 6480, pp. 192–206. Springer, Heidelberg (2010). https://doi.org/10.1007/978-3-642-17697-5_10
25. Jarecki, S., Krawczyk, H., Xu, J.: OPAQUE: an asymmetric PAKE protocol secure against pre-computation attacks. In: Nielsen, J.B., Rijmen, V. (eds.) EUROCRYPT 2018. LNCS, vol. 10822, pp. 456–486. Springer, Cham (2018). https://doi.org/10.1007/978-3-319-78372-7_15
26. Kainda, R., Flechais, I., Roscoe, A.: Usability and security of out-of-band channels in secure device pairing protocols. In: Proceedings of the 5th Symposium on Usable Privacy and Security, p. 11. ACM (2009)
27. Kainda, R., Flechais, I., Roscoe, A.: Secure mobile ad-hoc interactions: reasoning about out-of-band (OOB) channels. IWSSI/SPMU **2010**, 10–15 (2010)
28. Katz, J., Vaikuntanathan, V.: Round-optimal password-based authenticated key exchange. In: Ishai, Y. (ed.) TCC 2011. LNCS, vol. 6597, pp. 293–310. Springer, Heidelberg (2011). https://doi.org/10.1007/978-3-642-19571-6_18
29. Krawczyk, H.: Cryptographic extraction and key derivation: the HKDF scheme. In: Rabin, T. (ed.) CRYPTO 2010. LNCS, vol. 6223, pp. 631–648. Springer, Heidelberg (2010). https://doi.org/10.1007/978-3-642-14623-7_34
30. Kumar, A., Saxena, N., Tsudik, G., Uzun, E.: A comparative study of secure device pairing methods. Pervasive Mob. Comput. **5**(6), 734–749 (2009)
31. Naor, M., Rotem, L., Segev, G.: The security of lazy users in out-of-band authentication. In: Beimel, A., Dziembowski, S. (eds.) TCC 2018. LNCS, vol. 11240, pp. 575–599. Springer, Cham (2018). https://doi.org/10.1007/978-3-030-03810-6_21
32. Nguyen, L.H., Roscoe, A.W.: Authentication protocols based on low-bandwidth unspoofable channels: a comparative survey. J. Comput. Secur. **19**(1), 139–201 (2011)
33. OTRv4-development: Specification of OTR version 4, October 2019. https://github.com/otrv4/otrv4/blob/master/otrv4.md
34. pEp Security: Pretty Easy Privacy (pEp). https://www.pep.security

35. Microsoft Research, I.: F* (2020). https://fstar-lang.org/
36. Rivest, R.L., Shamir, A.: How to expose an eavesdropper. Commun. ACM **27**(4), 393–394 (1984)
37. Roscoe, A.W.: Detecting failed attacks on human-interactive security protocols (transcript of discussion). In: Anderson, J., Matyáš, V., Christianson, B., Stajano, F. (eds.) Security Protocols 2016. LNCS, vol. 10368, pp. 198–205. Springer, Cham (2017). https://doi.org/10.1007/978-3-319-62033-6_22
38. Roscoe, A.W., Ryan, P.Y.A.: Auditable PAKEs: approaching fair exchange without a TTP. In: Stajano, F., Anderson, J., Christianson, B., Matyáš, V. (eds.) Security Protocols 2017. LNCS, vol. 10476, pp. 278–297. Springer, Cham (2017). https://doi.org/10.1007/978-3-319-71075-4_31
39. Ruoti, S., Andersen, J., Monson, T., Zappala, D., Seamons, K.: A comparative usability study of key management in secure email. In: Fourteenth Symposium on Usable Privacy and Security, pp. 375–394 (2018)
40. Sasson, E.B., et al.: Zerocash: decentralized anonymous payments from bitcoin. In: 2014 IEEE Symposium on Security and Privacy, pp. 459–474 (2014)
41. Shirvanian, M., Saxena, N.: Wiretapping via mimicry: short voice imitation man-in-the-middle attacks on crypto phones. In: Proceedings of the 2014 ACM SIGSAC Conference on Computer and Communications Security, CCS 2014, pp. 868–879 (2014)
42. Signal: Improving registration lock with secure value recovery, February 2020. https://signal.org/blog/improving-registration-lock
43. Signal: Technology preview for secure value recovery (2020). https://signal.org/blog/secure-value-recovery
44. Stedman, R., Yoshida, K., Goldberg, I.: A user study of off-the-record messaging. In: 4th Symposium on Usable Privacy and Security, pp. 95–104 (2008)
45. Tan, J., Bauer, L., Bonneau, J., Cranor, L.F., Thomas, J., Ur, B.: Can unicorns help users compare crypto key fingerprints? In: Proceedings of the 2017 CHI Conference on Human Factors in Computing Systems, pp. 3787–3798. ACM (2017)
46. Unger, N., et al.: SoK: secure messaging. In: 2015 IEEE Symposium on Security and Privacy, pp. 232–249. IEEE (2015)
47. Vaudenay, S.: Secure communications over insecure channels based on short authenticated strings. In: Shoup, V. (ed.) CRYPTO 2005. LNCS, vol. 3621, pp. 309–326. Springer, Heidelberg (2005). https://doi.org/10.1007/11535218_19
48. Vazquez Sandoval, I., Atashpendar, A., Lenzini, G.: Authentication and key management automation in decentralized secure email and messaging via low-entropy secrets. In: Proceedings of the 17th International Joint Conference on e-Business and Telecommunications, ICETE 2020 - Volume 2: SECRYPT, Lieusaint, Paris, France (2020)
49. Warner, B.: Pure-Python SPAKE2 (2010). https://github.com/warner/python-spake2
50. Yao, A.C.: Protocols for secure computations. In: 23rd Annual Symposium on Foundations of Computer Science (SFCS 1982), pp. 160–164. IEEE (1982)

Practically Efficient Attribute-Based Encryption for Compartmented and Multilevel Access Structures

Ferucio Laurențiu Țiplea[1,2](✉) (iD), Alexandru Ioniță[2] (iD), and Anca Maria Nica[1] (iD)

[1] Department of Computer Science, Alexandru Ioan Cuza University of Iași, Iași, Romania
ferucio.tiplea@uaic.ro
[2] Simion Stoilow Institute of Mathematics of the Romanian Academy, Bucharest, Romania

Abstract. Compartmented access structures (CASs) regulate the access control by requesting the consent of various compartments. Thus, they are particularly useful to the Internet of Things or Wireless Sensor Networks applications with cloud support. The construction of practically efficient attribute-based encryption (ABE) schemes for CASs is faced with the fact that these access structures cannot be represented by Boolean formulas. The use of multilinear map based ABE schemes for general Boolean circuits is not only impractical but also suffers from the lack of secure multilinear map candidates. Also, the schemes based on lattice cryptography, even if they are secure, are highly inefficient in practice. We show in this paper that for CASs we can construct practically efficient ABE schemes based on secret sharing and just one bilinear map. The construction can also be applied to multilevel access structures. The security proof is performed in a general context that can apply to other similar access structures.

Keywords: Compartmented access structure · Attribute based encryption

1 Introduction

Recent developments in wireless sensor networks (WSN), internet of things (IoT), and cloud computing are raising increasing problems over access control. Standard access control techniques, such as *discretionary access control* (DAC), *mandatory access control* (MAC), or *role-based access control* (RBAC), prove to be inappropriate in such cases. For instance, DAC is not well suited for large-scale networks with high security requirements mainly because it does not offer any mechanism or method to manage the improper access control: if the software fails to restrict the user from predefined permissions then any hacker can hack into the system, can have access to the confidential files, and can also perform all the actions like read, write, or delete. Neither MAC does better in such cases. For instance, it is difficult to deploy MAC in cloud systems because it does not support separation of duties, delegation, or inheritance. Although RBAC alleviates some of the security issues with DAC and MAC, it is still not very well suited for cloud computing because it does not scale easily to systems with large number of users

---

This is an extension of the conference paper [9].

© Springer Nature Switzerland AG 2021
M. S. Obaidat and J. Ben-Othman (Eds.): ICETE 2020, CCIS 1484, pp. 129–150, 2021.
https://doi.org/10.1007/978-3-030-90428-9_6

and roles where the user's roles change frequently. Moreover, it is difficult to extended RBAC across administrative domains as it is difficult to decide a role's privileges.

Attribute based access control (ABAC) is one of the techniques that can overcome the shortcomings mentioned above. ABAC uses attributes (of users, objects, actions, environment) and defines policies based on them. Attributes make ABAC a more fine-grained access control model than RBAC. However, when working with encrypted data for example in cloud, it is good to have the access control policy directly embedded in data and the decryption be carried out only by authorized access structures. One of the best methods to do that is by *attributed-based encryption* (ABE) that allows us to define fine-grained access control on the decryption process.

Diversifying the roles of users and managers, increasing the number of resources and their type, subsidiaries and departments of companies, leads to the orientation of the access control more on groups of attributes than on individual objects. For instance, the Oracle Cloud Infrastructure [19] uses *compartments* to group related cloud resources. Compartments provide logical isolation, which makes it much easier to govern the management permission policies and track the costs incurred by the related groups of resources.

Often, compartments must be considered in a certain (partial or total) order, regardless of whether they consist of users or resources. The supply chain with products grouped in compartments must follow a certain order (which can be partial), the decision process often follows a total order between compartments, etc. The access control structures should then be defined by means of compartments. Existing approaches for such access structures include *multilevel access structures* (MASs) and *compartmented access structures* (CASs) [15, 26, 28, 30–32, 38].

Contribution. Access control through ABE has proven to be a necessary and important technology in the current context. There are two basic policies in using ABE: the key policy (KP-ABE) and the ciphertext policy (CP-ABE). In a KP-ABE, each message is encrypted together with a set of attributes and the decryption key is computed for the entire access structure; in a CP-ABE, each message is encrypted together with an access structure while the decryption keys are given for specific sets of attributes.

In this paper we focus on the KP-ABE paradigm. The most efficient KP-ABE scheme from the practical point of view is that in [16], which uses linear secret sharing and a single bilinear map. Unfortunately, the access structures supported by this scheme are only those that can be described by Boolean formulas, while compartmented access structures cannot be described by Boolean formulas (Proposition 1 in our paper). The extension to Boolean circuits by means of multi-linear maps as proposed in [14] is not secure due to the fact that no candidate multi-linear map proposed so far is secure [1, 8]. The extension of KP-ABE to Boolean circuits by means of lattice cryptography as proposed for instance in [4] is rather unpractical due to the large expansion of the ciphertext and the decryption key. The KP-ABE scheme in [10] may accommodate Boolean circuits. However, it is efficient in practice only if the fan-out gates it uses do not lead to an exponential increase of the size of the decryption key.

In this paper we prove first that CASs cannot be described by Boolean formulas. Then, we show that the KP-ABE scheme proposed in [10] can be applied quite efficiently to CASs. The ciphertext has the same size as in the case of the KP-ABE scheme in [16], while the size of the decryption key is four times larger than the one in [16]. This is even far more efficient than the scheme in [14] if it were to be secure with any multi-linear map candidate.

Due to the particularity of the CASs we show then that the fan-out gates can be removed, leading to an even more efficient KP-ABE scheme in which the size of the decryption key is only two times larger than the one in [14]. The same technique is also applied to MASs.

Boolean circuits describing CASs and MASs have an important feature: their input gates are the only gates of fan-out larger than one. We generalize this remark and present a KP-ABE scheme for Boolean circuits of this type (called *multiple-input Boolean trees*). This scheme's security proof also covers the schemes for CASs and MASs that have become particular cases. The generalization to multiple-input Boolean trees is a proper extension of the conference paper [9].

Related Work. During the last decade there has been a continuous increase in the use of ABE technology in IoT and WSN with cloud support. One of the most cited papers [37] addresses the problem of defining and enforcing access policies based on data attributes and, on the same time, allowing the data owner to delegate most of the computation tasks involved in fine-grained data access control to untrusted cloud servers without disclosing the underlying data contents.

[33] proposes a KP-ABE scheme for IoT applications based on cloud, with collaborative encryption. When a node with low computational capabilities must encrypt some message, it is assisted by more powerful neighboring nodes.

In order to have an efficient decryption cost and at the same time to offer protection to sensitive data, [17] came with the solution of outsourcing the decryption process in the case of ABE schemes to the cloud. Since then, this new paradigm presented a high interest, having several extensions and new systems being constructed upon it. A few examples of the extensions include support for verification of the decryption process [27], remote auditing [36], keyword search [22], and efficiency improvements [24].

The authors of [35] combine searchable encryption along with ABE, resulting in a multiple keyword search ABE scheme. Their system also supports attribute revocation without changing the ciphertext. The system uses a linear secret sharing scheme as access structure.

Another recent work on ABE in cloud system is presented in [34], where an ABE scheme with multiple functionalities is proposed: the scheme provides malicious user traceability, attribute revocation for malicious users, and updates over secret key and ciphertext in order to provide security against collusion attack between users. However, the system is limited to Boolean formulas as access structures.

In [6], a password-based user access control scheme with ABE support has been proposed to provide access control over WSNs. Because most ABE schemes are computationally heavy, sensor requests are grouped under cluster heads, where they are encrypted under some set of attributes, specific for the sensor information. Then each user is assigned a smart card, which stores an access tree. If a user's access structure is satisfied by the attributes from some ciphertext, then it can decrypt the information from the sensor. However, complex real life situations such as healthcare systems where the sensors must contain medical data, may require advanced access control structures that could be unable to express with Boolean formulas.

The necessity of using compartments to define access control policies has already been advocated by many researchers. [5] proposes a secure platform, called *TrApps*, to offer solutions for secure execution in untrusted cloud systems. The applications are divided in small trusted compartments in order to protect sensitive data.

We have already mentioned that the Oracle cloud infrastructure [19] uses a compartmented hierarchical form of grouping together related applications. One of the reasons for this is to facilitate access control granting of the resources. Such a system could benefit from an ABE scheme with compartmented access structure: each resource is assigned some attributes, and each application has its own access structure, based upon which it is granted access to resources.

[18] have proposed *MobInfoSec*, a system to protect sensitive information on mobile devices. The authors recognize the importance of multilevel access structures in order to have a good access control system, and tries to combine certificate public-key cryptography with general access structure.

One of the papers that tries to design ABE schemes for multi-level access control policies is [20]. The access control policy is based on a Boolean tree whose root is a threshold gate and the set of its children is partitioned into sets called security levels. A message is viewed as a vector of components, each of which being encrypted by a standard CP-ABE scheme. So, message components can be obtained by decryption depending on the security level of the user. The scheme does not offer a threshold multilevel access on security levels. So, the decryption entity has to satisfy a precise set of attributes to be able to decrypt a given sub-sets of data blocks with respect to a given security level. This aspect is somehow fixed in [21] by using two bilinear maps. We emphasize that the access control structures in these papers are different from MASs and CASs. A similar idea is used in [23], where the access control architecture is built on five entities: data owner, cloud service provider, center authority, department user, and user. Nor does this scheme use policies such as MAS or CAS.

Paper Structure. The paper is divided into six sections. The next one fixes the basic terminology and notation used throughout the paper. Section 3 includes our main contribution with respect to CASs and MASs. It starts by motivating our work on practically efficient ABE schemes for CASs and shows that CASs cannot be represented by Boolean formulas. Then, it proves efficiency of the KP-ABE scheme in [10] when applied to CASs. An improvement of this scheme is also proposed and it is shown that the technique can also be applied to the case of MASs. Section 5 generalizes the results in the previous section to multiple-input Boolean trees. It also constitutes a proper extension of the conference paper [9]. An implementation of the KP-ABE scheme for CASs is discussed in Sect. 5. The last section concludes the paper.

2   Preliminaries

We recall in this section the basic terminology and notation that is to be used throughout this paper.

The set of integers is denoted by $\mathbb{Z}$. A positive integer $a > 1$ is a *prime* number if the only positive divisors of it are 1 and a. Two integers a and b are called *congruent modulo n*, denoted $a \equiv b \bmod n$ or $a \equiv_n b$, if n divides $a - b$ (n is an integer too). The notation $a = b \bmod n$ means that a is the *remainder* of the integer division of b by n. The set of all congruence classes modulo n is denoted $\mathbb{Z}_n$. For a set A, $a \leftarrow A$ means that a is uniformly at random chosen from A.

Access Control Structures. Given a non-empty finite set $\mathcal{U}$ whose elements are called *attributes* in our paper, an *access structure* over $\mathcal{U}$ is any set $\mathcal{S}$ of non-empty subsets of $\mathcal{U}$ [29]. $\mathcal{S}$ is called *monotone* if it contains all subsets $B \subseteq \mathcal{U}$ with $A \subseteq B$, whenever $A \in \mathcal{S}$. The subsets (of $\mathcal{U}$) that are in $\mathcal{S}$ are called *authorized sets*, while those not in $\mathcal{S}$, *unauthorized sets*.

It is customary to represent (monotone) access structures by (monotone) Boolean circuits (for more details about Boolean circuits the reader is referred to [3]). Thus, given a finite set $\mathcal{U}$ of attributes, a *Boolean circuit C over $\mathcal{U}$* consists of:

- $|\mathcal{U}|$ *input gates*. An input gate does not have any input wire but only output wires. In our approach, the input gates are in a one-to-one correspondence with the elements of $\mathcal{U}$. By their output wires, the input gates feed the input wires of other gates by Boolean values assigned to their attributes;
- Just one output wire (which is not input wire of any gate);
- Arbitrarily many logic (u, v)-gates. A (u, v)-gate, where $1 \le u \le v$, has v input wires and one or more output wires. If the input wires of a (u, v)-gate are assigned Boolean values and at least u of them are 1, the output wires of the gate will get the value 1; otherwise they will get 0. $(1, 2)$- and $(2, 2)$-gates are usually referred to as OR- and AND-gates, respectively.

A NOT-*gate* has exactly one input wire and reverses the Boolean value that comes on its input wire to all its output wires. Boolean circuits without NOT-gates are usually referred to as *monotone*. In this paper we will only consider monotone Boolean circuits.

The number of outputs of a gate is called the *gate fan-out*. A *Boolean circuit of fan-out one*, also called *Boolean formula*, has all its gates of fan-out one.

In graphical representation, the input gates will be specified directly by their associated attributes; the other gates will be represented by circles containing the gate type (see, for instance, the Boolean circuit in Fig. 1(a)).

Each $A \subseteq \mathcal{U}$ evaluates the circuit C to one of the Boolean values 0 or 1 by simply assigning 1 to all input gates associated to elements in A, and 0 otherwise; then the Boolean values are propagated bottom-up to all gate output wires in a standard way. $C(A)$ stands for the Boolean value obtained by evaluating C for A. The access structure defined by C is the set of all subsets A of $\mathcal{U}$ with $C(A) = 1$.

Key-Policy Attribute Based Encryption. A *key-policy attribute based encryption* (KP-ABE) scheme consists of four probabilistic polynomial-time (PPT) algorithms [16]:

$Setup(\lambda)$: this is a PPT algorithm that takes as input the security parameter λ and outputs a set of public parameters PP and a master key MSK;

$Enc(m, A, PP)$: this is a PPT algorithm that takes as input a message m, a non-empty set of attributes $A \subseteq \mathcal{U}$, and the public parameters, and outputs a ciphertext E;

$KeyGen(\mathcal{C}, MSK)$: this is a PPT algorithm that takes as input an access structure $\mathcal{C}$ (given as a Boolean circuit) and the master key MSK, and outputs a decryption key D (for the entire Boolean circuit $\mathcal{C}$);

$Dec(E, D)$: this is a deterministic polynomial-time algorithm that takes as input a ciphertext E and a decryption key D, and outputs a message m or the special symbol $\perp$.

The following correctness property is required to be satisfied by any KP-ABE scheme: for any $(PP, MSK) \leftarrow Setup(\lambda)$, any Boolean circuit $\mathcal{C}$ over a set $\mathcal{U}$ of attributes, any message m, any $A \subseteq \mathcal{U}$, and any $E \leftarrow Enc(m, A, PP)$, if $\mathcal{C}(A) = 1$ then $m = Dec(E, D)$, for any $D \leftarrow KeyGen(\mathcal{C}, MSK)$.

We consider the standard notion of selective security for KP-ABE [16]. Specifically, in the *Init* phase the *adversary* (PPT algorithm) announces the set A of attributes that he wishes to be challenged upon, then in the *Setup* phase he receives the public parameters PP of the scheme, and in *Phase 1* oracle access to the decryption key generation oracle is granted for the adversary. In this phase, the adversary issues queries for decryption keys for access structures defined by Boolean circuits $\mathcal{C}$, provided that $\mathcal{C}(A) = 0$. In the *Challenge* phase the adversary submits two equal length messages m_0 and m_1 and receives the ciphertext associated to A and one of the two messages, say m_b, where $b \leftarrow \{0, 1\}$. The adversary may receive again oracle access to the decryption key generation oracle (with the same constraint as above); this is *Phase 2*. Eventually, the adversary outputs a guess $b' \leftarrow \{0, 1\}$ in the *Guess* phase.

The *advantage* of the adversary in this game is $P(b' = b) - 1/2$. The KP-ABE scheme is *secure* (in the selective model) if no adversary has more than a negligible advantage in the selective game described above.

Bilinear Maps and the Decisional BDH Assumption. Given G_1 and G_2 two multiplicative cyclic groups of prime order p, a map $e : G_1 \times G_1 \to G_2$ is called *bilinear* if it satisfies:

- $e(x^a, y^b) = e(x, y)^{ab}$, for any $x, y \in G_1$ and $a, b \in \mathbb{Z}_p$;
- $e(g, g)$ is a generator of G_2, for any generator g of G_1.

G_1 is called a *bilinear group* if the operation in G_1 and e are both efficiently computable.

The *Decisional Bilinear Diffie-Hellman* (DBDH) problem in the bilinear group G_2 is the problem to distinguish between $e(g, g)^{abc}$ and $e(g, g)^z$ given g, g^a, g^b, and g^c, where g is a generator of G_1 and a, b, c, and z are randomly chosen from $\mathbb{Z}_p$. The *DBDH assumption* for G_2 states that no PPT algorithm $\mathcal{A}$ can solve the DBDH problem in G_2 with more than a negligible advantage.

3 Our Contribution

3.1 Motivation and Main Goal

Compartmented Access Structures. Threshold access structures [2,7,12] are suitable when participants have the same degree of trust. However, many real-world applications such as cloud storage, healthcare systems, wireless sensor networks and so on need more complex access structures based on different degrees of trust and privileges associated to participants. Compartmented access structures can cope with this problem. Within such structures the set of participants is partitioned into groups called compartments, and thresholds are assigned on whose basis authorized sets are defined.

A *compartmented access structure* [28] over a finite set $U = \{1, \ldots, n\}$ of attributes is a tuple $(\overline{U}, \overline{c}, t, \mathcal{S})$, where:

- $\overline{U} = (U_1, \ldots, U_k)$ is a partition of U into $k \geq 1$ non-empty subsets called *compartments* (the number of participants in U_i is n_i, for all $1 \leq i \leq k$);
- $\overline{c} = (t_1, \ldots, t_k)$ is a vector of strictly positive integers called *thresholds* that satisfy $t_i \leq n_i$ for all $1 \leq i \leq k$;
- t is a global threshold satisfying $\sum_{i=1}^{k} t_i \leq t \leq n$;
- $\mathcal{S}$ is the set of all *authorized sets* defined by

$$\mathcal{S} = \{A \subseteq U | (\forall 1 \leq i \leq k)(|A \cap U_i| \geq t_i) \wedge (|A| \geq t)\}.$$

That is, an authorized set in such an access structure should include enough attributes from each compartment and should also be large enough (please see [32] for more details). The importance of CASs has been recognized by many researchers, as we have already mentioned in the first section of the paper.

CASs and Boolean Formulas. The ABE scheme in [16] is the most practically efficient scheme known so far when it comes to access structures defined Boolean formulas. Unfortunately, CASs cannot be described by Boolean formulas, as the following proposition shows.

Proposition 1 [9]. *Compartmented access structures cannot be defined by Boolean formulas.*

Proof. Assume that CASs can be represented by Boolean formulas (that is, by Boolean circuits of fan-out one). Consider then the following CAS:

- $\mathcal{U} = \{1, 2, 3, 4, 5\}$;
- $\mathcal{U}_1 = \{1, 2, 3\}, \mathcal{U}_2 = \{4, 5\}$;
- $t_1 = 1, t_2 = 1$, and $t = 3$.

Let $\mathcal{C}$ be a Boolean circuit of fan-out one that represents this CAS. This circuit has five input gates, namely the attributes 1, 2, 3, 4, and 5. We remark that at least two input gates must be directly connected. We have then the following cases:

1. There is a gate Γ that connects directly inputs only from the same compartment. Let us assume that Γ connects directly 1 and 2 and, moreover, Γ is evaluated to 1 whenever one of these two inputs is assigned to 1. Remark that $\{1, 4, 5\}$ and $\{2, 4, 5\}$ are authorized, but $\{1, 4\}, \{1, 5\}, \{2, 4\}$, and $\{2, 5\}$ are not. As the circuit is of fan-out one, the gates 1 and 2 cannot be connected to other logic gates. Therefore, the gates 4 and 5 must be connected to logic gates in such a way that the circuit is evaluated to one only if these two gates are simultaneously assigned to one. But then, $\mathcal{C}(1, 2, 4) = 0 = \mathcal{C}(1, 2, 5)$ because it does not matter that 1 or 2 or both evaluate Γ to 1 as long as these inputs are of fan-out one. Therefore, we have arrived at a contradiction;

2. There is a gate Γ that connects directly inputs only from the same compartment. Let us assume that Γ connects directly 1 and 2 and, moreover, Γ is evaluated to 1 whenever at least two of its inputs are assigned to 1. As $\mathcal{C}(1,4,5) = 1, \mathcal{C}(2,4,5) = 1$, and in both cases Γ is evaluated to 0, the fact that the circuit is of fan-out one leads to the conclusion that the evaluation of $\mathcal{C}$ to 1 does not depend on the value of Γ. But then we get $\mathcal{C}(4,5) = 1$, which is a contradiction;
3. The other cases, when Γ connects inputs only from the second compartment or when it connects inputs from both compartments, are treated in a similar way.

As in all possible cases we were led to a contradiction, we conclude that CASs cannot be represented by Boolean formulas.   □

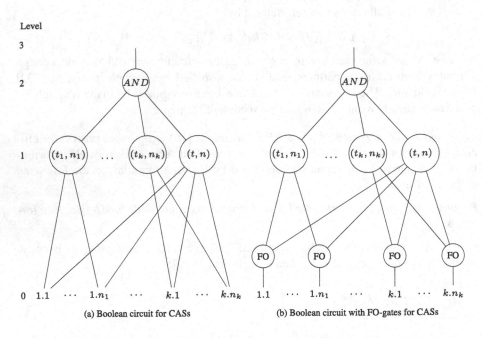

Fig. 1. Boolean circuit representation of compartmented access structure [9].

CASs can however be described by Boolean circuits of fan-out two. Before showing this let us adopt the following notation for CASs. If the set of attributes is $\mathcal{U} = \{1,\ldots,n\}$ and there are k compartments, then they will be denoted by $\mathcal{U}_i = \{i.1,\ldots,i.n_i\}$, for all $1 \le i \le k$. The attributes of the compartments are taken in order from 1 to n and, therefore, $i.j$ refers to the attribute $i.j = j+\sum_{\ell=1}^{i-1} n_\ell$, for all $1 \le i \le k$ and $1 \le j \le n_i$. The threshold for $\mathcal{U}_i$ is denoted by t_i, and the global threshold is t.

Given a CAS as above, it can be described by a Boolean circuit with input gates of fan-out two, as it is shown in Fig. 1(a). For the sake of readability, we have used a generalized AND-gate with more than two input wires; it can be regarded as the threshold $(k+1, k+1)$-gate.

Our Main Goal. Due to Proposition 1, the ABE scheme in [16] cannot be applied to CASs. The options we have then are the following:

1. Use the ABE scheme in [14] or even the more efficient one in [13]. Unfortunately, both are based on multi-linear maps and the recent results show clearly that no candidate multi-linear map proposed so far is secure [1,8];
2. Use ABE schemes based on lattice cryptography, such as [4]. They are secure schemes but, unfortunately, they generate very large ciphertexts and keys;
3. Use the ABE scheme in [10]. This is a solution based on secret sharing and just one bilinear map. Under this scheme, the sharing process produces multiple shares on the gates with fan-out greater than two. If such gates are chained, then the input gates may get too many shares, which means a large increase in the size of the decryption key. However, for certain access structures, the gates with fan-out greater than two are in a limited number and without overlapping. In such cases, the decryption key might have reasonable size and the scheme becomes, in terms of efficiency, comparable to that in [16].

In this paper we will show that the ABE scheme in [10] can efficiently be used for CASs. In this context, the scheme produces a decryption key of size $2n \log p$, together with a public key of the same size, where n is the number of attributes and p is a prime. Recall that the scheme in [16] produces a smaller decryption key of size $n \log p$, but it is limited to Boolean formulas.

Then, we will also show how to simplify the scheme above to one that does not need any public key. In this way, we probably get the most efficient ABE scheme for CASs, based on secret sharing and just one bilinear map.

3.2 Our Scheme for CASs

The aim of this section is to show that the ABE scheme in [10] can efficiently be used to accommodate CASs. Then, a more efficient ABE scheme will be derived.

Recall first the scheme in [10] adapted to CASs. The Boolean circuit for a CAS, as it is required in [10], looks like in Fig. 1(b). As one can see, the Boolean circuit uses FO-gates that simply multiply the output of the gates to which they are associated. These gates are just a technical ingredient used to help us better understand the secret sharing process.

The ABE scheme uses a secret sharing procedure $Share(y, C)$ that on a Boolean circuit C as above and a value $y \in \mathbb{Z}_p$, where p is a prime, shares y top-down on C. Even if the shares are associated only on (output) wires, the shares of the input gates' output wires will often be referred to as the shares of the input gates.

Procedure $Share(y, C)$ ($y \in \mathbb{Z}_p$, C Boolean circuit for CAS):

- Initially, y is assigned to the output wire of the circuit (the output wire of the AND-gate);
- Uniformly at random choose $y_1, \ldots, y_k \leftarrow \mathbb{Z}_p$, compute $y_{k+1} = y - (y_1 + \cdots + y_k) \bmod p$, and assign y_i to the i-th input wire of the AND-gate, for all $1 \leq i \leq k + 1$ (from left to right);

- Share y_1 at the (t_1, n_1)-gate as follows. If $t_1 = 1$, then y_1 is "copied" to all its input wires. Otherwise, choose uniformly at random $a_{1,1}, \ldots, a_{1,t_1-1} \leftarrow \mathbb{Z}_p$ and define the polynomial

$$f_1(x) = y_1 + a_{1,1}x + \cdots + a_{1,t_1-1}x^{t_1-1} \bmod p$$

Then, assign to the input wires of the gate the shares $f_1(1), \ldots, f_1(n_1)$ (in this order from left to right).

Share then $y_2, \ldots, y_k$ in the same way y_1 was shared. For y_{k+1} we choose uniformly at random $a_1, \ldots, a_{t-1} \leftarrow \mathbb{Z}_p$ and define the polynomial

$$f_{k+1}(x) = y_{k+1} + a_1 x + \cdots + a_{t-1}x^{t-1} \bmod p$$

Then, assign to the input wires of the gate the shares $f_{k+1}(i.j)$ in lexicographic order on i and j (please remark that y_{k+1} has to be shared at the (t, n)-gate which has n input wires);
- The FO-gate that splits the output of the input gate $i.j$ ($1 \le i \le k, 1 \le j \le n_i$) gets two shares: $f_i(j)$ and $f_{k+1}(i.j)$. Each of them is shared down as follows. Uniformly at random choose $a_{i,j}^1, a_{i,j}^2 \leftarrow \mathbb{Z}_p$ and compute $b_{i,j}^1 = f_i(j) - a_{i,j}^1 \bmod p$, $b_{i,j}^2 = f_{k+1}(i.j) - a_{i,j}^2 \bmod p$, $g^{b_{i,j}^1}$, and $g^{b_{i,j}^2}$. The values $a_{i,j}^1$ and $a_{i,j}^2$ are passed down to the input gate $i.j$ as shares, while $g^{b_{i,j}^1}$ and $g^{b_{i,j}^2}$ are public keys associated to the FO-gate.

At the end of the sharing procedure, each input gate $i.j$ gets two shares denoted $S(i.j, 1)$ and $S(i.j, 2)$, while its associated FO-gate is assigned two public values denoted $P(i.j, 1)$ and $P(i.j, 2)$ (please see Fig. 2).

Now, the ABE scheme can be described as follows (we will name it SSBM_1 as an acronym for *secret sharing and bilinear map based ABE scheme*).

SSBM_1 ABE Scheme [9]

Setup(λ, n): the setup algorithm uses the security parameter λ to choose a prime p, two multiplicative groups G_1 and G_2 of prime order p, a generator g of G_1, and a bilinear map $e : G_1 \times G_1 \to G_2$. Then, it chooses $y \in \mathbb{Z}_p$ and, for each attribute $i.j$, chooses $r_{i,j} \leftarrow \mathbb{Z}_p$ (please see the notation above). Finally, the algorithm outputs the public parameters

$$PP = (p, G_1, G_2, g, e, n, Y = e(g,g)^y, (T_{i,j} = g^{r_{i,j}} | i, j))$$

and the master key $MSK = (y, r_{i,j} \mid i, j)$;

Encrypt(m, A, PP): the encryption algorithm encrypts a message $m \in G_2$ by a non-empty set A of attributes as follows:
- $s \leftarrow \mathbb{Z}_p$;
- output $E = (A, E' = mY^s, (E_{i,j} = T_{i,j}^s = g^{r_{i,j}s} | i.j \in A), g^s)$;

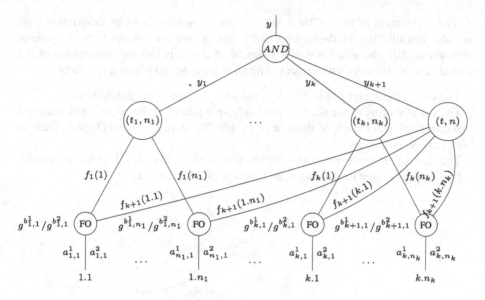

Fig. 2. Sharing procedure [9].

$KeyGen(\mathcal{C}, MSK)$: the decryption key generation algorithm generates a decryption key (D, P) for the CAS defined by the Boolean circuit $\mathcal{C}$ as follows:
- $(S, P) \leftarrow Share(y, \mathcal{C})$ (please see the notation above);
- output (D, P), where $D(i.j, \ell) = g^{S(i.j,\ell)/r_{i,j}}$ for all $1 \leq i \leq k$, $1 \leq j \leq n_i$, and $\ell = 1, 2$;

$Decrypt(E, (D, P))$: given E and (D, P) as above, the decryption works as follows:
- Compute $V_A(i.j, \ell)$ for all attributes $i.j$ and $\ell = 1, 2$ by

$$V_A(i.j, \ell) = \begin{cases} e(g, g)^{S(i.j,\ell)s}, & \text{if } i.j \in A \\ \perp, & \text{otherwise} \end{cases}$$

where $e(g, g)^{S(i.j,\ell)s} = e(g^{r_{i,j}s}, g^{S(i.j,\ell)/r_{i,j}})$ and $\perp$ means "undefined";
- For each attribute $i.j$ use the public key $P(i.j, 1)$ to compute $F_A(i.j, 1) = e(g, g)^{f_i(j)s}$ by

$$F(i.j, 1) = V_A(i.j, 1) \cdot e(P(i.j, 1), g^s).$$

In a similar way, $F_A(i.j, 2) = e(g, g)^{f_{k+1}(i.j)s}$ is computed by means of $P(i.j, 2)$. Remark that $F_A(i.j, \ell) = \perp$, whenever $i.j \notin A$;
- If the (t_1, n_1)-gate is satisfied (i.e., at least t_1 attributes from the first compartment are in A), then use the Lagrange interpolation formula to derive $e(g, g)^{y_1 s}$ from the corresponding attributes' F_A-values (as computed before). If the gate is not satisfied, then the value will be $\perp$. Do the same for all gates on the first level;
- If the values for the gates on the first level are all different than $\perp$, then multiply them and get $O = e(g, g)^{ys}$ as the value of the output wire of the AND-gate. Otherwise, $O = \perp$;
- $m := E'/O$.

The correctness of the SSBM_1 scheme simply follows from its description (one may also consult [10] for the general case), and its security follows from the general approach in [10] (the scheme we have described above is just an instantiation of the general case in [10]). As with respect to its efficiency, we list below a few facts:

1. The size of the secret key is $2n \log p$, and so is the size of the public key;
2. The secret sharing phase needs to randomly split y in $k+1$ shares, to apply Shamir's secret sharing for each of them, and to split $2k$ secrets at the FO-gates, each in exactly two shares;
3. The decryption phase needs $4n$ computations of the map e, $k + 1$ secret reconstruction by polynomial interpolation, and $2n + k$ multiplications.

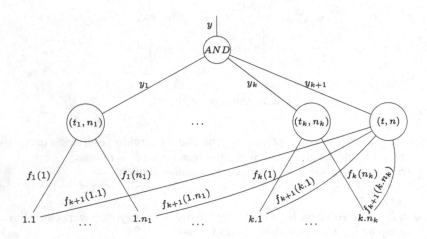

Fig. 3. Simplified secret sharing procedure [9].

Even if the SSBM_1 scheme is quite efficient for CASs, we may still improve its efficiency. The fundamental observation is that the FO-gates only duplicate the outputs of the input gates. As a result, it is no longer necessary for the shares coming to them from top to bottom be once again shared (this statement will be rigorously argued a little bit later). Therefore, the secret sharing scheme can be simplified as it is illustrated in Fig. 3. That is, the FO-gates are removed and the shares from the (t_i, n_i)-gate and from the (t, n)-gate come directly to the attribute $i.j$. In this way, the public keys are completely removed and each attribute $i.j$ gets the shares $S(i.j, 1) = f_i(j)$ and $S(i.j, 2) = f_{k+1}(i.j)$. We denote this new secret sharing procedure by $Share'(y, \mathcal{C})$.

Thus, we arrive at the following ABE scheme.

SSBM_2 ABE Scheme [9]

$Setup(\lambda, n)$: the same as in SSBM_1 scheme;
$Encrypt(m, A, PP)$: the same as in SSBM_1 scheme;
$KeyGen(\mathcal{C}, MSK)$: the decryption key generation algorithm generates a decryption key D for the CAS defined by the Boolean circuit $\mathcal{C}$ as follows:

- $S \leftarrow Share'(y, C)$ (please see the notation above);
- output D, where $D(i.j, \ell) = g^{S(i.j,\ell)/r_{i,j}}$ for all $1 \leq i \leq k$, $1 \leq j \leq n_i$, and $\ell = 1, 2$;

$Decrypt(E, D)$: given E and D as above, the decryption works as follows:
- Compute $F_A(i.j, \ell)$ for all attributes $i.j$ and $\ell = 1, 2$ by

$$F_A(i.j, \ell) = \begin{cases} e(g, g)^{S(i.j,\ell)s}, & \text{if } i.j \in A \\ \perp, & \text{otherwise} \end{cases}$$

where $e(g, g)^{S(i.j,\ell)s} = e(g^{r_{i,j}s}, g^{S(i.j,\ell)/r_{i,j}})$ and $\perp$ means "undefined";
- If the (t_1, n_1)-gate is satisfied (i.e., at least t_1 attributes from the first compartment are in A), then use the Lagrange interpolation formula to derive $e(g, g)^{y_1 s}$ from the corresponding attributes' F_A-values (as computed before). If the gate is not satisfied, then the value will be $\perp$. Do the same for all gates on the first level;
- If the values for the gates on the first level are all different than $\perp$, then multiply them and get $O = e(g, g)^{ys}$ as the value of the output wire of the AND-gate. Otherwise, $O = \perp$;
- $m := E'/O$.

It is straightforward to prove the correctness of this new scheme. Just remark that the recovering procedure produces the same result at the threshold gates on the first level as in the case of the SSBM_1 scheme.

The security of the SSBM_2 scheme is settled by the following theorem, whose proof will be derived as a special case from a more general result in Sect. 4 (one may also consult [9] for a direct proof).

Theorem 1. *The SSBM_2 ABE scheme is secure in the selective model under the decisional bilinear Diffie-Hellman assumption.*

3.3 Variations on the Same Theme: The Case of MASs

Multilevel Access Structures are another example of access structures that cannot be described by Boolean formulas. This was shown in [10], where the most efficient ABE scheme (at that time) for such access structures was proposed. However, the SSBM_2 scheme can also be adapted for multilevel access structures, leading to an even more efficient solution than the one in [10]. But, let us first recall the multilevel access structures.

A *disjunctive multilevel access structure* (DMAS) [28] over a set $\mathcal{U} = \{1, \ldots, n\}$ of attributes is a tuple $(\bar{t}, \bar{\mathcal{U}}, \mathcal{S})$, where $\bar{t} = (t_1, \ldots, t_k)$ is a vector of positive integers satisfying $0 < t_1 < \cdots < t_k$, $\bar{\mathcal{U}} = (\mathcal{U}_1, \ldots, \mathcal{U}_k)$ is a partition of $\mathcal{U}$ ($\mathcal{U}_i$ is the i-th level of $\mathcal{U}$), and $\mathcal{S}$ is defined by:

$$\mathcal{S} = \{A \subseteq \mathcal{U} | (\exists 1 \leq i \leq k)(|A \cap (\cup_{j=1}^{i} \mathcal{U}_j)| \geq t_i)\}.$$

If we replace "∃" by "∀" in the above definition, we obtain the concept of *conjunctive multilevel access structure* (CMAS) [30].

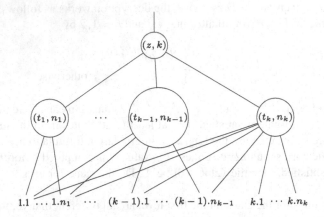

Fig. 4. Boolean circuit representation of multilevel access structure: $z = 1$ for the disjunctive case, and $z = k$ for the conjunctive case [9].

If we adopt the same notations for attributes and we do the same simplifications as in the case of CASs, then the Boolean circuit used in [10] to represent multilevel access structures looks like the one in Fig. 4, to which we can apply $Share'$. In this case, the attribute $i.j$ will get $k - i + 1$ shares denoted $S(i.j, \ell)$, with $1 \leq \ell \leq k - i + 1$ (remark that the number of shares only depends on the level i). The ABE scheme SSBM_2 can be applied in this case too, with the only difference that ℓ takes values as above. Remark also that for DMASs, $z = 1$ means that the (z, k)-gate is a generalized OR-gate and, therefore, the secret y is "copied" on all its input wires. When $z = k$, the (z, k)-gate is a generalized AND-gate as in the case of CASs.

The decryption key size produced by the ABE scheme SSBM_2 for multilevel access structures is

$$k \cdot n_1 + (k - 1) \cdot n_2 + \cdots + n_k \cdot 1$$

which gives on average $n(k + 1)/2$ (just take all levels of the same size). The approach in [10] generates a public key too of the same size. Therefore, we get a substantial improvement over the approach in [10] which, besides the one proposed in this paper, was the most efficient one (please see [10] for details).

4   Extension to Multiple-Input Boolean Trees

The Boolean circuits in Figs. 3 and 4 have the property that their input gates are the only gates of fan-out greater than one. Such Boolean circuits will generally be called *multiple-input Boolean trees*. The terminology comes from the fact that several logic gates in the circuit can use the same input gate; otherwise, it is like a tree. It is natural then to ask whether the SSBM_2 scheme in Sect. 3 can be generalized to such Boolean circuits. The answer is positive, as will be seen below.

Given a multiple-input Boolean tree $\mathcal{C}$ with n input gates, we will denote by (i, j) the jth output wire of the input gate i, where $1 \leq j \leq k_i$ and k_i is the fan-out of the gate i (without loss of generality, we may assume that the output wires of each input gate are totally ordered). We emphasize again that all logic gates of a multiple-input Boolean trees have exactly one output wire.

The first step we need to take to generalize the SSBM_2 scheme to multiple-input Boolean trees is to analyze how the sharing procedure on such circuits changes. In fact, we are dealing with the same sharing procedure $Share'(y, \mathcal{C})$. For clarity, we resume it below.

Procedure $Share'(y, \mathcal{C})$ ($y \in \mathbb{Z}_p$, $\mathcal{C}$ multiple-input Boolean tree):

– Initially, y is assigned to the output wire of the circuit to be shared top-down along $\mathcal{C}$;
– If z is to be shared at a (u, v)-gate, we do as follows:
  • If $u = 1$, then z is "copied" to all gate's input wires;
  • If $u > 1$, choose uniformly at random $a_1, \ldots, a_{u-1} \leftarrow \mathbb{Z}_p$ and define the polynomial

$$f(x) = z + a_1 x + \cdots + a_{u-1} x^{u-1} \bmod p$$

Then, assign to the input wires of the gate the shares $f(1), \ldots, f(v)$ (in this order from left to right).

At the end of the sharing procedure, each input gate i gets k_i shares on its output wires. Let us denote this shares by $S(i, j)$, for all i and j.

Now, we are able to describe our general KP-ABE scheme.

SSBM ABE Scheme

$Setup(\lambda, n)$: the setup algorithm uses the security parameter λ to choose a prime p, two multiplicative groups G_1 and G_2 of prime order p, a generator g of G_1, and a bilinear map $e : G_1 \times G_1 \rightarrow G_2$. Then, it chooses $y \in \mathbb{Z}_p$ and, for each attribute i and output wire $1 \leq j \leq k_i$, chooses $r_{i,j} \leftarrow \mathbb{Z}_p$, (please see the notation above). Finally, the algorithm outputs the public parameters

$$PP = (p, G_1, G_2, g, e, n, Y = e(g, g)^y, (T_{i,j} = g^{r_{i,j}} | i \in \mathcal{U}, 1 \leq j \leq k_i))$$

and the master key $MSK = (y, (r_{i,j} \mid i \in \mathcal{U}, 1 \leq j \leq k_i))$;

$Encrypt(m, A, PP)$: the encryption algorithm encrypts a message $m \in G_2$ by a non-empty set A of attributes as follows:
  – $s \leftarrow \mathbb{Z}_p$;
  – output $E = (A, E' = mY^s, (E_{i,j} = T_{i,j}^s = g^{r_{i,j}s} | i \in A, 1 \leq j \leq k_i), g^s)$;

$KeyGen(\mathcal{C}, MSK)$: the decryption key generation algorithm generates a decryption key D for the multiple-input Boolean circuit $\mathcal{C}$ as follows:
  – $S \leftarrow Share'(y, \mathcal{C})$ (please see the notation above);
  – output D, where $D(i.j) = g^{S(i.j)/r_{i,j}}$ for all $1 \leq i \leq n$ and $1 \leq j \leq k_i$;

$Decrypt(E, D)$: given E and D as above, the decryption works as follows:

– Compute $F_A(i,j)$ for each input gate i and output wire j of i by

$$F_A(i,j) = \begin{cases} e(g,g)^{S(i,j)s}, & \text{if } i \in A \\ \bot, & \text{otherwise} \end{cases}$$

where $e(g,g)^{S(i,j)s} = e(g^{r_{i,j}s}, g^{S(i,j)/r_{i,j}})$ and $\bot$ means "undefined";
– Propagate the F_A values from bottom to top as follows. For each (u,v)-gate with at least u input wires that satisfy the gate and for which the F_A values were already computed (and different than $\bot$), use the Lagrange interpolation formula to derive $e(g,g)^{zs}$ from the corresponding input wires, where z is the share associated to the gate's output wire. The F_A value such computed is associated with the output wire of the gate;
– $m := E'/O$, where O is the F_A value associated with the output wire of the circuit $\mathcal{C}$.

It is straightforward to prove the correctness of this new scheme. Then remark that the schemes for CASs and MASs from the previous section are special cases of this scheme.

The security of the SSBM scheme is settled by the following theorem.

Theorem 2. *The SSBM KP-ABE scheme is secure in the selective model under the decisional bilinear Diffie-Hellman assumption.*

Proof. Let $\mathcal{A}$ be an adversary against the SSBM scheme. We show that we can define an adversary $\mathcal{B}$ against the DBDH problem so that $\mathcal{B}$ has non-negligible advantage if $\mathcal{A}$ has. This will prove the security of the SSBM scheme under the decisional bilinear Diffie-Hellman assumption.

The adversary $\mathcal{B}$ we define plays the role of challenger for $\mathcal{A}$ in the selective game with the SSBM scheme. More precisely, consider a DBDH instance that is given to $\mathcal{B}$: two groups G_1 and G_2 of prime order p, a generator g of G_1, a bilinear map $e : G_1 \times G_1 \to G_2$, the values g^a, g^b, g^c, and $Z_v \leftarrow \{Z_0, Z_1\}$, where $Z_0 = e(g,g)^{abc}$, $Z_1 = e(g,g)^z$, and $a, b, c, z \leftarrow \mathbb{Z}_p$. $\mathcal{B}$ has to distinguish between Z_0 and Z_1. Its idea is to setup the SSBM scheme for $\mathcal{A}$ so that the challenge encryption for $\mathcal{A}$ looks like done with $y = ab$ and $s = c$, although $\mathcal{B}$ does not know ab and c (that is, the message is encrypted by $e(g,g)^{abc}$). If $\mathcal{A}$ quesses correctly in the challenge phase, then $\mathcal{B}$ concludes that $B_v = Z_0$.

Let us show how $\mathcal{B}$ plays the role of challenger for $\mathcal{A}$.

$\mathcal{B}$ *Prepares the init Phase for $\mathcal{A}$:* $\mathcal{B}$ asks $\mathcal{A}$ to choose a non-empty set A of attributes on which $\mathcal{A}$ wishes to be challenged upon ($\mathcal{B}$ will know this set A).

$\mathcal{B}$ *sets up the SSBM scheme:* $\mathcal{B}$ chooses at random $r_{i,j} \in \mathbb{Z}_p$ for all $i \in \mathcal{U}$ and $1 \leq j \leq k_i$ and computes $Y = e(g^a, g^b) = e(g,g)^{ab}$ and $T_{i,j}$ for all $i \in \mathcal{U}$ and $1 \leq j \leq k_i$, where

$$T_{i,j} = \begin{cases} g^{r_{i,j}}, & \text{if } i \in A \text{ and } 1 \leq j \leq k_i \\ (g^b)^{r_{i,j}} = g^{br_{i,j}}, & \text{otherwise.} \end{cases}$$

Then, $\mathcal{B}$ publishes the public parameters

$$PP = (p, G_1, G_2, g, e, n, Y, (T_{i,j} | i \in \mathcal{U}, 1 \leq j \leq k_i)).$$

$\mathcal{B}$ *delivers decryption key to* $\mathcal{A}$: Assume that $\mathcal{B}$ has to deliver a decryption key to $\mathcal{A}$ for a multiple-input Boolean tree $\mathcal{C}$ with $\mathcal{C}(A) = 0$.

Recall that, in the SSBM scheme, the integer $y = ab$ should be shared on $\mathcal{C}$ in order to compute the decryption key. $\mathcal{B}$ does not know $y = ab$ or g^{ab} (if $\mathcal{B}$ knew g^{ab} it could share ab at the exponent). However, it will improvise a sharing scheme, called $FakeShare$, that will finally generate a valid result to $\mathcal{A}$.

For the sake of clarity we will describe this procedure for the case of OR- and AND-gates (the extension to general (u, v)-gates is straightforward).

Let us first introduce some helpful notations. To distinguish between wires, assume that they are labeled. Among these labels, o stands for the output wire of the circuit and (i, j) stands for the jth wire of the input gate i, where $i \in \mathcal{U}$ and $1 \le j \le k_i$. If w is a wire, $S(w)$ stands for the share (if any) associated with w in the sharing process, and $\mathcal{C}_w(A)$ stands for the Boolean value that w gets when $\mathcal{C}(A)$ is computed. Given $X \in \{OR, AND\}$, denote by (w_1, w_2, X, w) the X-gate with the input wires w_1 and w_2 and output wire w.

The $FakeShare$ procedure is based on the following ideas:

1. If $\mathcal{C}_w(A) = 0$, then $S(w)$ is of the form g^x, for some $x \in \mathbb{Z}_p$; otherwise, it is an element from $\mathbb{Z}_p$;
2. Initially, the value g^a is to be shared at the output wire o of the circuit;
3. The value b will be added to the exponent after the sharing phase by means of g^b for shares in $\mathbb{Z}_p$, and by means of the shares in the other case (details are provided after the $FakeShare$ procedure).

Now, we are ready to describe the $FakeShare$ procedure.

$FakeShare(g^a, \mathcal{C}, A)$

1. Initially, all gates of $\mathcal{C}$ are unmarked;
2. $S(o) := g^a$;
3. If $\Gamma = (w_1, w_2, OR, w)$ is an unmarked OR-gate and $S(w) = x$, then mark Γ and do the followings:
   (a) if $\mathcal{C}_w(A) = \mathcal{C}_{w_1}(A) = \mathcal{C}_{w_2}(A)$, then $S(w_1) := S(w)$ and $S(w_2) := S(w)$;
   (b) if $\mathcal{C}_w(A) = 1 = \mathcal{C}_{w_1}(A)$ and $\mathcal{C}_{w_2}(A) = 0$, then $S(w_1) := S(w)$ and $S(w_2) := g^{S(w)}$;
   (c) if $\mathcal{C}_w(A) = 1 = \mathcal{C}_{w_2}(A)$ and $\mathcal{C}_{w_1}(A) = 0$, then $S(w_2) := S(w)$ and $S(w_1) := g^{S(w)}$.
   Remark that $S(w) \in \mathbb{Z}_p$ in the last two cases (b) and (c);
4. If $\Gamma = (w_1, w_2, AND, w)$ is an unmarked AND-gate, then mark Γ and do the followings:
   (a) if $\mathcal{C}_w(A) = 1$, then choose x uniformly at random from $\mathbb{Z}_p$ and assign $S(w_1) := x$ and $S(w_2) := S(w) - x \bmod p$;
   (b) if $\mathcal{C}_{w_1}(A) = 1$ and $\mathcal{C}_w(A) = 0 = \mathcal{C}_{w_2}(A)$ then choose x uniformly at random from $\mathbb{Z}_p$ and assign $S(w_1) := x$ and $S(w_2) = S(w)/g^x$;
   (c) if $\mathcal{C}_{w_2}(A) = 1$ and $\mathcal{C}_w(A) = 0 = \mathcal{C}_{w_1}(A)$ then do as above by swapping w_1 and w_2 between them;
   (d) if $\mathcal{C}_w(A) = \mathcal{C}_{w_1}(A) = \mathcal{C}_{w_2}(A) = 0$ then choose x uniformly at random from $\mathbb{Z}_p$ and assign $S(w_1) = g^x$ and $S(w_2) = S(w)/g^x$.

Remark that $S(w) \in \mathbb{Z}_p$ in the first case (a);

5. repeat the last two steps above until all gates get marked.

The algorithm $\mathcal{B}$ will deliver to the adversary $\mathcal{A}$ the decryption key $D = (D(i,j)|i \in \mathcal{U}, 1 \leq j \leq k_i)$, where

$$D(i,j) = \begin{cases} (g^b)^{S(i,j)/r_{i,j}}, & \text{if } i \in A \text{ and } 1 \leq j \leq k_i \\ S(i,j)^{1/r_{i,j}}, & \text{if } i \notin A \text{ and } 1 \leq j \leq k_i. \end{cases}$$

One has to remark the correspondence between the public parameter $T_{i,j}$ and the key component $D(i,j)$. More precisely, for $i \in A$ and $1 \leq j \leq k_i$ the key component is of the form

$$D(i,j) = g^{bS(i,j)/r_{i,j}}$$

while for $i \notin A$ and $1 \leq j \leq k_i$ it is of the form

$$D(i,j) = g^{y_{i,j}/r_{i,j}} = g^{by_{i,j}/br_{i,j}}$$

for some $y_{i,j} \in \mathbb{Z}_p$ because the shares that come to i are all powers of g.

Let us argue now that the distribution of this decryption key is identical to that in the original scheme. It is sufficient to show that to share the exponent $ab \bmod p$, we only need to share a. Moreover, based on the recursive procedure, it is sufficient to show this on a single AND-gate.

Clearly, any sharing $a \equiv_p x_1 + x_2$ of a gives rise to a sharing $ab \equiv_p x_1 b + x_2 b$ of $ab \bmod b$. If $ab \equiv_p y_1 + y_2$ is a sharing of $ab \bmod p$, the congruences $x_1 b \equiv_p y_1$ and $x_2 b \equiv_p y_2$ have unique solutions (in $\mathbb{Z}_p$) in the unknowns x_1 and x_2, respectively. Therefore, the sharing $ab \equiv_p y_1 + y_2$ is equivalent to a sharing of the form $ab \equiv_p x_1 b + x_2 b$. Moreover, it is straightforward to see that $a \equiv_b x_1 + x_2$.

$\mathcal{B}$ Answers to $\mathcal{A}$'s Challenge: The adversary $\mathcal{A}$ selects two messages m_0 and m_1 (of the same length) and sends them to $\mathcal{B}$. The adversary $\mathcal{B}$ encrypts m_u with Z_v, where $u \leftarrow \{0,1\}$, and sends it back to $\mathcal{B}$. The ciphertext is

$$E = (A, E' = m_u Z_v, (E_{i,j} = T_{i,j}^s = g^{r_{i,j}s} | i \in A, 1 \leq j \leq k_i), g^c)$$

If $v = 0$, E is a valid encryption of m_u (remark that $\mathcal{B}$ uses g^c as if it knew $s = c$); if $v = 1$, E' is a random element from G_2.

$\mathcal{B}$ Answers to $\mathcal{A}$'s Queries: $\mathcal{B}$ may answer to more queries submitted by $\mathcal{A}$ for decryption keys for multiple-input Boolean trees $\mathcal{C}$ with $\mathcal{C}(A) = 0$.

$\mathcal{B}$'s Decision: Let u' be $\mathcal{A}$'s guess. If $u' = u$, then $\mathcal{B}$ outputs $v' = 0$; otherwise, it outputs $v' = 1$.

We compute now the advantage of $\mathcal{B}$. Clearly,

$$P(v' = v) - \frac{1}{2} = P(v' = v|v = 0) \cdot P(v = 0) + P(v' = v|v = 1) \cdot P(v = 1) - \frac{1}{2}$$

Both $P(v = 0)$ and $P(v = 1)$ are 1/2. Then, remark that

$$P(v' = v|v = 0) = P(u' = u|v = 0) = \frac{1}{2} + \eta$$

and $P(v' = v|v = 1) = P(u' \neq u|v = 1) = \frac{1}{2}$, where η is $\mathcal{A}$'s advantage on the scheme.

Putting all together we obtain that the advantage of $\mathcal{B}$ is $\eta/2$. Therefore, if $\mathcal{A}$ has a non-negligible advantage against the SSBM scheme then $\mathcal{B}$ will have against the DBDH problem, contradictions the assumption in the theorem. $\square$

The SSBM scheme can also be applied to a Boolean circuit with larger fan-out logic gates than one if we previously transform this circuit into a multiple-input Boolean tree. In essence, the transformation is simple and consists of duplicating sub-trees that have as root fan-out logic gates larger than one but without multiplying the attributes, as Fig. 5 suggests.

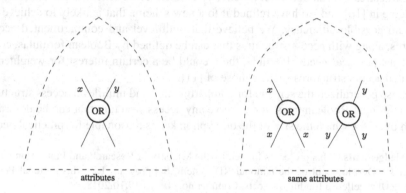

Fig. 5. Duplicating gates of fan-out greater than one [9].

As one can see, the sub-circuit with the OR-gate as root (in the left hand side picture) must be duplicated. Clearly, this can lead to a very large increase of the final circuit compared to the original one (just think that the duplicated sub-circuits contain other gates with fan-out greater than one, which means that the duplicating process must be repeated). However, the advantage is that the result will be a multiple-input Boolean tree. If the number of output gate wires is not too large, then the SSBM ABE scheme can be used.

Recall that the KP-ABE scheme in [10] can also be applied to Boolean circuits. It uses FO-gates and keeps the Boolean circuit of the same size.

5   Implementation

At https://github.com/Juve45/abe-cas one can find an implementation of our SSBM_2 ABE scheme. The programs are written in C for better portability. For bilinear map support we have used the PBC library [25] and also the GMP library for multi-precision arithmetic. Thus, our system should run in any operating system that supports GMP and PBC. The implementation was tested în Linux (Linux 4.9, Debian 9.12) and Windows 10.

6   Conclusions

Building access control policies based on compartments plays an important role in today's technologies, such as IoT and WSN with cloud support. In addition, the need to work with encrypted data in the cloud requires that such access policies be integrated with encryption techniques. Attribute-based Encryption (ABE) is an encryption technique that integrates access control policies defined in the most general way, namely, through Boolean circuits. However, ABE schemes developed to date are practically efficient only for Boolean formulas, while compartmented and multilevel access structures cannot be expressed by Boolean formulas.

In this paper we have shown that for the case of compartmented and multilevel access structures we can construct practically efficient ABE schemes. We started from the scheme in [10] and we have refined it to a new scheme that is likely to achieve the maximum possible efficiency. We believe that multilevel and compartmented access structures, along with access structures that can be defined by Boolean formulas, cover most of the practical needs. Possibly, there could be a certain interest for weighted or distributed access structures such as those of [11].

We also generalized the scheme for compartmented and multilevel access structures to multiple-input Boolean trees. It can serve any access structure that can be described by such trees, for which the size of the decryption key is reasonable for practical needs.

Acknowledgements. This project is funded by the Ministry of Research and Innovation within Program 1 – Development of the national RD system, Subprogram 1.2 – Institutional Performance – RDI excellence funding projects, Contract no.34PFE/ 19.10.2018.

References

1. Albrecht, M., Davidson, A.: Are graded encoding schemes broken yet? (2017). https://malb.io/are-graded-encoding-schemes-broken-yet.html
2. Barzu, M., Țiplea, F.L., Drăgan, C.C.: Compact sequences of co-primes and their applications to the security of CRT-based threshold schemes. Inf. Sci. **240**, 161–172 (2013)
3. Bellare, M., Hoang, V.T., Rogaway, P.: Foundations of garbled circuits. In: Proceedings of the 2012 ACM Conference on Computer and Communications Security, CCS 2012 pp. 784–796. ACM, New York (2012)
4. Boneh, D., Nikolaenko, V., Segev, G.: Attribute-based encryption for arithmetic circuits. IACR Cryptol. ePrint Arch. **2013**, 669 (2013). http://eprint.iacr.org/2013/669
5. Brenner, S., Goltzsche, D., Kapitza, R.: TrApps: secure compartments in the evil cloud. Association for Computing Machinery, New York (2017)
6. Chatterjee, S., Das, A.K.: An effective ECC-based user access control scheme with attribute-based encryption for wireless sensor networks. Secur. Commun. Netw. **8**(9), 1752–1771 (2015)
7. Țiplea, F.L., Drăgan, C.C.: A necessary and sufficient condition for the asymptotic idealness of the GRS threshold secret sharing scheme. Inf. Process. Lett. **114**(6), 299–303 (2014)
8. Țiplea, F.L.: Multi-linear maps in cryptography. In: Proceedings of 4th International Conference on Mathematical Foundations of Informatics, pp. 241–258, July 2018

9. Țiplea, F.L., Ioniță, A., Nica, A.M.: Practically efficient attribute-based encryption for compartmented access structures. In: Proceedings of the 17th International Joint Conference on e-Business and Telecommunications - Volume 3: SECRYPT, pp. 201–212. INSTICC, SciTePress (2020)

10. Țiplea, F.L., Drăgan, C.C.: Key-policy attribute-based encryption for Boolean circuits from bilinear maps. In: Ors, B., Preneel, B. (eds.) BalkanCryptSec 2014. LNCS, vol. 9024, pp. 175–193. Springer, Cham (2015). https://doi.org/10.1007/978-3-319-21356-9_12

11. Drăgan, C.C., Țiplea, F.L.: Distributive weighted threshold secret sharing schemes. Inf. Sci. **339**, 85–97 (2016)

12. Drăgan, C.C., Țiplea, F.L.: On the asymptotic idealness of the Asmuth-Bloom threshold secret sharing scheme. Inf. Sci. **463–464**, 75–85 (2018)

13. Drăgan, C.C., Țiplea, F.L.: Key-policy attribute-based encryption for general Boolean circuits from secret sharing and multi-linear maps. In: Pasalic, E., Knudsen, L.R. (eds.) BalkanCryptSec 2015. LNCS, vol. 9540, pp. 112–133. Springer, Cham (2016). https://doi.org/10.1007/978-3-319-29172-7_8

14. Garg, S., Gentry, C., Halevi, S., Sahai, A., Waters, B.: Attribute-based encryption for circuits from multilinear maps. In: Canetti, R., Garay, J.A. (eds.) CRYPTO 2013. LNCS, vol. 8043, pp. 479–499. Springer, Heidelberg (2013). https://doi.org/10.1007/978-3-642-40084-1_27

15. Ghodosi, H., Pieprzyk, J., Safavi-Naini, R.: Secret sharing in multilevel and compartmented groups. In: Boyd, C., Dawson, E. (eds.) ACISP 1998. LNCS, vol. 1438, pp. 367–378. Springer, Heidelberg (1998). https://doi.org/10.1007/BFb0053748

16. Goyal, V., Pandey, O., Sahai, A., Waters, B.: Attribute-based encryption for fine-grained access control of encrypted data. In: ACM Conference on Computer and Communications Security, pp. 89–98. ACM (2006)

17. Green, M., Hohenberger, S., Waters, B.: Outsourcing the decryption of ABE ciphertexts. In: Proceedings of the 20th USENIX Conference on Security, SEC 2011, p. 34. USENIX Association, USA (2011)

18. Hyla, T., Pejas, J., Fray, I.E., Macków, W., Chocianowicz, W., Szulga, M.: Sensitive information protection on mobile devices using general access structures. In: ICONS 2014 (2014)

19. Jakóbczyk, M.T.: Practical Oracle Cloud Infrastructure: Infrastructure as a Service, Autonomous Database, Managed Kubernetes, and Serverless, 1st edn. Apress, New York (2020)

20. Kaaniche, N., Laurent, M.: Attribute based encryption for multi-level access control policies. In: Proceedings of the 14th International Joint Conference on e-Business and Telecommunications - Volume 4: SECRYPT, (ICETE 2017), pp. 67–78. INSTICC, SciTePress (2017)

21. Kaaniche, N., Laurent, M.: SABE: a selective attribute-based encryption for an efficient threshold multi-level access control. In: Samarati, P., Obaidat, M.S. (eds.) Proceedings of the 15th International Joint Conference on e-Business and Telecommunications, ICETE 2018 - Volume 2: SECRYPT, Porto, Portugal, 26–28 July 2018, pp. 321–333. SciTePress (2018)

22. Li, J., Lin, X., Zhang, Y., Han, J.: KSF-OABE: outsourced attribute-based encryption with keyword search function for cloud storage. IEEE Trans. Serv. Comput. **10**(5), 715–725 (2016)

23. Li, Z., Huan, S.: Multi-level attribute-based encryption access control scheme for big data (2018)

24. Liao, Y., Zhang, G., Chen, H.: Cost-efficient outsourced decryption of attribute-based encryption schemes for both users and cloud server in green cloud computing. IEEE Access **8**, 20862–20869 (2020)

25. Lynn, B.: PBC library (2007). https://crypto.stanford.edu/pbc/

26. Pramanik, J., Roy, P.S., Dutta, S., Adhikari, A., Sakurai, K.: Secret sharing schemes on compartmental access structure in presence of cheaters. In: Ganapathy, V., Jaeger, T., Shyamasundar, R.K. (eds.) ICISS 2018. LNCS, vol. 11281, pp. 171–188. Springer, Cham (2018). https://doi.org/10.1007/978-3-030-05171-6_9

27. Qin, B., Deng, R.H., Liu, S., Ma, S.: Attribute-based encryption with efficient verifiable outsourced decryption. IEEE Trans. Inf. Forensics Secur. **10**(7), 1384–1393 (2015)

28. Simmons, G.J.: How to (really) share a secret. In: Goldwasser, S. (ed.) CRYPTO 1988. LNCS, vol. 403, pp. 390–448. Springer, New York (1990). https://doi.org/10.1007/0-387-34799-2_30

29. Stinson, D.: Cryptography: Theory and Practice, 3rd edn. Chapman and Hall/CRC, Boca Raton (2005)

30. Tassa, T.: Hierarchical threshold secret sharing. J. Cryptol. **20**(2), 237–264 (2007)

31. Tassa, T., Dyn, N.: Multipartite secret sharing by bivariate interpolation. J. Cryptol. **22**(2), 227–258 (2008)

32. Țiplea, F.L., Drăgan,C.C.: Asymptotically ideal CRT-based secret sharing schemes Cryptology ePrint Archive Report 2018/933, September 2018

33. Touati, L., Challal, Y.: Collaborative KP-ABE for cloud-based Internet of things applications. In: 2016 IEEE International Conference on Communications (ICC), pp. 1–7 (2016)

34. Wang, S., Guo, K., Zhang, Y.: Traceable ciphertext-policy attribute-based encryption scheme with attribute level user revocation for cloud storage. PLoS ONE **13**, e0203225 (2018)

35. Wang, S., Zhao, D., Zhang, Y.: Searchable attribute-based encryption scheme with attribute revocation in cloud storage. PLoS ONE **12**, e0183459 (2017)

36. Yu, J., Ren, K., Wang, C.: Enabling cloud storage auditing with verifiable outsourcing of key updates. IEEE Trans. Inf. Forensics Secur. **11**(6), 1362–1375 (2016)

37. Yu, S., Wang, C., Ren, K., Lou, W.: Achieving secure, scalable, and fine-grained data access control in cloud computing. In: 2010 Proceedings IEEE INFOCOM, pp. 1–9 (2010)

38. Yu, Y., Wang, M.: A probabilistic secret sharing scheme for a compartmented access structure. In: Qing, S., Susilo, W., Wang, G., Liu, D. (eds.) ICICS 2011. LNCS, vol. 7043, pp. 136–142. Springer, Heidelberg (2011). https://doi.org/10.1007/978-3-642-25243-3_11

Analysis of In-Place Randomized Bit-Flipping Decoders for the Design of LDPC and MDPC Code-Based Cryptosystems

Marco Baldi[1] , Alessandro Barenghi[2](✉) , Franco Chiaraluce[1] ,
Gerardo Pelosi[2] , and Paolo Santini[1]

[1] Università Politecnica delle Marche - DII, Via Brecce Bianche 12, Ancona, Italy
{m.baldi,f.chiaraluce,p.santini}@staff.univpm.it
[2] Politecnico di Milano - DEIB, Piazza Leonardo da Vinci 32, Milano, Italy
{alessandro.barenghi,gerardo.pelosi}@polimi.it

Abstract. We present a variant of the classic in-place bit-flipping decoder, frequently used with Low- and Moderate-Density Parity Check (LDPC/MDPC) codes, which allows a statistical analysis of the achievable decoding failure rate (DFR) in worst-case conditions. Such evaluation is of paramount importance in code-based post-quantum cryptography (PQC) where the ability to achieve indistinguishability under adaptive chosen ciphertext attacks strictly depends on being able to ensure very low DFR values (e.g., in the order of 2^{-128} or lower) that, as such, are practically impossible to validate via numerical simulation. We provide theoretical evidence of the proposed approach and demonstrate its correctness through numerical examples. Moreover, we investigate the effect of changing the bit flipping decision threshold on the provided worst case analysis. Finally, we give design parameters for code-based cryptosystems employing Quasi-Cyclic LDPC/MDPC codes, able to achieve the security levels required in the NIST PQC standardization initiative which is currently in progress.

Keywords: Bit-flipping decoding · Code-based cryptosystems · Decoding failure rate · LDPC codes · MDPC codes · Quasi-cyclic codes · Post-quantum cryptosystems

1 Introduction

Among the various options proposed for a new generation of asymmetric cryptosystems, able to counter the advent of quantum computers, a prominent role is played by code-based cryptosystems. McEliece [21] was the first to prove the computational hardness of decoding error affected codewords from random linear codes, in particular showing that determining the existence of such an error vector belongs to the NP-Complete class [20]. The original McEliece cryptosystem builds a trapdoor from an obfuscation of the generator matrix of a Goppa code, an algebraic code, and encodes the messages into codewords of the obfuscated code, subsequently adding a number of errors which are guaranteed to be correctable by the secret Goppa code. In a variant proposed by Niederreiter some years later [23], the generator matrix is replaced by the parity-check matrix and

© Springer Nature Switzerland AG 2021
M. S. Obaidat and J. Ben-Othman (Eds.): ICETE 2020, CCIS 1484, pp. 151–174, 2021.
https://doi.org/10.1007/978-3-030-90428-9_7

the message is encoded into syndrome vectors, thus achieving a significant reduction in the number of operations for encryption, at the cost of a moderate increase in the number of operations for decryption. After 40 years from its introduction, the original McEliece cryptosystem is still unbroken and, while requiring a scaling of its parameters [1], from its original proposal, it retains its security against quantum computing adversaries. However, cryptosystems adopting Goppa codes have some drawbacks. The most important one is the large size of the public key, in the order of hundreds of kilobytes to a megabyte range depending on the target security level. Wishing to reduce the key size, a valid alternative to Goppa codes is constituted by the adoption of Quasi-Cyclic (QC) codes. These codes are characterized by generator and parity-check matrices that are quasi-cyclic, i.e., composed by circulant square blocks, where all rows are obtained cyclically rotating the first one. Therefore, it is sufficient to store only the first row of such matrices to preserve their whole representation. The adoption of QC codes with an underlying algebraic structure is the most convenient choice from an efficiency viewpoint; nonetheless, it exposes the system to cryptanalytic attacks [15]. Such vulnerabilities disappear when using random or pseudo-random codes (i.e., without any underlying algebraic structure); indeed, the use of Quasi-Cyclic Low-Density Parity-Check (QC-LDPC) codes [8] or Quasi-Cyclic Moderate-Density Parity-Check (QC-MDPC) codes [22] allows to provide proper security guarantees from a mathematical and cryptanalytical perspective as well as satisfactory key sizes from an engineering standpoint. Currently, these kinds of codes are employed in the design of both the LEDAcrypt [7,9,10] and the BIKE [2] cryptosystem, which were also evaluated in the framework of the initiative promoted by the U.S.A. National Institute of Standards and Technology (NIST) for the standardization of post-quantum cryptosystems [24].

LDPC and MDPC codes are usually decoded through iterative algorithms which, in contrast with the bounded distance decoders typically used with algebraic codes, are not characterized by a deterministic decoding radius. As a consequence, there is a need to estimate the Decoding Failure Rate (DFR) performance of these codes through numerical simulations. This is not an issue whenever relatively large failure rates are satisfactory, as occurs, for example, in wireless communications, but it becomes an issue in those applications which require extremely low failure rates, as it is the case of code-based cryptographic applications.

In code-based cryptography, a non-null DFR implies that a decryption action may fail even on a valid ciphertext and this exposes the cryptosystem to Chosen Ciphertext Attacks (CCAs) such as those documented in [14,17,29], which exploit the availability of a decryption oracle (queried with ciphertexts properly built employing the public key) to derive information on the secret structure of the underlying QC-LDPC/QC-MDPC code. The only way to avoid these kinds of attacks, thus attaining Indistinguishability under Adaptively Chosen Ciphertext Attack is to apply state-of-the-art constructions such as the ones introduced in [11,19], which in turn require the failure rate of the underlying code to be negligible in the security parameter. As a consequence, it can be shown that a cryptosystem with security parameter λ requires a DFR $\leq 2^{-\lambda}$, with $\lambda \geq 128$. Such values are clearly impossible to simulate, even with the most powerful computer (or cluster of computers). This makes extremely important to assess models which allow to estimate the behavior of decoders for QC-LDPC and QC-MDPC codes, even though in conservative conditions. In this paper, we tackle such topic, focusing on the Bit-Flipping (BF) decoding technique [16] which is commonly used in this application as it offers an excellent trade-off between error correction capability and computational complexity.

In short, a BF algorithm performs syndrome decoding through an iterative procedure, in which the bit locations where the received message is erroneous are estimated starting from the value of the received syndrome. More precisely, the decoder starts from an estimate of the error vector with all bits set to zero and applies a sequence of *iteration functions*, each of which evaluates whether or not to flip (i.e., change) the j-th bit of the estimated error vector. The flipping action is made depending on the result of a check on whether the number of unsatisfied parity-check equations involving the estimated error vector bit exceeds a predefined threshold. If a flip is performed, the value of the syndrome is updated to reflect the change in the estimate. The decoder stops when the updated syndrome value is equal to zero (indicating a decoding success), or a predefined maximum number of iterations is reached.

Depending on the strategy employed by the iteration function to update the syndrome, BF decoders are classified in two main groups: in-place algorithms and out-of-place algorithms. The distinguishing point between an in-place and an out-of-place iteration function lies on when the update of the syndrome value is executed. In the in-place iteration function, the syndrome is updated just after each test establishing if the j-th bit value in the estimated error vector should be flipped or not. In the out-of-place iteration function, instead, the syndrome is updated after the tests over all the bits in the estimated error vector are executed and the corresponding bit-flips are performed.

In this paper, we consider a simple variant of the in-place BF strategy, which consists in randomizing the order in which the estimated error positions are processed. This modification permits us to derive a worst-case analysis for the DFR of syndrome-decoding based systems, which is employed to design code parameters for QC-LDPC/QC-MDPC based cryptosystems matching the DFR figures of merit needed to provide IND-CCA2 guarantees. A preliminary version of this paper appeared in [6], where we showed that, employing well-established assumptions in coding theory, it is possible to develop a closed-form statistical model of such a decoder, by studying the worst-case execution at each iteration for the average QC-LDPC/QC-MDPC code performance. In this work we revise and expand the theoretical tractation of the subject, adding the demonstration of some core lemmas and propositions,that were omitted in [6]. Moreover, we provide an extended experimental evaluation in which we analyze the effect of changing the BF decoder thresholds in both a single iteration decoder and a two iterations one.

2 Notation and Background

Throughout the paper, we will use uppercase (resp. lowercase) bold letters to denote matrices (resp. vectors). Given a matrix $\mathbf{A}$, its i-th row and j-th column will be denoted as $\mathbf{A}_{i,:}$ and $\mathbf{A}_{:,j}$, respectively, while an entry on the i-th row and the j-th column will be denoted as $a_{i,j}$. A null vector of length n will be denoted as $\mathbf{0}_n$. Given a vector $\mathbf{a}$, its length will be denoted as $|\mathbf{a}|$, while its i-th element as a_i, with $0 \leq i \leq |\mathbf{a}| - 1$. Finally, the *support* (i.e., the set of positions/indexes of the asserted elements in a sequence) and the Hamming weight of $\mathbf{a}$ will be reported as $\mathrm{Supp}(\mathbf{a})$ and $\mathrm{w_H}(\mathbf{a})$, respectively. We will use $\mathcal{P}_n$ to denote the set of permutations of n elements, represented as bijections on the set of integers $\{0, \ldots, n-1\}$. Given a permutation $\pi \in \mathcal{P}_n$ and an integer $i \in \{0, \ldots, n-1\}$, we will write $\pi(i) = j$ if the image of i, according to permutation π, is j. Given a vector $\mathbf{a} \in \mathbb{F}_2^n$, we will use $\pi(\mathbf{a})$ to denote the vector that is obtained by permuting each of the entries of $\mathbf{a}$ according to π. We will write $\pi \xleftarrow{\$} \mathcal{P}_n$ to denote a permutation π that is randomly and uniformly picked among the elements in $\mathcal{P}_n$.

As far as the cryptosystems are concerned, in the following we will make use of a QC-LDPC/QC-MDPC code $\mathcal{C}$, with length $n = n_0 p$, dimension $k = (n_0 - 1)p$, $n_0 \geq 2$, and redundancy $r = n - k = p$ to correct t intentional errors. The private-key will coincide with the parity-check matrix $\mathbf{H} = [\mathbf{H}_0, \mathbf{H}_1, \cdots, \mathbf{H}_{n_0-1}] \in \mathbb{F}_2^{r \times n}$, where each $\mathbf{H}_i$, $0 \leq i \leq n_0 - 1$, is a binary circulant matrix of size $p \times p$ and fixed Hamming weight v of each column/row.

In the case of a Niederreiter scheme, the public-key is defined as the systematic parity-check matrix of the code $\mathbf{M} \in \mathbb{F}_2^{r \times n}$ and derived from the private-key as $\mathbf{M} = \mathbf{H}_{n_0-1}^{-1}\mathbf{H}$, while the plaintext message is mapped to an error vector $\mathbf{e} \in \mathbb{F}_2^{1 \times n}$ having $\mathrm{w_H}(\mathbf{e}) = t$ asserted bits. The encryption algorithm outputs as a ciphertext the syndrome $\mathbf{c} = \mathbf{e}\mathbf{M}^\top \in \mathbb{F}_2^{1 \times r}$. The decryption algorithm takes as input $\mathbf{c}$ and the private-key $\mathbf{H}$ to compute a private-syndrome $\mathbf{s} \in \mathbb{F}_2^{1 \times r}$ such that $\mathbf{s} = \mathbf{c}\mathbf{H}_{n_0-1}^\top = \mathbf{e}\mathbf{M}^\top\mathbf{H}_{n_0-1}^\top = \mathbf{e}\mathbf{H}^\top(\mathbf{H}_{n_0-1}^\top)^{-1}\mathbf{H}_{n_0-1}^\top = \mathbf{e}\mathbf{H}^\top$. Subsequently, to derive the original plaintext message $\mathbf{e}$, the decryption algorithm feeds with the private-key and the computed private-syndrome a BF *syndrome decoding* algorithm.

In the case of the McEliece scheme, the public-key is chosen as the systematic generator matrix of the code: $\mathbf{G} \in \mathbb{F}_2^{k \times n}$. The ciphertext is in the form $\mathbf{c} = \mathbf{m}\mathbf{G} + \mathbf{e} \in \mathbb{F}_2^{1 \times n}$, where $\mathbf{m} \in \mathbb{F}_2^{1 \times k}$ is a plaintext message encoded with k bits, and $\mathbf{e} \in \mathbb{F}_2^{1 \times n}$ is a n-bit error vector with exactly $\mathrm{w_H}(\mathbf{e}) = t$ asserted bits. The decryption algorithm takes as input the ciphertext $\mathbf{c}$ and the private-key $\mathbf{H}$ to compute the syndrome $\mathbf{s} = \mathbf{c}\mathbf{H}^\top = \mathbf{e}\mathbf{H}^\top \in \mathbb{F}_2^{1 \times r}$ and feeds a *syndrome decoding* algorithm, which in turn yield the error vector and allows to recover the original plaintext $\mathbf{m}$ employing the generation matrix and the vector $\mathbf{c} - \mathbf{e}$.

The syndrome decoding procedure analyzed in this paper originated from the BF decoding strategy that was originally proposed by Gallager in [16]. The original BF algorithm takes as input a syndrome $\mathbf{s} = (\mathbf{c} + \mathbf{e})\mathbf{H}^\top = \mathbf{e}\mathbf{H}^\top \in \mathbb{F}_2^{1 \times r}$ computed multiplying the codeword $\mathbf{c} \in \mathbb{F}_2^{1 \times n}$ corrupted by an unknown error vector $\mathbf{e} \in \mathbb{F}_2^{1 \times n}$ by the matrix obtained transposing the parity-check matrix of the code. The algorithm yields an estimate of the unknown error vector, that we denote as $\hat{\mathbf{e}}$, which is initially assumed to be a null vector. For each bit position in the error estimate (and correspondingly also in the unknown error vector), a decision about flipping or not the bit value at hand is taken on the ground of the *number of unsatisfied parity-check* (upc) equations in which such a bit value/position participates. Considering a generic error bit in position $0 \leq j \leq n-1$, such a quantity is computed as follows [6].

$$\mathrm{upc}_j = \sum_{i \in \{\mathrm{Supp}(\mathbf{H}_{:,j}) \cap \{0, \ldots, r-1\}\}} s_i.$$

Indeed, note that the constant term of the i-th parity-check equation ($0 \leq i \leq r - 1$) corresponds to the i-th entry in $\mathbf{s} = \mathbf{eH}^\top$, and that the equations influenced by the j-th bit of the error vector coincide with the ones having an asserted bit at the j-th column of $\mathbf{H}$. As a consequence, the number of unsatisfied parity-check equations in which the j-th bit participates can be obtained by summing the entries of the syndrome which are indexed by the set of positions in $\mathrm{Supp}(\mathbf{H}_{:,j})$. When upc_j exceeds a given threshold (e.g., when more than a half of the parity check equations in which the j-th error bit is involved – as in the original proposal by Gallager), then the bit value in the considered position of the estimated error vector is flipped and the syndrome is coherently updated by replacing its current value with $\mathbf{s} \oplus \mathbf{H}_{:,j}$. In a single decoding iteration, all error bits are evaluated following their positional order from 0 to $n - 1$. A syndrome decoder, which applies an in-place decoding strategy, executes multiple iterations, each of which repeats the steps previously described until either a null syndrome is obtained or a prefixed maximum number of iterations is reached.

When an out-of-place strategy is employed, every error bit is assessed relying on the same syndrome value provided (as input) at the beginning of the iteration, while the updates of both the error vector estimate and the syndrome are postponed after all error bits have been evaluated.

3 In-Place Randomized Bit-Flipping Decoder

In this section we describe a simple modification to the canonical in-place decoder proposed by Gallager, for which we are able to provide a closed form estimate of the DFR in a worst-case scenario.

3.1 An In-Place, Randomized Bit-Flipping Decoder

Algorithm 1 reports an in-place BF decoder where the estimates on the error vector bits are computed in the order driven by a randomly picked permutation π. For this reason, we denote this decoder as In-place Randomized Bit-Flipping (IR-BF) decoder. Introducing this randomization of the bit estimate evaluation order allows us to derive an effective worst case analysis for the DFR, as we describe in Sect. 3.2.

The inputs to the decoding algorithm are the binary parity-check matrix $\mathbf{H}$, the syndrome $\mathbf{s}$, the maximum number of iterations imax and a vector $\mathbf{b}$ of length imax, such that its k-th entry, $\mathbf{b}_k$, with $0 \leq k \leq \mathtt{imax}-1$, is employed during the k-th iteration as a threshold on the value of the unsatisfied parity-check counters to trigger a flip of the corresponding error bit estimates or not. For each outer loop iteration (beginning at line 3), a permutation is randomly generated (line 4) to establish the evaluation order of the bits in the estimated error vector, for the current iteration. The algorithm proceeds applying the said permutation to each value taken by the counter $j \in \{0, 1, \ldots, n-1\}$ of the inner loop iterations (line 5) to obtain the bit position $\ell = \pi(j)$ of the estimated error vector to be processed during the inner loop iteration at hand. The number of unsatisfied parity-checks (upc) in which the ℓ-th bit of the error estimate $\hat{\mathbf{e}}$ is involved is computed by summing the syndrome bits having a position corresponding to the asserted elements of the ℓ-th column of the parity check matrix $\mathbf{H}$ (lines 7–9). If the number of unsatisfied

---

Algorithm 1. In-place, Randomized Bit-flipping (IR-BF) decoder [6].

Input: $\mathbf{s} \in \mathbb{F}_2^{1 \times r}$: syndrome
$\quad\quad\quad \mathbf{H} \in \mathbb{F}_2^{r \times n}$: parity-check matrix with column-weight v

Output: $\hat{\mathbf{e}} \in \mathbb{F}_2^{1 \times n}$: recovered error value
$\quad\quad\quad\quad \mathbf{s} \in \mathbb{F}_2^{1 \times r}$: syndrome; if error $\hat{\mathbf{e}} = \mathbf{e}$ then $\mathbf{s}$ is null

Data: $\mathtt{imax} \geq 1$: maximum number of (outer loop) iterations;
$\quad\quad\quad \mathbf{b} = [\mathbf{b}_0, \ldots, \mathbf{b}_k, \ldots, \mathbf{b}_{\mathtt{imax}-1}]$, with $\mathbf{b}_k \in \{\lceil \frac{v}{2} \rceil, \ldots, v\}$: flip thresholds

1   $\mathtt{iter} \leftarrow 0$
2   $\hat{\mathbf{e}} \leftarrow \mathbf{0}_n$ // estimated error initialization
3   **while** ($\mathtt{iter} < \mathtt{imax}$) $\wedge$ ($\mathrm{w_H}(\mathbf{s}) > 0$) **do**

4      $\pi \xleftarrow{\$} \mathcal{P}_n$ // random permut. of size n
5   **for** $j \leftarrow 0$ **to** $n-1$ **do**
6         $\ell \leftarrow \pi(j)$ // permuted bit index
7         $\mathtt{upc} \leftarrow 0$ // integer value
8   **for** $i \in \mathrm{Supp}(\mathbf{H}_{:,\ell})$ **do**
9            $\mathtt{upc} \leftarrow \mathtt{upc} + s_i$
10   **if** $\mathtt{upc} \geq \mathbf{b}_{\mathtt{iter}}$ **then**
11           $\hat{e}_\ell \leftarrow \hat{e}_\ell \oplus 1$ // error update
12           $\mathbf{s} \leftarrow \mathbf{s} \oplus \mathbf{H}_{:,\ell}$ // syndrome update
13      $\mathtt{iter} \leftarrow \mathtt{iter} + 1$ // counter update

14   **return** $\{\hat{\mathbf{e}}, \mathbf{s}\}$

---

parity-checks in which the ℓ-th bit participates exceeds the threshold, $\mathbf{b}_{\mathtt{iter}}$, chosen for the current outer loop iteration, then the value of the ℓ-th position of the estimated error vector, $\hat{e}_\ell$, is changed (i.e., flipped, hence the name of the decoding technique) and the value of the syndrome is updated to reflect this change, adding to it the ℓ-th column of $\mathbf{H}$ (lines 10–12). Once the inner loop at lines 5–12 terminates, the decoder has completed the iteration, and thus proceeds to increment the iteration counter $\mathtt{iter}$ and checks whether the syndrome is the null vector, or not, or if the maximum number of iterations is reached. We note that this classical formulation of the IR-BF decoder does not entail a constant iteration number. However, it is readily transformed into one with a constant iteration number substituting the while loop at lines 3–13 with a countable $\mathtt{for}$ loop executing exactly $\mathtt{imax}$ iterations. Indeed, executing extra iterations of the IR-BF algorithm when the syndrome is already the null vector does not alter the correctness of the results. Indeed, once the syndrome is the null vector, all the $\mathtt{upc}$ values will be equal to zero, and, since the least functional threshold is strictly positive, the execution path controlled by the estimate-changing *if statement* at lines 10–12 is never taken.

3.2 Modeling of the Bit-Flipping Probabilities

In the following we describe a statistical approach to model the behaviour of the IR-BF decoder [6]. From now on, we will employ the following notation:

– $\mathbf{e}$ denotes the actual error vector, with Hamming weight weight t;

- $\bar{e}$ denotes the error estimate at the beginning of the outer loop of Algorithm 1 (line 3), while $\hat{e}$ will denote the error estimate at the beginning of the inner loop of Algorithm (line 5). In other words, $\bar{e}$ is a snapshot of the error estimate made by the IR-BF decoder before a sweep of n estimated error bit evaluations is made, while $\hat{e}$ is the value of the estimated error vector before each estimated error bit is evaluated;
- $\bar{e}' = e \oplus \bar{e}$ denotes the vector such that its asserted positions are only those corresponding to positions in which (the unknown) e and $\bar{e}$ are different; the number of such mismatches is denoted as $\bar{t} = w_H(\bar{e}')$. In analogous way, we define $\hat{e}' = e \oplus \hat{e}$ and $\hat{t} = w_H(\hat{e}')$.

We remark that, for the first outer-loop iteration of the decoding algorithm, we have $\bar{e} = 0_n$, $\bar{e}' = e$ and $\bar{t} = t$. To avoid cumbersome notation, we will not introduce analogous formalism for the syndrome and will always use s to denote it. At the beginning of the outer loop iteration in Algorithm 1, the syndrome corresponds to $(e \oplus \bar{e})H^\top = \bar{e}'H^\top$ while, inside the inner loop iteration, an estimate $\hat{e}$ will be associated to the syndrome $(e \oplus \hat{e})H^\top = \hat{e}'H^\top$.

Assumption 1. *The probability* $P_{f|1}^{\mathrm{th}} = \Pr\left[upc_j \geq \mathtt{th} \mid e_j \neq \hat{e}_j\right]$, *with* $j \in \{0,1, \ldots, n-1\}$, *that the number of the unsatisfied parity checks involving the j-th bit of the error vector, i.e.,* upc_j, *is large enough to trigger a flip of* $\hat{e}_j$, *given that its current value does not match the value of the j-th bit in the unknown error vector, i.e.,* $\hat{e}'_j = e_j \oplus \hat{e}_j = 1$, *is a function of only the total number* $\hat{t} = w_H(\hat{e} \oplus e)$ *of positions over which the estimated error vector $\hat{e}$ and the unknown error vector e differ.*

Analogously, the probability $P_{m|0}^{\mathrm{th}} = \Pr\left[upc_j < \mathtt{th} \mid e_j = \hat{e}_j\right]$ *that the number of the unsatisfied parity checks involving the j-th bit of the error vector, i.e.,* upc_j, *is low enough to maintain the current value $\hat{e}_j$ of the j-th estimated error vector bit, given that its current value matches the value of the j-th bit in the unknown error vector, i.e.,* $\hat{e}'_j = e_j \oplus \hat{e}_j = 0$, *is a function of only the total number* $\hat{t} = w_H(\hat{e} \oplus e)$ *of positions over which the estimated error vector $\hat{e}$ and the unknown error vector e differ.*

Informally, we are stating that the statistical behaviour of the single given upc_j does not depend on its location j, but only on the number of discrepancies between the estimated error vector and the actual one, and the fact that the j-th position of $\hat{e}$ is in accordance or not with e.

The following probabilities referred to flipping (f) or maintaining (m) the value of each bit of $\hat{e}$ will be used to characterize the iteration behaviour [6]

$$P_{f|1}^{\mathrm{th}}(\hat{t}) = \Pr\left[upc_j \geq \mathtt{th} \mid e_j \neq \hat{e}_j, \ w_H(e \oplus \hat{e}) = \hat{t}\right],$$

$$P_{m|1}^{\mathrm{th}}(\hat{t}) = 1 - P_{f|1}^{\mathrm{th}}(\hat{t}) = \Pr\left[upc_j < \mathtt{th} \mid e_j \neq \hat{e}_j, \ w_H(e \oplus \hat{e}) = \hat{t}\right],$$

$$P_{m|0}^{\mathrm{th}}(\hat{t}) = \Pr\left[upc_j < \mathtt{th} \mid e_j = \hat{e}_j, \ w_H(e \oplus \hat{e}) = \hat{t}\right],$$

$$P_{f|0}^{\mathrm{th}}(\hat{t}) = 1 - P_{m|0}^{\mathrm{th}}(\hat{t}) = \Pr\left[upc_j \geq \mathtt{th} \mid e_j = \hat{e}_j, \ w_H(e \oplus \hat{e}) = \hat{t}\right].$$

To derive closed formulae for both $P_{f|1}$ and $P_{m|0}$, we focus on QC-LDPC/QC-MDPC parity-check matrices, as described in Sect. 2, with column weight v and row weight

$w = n_0 v$. We observe that Algorithm 1 uses the columns of the parity-check matrix, for each outer loop iteration, in an order chosen by the random permutation at line 4, and that the computation accumulating the syndrome bits into the upc at lines 8–9 is independent of the order in which they are added.

According to this, in the following we assume that each row of the parity-check matrix H is independent of the others and modeled as a sample of a uniform random variable, distributed over all possible sequences of n bits with weight w, and name a parity-check matrix (v, w)-regular if all its columns have weight v and all its rows have weight w. We share this assumption with a significant amount of literature on the prediction of the DFR of QC-LDPC decoders, ranging from the original work by Gallager on LDPCs [16, Section 4.2] to more recent ones, namely [32, Section 3] and [27, Section 4].

Formally, the following statement is assumed to hold:

Assumption 2. *Let H be a $p \times n_0 p$ quasi-cyclic block-circulant (v, w)-regular parity-check matrix and let s be the $1 \times p$ syndrome corresponding to a $1 \times n_0 p$ error vector $\hat{e}' = e \oplus \hat{e}$ that is modeled as a sample from a uniform random variable distributed over the elements in $\mathbb{F}_2^{1 \times n_0 p}$ with weight $\hat{t}$.*
We assume that each row $h_{i,:}$, $0 \leq i \leq p - 1$, of the parity-check matrix H is well modeled as a sample from a uniform random variable distributed over the elements of $\mathbb{F}_2^{1 \times n_0 p}$ with weight w.

Note that the assumption on the fact that the syndrome at hand is obtained from a vector $\hat{e}' = \hat{e} \oplus e$ of weight $\hat{t}$ is trivially true if the iteration of the decoder being considered is the first one being computed, since the error estimate $\hat{e}$ is null and the error vector e is drawn at random with weight $t = \hat{t}$. This in turn states that, when employing Assumption 2 in estimating the correction capability of the first iteration of a decoder, we are only relying on the fact that the rows of the matrix H can be considered independent, neglecting the effects of the quasi-cyclic structure.

In the following Lemma we establish how, upon relying on the previous assumption, the probabilities that characterize the choices on the bits of the estimated error vector, made by a either an in-place or an out-of-place iteration function, can be expressed [6].

Lemma 1. *Let H be a $p \times n_0 p$ quasi-cyclic block-circulant (v, w)-regular parity-check matrix; let $\hat{e}' = \hat{e} \oplus e$ be an unknown vector of length n and weight $\hat{t}$ such that $H(\hat{e}')^T = s$.*
From Assumption 1 and Assumption 2, the probabilities $\rho_{0,u}(\hat{t}) = \Pr[s_i = 1 | \hat{e}'_z = 0]$ and $\rho_{1,u}(\hat{t}) = \Pr[s_i = 1 | \hat{e}'_z = 1]$ that the i-th parity-check equation having $h_{i,z} = 1$, for any $0 \leq z \leq n - 1$, is unsatisfied (i.e., $s_i = h_{i,:}(\hat{e}')^T = 1$) given the value of $\hat{e}'_z$, can be derived as follows

$$\rho_{0,u}(\hat{t}) = \Pr\left[h_{i,:}(\hat{e}')^T = 1 \mid \hat{e}'_z = 0\right] = \frac{\sum_{l=1,\, l\ odd}^{\min\{w-1,\hat{t}\}} \binom{w-1}{l}\binom{n_0 p - w}{\hat{t}-l}}{\binom{n_0 p - 1}{\hat{t}}}$$

$$\rho_{1,u}(\hat{t}) = \Pr\left[h_{i,:}(\hat{e}')^T = 1 \mid \hat{e}'_z = 1\right] = \frac{\sum_{l=0,\, l\ even}^{\min\{w-1,\hat{t}-1\}} \binom{w-1}{l}\binom{n_0 p - w}{\hat{t}-1-l}}{\binom{n_0 p - 1}{\hat{t}-1}}$$

Consequently, the probability $P_{f|1}(\hat{t}) = \Pr\left[\mathrm{upc}_z \geq \mathrm{th} \mid \hat{e}'_z = \hat{e}_z \oplus e_z = 1\right]$ *of changing (flipping) the z-th bit of the estimated error vector $\hat{e}_z$ assuming that $\hat{e}'_z = 1$, and the probability* $P_{m|0}(\hat{t}) = \Pr\left[\mathrm{upc}_z < \mathrm{th} \mid \hat{e}'_z = \hat{e}_z \oplus e_z = 0\right]$ *of maintaining $\hat{e}_z$ assuming that $\hat{e}'_z = 0$, are computed as follows*

$$P_{f|1}^{\mathrm{th}}(\hat{t}) = \sum_{\sigma=\mathrm{th}}^{v} \binom{v}{\sigma} \left(\rho_{1,\mathrm{u}}(\hat{t})\right)^{\sigma} \left(1 - \rho_{1,\mathrm{u}}(\hat{t})\right)^{v-\sigma},$$

$$P_{m|0}^{\mathrm{th}}(\hat{t}) = \sum_{\sigma=0}^{\mathrm{th}-1} \binom{v}{\sigma} \left(\rho_{0,\mathrm{u}}(\hat{t})\right)^{\sigma} \left(1 - \rho_{0,\mathrm{u}}(\hat{t})\right)^{v-\sigma}.$$

Proof. For the sake of brevity, we consider the case of $\hat{e}'_z = 1$ deriving the expression of $P_{f|1}^{\mathrm{th}}(\hat{t})$; the proof for $P_{m|0}^{\mathrm{th}}(\hat{t})$ can be carried out with similar arguments. Given a row $h_{i,:}$ of the parity-check matrix H, such that $z \in \mathrm{Supp}(h_{i,:})$, the equation $\bigoplus_{j=0}^{n_0p-1} h_{i,j}\hat{e}'_j$ (in the unknown $\hat{e}'$) yields a non-null value for the i-th bit of the syndrome, $\hat{s}_i$, (i.e., the equation is unsatisfied) if and only if the support of $\hat{e}'$ is such that $\bigoplus_{j=0}^{n_0p-1} h_{i,j}\hat{e}'_j = 2a + 1, a \geq 0$, including the term having $j = z$, i.e., $h_{i,z}\hat{e}'_z = 1$. This implies that the cardinality of the set obtained intersecting the support of $h_{i,:}$ with the one of $\hat{e}'$, $|(\mathrm{Supp}(h_{i,:}) \setminus \{z\}) \cap (\mathrm{Supp}(\hat{e}') \setminus \{z\})|$, must be an even number, which in turn cannot be larger than the minimum between $|\mathrm{Supp}(h_{i,:}) \setminus \{i\}| = w-1$ and $|\mathrm{Supp}(\hat{e}') \setminus \{i\}| = \hat{t} - 1$.

The probability $\rho_{1,\mathrm{u}}(\hat{t})$ is obtained considering the fraction of the number of values of $\hat{e}'$ having an even number of asserted bits matching the asserted bits ones in a row of H (noting that, for the z-th bit position, both the error and the row of H are set) on the number of $\hat{e}'$ values having $\hat{t} - 1$ asserted bits over $n_0p - 1$ positions, i.e., $\binom{n_0p-1}{\hat{t}-1}$. The numerator of the said fraction is easily computed as the sum of all $\hat{e}'$ configurations having an even number $0 \leq l \leq \min\{w - 1, \hat{t} - 1\}$ of asserted bits. Considering a given value for l, the counting of $\hat{e}'$ values is derived as follows. Picking one vector with l asserted bits over w possible positions, i.e., one vector over $\binom{w-1}{l}$ possible ones, there are $\binom{n_0p-w}{\hat{t}-1-l}$ possible values of the error vector exhibiting $\hat{t} - 1 - l$ null bits in the remaining $n_0p - w$ positions; therefore, the total number of vectors with weigh l is $\binom{w-1}{l}\binom{n_0p-w}{\hat{t}-1-l}$.

Repeating the same line of reasoning for each value of l allows to derive the numerator of the formula defining $\rho_{1,\mathrm{u}}(\hat{t})$.

From Assumption 2, the observation of any unsatisfied parity check involving the z-th bit of the error vector $\hat{e}'_z$ (i.e., $h_{i,:}(\hat{e}')^T = 1$) given that $\hat{e}'_z = \hat{e}_z \oplus e_z = 1$, is modeled as a random variable with a Bernoulli distribution having parameter (or expected value) $\rho_{1,\mathrm{u}}(\hat{t})$, and each of these random variables is independent of the others. Consequentially, the probability that the decoder performs a bit-flip of an element of the estimated error vector when the corresponding bit of the error vector is asserted and the counter of the unsatisfied parity checks (upc) is above or equal to a given threshold th, is derived as the binomial probability obtained adding the outcomes of v (column-weight of H) i.i.d. Bernoulli trials. □

Worst-Case Iteration Scenario for the IR-BF Decoder. In the following we focus on a single iteration of the outer loop of Algorithm 1 and derive a statistical model for the IR-BF decoder, employing the probabilities $P_{f|1}$ and $P_{m|0}$ as previously derived [6].

In particular, we consider a *worst-case* evolution for the decoder, proving what is the computation path which ends in a decoding success with the lowest probability. To this end, we denote a decoding success the case when the decoder terminates the inner loop iteration in the state where the estimate of the error $\hat{e}$ matches the actual error e. Indeed, in such a case, we have $w_H(e \oplus \hat{e}) = 0$.

Considering the error estimate at the beginning of the outer-loop iteration $\bar{e}$ and the corresponding number of residual mismatched bit estimations $\bar{t} = w_H(e \oplus \bar{e})$, we will study, in statistical terms, the evolution of the number of mismatches between the vectors e and $\hat{e}$, which we denote with $\hat{t}$.

We denote as π the permutation picked in line 4 of Algorithm 1 and as π^* an element of the subset $\mathcal{P}_n^*$ of permutations ($\mathcal{P}_n^* \subset \mathcal{P}_n$) such that

$$\text{Supp}(\pi^*(e \oplus \bar{e})) = \{n - \bar{t}, n - \bar{t} + 1, \cdots, n - 1\}, \ \forall \pi^* \in \mathcal{P}_n^*.$$

Let $\text{Prob}(\hat{e} \neq e| \ \pi \in \mathcal{P}_n)$ be the probability that the estimated error vector $\hat{e}$ at the end of the current inner loop iteration is different from e, conditional on the fact that the permutation π was applied before the inner loop execution started. Similarly, we define $\text{Prob}(\hat{e} \neq e| \ \pi^* \in \mathcal{P}_n^*)$, by considering π^* in place of π.

It can be verified that $P_{f|1}(\hat{t}) \geq P_{f|1}(\hat{t} + 1)$, and $P_{m|0}(\hat{t}) \geq P_{m|0}(\hat{t} + 1)$, $\forall \hat{t}$, as increasing the number of current mis-estimated error bits, increases the likelihood of a wrong decoder decision. By leveraging Assumptions 1 and 2, we now prove how the decoder reaches a correct decoding at the end of the outer loop, with the lowest probability.

Lemma 2. *The execution path of the inner loop in Algorithm 1, yielding the worst possible decoder success rate is the one taking place when $\pi^* \in \mathcal{P}_n^*$ is applied at the beginning of the outer loop. In other words, $\forall \pi \in \mathcal{P}_n$, and $\forall \pi^* \in \mathcal{P}_n^*$, the following inequality holds*

$$\text{Prob}(\hat{e} \neq e| \ \pi \in \mathcal{P}_n) \leq \text{Prob}(\hat{e} \neq e| \ \pi^* \in \mathcal{P}_n^*).$$

Proof. We consider one execution of the outer loop in Algorithm 1, and denote with $\bar{t}$ the initial number of mismatches between the actual error (that is, e) and its estimate (that is, $\bar{e}$). We can write $\text{Prob}(\hat{e} \neq e| \ \pi \in \mathcal{P}_n) = 1 - \beta(\pi)$, where $\beta(\pi)$ is the probability that all bits, evaluated in the order specified by π, are correctly processed. To visualize the effect of a permutation $\pi^* \in \mathcal{P}_n^*$, we can consider the following representation

$$\pi^*(e) \oplus \pi^*(\bar{e}) = [\underbrace{0, 0, \cdots, 0}_{\text{length } n - \bar{t}}, \underbrace{1, 1, \cdots, 1}_{\text{length } \bar{t}}], \ \forall \pi^* \in \mathcal{P}_n^*.$$

The decoder will hence analyze first a run of $n - \bar{t}$ positions where the differences between the permuted error $\pi^*(e)$ vector and $\pi^*(\bar{e})$ contain only zeroes, followed by a run of $\bar{t}$ positions containing only ones. Thus, we have that

$$\beta(\pi^*) = \left(P_{m|0}(\bar{t})\right)^{n-\bar{t}} \cdot P_{f|1}(\bar{t}) \cdot P_{f|1}(\bar{t} - 1) \cdots P_{f|1}(1).$$

The former expression can be derived thanks to Assumption 1 as follows. Note that, the first elements in the first $n-\bar{t}$ positions of $\pi^*(\bar{e})$ and $\pi^*(e)$ match, therefore the decoder makes a correct evaluation if it does not change the corresponding entries in $\hat{e}$. This implies that, in case a sequence of $n-\bar{t}$ correct decisions are made in the corresponding iterations of the inner loop, each iteration will have the same probability $P_{m|0}(\bar{t})$ of correctly evaluating the current estimated error bit. This leads to a probability of performing the first $n-\bar{t}$ iterations taking a correct decision equal to $\left(P_{m|0}(\bar{t})\right)^{n-\bar{t}}$.

Through an analogous line of reasoning, we observe that the decoder will need to change the value of the current estimated error bit during the last $\bar{t}$ iterations of the inner loop. As a consequence, if all correct decisions are made, the number of residual errors will decrease by one at each inner loop iteration, yielding the remaining part of the expression.

Considering a generic permutation π, such that the support of $\pi(e)$ is $\{u_0, \cdots, u_{\bar{t}-1}\}$; we have

$$
\begin{aligned}
\beta(\pi) &= \quad [P_{m|0}(\bar{t})]^{u_0} P_{f|1}(\bar{t}) [P_{m|0}(\bar{t}-1)]^{u_1-u_0-1} P_{f|1}(\bar{t}-1) \cdots P_{f|1}(1) [P_{m|0}(0)]^{n-1-u_{\bar{t}-1}} \\
&= \quad [P_{m|0}(\bar{t})]^{u_0} [P_{m|0}(0)]^{n-1-u_{\bar{t}-1}} \prod_{j=1}^{\bar{t}-1} [P_{m|0}(\bar{t}-j)]^{u_j-u_{j-1}-1} \prod_{l=0}^{\bar{t}-1} P_{f|1}(\bar{t}-l).
\end{aligned}
$$

We now show that we always have $\beta(\pi) \geq \beta(\pi^*)$.

Indeed, since $P_{m|0}(0) = 1$, due to the monotonic trends of the probabilities $P_{m|0}(\hat{t})$ and $P_{f|1}(\hat{t})$, the following chain of inequalities can be derived

$$
\begin{aligned}
\beta(\pi) &= \\
&= [P_{m|0}(0)]^{n-1-u_{\bar{t}-1}} [P_{m|0}(\bar{t})]^{u_0} \prod_{j=1}^{\bar{t}-1} [P_{m|0}(\bar{t}-j)]^{u_j-u_{j}-1-1} \prod_{l=0}^{\bar{t}-1} P_{f|1}(\bar{t}-l) \\
&\geq [P_{m|0}(0)]^{n-1-u_{\bar{t}-1}} [P_{m|0}(\bar{t})]^{u_0} \prod_{j=1}^{\bar{t}-1} [P_{m|0}(\bar{t})]^{u_j-u_{j-1}-1} \prod_{l=0}^{\bar{t}-1} P_{f|1}(\bar{t}-l) \\
&= [P_{m|0}(0)]^{n-1-u_{\bar{t}-1}} [P_{m|0}(\bar{t})]^{u_0} [P_{m|0}(\bar{t})]^{u_{\bar{t}-1}-u_0-(\bar{t}-1)} \prod_{l=0}^{\bar{t}-1} P_{f|1}(\bar{t}-l)) \\
&= [P_{m|0}(0)]^{n-1-u_{\bar{t}-1}} [P_{m|0}(t)]^{u_{\bar{t}-1}-(\bar{t}-1)} \prod_{l=0}^{\bar{t}-1} P_{f|1}(\bar{t}-l) \\
&\geq [P_{m|0}(\bar{t})]^{n-1-u_{\bar{t}-1}} [P_{m|0}(\bar{t})]^{u_{\bar{t}-1}-(\bar{t}-1)} \prod_{l=0}^{\bar{t}-1} P_{f|1}(\bar{t}-l) \\
&= [P_{m|0}(\bar{t})]^{n-\bar{t}} \prod_{l=0}^{\bar{t}-1} P_{f|1}(\bar{t}-l) = \beta(\pi^*).
\end{aligned}
$$

$\square$

A Worst-Case DFR Estimate for the IR-BF Decoder. We consider one outer loop iteration with $\bar{e}$ being the error vector estimate before the beginning of the loop, exhibiting $\bar{t} = w_H(e \oplus \bar{e})$ mismatches with the unknown error vector e. From now on we will assume that, in each inner-loop iteration, a permutation from the set $\mathcal{P}_n^*$ is picked; in other words, we are assuming that the decoder is always constrained to reach a decoding success through the worst possible execution path [6].

Let us consider the following two sets bit-positions/indexes in the error vector esti-mate: $E_1 = S(\mathbf{e} \oplus \bar{\mathbf{e}})$ and $E_0 = \{0, \ldots, n-1\} \setminus E_1$. Denote with $\hat{t}_0$ the number of places/positions where the estimated error differs from the actual unknown $\mathbf{e}$ and the positions are also included in E_0. At the beginning of the outer loop iteration, we have

$$\hat{t}_0 = |\mathrm{Supp}(\mathbf{e} \oplus \bar{\mathbf{e}}) \cap E_0| = 0.$$

Analogously, denoting with $\hat{t}_1$ the number of positions in which the estimated error and the actual one differ and the positions are also included in E_1; at the beginning of the outer loop iteration, we have

$$\hat{t}_1 = |\mathrm{Supp}(\mathbf{e} \oplus \bar{\mathbf{e}}) \cap E_1| = \bar{t}.$$

i) Let $\mathrm{Prob}_{\mathcal{P}_n^*}\left(\omega \xrightarrow{E_0} x\right)$ denote the probability that the decoder in Algorithm 1, starting from a state where $\mathrm{w_H}(\bar{\mathbf{e}} \oplus \mathbf{e}) = \omega$, and acting in the order specified by a worst case permutation $\pi^* \in \mathcal{P}_n^*$, ends in a state with $\hat{t}_0 = x$ residual errors among the bits indexed by E_0 after completing the inner loop at lines $5 - 12$;

ii) Let $\mathrm{Prob}_{\mathcal{P}_n^*}\left(\omega \xrightarrow{E_1} x\right)$ denote the probability that the decoder in Algorithm 1, starting from a state where $\mathrm{w_H}(\bar{\mathbf{e}} \oplus \mathbf{e}) = \omega$, and acting in the order specified by a worst case permutation $\pi^* \in \mathcal{P}_n^*$ ends in a state with $\hat{t}_1 = x$ residual errors among the bits indexed by E_1 after completing the loop at lines 5–12;

iii) Let $\mathrm{Prob}_{\mathcal{P}_n^*}\left(\omega \xrightarrow{i} x\right)$ be the probability that, starting from a state such that $\mathrm{w_H}(\bar{\mathbf{e}} \oplus \mathbf{e}) = \omega$, after i iterations of the outer loop at lines 5–12 of Algorithm 1, each one operating with a worst case permutation, ends in a state where $\mathrm{w_H}(\hat{\mathbf{e}} \oplus \mathbf{e}) = x$.

The expressions of the probabilities i) and ii) describe the statistical distributions of $\hat{t}_0$ and $\hat{t}_1$ after that all n iterations of the inner loop of Algorithm 1 have been exe-cuted and all the bits in the estimated error vector have been processed in the order pointed out by the permutation $\pi^* \in \mathcal{P}_n^*$, selected at the beginning of the outer loop. To show how the said distributions are computed and that they only depend on $\mathrm{P}_{f|1}(\hat{t})$ and $\mathrm{P}_{m|0}(\hat{t})$, respectively, we employ the framework of Probabilistic Finite State Automata (PFSA) [26].

Informally, a PFSA is a Finite State Automaton (FSA) characterized by transition probabilities for each of the transitions of the FSA. The state of a PFSA is a discrete probability distribution over the set of FSA states and the probabilities of the transitions starting from the same FSA state, reading the same symbol, must add up to one. A transition from a PFSA state to its subsequent one in the computation is computed taking, for each automaton state for which an admissible transition is present (i.e. the read symbol matches the one on the input tape), the probability mass related to the automaton state itself and, adding the product of the probability mass multiplied by the transition probability to the destination automaton state probability mass.

We model the statistical distribution of $\hat{t}_0$ as the state of a PFSA having $n - t$ FSA states, each one mapped onto a specific value for $\hat{t}_0$, as depicted in Fig. 1. We consider the underlying FSA to be accepting the input language constituted by binary strings

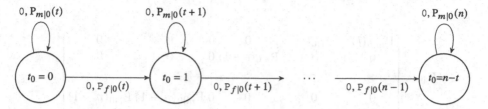

Fig. 1. Structure of the probabilistic FSA modeling the evolution of the distribution of the $\hat{t}_0$ variable. Read characters are reported in black, transition probabilities in red. This figure also appeared in the appendix of the conference version of this paper [6].

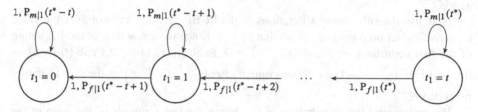

Fig. 2. Structure of the probabilistic FSA modeling the evolution of the distribution of the $\hat{t}_1$ variable. Read characters are reported in black, transition probabilities in red. This figure also appeared in the appendix of the conference version of this paper [6].

obtained as the sequences of $\hat{e}_j \neq e_j$ values, where j is the error estimate position being processed by the IR-BF decoder at a given inner loop iteration. We therefore have that, for the PFSA modeling the evolution of $\hat{t}_0$ while the IR-BF decoder acts on the first $n - t$ positions specified by π^*, all the read bits will be equal to 0, as π^* sorts the positions of $\hat{e}$ so that the ($n - t$, at the first iteration) positions with no discrepancy between $\bar{e}$ and e come first. The transition probability for the PFSA transition from a state $\hat{t}_0 = i$ to $\hat{t}_0 = i + 1$ requires the IR-BF decoder to flip a bit of $\hat{e}$ equal to zero, and matching the one in the same position of e, causing a discrepancy. Because of Assumption 1, the probability of such a transition is $P_{f|0}(t + i)$, while the probability of the self-loop transition from $\hat{t}_0 = i$ to $\hat{t}_0 = i$ itself is $P_{m|0}(t + i)$.

Note that, during the inner loop iterations of the IR-BF decoder acting on positions of $\hat{e}$ which have no discrepancies, it is not possible to decrease the value $\hat{t}_0$, as no reduction on the number of discrepancies between $\hat{e}$ and e can be done changing values of $\hat{e}$ which are already equal to the ones in e. Hence, we have that the probability of transitioning from $\hat{t}_0 = i$ to $\hat{t}_0 = i - 1$ is zero.

The evolution of a PFSA can be efficiently computed simply taking the current state, represented as the vector **y** of probabilities for each FSA state, and multiplying it by an appropriate matrix which characterizes the transitions in the PFSA. Such a matrix is derived as the adjacency matrix of the PFSA graph representation, keeping only the edges for which the read character matches the edge label, and substituting the one-values in the adjacency matrix with the probability labelling the corresponding edge. We obtain the transition matrix modeling an iteration of the IR-BF decoder acting on an $\hat{e}_j = e_j$ (i.e., reading a 0) as the $(n - t + 1) \times (n - t + 1)$ matrix

$$\mathbf{K}_0 = \begin{bmatrix} P_{m|0}(t) & P_{f|0}(t) & 0 & 0 & 0 & 0 \\ 0 & P_{m|0}(t+1) & P_{f|0}(t+1) & 0 & 0 & 0 \\ \vdots & \vdots & \vdots & \vdots & \vdots & \vdots \\ 0 & 0 & 0 & 0 & P_{m|0}(n-1) & P_{f|0}(n-1) \\ 0 & 0 & 0 & 0 & 0 & P_{m|0}(n) \end{bmatrix}.$$

Since we want to compute the effect on the distribution of $\hat{t}_0$ after $n - t$ iterations of the IR-BF decoder acting on positions j such that $\hat{e}_j = e_j$, we can obtain it simply as $\mathbf{y}\mathbf{K}_0^{n-t}$.

Note that the subsequent t iterations of the IR-BF decoder will not alter the value of $\hat{t}_0$ as they act on positions j such that $e_j = 1$. Since we know that, at the beginning of the first iteration $\mathbf{y} = [\text{Prob}\,(\hat{t}_0 = 0) = 1, \text{Prob}\,(\hat{t}_0 = 1) = 0, \text{Prob}\,(\hat{t}_0 = 2) = 0, \cdots, \text{Prob}\,(\hat{t}_0 = n - t) = 0]$, we compute $\text{Prob}_{\mathcal{P}_n^*}\left(\omega \xrightarrow{E_0} x\right)$ as the $(x+1)$-th element of $\mathbf{y}\mathbf{K}_0^{n-t}$.

We now model the distribution of $\hat{t}_1$, during the last $\hat{t}$ rounds of the loop in the randomized in-place iteration function. Note that, to this end, the first $n - t$ iterations of the inner loop have no effect on $\hat{t}_1$. Denote with $\tilde{t}$ the incorrectly estimated bits in $\hat{e}' = \mathbf{e} \oplus \hat{e}$, that is, $\tilde{t} = \text{w}_{\text{H}}\,(\hat{e}')$, when the iteration function is about to evaluate the first of the positions j where $\hat{e}_j \neq e_j$. Note that, at the beginning of this second phase of the outer loop we have $\tilde{t} = \tilde{t}_0 + \hat{t}_1$, where $\tilde{t}_0$ is the number of discrepancies in the first $n - \hat{t}$ positions when the iteration is about to analyze the first position of $\hat{e}$ for which $\text{w}_{\text{H}}\,(\mathbf{e} + \hat{e})$.

Analogously to the PFSA describing the evolution for $\hat{t}_0$, we obtain the PFSA modeling the evolution of $\hat{t}_1$, reported in Fig. 2. The initial distribution of the values of $\hat{t}_1$, constituting the initial state of the PFSA in Fig. 2, is such that $\text{Prob}\,(\hat{t}_1 = t) = 1$, corresponding to the $\hat{t}_1$-element vector $\mathbf{z} = [0, 0, \ldots, 0, 1]$. The transition matrix of the PFSA is

$$\mathbf{K}_1 = \begin{bmatrix} P_{m|1}(\tilde{t} - t) & 0 & 0 & 0 & 0 & 0 \\ P_{f|1}(\tilde{t} - t + 1) & P_{m|1}(\tilde{t} - t + 1) & 0 & 0 & 0 & 0 \\ \vdots & \vdots & \vdots & \vdots & \vdots & \vdots \\ 0 & 0 & 0 & P_{f|1}(\tilde{t} - 1) & P_{m|1}(\tilde{t} - 1) & 0 \\ 0 & 0 & 0 & 0 & P_{f|1}(\tilde{t}) & P_{m|1}(\tilde{t}) \end{bmatrix}.$$

We are thus able to obtain the $\text{Prob}_{\mathcal{P}_n^*}\left(\omega \xrightarrow{E_1} x\right)$ computing $\mathbf{z}\mathbf{K}_1^t$ and taking its $(x+1)$-th element.

Having shown how to compute $\text{Prob}_{\mathcal{P}_n^*}\left(\omega \xrightarrow{E_0} x\right)$, and $\text{Prob}_{\mathcal{P}_n^*}\left(\omega \xrightarrow{E_1} x\right)$, we proceed to show how they can be used together to derive $\text{Prob}_{\mathcal{P}_n^*}\left(\omega \xrightarrow{i} x\right)$ and express the worst case DFR after $\texttt{imax}$ iterations of the outer-loop of Algorithm 1, which we denote as $\text{DFR}^*_{\texttt{itermax}}$.

First of all, it is easy to observe have

$$\text{Prob}_{\mathcal{P}_n^*}\left(\omega \xrightarrow[1]{} x\right) = \sum_{\delta=\max\{0\,;\,x-(n-\omega)\}}^{\omega} \text{Prob}_{\mathcal{P}_n^*}\left(\omega \xrightarrow{E_0} x-\delta\right)\text{Prob}_{\mathcal{P}_n^*}\left(\omega \xrightarrow{E_1} \delta\right).$$

From now on, we will denote with $\hat{e}^{(\texttt{iter})}$ the error vector estimate after the $\texttt{iter}+1$ outer loop iterations; coherently, we write $\hat{t}^{(i)} = \text{w}_\text{H}\left(e \oplus \hat{e}^{(\texttt{iter})}\right)$, that is: $\hat{t}^{(i)}$ corresponds to the number of residual errors after the i-th outer loop iteration.

As a consequence, by considering all possible configurations of such values, and taking into account that the first iteration begins with t residual errors, we have

$$\text{Prob}_{\mathcal{P}_n^*}\left(t \xrightarrow[\texttt{imax}-1]{} \hat{t}^{(\texttt{imax}-1)}\right) = \sum_{\hat{t}^{(0)}=0}^{n} \cdots$$

$$\cdots \sum_{\hat{t}^{(\texttt{imax}-2)}=0}^{n} \text{Prob}_{\mathcal{P}_n^*}\left(\hat{t}^{(\texttt{imax}-2)} \xrightarrow[1]{} \hat{t}^{(\texttt{imax}-1)}\right) \prod_{j=0}^{\texttt{imax}-2} \text{Prob}_{\mathcal{P}_n^*}\left(\hat{t}^{(j-1)} \xrightarrow[1]{} \hat{t}^{(j)}\right)$$

where, to have a consistent notation, we consider $\hat{t}^{(-1)} = t$. The above formula takes into account all possible transitions starting from an initial number of residual errors equal to t and ending in $\hat{t}^{(\texttt{imax}-1)}$ residual errors. Taking this probability into account, the DFR after $\texttt{imax}$ iterations is

$$\text{DFR}_{\texttt{imax}}^* = 1 - \sum_{\hat{t}^{(\texttt{imax}-1)}=0}^{n} \text{Prob}_{\mathcal{P}_n^*}\left(t \xrightarrow[\texttt{imax}-1]{} \hat{t}^{(\texttt{imax}-1)}\right)\text{Prob}_{\mathcal{P}_n^*}\left(\hat{t}^{(\texttt{imax}-1)} \xrightarrow[1]{} 0\right).$$

In the case of the decoder performing just one iteration, the expression of the DFR, keeping into account Lemma 2, is

$$\text{DFR}_1^* = 1 - \text{Prob}_{\mathcal{P}_n^*}\left(t \xrightarrow[1]{} 0\right) = 1 - \left(\text{P}_{m|0}(t)\right)^{n-t}\prod_{j=1}^{t}\text{P}_{f|1}(j).$$

A bonus point of the analysis we propose is that it is easy to obtain also an estimate for the average DFR of a single-iteration decoder, (i.e., corresponding to one outer loop iteration, using a random permutation π). Indeed, let $\pi(e)$ be the vector obtained by applying the permutation π on e, with support $\text{Supp}(\pi(e))$. Let a_i, a_{i+1} be two consecutive elements of $\text{Supp}(\pi(e))$, with $0 \leq i \leq t-2$, and denote as d the average zero-run length in e. It can be easily seen that, when π is randomly drawn from $\mathcal{P}_n$ and e is uniformly distributed over all binary n-uples, then the average zero-run length between two consecutive set entries in e corresponds to $d = \frac{n-t}{t+1}$. Consequently, we can obtain a simple estimate for the average DFR after one iteration as

$$\text{DFR}_1 \approx 1 - \left(\prod_{j=1}^{t}\left(\text{P}_{m|0}(j)\right)^d\right)\prod_{\ell=1}^{t}\text{P}_{f|1}(\ell).$$

4   Validation of DFR Models and Cryptosystem Design

In this section we perform a numerical validation of the proposed analysis of IR-BF decoders and employ the our model to design practical sets of code parameters for QC-LDPC/QC-MDPC code-based cryptosystems employing a two-iteration IR-BF decoder. First, we consider the accuracy of the new model for a single decoding iteration showing that it is fully accurate regardless of both the choice of the thresholds employed to perform the bit-flipping evaluations and the code parameters. Subsequently, we consider more than one decoding iteration and comment on the differences between the modeled and the experimental DFRs of Algorithm 1. In particular, we observe that differences between the proposed model and the experimental behavior arise only when the threshold values selected to perform the bit-flipping evaluations in Algorithm 1 are significantly larger than $v/2$, and provide qualitative justifications for such a phenomenon. Furthermore, we provide experimental evidence that when the values of the bit-flipping thresholds adopted by Algorithm 1 are close to $v/2$, the worst case model we developed for the IR-BF decoder well fits the behavior observed through numerical simulations.

4.1   Experimental Validation of DFR Models

We consider a QC-MDPC code having the-parity check matrix $\mathbf{H}$ formed by a row of $n_0 = 2$ circulant blocks of size $p = 4,801$ and column weight $v = 45$. The error correction capability of this code via IR-BF decoding has been assessed through Monte Carlo simulations. For this purpose, the IR-BF decoder has been implemented in C99 while the whole simulation software has been compiled with the GCC 8.3.0 on a Debian GNU/Linux 10.2 (stable) operating system. Numerical simulations have been performed on a machine equipped with an Intel Core i5-6500 CPU running at 3.20 GHz.

The DFR has been estimated by varying the error vector weight t from 10 to 100, and generating and decoding $10^6 \approx 2^{20}$ randomly generated error vectors for each value of the weight. The bit-flipping threshold has been considered equal for all iterations. The DFR curves obtained through the said experimental simulations are compared with one obtained applying the theoretical worst case DFR estimate computed according to Sect. 3.2, which has been implemented employing the NTL library.[1]

Let us first consider a bit-flipping threshold $b = 25$ ($\geq \lceil \frac{v}{2} \rceil = 23$). In Fig. 3 we report the results of numerical simulations of the DFR of the IR-BF decoder (*Sim.* datasets in Fig. 3) running for either one or two iterations (see DFR_1 and DFR_2, respectively). The DFR curves corresponding to a permutation selected among the worst case ones are also reported, for either one or two decoding iterations (see DFR_1^* and DFR_2^*, respectively). For the case of one iteration, also the simulated DFR without the initial permutation, noted as DFR^{id}, is considered. Note that we are able to pick one of the worst-case permutations in practice since the actual error vector $\mathbf{e}$ is known to us, thus allowing the computation of the discrepancies between the current error estimate and the actual error itself. The results are matched against the closed-form estimates as derived in the previous section.

---

[1] NTL: A Library for doing Number Theory. https://www.shoup.net/ntl/.

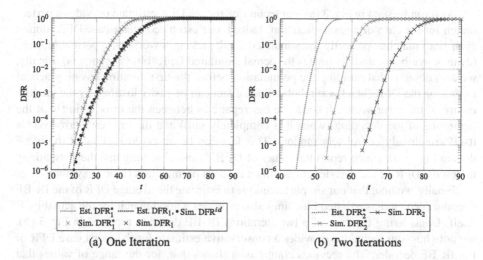

(a) One Iteration

(b) Two Iterations

Fig. 3. Numerical validation of the DFR estimates (Est.) through numerical simulations (Sim.), appeared also as Fig. 1 in the conference version of this paper [6]. The QC-MDPC code parameters are $n_0 = 2$, $p = 4801$ and $v = 45$. Figure (a) refers to the case of one decoding iteration (i.e., imax = 1), figure (b) refers to a maximum number of decoding iterations equal to 2 (i.e., imax = 2). The chosen decoding threshold, for both cases, is b = 25. The results marked with "Est." are obtained via the computation of closed formulas as opposed to the ones marked "Sim." which are the result of a numerical simulation.

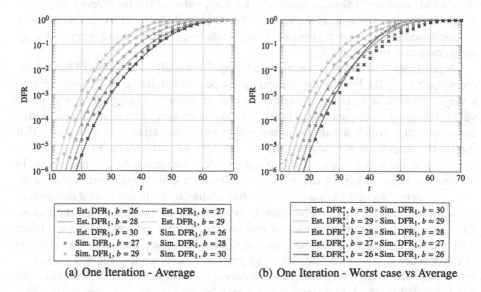

(a) One Iteration - Average

(b) One Iteration - Worst case vs Average

Fig. 4. Numerical validation of the DFR estimates (Est.) through numerical simulations (Sim.), for one decoding iteration. The QC-MDPC code parameters are $n_0 = 2$, $p = 4801$ and $v = 45$. The results marked with "Est." are obtained via the computation of closed formulas as opposed to the ones marked "Sim." which are the result of a numerical simulation.

As it can be seen in Fig. 3 (a), our technique for the DFR estimate provides a perfect match for the case of a single iteration. Indeed, our estimated worst-case DFR (dotted cyan line) matches perfectly the simulated DFR picking a worst-case permutation π^* (cyan × symbols), and dominates the actual simulated DFR (blue × symbols). Finally, we also observe that omitting the permutation before the first iteration has no practical impact on the DFR (black ● symbols). Such a fact can be easily justified by the random nature of the error vector. Indeed, the discrepancies between the error estimate at the beginning of the decoding (when it is completely null) and the unknown error vector itself are already completely random. This fact can be observed looking at the black dots in Fig. 3 (a), which report the values of DFR^{id}, and observing that they essentially match the DFR of the decoder employing a random permutation (blue × symbols).

Finally, we note that our simple technique to estimate the average DFR of the IR-BF decoder (depicted as a dotted blue line) also provides a good match for the actual DFR itself. Considering the case of a two iterations IR-BF decoder, reported in Fig. 3 (b), we note how our technique provides a conservative estimate for the worst case DFR of the IR-BF decoder. The previous comparison shows that, for the range of values that can be reached with numerical simulations, the presented theoretical analysis yields conservative estimates for the DFR of the IR-BF decoder.

Let us now consider different choices for the bit-flipping threshold, namely, b ∈ $\{26, 27, 28, 29, 30\}$. We first focus on a single decoding iteration and, again, compare the DFR values derived from the theoretical model with the ones obtained via numerical simulations; the corresponding results are reported in Fig. 4. For every threshold value, there is a tight match between the pair of DFR curves reporting theoretically estimated values and simulated values, respectively, for each value of the bit-flipping threshold. A noteworthy point is that, as the value of the employed threshold increases, the DFR values provided by our worst case modeling tends to coincide with those provided by an average case modeling.

A justification of this phenomenon can be provided analyzing the role of the threshold value b when the bit-flipping evaluations are performed. In the IR-BF decoder with a single iteration, a decoding failure can be caused either by *i)* flipping error estimate values where no discrepancy with the actual error is present or by *ii)* not flipping error estimate values which are in discrepancy with the actual error. The probability that the IR-BF outer-loop iteration flips (either wrongly or correctly) a bit value rapidly decreases as the value of the bit-flipping threshold b increases. As a consequence, in the decoder behaviour it is extremely unlikely that a non discrepant error estimate bit value is flipped (decoding failure cause i)), thus leading to the failures being caused preeminently by missed flips on discrepant error estimate values (decoding failure cause ii)). Since the non flipping actions on non discrepant error estimate values are taken with increasing probability as the decoding threshold is risen, the inner loop iteration of the decoder in which the said values are processed becomes less and less important. Indeed, as more and more of such non-flip decisions are correctly made, their effect on the number of residual discrepancies to be dealt by the decoder vanishes. Such a phenomenon is well represented by both our model and the simulation results reported in Fig. 4, where it can be seen that the worst-case and average-case behavior of the decoder

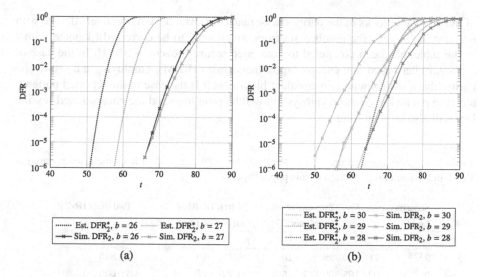

(a)   (b)

Fig. 5. Comparison between the worst case theoretical model for the DFR of a two iterations decoder, and the average simulated one. The QC-MDPC code parameters are $n_0 = 2, p = 4801$ and $v = 45$. The results marked with "Est." are obtained via the computation of closed formulas as opposed to the ones marked "Sim." which are the result of a numerical simulation.

for higher values of b becomes more and more similar, becoming substantially the same for $b = 30$.

We also note that, whenever the threshold is risen, the likelihood of the BF decoding missing a flip on discrepant location of the error estimate raises, therefore leading to an increased number of decoding failures (assuming all the remaining code parameters and the weight of the error are unchanged). This is also evident in Fig. 4. A phenomenon analogous to the one observed in the single iteration case takes place in the case of a multi-iteration decoder. Indeed, our proposed model yields a worst case estimate for the DFR, as reported in Fig. 5(a) up to a threshold of $b = 27$. When considering higher threshold values, as the ones depicted in Fig. 5(b) where larger threshold values starting at b = 28 are employed, we have that the effect of decoding failures being determined by a larger amount of missed flipping actions on discrepant error estimate locations is amplified in a two iteration decoder. This in turn leads, for larger threshold values to a predicted worst-case DFR value which is lower than the actual simulated one. We note that this phenomenon can be practically counteracted picking low thresholds for the IR-BF decoder iterations, thus having it work in the regime where our DFR analysis provides conservative results.

4.2 Design of Code-Based Cryptosystems

We can employ the presented DFR model to design parameters for code-based cryptosystems employing QC-LDPC/QC-MDPC codes, targeting a security level equivalent to breaking an instance of the AES block cipher with a key size equal to 128, 192, or 256 bits. Focusing on the case of $n_0 = 2$, we provide the resulting size and column weight of the circulant blocks in the parity-check matrix $\mathbf{H}$, which we respectively denote with p and v, in Table 1; the number of errors which need to be corrected (denoted with t in the table) has been computed to guarantee security levels of 2^λ [4]. In the case of a Niederreiter-based key encapsulation mechanism (KEM), employing a quasi-cyclic parity-check matrix with two circulant blocks, as it is the case in the reported parameters, the public key of the cryptosystem will be p-bit long and the encapsulated session key will also be p-bit long.

Table 1. Cryptosystem parameters; DFR$=2^{-\lambda}$, $\lambda=\{128, 192, 256\}$ (this table also appeared as Tab. 1 in the conference version of this paper [6]).

Security Level	v	t	Two out-of-place iterations [27]		1st iter. IR-BF + 2nd out-of-place iter. [7]		Two iter.s IR-BF
			p	τ	p	τ	p
2^{128}	71	130	28, 277	10	26, 171	10	19, 813
2^{192}	103	195	52, 667	15	50, 227	15	38, 069
2^{256}	137	260	83, 579	18	80, 309	18	61, 211

Table 1 compares the parameter sets for the two-iterations out-of-place decoder proposed in [27], a decoder obtained with one iteration of the IR-BF decoder, followed by one iteration of the out-of-place LEDAcrypt decoder [7], computing the resulting DFR on the base of the number of residual error distribution after the first iteration provided by our technique, and a two-iterations IR-BF decoder. In the table, the values of τ refer to the number of errors that can be corrected with certainty by an iteration of an out-of-place BF decoder. As it can be seen from the reported results, even employing a hybrid approach, where the first decoder iteration is performed in-place by the IR-BF decoder, and the second one is performed out-of-place, allows a small reduction of the key size. Moving to our in-place decoding strategy allows to reduce the public key and ciphertext size by $\approx 25\%$ with respect to the approach described in [27].

5   Related Work and Discussion

A code-specific analysis to establish the total error correction capability (i.e., null DFR) for a single BF iteration has first appeared in [32] and has then been improved in [27]. With similar arguments, an assumption-free, conservative upper bound for the DFR of a single decoder iteration was derived in [28]. However, employing such approaches to design the secret code parameters results in impractically large public-key sizes. To obtain keys with smaller size, in [3,5,27,32] the DFR of a two-iterations out-of-place decoder is analyzed, providing a closed-form method to derive an upper bound on the average DFR over all the QC-LDPC/QC-MDPC codes with the same length, rate and density, under reasonable assumptions. However, the second and final decoding iteration is analyzed in a conservative way, thus designing code parameters which may be further improved.

In [31], the authors propose a characterization of a variant of the out-of-place decoder based on the extrapolation of the DFR curve in the desired regime of low DFR values, starting from higher DFR values estimated through numerical simulations. This method assumes that the exponentially decreasing trend of the DFR curve is steady as the code length increases, while all the other parameters are kept constant. This assumption is made in the scenario where numerical simulations allow to examine a DFR in the range of 2^{-27}, assuming that the trend is still the same for DFR values of 2^{-128} and lower. A qualitative justification is provided for this assumption in the appendix of [30]. In the said appendix, the authors rely on the so-called *concavity assumption*, according to which the DFR curve remains concave for all values of practical interest. Such an assumption implies that the so-called *error floor* region of the DFR curve, where the said curve changes concavity, and that is present in all LDPC/MDPC codes, after the so-called *waterfall* region, does not occur for DFR values of practical interest.

We find this assumption to be difficult to maintain, since predicting the beginning of the error floor region is an extremely challenging task, which has currently no satisfactory closed form solution. Indeed, phenomena such as the existence of the so-called *trapping sets* (particular sets of error patterns which cause an iterative decoder to fail), which are deemed to have a negligible impact in the assumption made in [30], are one of the prime objects of study to determine the location of the error floor region [18,25].

We note that if either a concavity change, or simply the change in the rate of the exponential decrease of the DFR curve before the concavity change, takes place before the region of practical interest, the extrapolations made in [30] will provide cryptosystem parameters which are not matching the DFR needed in IND-CCA2 constructions. Thus, we believe that relying on DFR curve extrapolations may provide overly optimistic cryptosystem parameter designs [12,13].

In [30], the authors also analyze an in-place decoding algorithm, called *Step-by-step* decoder, modeling its DFR. The proposed analysis however, obtains a DFR estimate which is lower than the actual DFR obtained via numerical simulation, and thus cannot be employed when an upper bound on the DFR value is desired. Furthermore, the proposed analysis considers the asymptotic behaviour of the *Step-by-step* decoder when an infinite number of iterations is performed. Such an approach provides a practical hindrance in principle to the implementation of the decoding procedure as a constant time one, as there is no fixed upper bound to the number of iterations a-priori.

In this work, we have obtained a characterization of a simple in-place decoder with a finite number of iterations, allowing its constant-time implementation in practice. Our characterization provides a statistical model which, by considering the worst case evaluation of the decoder, provides a conservative estimate of the decoder evolution. As a result, we do not rely on any specific *a-priori* assumption on the behaviour of the DFR curve but, on the contrary, completely derive it as a function of the scheme parameters and the decoder setting.

6 Conclusion

In this work, we presented a closed form analysis of the error correction capability of a randomized variant of the classic in-place bit flipping decoder. Considering this randomized variant allowed us to provide closed form worst case DFR estimates, for the said bit-flipping decoder, allowing its evaluation even in regimes where the actual DFR cannot be derived by numerical simulations. This in turn allowed us to provide sound parameters for code-based cryptosystems relying on QC-LDPC/QC-MDPC codes, where providing extremely low DFRs is a requirement to achieve IND-CCA2 security guarantees. Our worst case analysis provides a perfect match of the IR-BF decoder behaviour when considering single iteration decoders, and a conservative bounding of the DFR in case a two-iteration IR-BF decoder is employed with a threshold close to the one of a canonical majority decoder. We foresee, as a interesting future research direction, the analysis of the emerging phenomena in two-iteration IR-BF decoders, whenever they are operating with thresholds far from the majority one.

References

1. Albrecht, M.R., et al.: Classic McEliece website. https://classic.mceliece.org (2020)
2. Aragon, N., et al.: BIKE website. https://bikesuite.org (2020)
3. Baldi, M., Barenghi, A., Chiaraluce, F., Pelosi, G., Santini, P.: LEDAkem: a post-quantum Key encapsulation mechanism based on QC-LDPC codes. In: Lange, T., Steinwandt, R. (eds.) PQCrypto 2018. LNCS, vol. 10786, pp. 3–24. Springer, Cham (2018). https://doi.org/10.1007/978-3-319-79063-3_1
4. Baldi, M., Barenghi, A., Chiaraluce, F., Pelosi, G., Santini, P.: A finite regime analysis of information set decoding algorithms. Algorithms **12**, 209 (2019)
5. Baldi, M., Barenghi, A., Chiaraluce, F., Pelosi, G., Santini, P.: LEDAcrypt: QC-LDPC code-based cryptosystems with bounded decryption failure rate. In: Baldi, M., Persichetti, E., Santini, P. (eds.) Code-Based Cryptography. CBC 2019. Lecture Notes in Computer Science, vol. 11666, pp. 11–43. Springer, Cham (2019). https://doi.org/10.1007/978-3-030-25922-8_2
6. Baldi, M., Barenghi, A., Chiaraluce, F., Pelosi, G., Santini, P.: A failure rate model of bit-flipping decoders for QC-LDPC and QC-MDPC code-based cryptosystems. In: Samarati, P., di Vimercati, S.D.C., Obaidat, M.S., Ben-Othman, J. (eds.) Proceedings of the 17th International Joint Conference on e-Business and Telecommunications, ICETE 2020, vol. 2, pp. 238–249 SECRYPT, Lieusaint, Paris, France, ScitePress (2020). https://doi.org/10.5220/0009891702380249
7. Baldi, M., Barenghi, A., Chiaraluce, F., Pelosi, G., Santini, P.: LEDAcrypt website. https://www.ledacrypt.org (2020)
8. Baldi, M., Chiaraluce, F., Garello, R., Mininni, F.: Quasi-cyclic low-density parity-check codes in the McEliece cryptosystem. In: Proceedings of IEEE International Conference on Communications, ICC 2007, Glasgow, Scotland, UK, pp. 951–956 (2007). https://doi.org/10.1109/ICC.2007.161
9. Barenghi, A., Pelosi, G.: A comprehensive analysis of constant-time polynomial inversion for post-quantum cryptosystems. In: Palesi, M., Palermo, G., Graves, C., Arima, E. (eds.) Proceedings of the 17th ACM International Conference on Computing Frontiers, CF 2020, pp. 269–276. Catania, Sicily, Italy, 2020. ACM (2020). https://doi.org/10.1145/3387902.3397224
10. Barenghi, A., Pelosi, G.: Constant weight strings in constant time: a building block for code-based post-quantum cryptosystems. In: Palesi, M., Palermo, G., Graves, C., Arima, E. (eds.) Proceedings of the 17th ACM International Conference on Computing Frontiers, CF 2020, pp. 132–141. Catania, Sicily, Italy 2020, ACM (2020). https://doi.org/10.1145/3387902.3392630

11. Bindel, N., Hamburg, M., Hövelmanns, K., Hülsing, A., Persichetti, E.: Tighter proofs of CCA security in the quantum random oracle model. Cryptology ePrint Archive, Report 2019/590 (2019). https://eprint.iacr.org/2019/590
12. Drucker, N., Gueron, S.: A toolbox for software optimization of QC-MDPC code-based cryptosystems. J. Cryptograph. Eng. **9**(4), 341–357 (2019). https://doi.org/10.1007/s13389-018-00200-4
13. Drucker, N., Gueron, S., Kostic, D.: QC-MDPC decoders with several shades of gray. Cryptology ePrint Archive, Report 2019/1423 (2019). https://eprint.iacr.org/2019/1423
14. Fabšič, T., Hromada, V., Stankovski, P., Zajac, P., Guo, Q., Johansson, T.: A reaction attack on the QC-LDPC McEliece cryptosystem. In: Lange, T., Takagi, T. (eds.) PQCrypto 2017. LNCS, vol. 10346, pp. 51–68. Springer, Cham (2017). https://doi.org/10.1007/978-3-319-59879-6_4
15. Faugère, J.C., Otmani, A., Perret, L., Tillich, J.P.: Algebraic cryptanalysis of McEliece variants with compact keys. In: EUROCRYPT. Lecture Notes in Computer Science, vol. 6110, pp. 279–298. Springer (2010). https://doi.org/10.1007/978-3-642-13190-5_14
16. Gallager, R.G.: Low-density parity-check codes. Ph.D. Thesis, M.I.T. (1963)
17. Guo, Q., Johansson, T., Stankovski, P.: A key recovery attack on MDPC with CCA security using decoding errors. In: Cheon, J.H., Takagi, T. (eds.) ASIACRYPT 2016. LNCS, vol. 10031, pp. 789–815. Springer, Heidelberg (2016). https://doi.org/10.1007/978-3-662-53887-6_29
18. Hashemi, Y., Banihashemi, A.H.: Characterization and efficient search of non-elementary trapping sets of LDPC codes with applications to stopping sets. IEEE Trans. Inf. Theory **65**(2), 1017–1033 (2019)
19. Hofheinz, D., Hövelmanns, K., Kiltz, E.: A modular analysis of the Fujisaki-Okamoto transformation. In: Kalai, Y., Reyzin, L. (eds.) Theory of Cryptography. TCC 2017. Lecture Notes in Computer Science, vol. 10677, pp. 341–371. Springer (2017). https://doi.org/10.1007/978-3-319-70500-2_12
20. Karp, R.M.: Reducibility among combinatorial problems. In: Miller, R.E., Thatcher, J.W., Bohlinger, J.D. (eds.) Complexity of Computer Computations. pp. 85–103. The IBM Research Symposia Series, Springer, Boston, MA (1972). https://doi.org/10.1007/978-1-4684-2001-2_9
21. McEliece, R.J.: A public-key cryptosystem based on algebraic coding theory. Deep Space Netw. Prog. Report **44**, 114–116 (1978)
22. Misoczki, R., Tillich, J.P., Sendrier, N., Barreto, P.L.: MDPC-McEliece: new McEliece variants from moderate density parity-check codes. In: Proceedings of IEEE International Symposium on Information Theory (ISIT 2013), pp. 2069–2073. Istanbul, Turkey (2013). https://doi.org/10.1109/ISIT.2013.6620590
23. Niederreiter, H.: Knapsack-type cryptosystems and algebraic coding theory. Prob. Con. Inf. Theory **15** (1986)
24. NIST: Post-quantum cryptography. https://csrc.nist.gov/projects/post-quantum-cryptography/post-quantum-cryptography-standardization
25. Richardson, T.: Error floors of LDPC codes. In: Proceedings of 41st Annual Allerton Conference Communication Control Computing, pp. 1426–1435. Monticello, IL, USA (2003)
26. Salomaa, A.: Finite non-deterministic and probabilistic automata. In: Theory of Automata, Chapter II, Monographs on Pure and Applied Mathematics, vol. 100. Pergamon (1969)
27. Santini, P., Battaglioni, M., Baldi, M., Chiaraluce, F.: Hard-decision iterative decoding of LDPC codes with bounded error rate. In: Proceedings of IEEE Conference on Communications (ICC 2019), Shanghai, China (2019). https://doi.org/10.1109/ICC.2019.8761536
28. Santini, P., Battaglioni, M., Baldi, M., Chiaraluce, F.: A theoretical analysis of the error correction capability of LDPC and MDPC codes under parallel bit-flipping decoding and application to cryptography. IEEE Trans. Commun. **68**(8), 1017–1033 (2020)

29. Santini, P., Battaglioni, M., Chiaraluce, F., Baldi, M.: Analysis of reaction and timing attacks against cryptosystems based on sparse parity-check codes. In: Code-Based Cryptography. CBC 2019. Lecture Notes in Computer Science, vol. 11666, pp. 115–136. Springer, Cham (2019). https://doi.org/10.1007/978-3-030-25922-8_7

30. Sendrier, N., Vasseur, V.: About low DFR for QC-MDPC decoding. Cryptology ePrint Archive, Report 2019/1434 (2019). https://eprint.iacr.org/2019/1434

31. Sendrier, N., Vasseur, V.: On the decoding failure rate of QC-MDPC bit-flipping decoders. In: Ding, J., Steinwandt, R. (eds.) PQCrypto 2019. Lecture Notes in Computer Science, vol. 11505, pp. 404–416. Springer, Cham (2019). https://doi.org/10.1007/978-3-030-25510-7_22

32. Tillich, J.: The decoding failure probability of MDPC codes. In: Proceedings of IEEE International Symposium on Information Theory (ISIT 2018), Vail, CO, USA, pp. 941–945 (2018). https://doi.org/10.1109/ISIT.2018.8437843

Business Analyst Tasks for Requirement Elicitation

Małgorzata Pańkowska(✉) 🆔

University of Economics in Katowice, Katowice, Poland
pank@ue.katowice.pl

Abstract. This paper is based on literature survey as well as on case study for the presentation of business analysis tasks and decision modeling for the presentation of business analysis tasks and decision modeling for Non-Formal Education System analysis and development. These studies identify the need to emphasize the role of business analysts for revealing opportunities in data governance and reduce the risks of information system implementation. The paper contributes to the understanding of business analysts in requirement elicitation and mapping. The study highlights the gap in the discussion on business analysts' role in information management and system development. Findings of this paper show that analysts can support information system developers in capturing the opportunities and in requirement elicitation by particular abilities of requirement mapping a cooperation with stakeholders.

Keywords: Business analyst · Requirement elicitation · e3 Value model · BPMN · ArchiMate

1 Introduction

Business analysis has a long history and as such is root of the subject of management itself. Analysis and diagnosis were always at the beginning of the decision making process. The decision maker was involved in the recognition of context, data, processes, and their outcomes just to recognize the economic solutions or select the best option. Consultants started to provide analysis services to organizations and they were able to work directly with their business clients. Later, business analysts began to be employed to assist managers and to take on some analytics roles, especially in reporting. In this paper, a basic question is what tasks, tools, and decision-making processes belong to business analysts. Therefore, the paper consists of two main parts. The first subchapter covers the presentation of literature review results and discussion on the role of business analysts in information system development processes. The second subchapter concerns the presentation of a case study on Non-Formal Education (NFE) system development at a university. This case study is to reveal the roles, tasks and decisions, as well as tools and techniques used by business analysts. Conclusions cover summarizing the literature review, revealed knowledge gaps and challenges important for business analysts in requirement elicitation and tasks mapping.

© Springer Nature Switzerland AG 2021
M. S. Obaidat and J. Ben-Othman (Eds.): ICETE 2020, CCIS 1484, pp. 175–193, 2021.
https://doi.org/10.1007/978-3-030-90428-9_8

2 Systematic Literature Review

Systematic literature review (SLR) is accepted as a research methodology and as such is employed within different disciplines of science as a way to synchronize research findings in a systematic and transparent way. This method is applied as a process for identification of relevant research as well as to reveal the gaps in research studies. Its aim is to recognize all empirical evidence to answer particular questions or to verify hypotheses. In this way, researchers are able to learn which particular issues are challenging. Detailed steps of the research on business analyst's characteristics and activities are included in Table 1.

Table 1. Detailed steps in literature survey.

Steps	Tasks
Collecting literature on business analysts	• Creating a search strategy • Selecting databases • Reading abstracts and full papers
Analyzing literature on business analysts	• Eliminating unrelated papers • Copying abstracts and available full papers • Supplementing additional literature • Removing duplicates that appear in different databases
Identification of business analysts' characteristics, competences, tools, techniques, tasks, methods, roles, and decision processes	• Reading titles, abstracts, keywords, and conclusions • Getting words, phrases, sentences associated with business analysts • Focusing on research results and findings in studies
Grouping research articles into classes on similar topics of studies	• Eliminating irrelevant papers • Classifying according to semantic similarity • Recognition of the best representative papers in classes
Identification of knowledge gaps in literature	• Summarizing the review results • Defining each gap in literature review • Considering identified gaps as challenges of further research • Discussion on the need to undertake the further research

The fundamental research question was formulated as follows: RQ1: How do business analysts support requirement elicitation? The proposed literature review research method was supplemented by the studies of guidelines on business analysis, i.e., Business Analysis Body of Knowledge (BABOK) [5], CBAP [30], and PMI Guide for Business Analysis [31], and BIZBOK [1]. The fundamental reviews were done using the following databases: Association for Information Systems Electronic Library (AIS eLibrary),

IEEE Explore Digital Library (IEEE Xplore), SAGE journals, Science Direct, Scopus, and Web of Science (WoS). The numbers of searching results were summarized in Fig. 1. According to the suggestions on literature review process, at first, taking into account the mentioned above repositories, the phrase "business analyst" was searched. The searching was conducted via the search string "business" AND "analyst". In the survey, papers and book chapters published in 2009–2020 were included. The reviewed papers classification was carried out by reading the articles and finding references to specific criteria, i.e., requirement elicitation and other tasks of business analysts, their competencies, roles, involvement in bridging the gaps between Information Technology (IT) and business needs, and finally – business analysts' challenges.

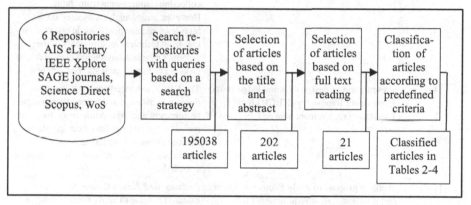

Fig. 1. The selection of articles considered for this research.

After the deduplication of founded results and the removal of inappropriate publication, finally, only 21 papers were selected as valuable examples for the discussion on business analyst' activities. The selected 21 papers were summarized in Tables 2, 3, and 4. According to the survey, there are thousands of papers, which concern analyst activity in different research area. However, only about 200 publications were written on business analyst for business systems. Authors of that papers prefer to write about the objects of business analyses instead about the actors, i.e., analysts. Eventually taking into account popular information system development methodologies, languages and tools, 21 publications are selected as the most suitable for this study. The content analysis revealed the primary activities of business analysts. The requirement elicitation is considered as a fundamental task of business analyst (Table 2).

Requirement elicitation process is a communication process oriented towards mutual understanding, negotiation, problem solution, and partnership cooperation. The business analysts' competencies are recognized and presented in reviewed literature in Table 3. In the time of business analytics development, the exceptional role belongs to business analysts and they have many new responsibilities, i.e., validation rules, progress reporting, visualization of data structures and algorithms, data collection and integration. Business analysts may be required to play a role of the recipient of information and knowledge, and provider of methodology. Therefore, both business as well as technology competencies are required. In some papers, the discussion on the role of business analyst are undertaken (Table 3). However, there are many interpretations of analyst roles.

Table 2. Publications on requirement elicitation task of business analyst.

No	Research item	Research questions	Results
1	[4]	Importance of the competency of business analyst involved in requirement elicitation	Indication that senior, intermediate, and junior business analysts performed similarly in selecting stakeholders' viewpoints and collecting requirements from them. However, senior analysts focused on high-level requirements, while others – on low-level technical requirements of the system. Organizations should clearly define tasks according to analysts' competencies
2	[43]	Presentation of design of Knowledge Based Component Repository (KBCR) for facilitating requirement analysis	The KBCR enhanced analysts' business domain knowledge and helped them prepare requirement analysis. While repositories of reusable components have been employed for some time, no one has used such repositories to help analysts acquire domain knowledge
3	[14]	Authors propose to apply Focus Groups in order to better elicit requirements for complex information system projects	Authors used Action Research as the research method to apply Focus Group in experiments
4	[11]	Authors intend that term consultant to be synonymous with business analyst, analyst programmer, and senior analyst	Structured interviews gather more information than unstructured interviews and techniques of sorting and ranking. The process of requirement elicitation is perceived as mutual learning by analyst and client
5	[24]	Authors propose a design framework for aligning business processes and IT across diverse collaborating organisations	Authors developed an architectural design framework BITA* that is composed of three coherent architectural design viewpoints. The BP2BP alignment viewpoint provides alignment modelling abstractions for business analysts to be used to align business collaboration processes. The IT2IT alignment viewpoint provides alignment modelling abstractions for software architects to be used to align distributed IT systems. The BP2IT alignment viewpoint provides alignment modelling abstractions for interdisciplinary teams of business and IT specialists

(continued)

Table 2. (*continued*)

No	Research item	Research questions	Results
6	[34]	The difficulties in communication between engineers, architects, business analysts, and the client should be removed to ensure mutual understanding in defining requirements, transposing into specifications, and a software	Authors share their experiences and explain how to leverage that knowledge through project-based learning, active and collaborative learning, delivered as face-to-face, self-paced e-learning, and online training courses, under the mentorship of experienced business analysts

Table 3. Business analysts' competencies, roles and involvement in bridging the gaps.

No	Research Item	Research Questions	Results
1	[27]	The authors offer a set of laboratory works to the formation of professional competencies and labor functions of a future specialist (business analyst) as part of the development of SAP Analytic Cloud technology	The use of situational tasks and cases helps to effectively implement the development of a complex of professional competencies, which are elements of generalized labor functions. The format of the description of the methodology is presented in the form of the traditional KeybyKey technology widely used in obtaining professional competencies in the field of IT
1	[19]	Authors focus on Design Thinking for requirement elicitation and learning	The competencies of Design Thinking are recommended to business analysts
2	[39]	Differentiation of the role of a business analyst by defining the appropriate skill level and breadth of required knowledge	Business analysts are to fill the gap between the experts (data scientists) and the day-to-day users
3	[38]	Authors focus on Business Process Analyst critical role for enterprise modelling	Proposal of framework of organizational learning to describe interventions and interactions that organizations use to build the required analyst's competencies
4	[41]	Approaches and challenges to create value from Big Data and from the business analytics	Authors emphasize the new roles of data scientists, business analysts, and IT professionals, as well as the need of their cooperation

(*continued*)

Table 3. (*continued*)

No	Research Item	Research Questions	Results
5	[12]	Author explores analyst's abilities to bridge the gaps between domains of users and of consultants	Analysts develop a shared interpretation scheme to translate concepts from the language of users to the language of experts
6	[7]	Problem of gaps between technical staff and business world	Authors propose a novel system named SODA (Searched Over DAta warehouse) that bridges the gap by enabling extended keyword search in a data warehouse
7	[32]	Business Intelligence and analytics involve several stakeholders, including IT people, analysts, business users, and data scientists	Author noticed a scarcity of research on conceptual models and mechanisms for creating business value by these stakeholders
8	[2]	Currently business analysts activities concern business process intelligence for agile decision making	Author argues that business analysts will identify opportunities for continuous business process improvement by providing contextualized, high quality and secure information
9	[28]	Data mining technology can be applied to support business analysts' work	Authors propose a framework that takes the results of the data mining process to improve the business performance, and to reduce time needed for data analysis

Dennis et al. [13] proposed a classification covering business analyst, system analyst, infrastructure and change management analyst, and project manager. Business analyst is assumed to focus on business value creation, but information system modeling should belong to system analyst. The final table covers publications including discussions on challenges formulated for business analysts. In general, information communication technology (ICT) constantly forces business analysts to look for new practices, methods,

Table 4. Publications on business analysts' challenges.

No	Research item	Research questions	Results
1	[3]	Empowering the business analysts to increase their expertise at many phases of the software development life cycle	Presentation of case study on usage of Grammar-Oriented Object Design (GOOD) method for creating and maintaining dynamically reconfigurable software architecture

(*continued*)

Table 4. (*continued*)

No	Research item	Research questions	Results
2	[36]	Business analyst involvement in Big Data architecture development	Business analyst is to be involved in requirement modelling process for Big Data governance, as well as in enterprise architecture development
2	[33]	Big Data governance is understood as a subsystem of corporate governance system, but also it covers data and information management, as well as Business Intelligence, therefore business organizations must standardize and systematize their handling of information and data	Business analysts are to be engaged in processes for having complete, current, actual policies, processes, and technologies for managing and controlling data flows, and for the management of volumes of data. Business analysts should be involved in data governance, accountability for data quality, economics of information, and providing value to information recipients
4	[45]	Authors argue that customer can be Data Provider (CDP) as well as Data Analyst (CDA)	Using survey data of 148 innovation projects, the authors find that both types of customer involvement facilitate business-to-business product innovation
5	[9]	This paper examines the analysts facing threat events to lay the groundwork for tacit knowledge management in Security Operational Centre (SOC)	The results highlight a unanimous pursuit of Root Cause Analysis (RCA) upon the outbreak of an incident and stages of decision-making when escalating to third party support providers. The results also suggest that simulation environments and physical proximity with analysts and vendors can facilitate the transfer of tacit knowledge more effectively in SOCs
6	[42]	Authors perceive a need for automatic methods to facilitate the search, retrieval, and analysis of large amounts of information	They propose a web tool to support the tasks performed by an Online Reputation Analyst (ORA). The proposed visualization techniques make it possible to immediately identify the relevance and scope of the opinions generated on Twitter

modelling languages, and tools supporting the modeling process. However, lately, Big Data and data science are strongly impacting business analysts' activities (Table 4).

The literature survey was supplemented by additional guidelines and standards review. In BABOK [5], business analyst should focus on understanding enterprise problems and goals, needs and solutions, strategy formulation, change specification, and facilitation of stakeholders' collaboration. Analysts are assumed to use various types of information, e.g., diagrams, legacy data, user stories, customer feedback, schema, user guides and spreadsheets. Therefore, they are required to understand the user decision-making process and to reduce the uncertainty in requirement elicitation process. They must understand the conditions, environment, and measures, in which the end-user decisions are made. According to Walliser [37], business analysts are to define a plan of action and prepare the processes for deliberation and decision-making. In the deliberation process, they combine cognitive thinking techniques, evaluate options and scenarios in order to form an intentional solution, and choose modelling techniques and software tools.

The CBAP [30] includes a more extended set of business analyst activities. They are responsible for the preparation and validation of feasibility studies, business cases, decision packages, project scope and requirements, and project deliverables [21]. Business analyst is involved in defining the business architecture, covering vision and mission, enterprise policies, procedures, geographical location, and organizational structures. The PMI Guide to Business Analysis [31] emphasizes the information need assessment, requirement traceability, monitoring, and solution evaluation.

BIZBOK [1] is assumed to provide a framework for business architects to address business challenges. This Guide is to include a comprehensive and complete vision of business architecture, combining together various concepts, disciplines, principles, and best practices. Authors of this approach focus on holistic and multidimentional business views, value delivering to stakeholders, the whole business ecosystem presentation, and integration community of individuals and assets. They emphasize constructivism in the activities, however they argue that business transparency is needed to streamline planing and evaluate alternative initiatives. The BIZBOK Guide topics do not refer directly to business analysis issues, but they cover principles that guide practices of architect business solution providing.

3 Business Analyst for Agile Method Driven Requirement Elicitation

Business organizations always have wanted to reduce risk of the current activities and minimize its impact on daily operations. Although workers are directed on what to do and how to do it, they expect a motivation and facilitation instead of management. According to Kuusinen et al. [25], agile methods focus on team collaboration and knowledge sharing. Agile processes employ intensive team work, face-to-face communication and trust as critical factors of working practices. Agility is a way of work grounded in the reality of learning. Research evidence shows that agile methods improve project stakeholders' communication, facilitate team and organizational cooperation. Business organizations are adopting agile methods, hoping to cope with rapidly changing environments and increase their opportunities for customer satisfaction. As Karvonen et al. [23] mention there is no single definition of business agility, but there is a set of desirable factors that affect the whole organization. Four fundamental values, (i.e., individuals and interactions over processes and tools, working software over comprehensive documentation, customer collaboration over contracting negotiation, responding to change over following a plan) are included in agile manifesto. Agile thinking is a holistic enterprise-wide approach that combines together the tools, methods, processes, standards, frameworks of an organization, resulting in a certain comprehensive approach [36]. Such approach includes the best practices and effective deliverables. Agile methods encourage to highly cooperative work between customers and product development teams. They focus on the early and frequent delivery of tangible solutions and in an iterative approach – sufficiently well response to changing customer requirements [15]. Agile methods emphasize the business analyst role and tasks. Business analyst need to understand the philosophy and rationale that underpin the agile approach. Girvan and Paul [15] consider the following business analyst values: collaborative working, self-organizing teams, doing the right thing and the thing right, continuous learning and improvement, planning for change, iterative development, and incremental delivery. Business units are expected to adapt and respond quickly to internal or external pressures. Business analysts are required to contribute to achieving organizational agility by ensuring an adaptability to change. Business analysts can support organizational agility by understanding the strategic context of the business organization, supporting the business architecture blueprinting, lean systems and services thinking implementation, and the investigation of business models and techniques.

The agile project community comprises computerized system users, business owners, stakeholders, sponsors, technical staff, information technology experts, and project managers. Frequent collaboration between the technical and business people is critical to success [10]. The agile project relies on self-organizing and self-managing teams. They apply the best practices and frequent communication to continuously look for feedback from the end users. The business analysts are just in the middle between business representatives and information technology staff. They are searching for the best solutions, which are a certain compromise and the results of deliberation and negotiations. Business analysts should identify issues, which are insuffiently explained or problematic. They must be strongly committed to the frequent delivery of high-quality software product features. Collier [10] considers characteristics of the agile project self-organizing team. He emphasizes people willingness to have control over their work, propensity to be better at what they are doing, and people preference to be part of a social group. These features encourage people to autonomy, self-organizing and self-discipline. People seek methods and techniques to continuously improve their practices and performances. They know they must respect norms and constraints, but they want to be free in what they are doing, because this freedom allows them to be creative. Self-organization requires shared responsibility and mutual support through recommendations and opinions sharing. As Collier [10] perceives, values and working agreements are self-imposed by the agile team members, and they must be consistent with organizational values and guidelines. Working rules are established just by this self-organizing team, so they are not imposed by external stakeholders. The self-organization requires mutual trust, commitments, responsibility, self-control, self-evaluation, and capacity planning.

Unlike traditional methods, agile methods focus on self-management, emergent processes, and informal coordinating mechanisms [6]. Therefore, the business analysts are necessary to facilitate frequent and problem-solving communication. Also Taylor [35] argues that agile methods encourages frequent inspection, communication, adaptation, self-organization, and accountability. The primary benefit of self-organizing teams is that when project participant feel they own the work, they tend to have more passion, time, and energy [26]. Van Oosterhout et al. [40] argue that agility is a way to cope with business organization changes, which are highly uncertain. The business uncertainty relates to the inability to predict the future impact of external forces on business. Beyond that, there are changes, which are quite predictable and the risks can be estimated. However, business organization are looking for people, who are not risk-averse. Business agility is implemented to response to problems and face challenges.

4   Business Analyst in Ontology Driven Requirement Engineering

Requirement engineering is critical stage in the software development life cycle. Communication problems and cultural differences do not facilitate work of developers and stakeholders. Many methods for requirement elicitation and analysis have been proposed to align business needs and information technology solutions. Usage of machine-learning capabilities is a way to solve the problem of business – information technology alignment and support requirement engineering. Business analysts organize deliberation and negotiation sessions, interviewing processes, brainstorming meetings, end user behaviour monitoring. In this way, they learn how end users work and how they communicate with their customers. Usually, beyond these techniques, experts are employed or expert systems are implemented to collect business requirements using various techniques like scenario analysis and simulation, interviews, questionnaire study, and case study analysis. Experts are responsible for domain knowledge collecting and providing it to business and system analysts. For business information system development, business analysts are usually involved in the business process modelling. Domain ontologies as formal representations of domain-specific knowledge are effective tools for process modeling and eliminating the semantic obstacles that unable understanding of specific domains.

Jenz [20] proposed to use business process ontologies to speed up business process implementation by eliminating the semantic gap between business analysts and software developers. Process analysts should rely on the experience of expert system managers to achieve process models with high comprehensibility, also known as pragmatic quality. According to Junior et al. [22], it is a challenge to help the business modelers to consolidate the knowledge in the process modelling guidelines and to reduce the process complexity. Therefore, the correctness of process models can be verified by means of ontologies. An ontology is developed to define process types, properties and relations. Junior et al. [22] argue that it is possible to use an ontology to represent business process model as a meta-model with inference capability to verify another process model's correctness. The use of ontologies may support the identification of problems that reduce a process model's comprehensibility. Integration of ontologies with business process modelling has gained attention in recent years, because this approach enriches process data usage and process knowledge reuse at the semantic level. Gurbiz et al. [16] have proposed a process ontology population methodology and tool for an event-driven process chain ontology populating in a fully automated or semi automated (user assisted) manner. The resulting ontologies are evaluated in terms of time-effort and precision metrics.

Yoon [44], using the ontology development method and the Protégé platform, introduced financial fraud ontology and an ontology-oriented financial fraud management system to enable analysts to increase the effectiveness of their work through rich financial fraud ontology knowledge. Cao and Woo [8] presented study focused on an ontological approach for providing domain knowledge to system analysts and designers. System analysts supported the reviewing and selection of components in domain model repository, and generating requirements for a new system.

Ontologies are used for the support of knowledge extraction, but still this approach is not fully utilised. There are proposals of new approaches that emphasize domain ontologies significance for business information development. Gutierrez et al. [17] proposed a novel approach by applying business architecture concepts for the definition of adaptive case management applications in combination with domain-specific ontologies and business rules. Therefore, business domain analysts can use domain- specific ontologies to support specification of goals, activities, and rules. Although business analysts use knowledge acquired from domain experts to develop high-level organizational strategic objectives, their roles in the process of knowledge acquisition and the domain ontologies development is not widely discussed in literature. Researchers rather focus on methodologies instead of business analysts tasks.

5   Case Study on Non-formal Education System Development

In this paper, non-formal education (NFE) is defined as an academic education form for adults. This education is ensured by university community as well as by volunteers from business. NFE facilitates learning by participation in events, e.g., night university visits, open lectures, game competitions, conferences, seminars, summer schools, and company visits. These activities are also known and university social responsibility (USR) events. The USR persuades academicians and students to undertake challenges to solve local community problems, to distribute knowledge and the latest technology solutions within local communities. In NFE community, the win-to-win strategy has significant priority. Local communities learn, but they also provide knowledge, experiences, observations, and opinions to academicians and university students. The complexity of tasks realized by NFE community forces its managers to implement business information systems for administration of different events. Main goal of this case study is to emphasize the role of business analyst in NFE information system development process. Therefore, the NFE architecture is presented in ArchiMate model (Fig. 2), e3 Value model (Fig. 3), and business process in BPMN Bizagi model (Figs. 4, 5, and 6).

There are some criticism that business analyst should focus on business requirements and leave system requirements with system analysts and software engineers [15,
18]. However, the primary role should belong to the business analyst, who understands
business goals, determines the information system goals and who should transform business requirements into system requirements. This transformation, known as requirement
mapping (Table 5), is extremely important to bridge the gaps between the expectations
of business people and preferences of IT specialists.

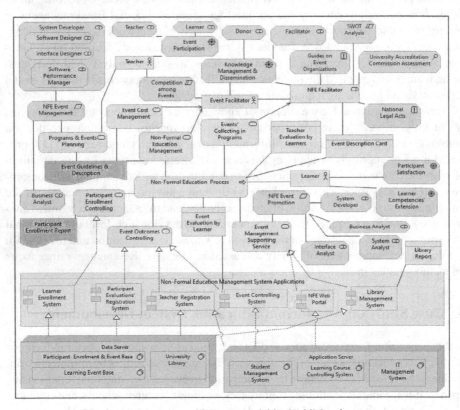

Fig. 2. NFE system architecture model in ArchiMate language.

The requirements mapped in Table 5 are subject of transactions in e3 Value model
(Fig. 3). This model enables discussion on communication between information system
development stakeholders and visualizes how joint efforts create value of the information
system. In this model, exchange of information among analysts and designers allow to
create new value of system artefacts. The e3 Value model emphasizes role of the business
analyst in comparison with other roles.

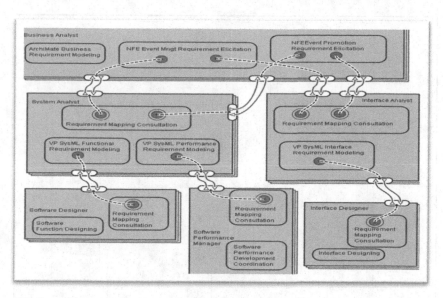

Fig. 3. e3 Value model of value exchange among Business Analyst and stakeholders.

Traditionally, initial analysis realized for business system development requires process modeling (Fig. 4). Figures 5 and 6 include extended sub-processes for process in Fig. 4. In the process model (see Fig. 4), tasks of business stakeholders, business analyst and system developer are interrelated. The two roles, i.e., Business Analyst and Education Facilitator, who is a domain knowledge expert, should be broken down and played by two persons of different competencies, to reduce risk and ensure high quality of requirement elicitation and system development. As it was presented in literature review, business analyst is expected to bridge the gap between the business requirements as they are specified in ArchiMate language in Fig. 2 and system requirements. The last ones can be specified in SysML or UML language and written in Visual Paradigm or any other computer aided software engineering (CASE) tool, e.g., Modelio, Camunda.

New opportunities of system modeling are created by the application of SysML, because SysML Requirement Diagram is suitable for requirement mapping. SysML requirement specification enables defining requirement attributes, project for requirement implementation, and other SysML diagrams connected with particular requirement diagram. SysML requirements are grouped into three classes, i.e., functional requirements, interface and performance requirements. The last ones define conditions, under which certain functions are performed.

Just e3 Value model is slightly different in comparison with ArchiMate and SysML models. These models focus on the analysis of system architecture and system requirement. However, the e3 Value model presents communication and transfer of values in this communication. Requirements elicitation and modelling are the key points in system analysis, but e3 Value model supports modelling the system stakeholders' roles in business information system development project. System requirements modelling belongs to system analysts, who for years have applied UML analytical tools to deal with this task [29].

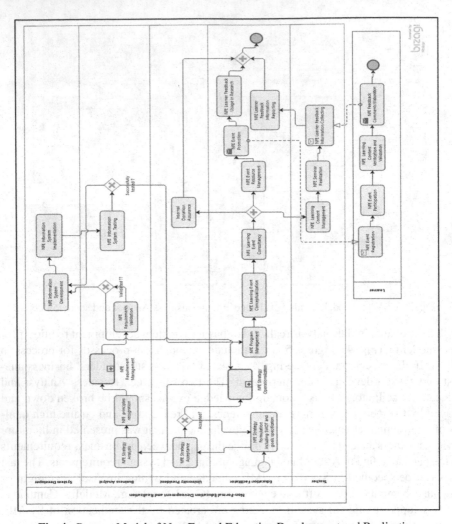

Fig. 4. Process Model of Non-Formal Education Development and Realization.

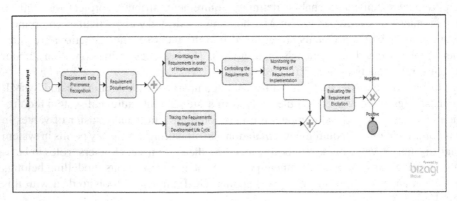

Fig. 5. Sub- Process on Non-Formal Education Requirement Management by Business Analyst.

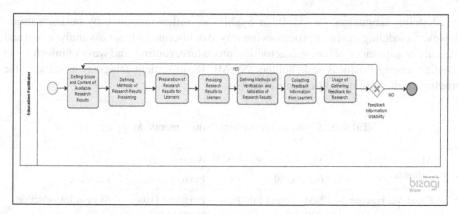

Fig. 6. Sub-Process on Non-Formal Education Strategy Operationalization by Education Facilitator.

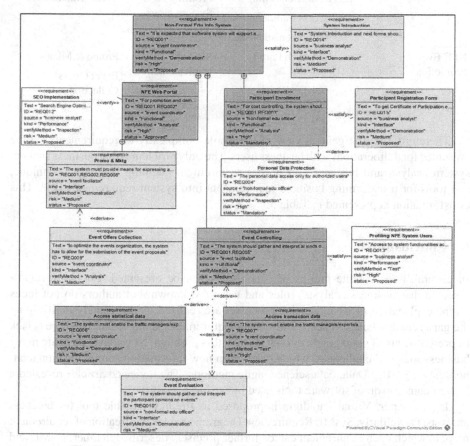

Fig. 7. Structure of Requirements in SysML Requirement Diagram.

Modeling languages, i.e., UML or SysML are rather unknown by business users. However, modeling business processes is a way to deliberate by business analysts and end users about sequences of business activities, procedure, routine, and ways of information transfers among business stakeholders. SysML Requirement Diagram is suitable for structuring all system requirements (Fig. 7).

Table 5. Business into System Requirements' Mapping.

ArchiMate Business Requirements	Visual Paradigm SysML Requirements		
	Functional	Performance	Interface
NFE Event Management	Non-Formal Edu Info System	Personal Data Protection	System Introduction
	Participant Enrollment		Participant Registration Form
	Event Controlling	Profiling NFE System Users	Event Evaluation
	Access transaction data		
	Access statistical data		
NFE Event Promotion	NFE Web Portal	SEO Implementation	Promo & Mktg
			Event Offers Collection

Therefore, the first general view of the whole complexity of requirements can be presented for deliberations with business users. The only problem is that business analyst, system analyst, and business user need a requirement mapping language, technique, and tools for transforming business requirements into system requirements [29]. This transformation is presented in Table 5.

6 Conclusions

In general, two separate groups of conclusions can be presented. Literature review revealed that business analysts' roles and tasks are known, but authors do not focus on the explanation of what decision processes are realized by these analysts. Bridging the gaps between business needs and system requirements is important, but there is lack of presentations of good practices how to solve this problem. Nowadays, there are many business analysts' challenges, which result from new information communication technologies, e.g., Big Data, data science, agile methods. The reviewed articles revealed a lack of comparison of software tools used by business analysts.

In this paper, Visual Paradigm is proposed as the best suitable tool for business analysts. Particularly, SysML Requirement Diagram enables the creation of requirement map, in which each requirement can be further precisely described in other SysML and UML diagrams included in one unique project. Finally, the requirement mapping is proposed as necessary to fill the gaps between the needs of business people and the proposals of software engineers. It should be emphasized that Visual Paradigm tool set in its professional version is an integrated software, which includes ArchiMate language and BPMN diagramming possibilities. Unfortunately, the e3 Value modelling is not possible there. The e3 Value model presents the value exchange among the information system project stakeholders. The values are included in communication messages and artefacts exchanged between actors. The values are not quantitatively measured, but just signaled as blue lines (see Fig. 3). The e3 Value model and BPMN diagram present actors, e.g., business analysts and their tasks and roles. The CMMN diagram focuses on actors' roles and tasks, but this modelling will be a research topic for the future work.

References

1. A Guide to the Business Architecture Body of Knowledge® (BIZBOK® Guide). Version 8.5 (2020). https://cdn.ymaws.com/www.businessarchitectureguild.org/resource/resmgr/biz bok_8_5/bizbok_v8.5_final_toc.pdf. Accessed 05 May 2020
2. Apine, B.: A new contract between business and business analysts. In: Grabis, J., Kirikova, M., Zdravkovic, J., Stirna, J. (eds.) The Practice of Enterprise Modeling, pp. 1–8. Springer, Heidelberg (2013). https://doi.org/10.1007/978-3-642-41641-5_1
3. Arsanjani, A.: Empowering the business analyst for on demand computing. IBM Syst. J. **44**(1), 67–80 (2005)
4. Babar, A., Bunker, D., Gill, A.: Investigating the relationship between business analysts' competency and IS requirements elicitation: a thematic-analysis approach. Commun. Assoc. Inf. Syst **42**(1), 334–362 (2018)
5. BABOK v3. A Guide to the Business Analysis Body of Knowledge, International Institute of Business Analysis, Toronto (2015)
6. Berntzen, M., Brede Moe, N., Stray, V.: The product owner in large-scale agile: an empirical study through the lens of relational coordination theory. In: Kruchten, P., Frase, S., Coallier, F. (Eds.) Agile Processes in Software Engineering and Extreme Programming, pp. 121–136, Springer, Cham (2019). https://doi.org/10.1007/978-3-030-19034-7_8
7. Blunschi, L., Jossen, C., Kossmann, D., Mori, M., Stockinger, K.: Data-thirsty business analysts need SODA: Search over data warehouse. In: International Conference on Information and Knowledge Management, Proceedings, pp. 2525–252 (2011)
8. Cao, L., Woo, H.: An ontological approach to support domain knowledge in information systems development, AMCIS 2004 conference proceedings (2004). https://aisel.aisnet.org/amcis2004/534/. Accessed 09 Sep 2020
9. Cho, S.Y., Happa, J., Creese, S.: Capturing tacit knowledge in security operation centers. IEEE Access **8**, 42021–42041 (2020)
10. Collier, K.: Agile Analytics, a Value-Driven Approach to Business Intelligence and Data Warehousing. Addison-Wesley, Upper Saddle River (2012)
11. Davey, B., Cope, Ch.J.: Consultants Experience of Requirements Elicitation Conversations – An Empirical Model, ECIS 2009 Proceedings (2009). http://aisel.aisnet.org/ecis2009/33. Accessed 05 May 2020
12. Deng, X.: Acting as translators between consultants and users in ERP implementation: an exploratory study of analysts' boundary spanning expertise. In: International Research Workshop on IT Project Management, pp. 30–42 (2010)
13. Dennis, A., Haley Wixom, B., Roth, R.M.: System Analysis and Design. Wiley, Hoboken (2015)

14. Farinha, C., da Silva Miguel, M.: Focus groups for eliciting requirements. In: Information Systems Development, UK Academy for Information Systems Conference Proceedings (2009). http://aisel.aisnet.org/ukais2009/26. Accessed 05 May 2020

15. Girvan, L., Paul, D.: Agile and Business Analysis, Practical Guidance for IT Professionals, BCS. The Chartered Institute for IT, Swindon (2017)

16. Gurbiz, O., Rabhi, F., Demirors, O.: Process ontology development using natural language processing: a multiple case study. Bus. Process. Manag. J. **25**(6), 1208–1227 (2019)

17. Gutiérrez Fernández, A.M., et al.: Applying business architecture principles with domain-specific ontology for ACM modelling: a building construction project example. In: Di Francescomarino, C., Dijkman, R., Zdun, U. (eds.) BPM 2019. LNBIP, vol. 362, pp. 388–399. Springer, Cham (2019). https://doi.org/10.1007/978-3-030-37453-2_32

18. Haugen, Ø., Reed, R., Gotzhein, R. (eds.): SAM 2012. LNCS, vol. 7744. Springer, Heidelberg (2013). https://doi.org/10.1007/978-3-642-36757-1

19. Hehn, J., Uebernickel, F.: Towards an understanding of the role of design thinking for requirements elicitation – findings from a multiple-case study. In: Twenty-Fourth Americas Conference on Information Systems, New Orleans, pp. 1–10 (2018)

20. Jenz, D.E.: Business Process Ontologies: Speeding up Business Process Implementation (2003). http://www.bptrends.com/publicationfiles/07-03%20WP%20BP%20Ontologies%20Jenz.pdf. Accessed 09 Sep 2020

21. Jonasson, H.: Determining Project Requirements, Mastering the BABOK and the CBAP Exam. CRC Press, Taylor & Francis Group, Boca Raton, London (2013)

22. Junior, V.H.G., Thom, L.H., De Oliveira, J.P.M., Fantinato, M., Avila, D.T.: A semiautomatic process model verification method based on process modeling guidelines. In: ICEIS 2017 – Proceedings of the 19th International Conference on Enterprise Information Systems, vol. 3, pp. 274–281 (2017). https://www.scitepress.org/ProceedingsDetails.aspx?ID=f3RlY9HqM8w=&t=1. Accessed 09 Sep 2020

23. Karvonen, T., Sharp, H., Barroca, L.: Enterprise agility: why is transformation so hard? In: Garbajosa, J., Wang, X., Aguiar, A. (eds.) XP 2018. LNBIP, vol. 314, pp. 131–145. Springer, Cham (2018). https://doi.org/10.1007/978-3-319-91602-6_9

24. Kassahun, A., Tekinerdogan, B.: BITA*: Business-IT alignment framework of multiple collaborating organizations. Inf. Softw. Technol. **127**, 106345 (2020)

25. Kuusinen, K., Gregory, P., Sharp, H., Barroca, L., Taylor, K., Wood, L.: Knowledge sharing in a large agile organisation: a survey study. In: Baumeister, H., Lichter, H., Riebisch, M. (eds.) XP 2017. LNBIP, vol. 283, pp. 135–150. Springer, Cham (2017). https://doi.org/10.1007/978-3-319-57633-6_9

26. Moreira, M.E.: The Agile Enterprise, Building and Running Agile Organizations. Springer, New York (2017). https://doi.org/10.1007/978-1-4842-2391-8

27. Nazarov, D.M., Morozova, A.S., Kokovikhin, A.Yu.: SAP analytic cloud: a tool for the formation of professional competencies of business analyst. In: 1st International Conference of Information Systems and Design, ICID 2019, Moscow Russian Federation, 8 March 2020, CEUR Workshop Proceedings. http://ceur-ws.org/Vol-2570/. Accessed 09 Sep 2020

28. Palpanas, T.: A knowledge mining framework for business analysts. Data Base Adv. Inf. Syst. **43**(1), 46–60 (2012)

29. Pańkowska, M.: Business to System Requirements Agile Mapping. In: ICE-B 2020 17th International Conference on e-Business Proceedings. INSTICC, ACM SIMIS, ABPMP, pp. 29–40 (2020). http://www.ice-b.icete.org. Accessed 09 Sep 2020

30. Phillips, J.: CBAP Certified Business Analysis Professional, Exam Guide, McGraw Hill, New York (2009)

31. PMI Guide to Business Analysis. Project Management Institute. Newtown Square, Pennsylvania (2017)

32. Prat, N.: Augmented analytics. Bus. Inf. Syst. Eng. **61**(3), 375–380 (2019)
33. Smallwood, R.F.: Information Governance. Wiley, Hoboken (2014)
34. Stevanoviu, J., Atanasijeviu, S., Atanasijeviu, T., Zahar, M.: Expanding the level of engineer knowledge for software modeling within corporate education by active and collaborative learning. In: IEEE Global Engineering Education Conference, EDUCON, April, 9125250, pp. 1807–1814 (2020)
35. Taylor, P.: The Lazy Project Manager. Infinite Ideas, Oxford (2009)
36. Unhelkar, B.: Big Data Strategies for Agile Business, Framework, Practices, and Transformation Roadmap. CRC Press, Boca Raton (2018)
37. Walliser, B.: Cognitive Economics. Springer, Berlin (2008). https://doi.org/10.1007/978-3-540-71347-0
38. Wamicha, E., Seymour, L.F.: Organizational interventions to build the ERP business process analyst: the 4 frameworks perspective. In: ACM International Conference Proceeding Series, Part F130806 (2017)
39. Wilder, C.R., Ozgur, C.: Business analytics for business analysts in manufacturing. In: Khosrow-Pour, M. (ed.) Operations and Service Management: Concepts, Methodologies, Tools, and Applications, pp. 272–280. IGI Global, Hershey (2017)
40. Van Oosterhout, M., Waarts, E., van Heck, E., van Hillegersberg, J.: Business agility: need, readiness and alignment with IT strategies. In: Desouza, K.C. (ed.) Agile Information Systems, Conceptualization, Construction, and Management, pp. 52–69. Butterworth-Heinemann, Oxford (2007)
41. Vidgen, R., Shaw, S., Grant, D.G.: Management challenges in creating value from business analytics. Eur. J. Oper. Res. **261**(2), 626–639 (2017)
42. Viloria, A., Varela, N., Vargas, J., Lezama, O.B.P.: Web platform for the identification and analysis of events on Twitter. In: Singh, V., Asari, V.K., Kumar, S., Patel, R.B. (eds.) Computational Methods and Data Engineering. AISC, vol. 1227, pp. 499–508. Springer, Singapore (2021). https://doi.org/10.1007/978-981-15-6876-3_39
43. Vitharana, P., Jain Hemant, K., Zahedi, F.M.: A knowledge based component/service repository to enhance analyst's domain knowledge for requirement analysis. Inf. Manag. **49**(1), 24–35 (2012)
44. Yoon, J.: An Ontlogy Guided Financial Fraud Knowledge Management System. University of Manchester, Manchester (2009). http://www.dissertationtools.com/mmu/2009/7091370.pdf. Accessed 09 Sep 2020
45. Zhang, H., Xiao, Y.: Customer involvement in big data analytics and its impact on B2B innovation. Indust. Market. Manag. **86**, 99–108 (2020)

Chained Transaction Protocol Automated Verification Using Cl-AtSe

Cătălin V. Bîrjoveanu[1(✉)] and Mirela Bîrjoveanu[2]

[1] Department of Computer Science, "Al.I.Cuza" University of Iaşi, Iaşi, Romania
cbirjoveanu@info.uaic.ro
[2] Vitesco Technologies, Iaşi, Romania

Abstract. The multi-chained complex transactions protocol from [4] is build around the chained transactions protocol. So, the formal proof of multi-chained complex transactions protocol correctness reduces to the formal proof of chained transactions protocol correctness. In this paper, we formally prove the correctness of the chained transaction protocol using Cl-AtSe model checker. The verification results obtained using Cl-AtSe demonstrate that all security requirements are met.

Keywords: Formal verification · Cl-AtSe · Multi-party electronic commerce · Chained transactions

1 Introduction

Complex transactions [3] are an important type of e-commerce transactions, allowing the combination in any form of *aggregate* and *optional* transactions. To be even closer to real world e-commerce transactions, there is a need to consider *chained transactions* in the transaction model that considers complex transactions. So, we introduced the chained transactions in [4].

In a chained transaction the customer obtains a physical product from a provider using one or more brokers. A *broker* is an agent that receives from another broker (or customer) a request to supply a physical product, and to accomplish this, he buys the product from another broker (or a provider) an sells it to the requesting party. The relevance of chained transactions is highlighted, for example when a broker makes available the products from many others brokers/providers as a single interface to the customer. These scenarios are often used in practice.

Related work proposes multi-party fair exchange protocols with applications in e-commerce transactions for buying physical products [3], buying digital products [11], digital signature of contracts [8], exchange of digital items [16] and certified e-mail [17].

Intermediaries are also considered in multi-party fair exchange protocols under different scenarios: digital signature of contracts [9], exchange of electronic items [10] and non-repudiation [12]. However, none of these solutions can be used in multi-chained complex transactions. More details regarding this can be found in [4].

M. S. Obaidat and J. Ben-Othman (Eds.): ICETE 2020, CCIS 1484, pp. 194–214, 2021.
https://doi.org/10.1007/978-3-030-90428-9_9

A multi-chained complex transactions protocol is proposed in [4] considering complex transactions in which the customer acquires each physical product in a chained transaction. Use cases of the multi-chained complex transactions protocol for Business to Consumer (B2C) and Business to Business (B2B) scenarios are described in [4].

The multi-chained complex transactions protocol from [4] is build around the chained transactions protocol. So, the formal proof of multi-chained complex transactions protocol correctness reduces to the formal proof of chained transactions protocol correctness. In this paper, we formally prove the correctness of the chained transaction protocol using Cl-AtSe [14] model checker from AVISPA [15]. The chained transaction protocol is a large multi-party protocol, therefore its formal proof is a challenging issue. The verification results obtained using Cl-AtSe demonstrate that all security requirements are met. Due to the multi-party aspect, during automated verification, an impressive number of states are analyzed as we can see in the Sect. 4.

The paper is structured as follows: Sect. 2 reminds the chained transaction protocol from [4], Sect. 3 provides an overview of AVISPA tool, Sect. 4 presents the formal specification and verification of the chained transaction protocol using Cl-AtSe, and Sect. 5 contains the conclusion.

2 Chained Transaction Protocol

In the *Chained Transaction Protocol (CTP)* from [4], we consider that the customer buys a physical product from a provider using one or more brokers.

CTP has the following participants: the customer, the provider, the brokers, the payment gateway and the bank. Table 1 presents the notations used in the description of *CTP*.

In *CTP* the following roles are identified: *initiator*, *receiver* and *payment processing*. An *initiator* agent initiates an exchange with a *receiver* by sending a request to buy a product. A *receiver* agent responds to the *initiator*'s request by sending the corresponding evidence of product's buying. The *payment processing* agent performs payments between initiators and receivers. C can only play the initiator role, as he initiates the chained transaction. P can play only the receiver role, as he provides a product to the agent that initiates an exchange with him. A broker is an intermediary agent in a chained transaction, communicating with both initiators and receivers. A broker plays the receiver role in an exchange in that he provides a product to an initiator. Also, a broker plays the initiator role in an exchange in that he buys a product from a receiver. The *payment processing* role is played by PG that is a trusted party.

We consider that each participant has the digital certificates for the public keys of each participant he communicates with. The communication channels between initiators and receivers are considered unreliable (messages can be lost) , and between PG and the other participants are resilient (messages can be delayed but not lost).

A *subtransaction* is an exchange in which an initiator buys a physical product from a receiver. A *chained transaction* in which C buys a certain physical product using the brokers $B_1, \ldots, B_n$ and the provider P is a sequence of subtransactions $s_0 s_1 \ldots s_n$, where C is the initiator in s_0, B_i is receiver in s_{i-1} and initiator in s_i, with $1 \leq i \leq n$, and P is receiver in s_n. In a chained transaction, C knows only the identity of the broker

Table 1. Notations used in CTP.

Notation	Interpretation
C, P, PG	Identity of Customer, Provider, Payment Gateway
B_i	Identity of Broker i, where $1 \le i \le n$. If $i = 0$, then B_i denotes C. If $i = n$, then B_{i+1} denotes P, and E_{i+1} is $Cert_P$.
PkA	RSA public key of the party A
$\{m\}_{PkA}$	$\{m\}_K, \{K\}_{PkA}$, where K is an AES session symmetric key. Hybrid encryption of the message m with PkA
$h(m)$	Digest of m obtained by applying of a hash function h
$SigA(m)$	RSA digital signature of A on $h(m)$
$PO_{i,i+1}$	$\{PM_i, OI_i\}_{PkB_{i+1}}$ - Purchase Order of B_i to B_{i+1}
PM_i	$\{PI_i, SigB_i(PI_i)\}_{PkPG}$ $PI_i = B_i, CardN_i, CCode_i, Id_i, Am_i, B_{i+1}$
OI_i	$B_i, B_{i+1}, Pid, Id_i, Am_i, SigB_i(B_i, B_{i+1}, Pid, Id_i, Am_i)$
Id_i	$Id_{i-1}N_i$ (If $i = 0$, then Id_{i-1} is the empty string)
$PR_{i,i+1}$	$\{PM_i, SigB_{i+1}(Id_i, B_i, B_{i+1}, Am_i)\}_{PkPG}$ Payment Request of B_{i+1} to get payment from B_i
$CE_{i,i+1}$	$Resp, B_i, B_{i+1}, Id_i, SigPG(Resp, B_i, B_{i+1}, Id_i, Am_i), SigPG(Resp, Id_i)$ Current Payment Evidence of B_i and B_{i+1} in s_i
E_i	Payment Evidence in s_i that B_i sends to B_{i-1} $Resp, Id_i, SigPG(Resp, Id_i)$
$CE_{i,i+1}.Resp$	The response $Resp$ in $CE_{i,i+1}$
$E_i.Resp$	The response $Resp$ in E_i
$A \to B : m$	A sends the message m to B

he communicates with in s_0, because C participates only in s_0. Also, B_i knows only the identities of the agents from s_{i-1} and s_i in which he participates, and P knows only the identity of the broker B_n.

C is browsing through the online catalog where the products from brokers are posted. After C decides the product he wants to buy, he clicks a"submit" button on the online catalog initiating CTP by sending to B_1 the purchase order $PO_{0,1}$ for buying a physical product. To fulfill C's request, B_1 initiates a new subtransaction by sending the purchase order $PO_{1,2}$ to B_2. In the same manner, B_2 initiates a new subtransaction with B_3, and so on until B_n initiates a new subtransaction with P. In this step, $n + 1$ subtransactions $s_0, s_1, \ldots, s_n$ are started. The successful finish of the entire chained transaction starts successfully finishing the subtransaction s_n, s_{n-1}, until successfully finishing s_0. Successful finish of s_n means that B_n and P received in s_n the same successful current payment evidence $CE_{n,n+1}$. This means that B_n received from P the successful current payment evidence for product, and P received the payment for product from B_n. Only after successful finish of s_n, B_n sends as receiver in s_{n-1} the payment request $PR_{n-1,n}$ to PG. Successful finish of s_{n-1} means that B_{n-1} and B_n received in s_{n-1} the same successful current payment evidence $CE_{n-1,n}$, and B_{n-1} received from B_n the successful payment evidence E_n in s_n. In this manner, any subtransaction s_i from chain is successfully finished only after the successful finish of $s_{i+1}, \ldots, s_n$ subtransactions.

CTP for a chained transaction $s_0 s_1 \ldots s_n$ consists of the *Exchange* sub-protocol for each subtransaction s_i, and two *Resolution* sub-protocols. Next, we will describe the *CTP*'s sub-protocols.

2.1 Exchange Sub-protocol

The *Exchange* sub-protocol for an arbitrary subtransaction s_i, where $0 \leq i \leq n$, that is presented in Table 2 [4]. In s_i, B_i sends to B_{i+1} the purchase order $PO_{i,i+1}$ to buy a physical product. $PO_{i,i+1}$ contains a payment message PM_i and the order information OI_i both encrypted with PkB_{i+1}. PM_i is build by B_i encrypting with PG's public key the payment information PI_i of B_i and the signature of B_i on PI_i.

PI_i contains the data provided by user as initiator: card number $CardN_i$ and a challenge code $CCode_i$ issued by bank. The challenge code is provided to user by bank via SMS. In each subtransaction s_i from chained transaction, B_i generates a fresh random number N_i. The identifier Id_i of s_i is built by concatenating the identifier Id_{i-1} of s_{i-1} with N_i. So, the identifier Id_i of s_i is the sequence of numbers $N_0 N_1 \ldots N_i$ generated in all subtransactions $s_0, s_1, \ldots, s_i$. In the case of a latter dispute, the identification of the subtransactions from chain is easily done by assigning identifiers to subtransactions in this manner.

OI_i contains the identity of the initiator B_i, of the receiver B_{i+1}, the product identifier Pid, the subtransaction identifier Id_i, the amount Am_i, and the signature of B_i on all these.

In each s_i, the receiver decrypts $PO_{i,i+1}$ and checks the signature of the initiator. If the receiver B_{i+1} is not the provider P $(i < n)$, then he stores $PO_{i,i+1}$ and sends $PO_{i+1,i+2}$ to B_{i+2} for buying the product requested by B_i.

At the line 2, if the receiver B_{i+1} is the provider P $(i = n)$, then s_i is the last subtransaction from chain. So, B_{i+1} stores $PO_{i,i+1}$ and sends the payment request $PR_{i,i+1}$ to PG to get payment from B_i. $PR_{i,i+1}$ is built from the payment message PM_i and B_{i+1}'s signature on Id_i, B_i, B_{i+1}, and Am_i. Upon receiving $PR_{i,i+1}$, PG decrypts it, checks B_i's signature on PI_i, checks B_{i+1}'s signature and checks if B_i is authorized to use the card by checking if the combination of $CardN_i$ and $CCode_i$ is valid. If some check is not satisfied, then PG sends to B_{i+1} an aborted current payment evidence $CE_{i,i+1}$ (with $Resp = ABORT$). If all checks are successful, PG sends the payment message to the bank. If the check on B_i's account balance, is satisfied, then the bank makes the transfer in B_{i+1}'s account providing a successful current payment evidence $CE_{i,i+1}$ (with $Resp = YES$) to PG that forwards it to B_{i+1} at the line 3. Otherwise, if checking B_i's account balance fails, then the bank provides an aborted current payment evidence $CE_{i,i+1}$ to PG that forwards it to B_{i+1} as a proof of s_i's abortion. We remark that $CE_{i,i+1}$ in s_i includes the evidence E_i that will be latter send by B_i to B_{i-1} to inform B_{i-1} if s_i was successfully finished or aborted. Also, PG stores $PR_{i,i+1}$ and $CE_{i,i+1}$ in its database. Upon receiving $\{CE_{i,i+1}\}_{PkB_{i+1}}$, B_{i+1} decrypts it and sends to B_i (line 4) the current evidence $CE_{i,i+1}$ and the provider certificate $Cert_P$. B_i checks the authenticity of $Cert_P$ and $CE_{i,i+1}$.

In each subtransaction s_i that is not the last from chain $(i < n)$, to answer the request received from B_i, the receiver B_{i+1} must ensure that either all the subtransactions that follows s_i in chain have been successfully completed, or all the subtransactions that follows s_i in chain have been aborted. An arbitrary subtransaction s_j is successful if

Table 2. Exchange sub-protocol for the subtransaction s_i.

---

1. $B_i \rightarrow B_{i+1} : PO_{i,i+1}$

2. **if** $(i = n)$ $B_{i+1} \rightarrow PG : PR_{i,i+1}$

3. $\qquad PG \rightarrow B_{i+1} : \{CE_{i,i+1}\}_{PkB_{i+1}}$

4. $\qquad B_{i+1} \rightarrow B_i : \{CE_{i,i+1}, Cert_P\}_{PkB_i}$

5. **else if** $(B_{i+2} \rightarrow B_{i+1} : \{CE_{i+1,i+2}, E_{i+2}\}_{PkB_{i+1}}$ in s_{i+1},

6. $\qquad$ with $CE_{i+1,i+2}.Resp{=}YES$ and $E_{i+2}.Resp{=}YES)$

7. $\qquad\qquad B_{i+1} \rightarrow PG : PR_{i,i+1}$

8. $\qquad\qquad PG \rightarrow B_{i+1} : \{CE_{i,i+1}\}_{PkB_{i+1}}$

9. $\qquad\qquad$ **if** $(CE_{i,i+1}.Resp{=}YES)$ $B_{i+1} \rightarrow B_i : \{CE_{i,i+1}, E_{i+1}\}_{PkB_i}$

10. $\qquad\qquad$ **else** *Resolution 1*

11. $\qquad\qquad$ **end if**

12. $\qquad$ **else if** $(B_{i+2} \rightarrow B_{i+1} : \{CE_{i+1,i+2}\}_{PkB_{i+1}}$ in s_{i+1},

13. $\qquad\qquad$ with $CE_{i+1,i+2}.Resp{=}ABORT)$ *Resolution 1*

14. $\qquad\qquad$ **else** *Resolution 2*

15. $\qquad\qquad$ **end if**

16. $\qquad$ **end if**

17. **end if**

B_j and B_{j+1} received in s_j the same successful $CE_{j,j+1}$. s_j is aborted if B_j and B_{j+1} received in s_j the same aborted $CE_{j,j+1}$.

So, at line 5, B_{i+1} waits to receive from B_{i+2} the current evidence $CE_{i+1,i+2}$ in s_{i+1} and the evidence E_{i+2} in s_{i+2}. If both evidences $CE_{i+1,i+2}$ and E_{i+2} received by B_{i+1} are successful, then $s_{i+1}, s_{i+2}, \ldots, s_n$ are successfully finished. In this case, B_{i+1} sends $PR_{i,i+1}$ to PG in s_i at line 7.

If B_{i+1} receives from PG (line 8) a successful $CE_{i,i+1}$, then he sends $CE_{i,i+1}$ and E_{i+1} to B_i (line 9). B_i verifies evidence's authenticity, and identifiers from both evidences to ensure the freshness of evidences and that these belong to successive subtransactions. If both evidences are successful, then $CE_{i,i+1}$ ensures B_i that s_i was successful and E_{i+1} ensures B_i that s_{i+1} was successful. If B_{i+1} receives from PG an aborted $CE_{i,i+1}$, then *Resolution 1* sub-protocol is applied (line 10) to abort all subtransactions from chain. The *Resolution 1* sub-protocol will be detailed below in Sect. 2.2.

If B_{i+1} receives from B_{i+2} an aborted $CE_{i+1,i+2}$, then *Resolution 1* sub-protocol is applied (line 13) to abort all subtransactions from chain. Otherwise, if B_{i+1} receives from B_{i+2} a successful $CE_{i+1,i+2}$, but E_{i+2} is missing or aborted, then *Resolution 2* sub-protocol is applied (line 14) to obtain a successful E_{i+2} or to abort all subtransactions from chain. The *Resolution 2* sub-protocol will be detailed below in Sect. 2.3.

Therefore, *CTP* continues until either all subtransactions initiated in chain transaction are successfully finished, or all aborted, ensuring in this way fairness.

If all parties involved in *CTP* behaves according to protocol's steps and no communication errors appear, then in each subtransaction s_i from chain the initiator B_i obtains the successful current payment evidence and the receiver B_{i+1} obtains the payment for the corresponding product.

Table 3. Resolution 1 sub-protocol.

$\text{if } (i < n) \; B_{i+1} \to PG : \{CE_{i,i+1}, \; CE_{i+1,i+2}\}_{PkPG}$

$\qquad\qquad PG \to B_{i+1} : \{\overline{CE}_{i+1,i+2}\}_{PkB_{i+1}}$

$\qquad\qquad PG \to B_{i+2} : \{\overline{CE}_{i+1,i+2}\}_{PkB_{i+2}}$

end if

for $(j = i + 1; j \le n - 1; j = j + 1)$

$\qquad B_{j+1} \to PG : \{\overline{CE}_{j,j+1}, \; CE_{j+1,j+2}\}_{PkPG}$

$\qquad PG \to B_{j+1} : \{\overline{CE}_{j+1,j+2}\}_{PkB_{j+1}}$

$\qquad PG \to B_{j+2} : \{\overline{CE}_{j+1,j+2}\}_{PkB_{j+2}}$

end for

for $(j = i; j \ge 1; j = j - 1)$

$\qquad B_j \to PG : \{CE_{j,j+1}, PM_{j-1}, OI_{j-1}\}_{PkPG}$

$\qquad PG \to B_j : \{CE_{j-1,j}\}_{PkB_j}$

$\qquad PG \to B_{j-1} : \{CE_{j-1,j}\}_{PkB_{j-1}}$

end for

2.2 Resolution 1 Sub-protocol

Let be s_i, where $0 \le i \le n$, the first subtransaction (in reverse order: from s_n to s_0) from the chained transaction $s_0 s_1 \ldots s_n$ in which B_{i+1} receives from PG an aborted $CE_{i,i+1}$ and forwards it to B_i. So, s_i is aborted, and fairness in CTP is not ensured. Therefore, to restore fairness in CTP, *Resolution 1* sub-protocol described in Table 3 [4] is applied to abort all subtransactions from chain.

If s_i is not the last subtransaction from chain, then B_{i+1} initiates *Resolution 1* by sending to PG a request to abort s_{i+1}. The request contains the aborted $CE_{i,i+1}$ in s_i and the successful $CE_{i+1,i+2}$ in s_{i+1}. PG verifies if the evidences belongs to successive subtransactions and if this checks, PG generates the aborted evidence $\overline{CE}_{i+1,i+2}$ that aborts the successful $CE_{i+1,i+2}$. As a proof of aborting s_{i+1}, PG sends $\overline{CE}_{i+1,i+2}$ to B_{i+1} and B_{i+2}. The first **for** loop aborts in a similar manner the subtransactions $s_{i+2}, \ldots, s_n$.

PG sends to the bank the request received from B_{i+1} and obtains $\overline{CE}_{i+1,i+2}$. The bank aborts the successful $CE_{i+1,i+2}$ by canceling the transfer and building $\overline{CE}_{i+1,i+2}$ as follows:

1. $\overline{E}_{i+1} = SigPG(ABORT, \; Id_{i+1}, \; E_{i+1})$
2. $\overline{CE}_{i+1,i+2} = ABORT, B_{i+1}, B_{i+2}, Id_{i+1}, SigPG(ABORT, B_{i+1}, B_{i+2}, Id_{i+1}, Am_{i+1}, CE_{i+1,i+2}), \overline{E}_{i+1}$

The second **for** loop aborts $s_{i-1}, \ldots, s_0$ in this order. In the first iteration, B_i sends to PG a request to abort s_{i-1}. The request contains the aborted $CE_{i,i+1}$ in s_i and the content of $PO_{i-1,i}$ received by B_i in s_{i-1}. PG verifies $CE_{i,i+1}$, $PO_{i-1,i}$'s content, and if identifiers belongs to successive subtransactions. If all checks are passed, PG generates an aborted evidence $CE_{i-1,i}$ and sends it to B_i and B_{i-1} as a proof of aborting s_{i-1}. Each iteration continues in a similar manner aborting a new subtransaction from chain until aborting s_0.

2.3 Resolution 2 Sub-protocol

Let be s_i, where $0 \leq i \leq n$, the first subtransaction (in reverse order: from s_n to s_0) from the chained transaction $s_0 s_1 \ldots s_n$ in which B_i sends $PO_{i,i+1}$ to B_{i+1}, but B_i does not receive the payment evidence from B_{i+1}. In this case, fairness in *CTP* is not ensured. So, to restore fairness in *CTP*, in any subtransaction s_i from chain, a timeout interval t is defined, in which B_i waits the payment evidence from B_{i+1}. If t expires and B_i does not receive the payment evidence from B_{i+1}, then B_i initiates *Resolution 2* by sending $\{PM_i, OI_i\}_{PkPG}$ to PG. On reception, PG decrypts it and checks B_i's signatures from PM_i and OI_i. If all checks are passed, then PG checks if $CE_{i,i+1}$ has been generated for the entry B_i, B_{i+1}, Id_i and Am_i, as follows:

1. If PG finds in its database the successful $CE_{i,i+1}$ and the successful E_{i+1}, then PG sends these evidences to B_i and *CTP* continues with s_{i-1}. If PG finds in its database the successful $CE_{i,i+1}$, and an aborted E_{i+1} or doesn't find E_{i+1}, then PG generates the aborted $\overline{CE}_{i,i+1}$ and sends it to B_i and B_{i+1} as a proof of aborting s_i. Further, for the last case, *Resolution 1* is applied to abort $s_{i+1}, \ldots, s_n$ if these are successful, and also to abort $s_{i-1}, \ldots, s_0$.
2. If PG finds in its database the aborted $CE_{i,i+1}$, then PG sends $CE_{i,i+1}$ to B_i and B_{i+1} as a proof of aborting s_i. *Resolution 1* is applied as in item 1.
3. If PG does not find an evidence, then PG generates the aborted evidence $CE_{i,i+1}$ and sends it to B_i and B_{i+1} as a proof of aborting s_i. *Resolution 1* is applied as in item 1.

A chained transaction successfully finished *CTP* if all its subtransactions are successfully finished. A chained transaction is aborted if all its subtransactions are aborted. As we can see, after running *CTP*, either the chained transaction successfully finished *CTP*, or is aborted.

Example. In Fig. 1, an instance of *CTP* considering a customer C, a broker B_1 and a provider P is described. The chained transaction is the sequence of the subtransactions $s_0 s_1$. In s_0, C initiates *CTP* by sending $P_{0,1}$ to B_1 for buying a physical product. To acquire the product requested by C, B_1 initiates a new subtransaction s_1 by sending $PO_{1,2}$ to P. P sends $PR_{1,2}$ to PG to get the payment for his product from B_1. After PG successfully verifies $PR_{1,2}$, he sends to P the successful $CE_{1,2}$. To complete s_1, P sends to B_1 the successful $CE_{1,2}$ and $Cert_P$. After receiving message 5, B_1 is ensured that s_1 is successfully finished. As a result, B_1 continues s_0 by sending in message 6, $PR_{0,1}$ to PG that responds to him with a successful $CE_{0,1}$. B_1 completes s_0 by sending $CE_{0,1}$ and E_1 to C. The successful $CE_{0,1}$ ensures C that s_0 successfully finished and the successful E_1 ensures C that s_1 successfully finished. In this case, the chained transaction is successful.

On the other side, if s_1 was successfully finished and s_0 was aborted because B_1 receives in message 7 an aborted $CE_{0,1}$, then fairness in *CTP* is not ensured. In this case, B_1 initiates *Resolution 1* sub-protocol with PG to abort s_1. So, the chained transaction becomes aborted.

Also, if B_1 sends the message 2 to P, but B_1 does not receive the corresponding evidence CE_{12} and the timeout expires, then B_1 initiates *Resolution 2* sub-protocol with

PG to receive the corresponding CE_{12}. Depending on successful or aborted CE_{12}, *CTP* continues or *Resolution 1* sub-protocol is applied. As a result, either s_0 and s_1 are successful or both are aborted.

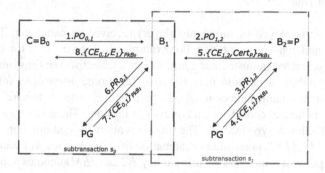

Fig. 1. *CTP* message flow.

3   Overview of AVISPA Tool

In this section, we provide an overview of AVISPA tool for automated validation of large-scale Internet security protocols [15], which we will use in the Sect. 4 for verification of *CTP*.

3.1   AVISPA Tool

In AVISPA, a protocol has to be specified in the High Level Protocol Specification Language (HLPSL) [1,2,6]. A HLPSL specification is automatically translated, using the hlpsl2if translator, into the Intermediate Format (IF) that is the input for Cl-AtSe backend that will be used for our verification from the Sect. 4. Cl-AtSe (Constraint-Logic-based Attack Searcher) is a model checker that uses constraint solving techniques [14], widely used to analyze security protocols. Security protocols verification using Cl-AtSe considers the perfect cryptography assumption, and a Dolev-Yao intruder model [7].

3.2   High Level Protocol Specification Language

Basic Roles. HLPSL is a role based language. The actions of each participant in a protocol session are specified by a basic role. The structure of a basic role is described below.

>   **role** name of role (typed parameters) **played by** player **def=**
>   **local**
>   declaration of typed local variables
>   **const**
>   declaration of typed constants
>   **init**

    initialization of variables
transition
    list of transitions
end role

A basic role is played by an agent (player) received as parameter. The parameters, variables and constants are typed. For example, the type *agent* is for agent names, *text* for fresh generated numbers, *nat* for numbers, *symmetric_key* for symmetric keys, *public_key* for public keys, *hash_func* for hash functions, *protocol_id* for labels and *channel(dy)* for communication channels. The attribute *dy* from *channel(dy)* specifies a communication channel considering a Dolev-Yao intruder. There is a data type *set* for unordered collection of typed values. The functions allow the combination of messages. For example, $M1.M2$ denotes the concatenation of the messages $M1$ and $M2$, M_K denotes encryption of a message M using a key K, and *H(M)* denotes application of a hash function H on the message M.

Transitions represents the actions of a basic role. A transition consists of a precondition and an action performed when the precondition is satisfied. The general form of a transition is described as follows:

$$S = 1 \wedge Rcv(M1) \ = \ | > \ S' := 2 \wedge Snd(M2)$$

S variable is used to define the state of the role instance. The agent that plays the role will communicate using parameters Snd and Rcv of type *channel*. The precondition of this transition is satisfied if the value of S is 1 and the message $M1$ is received on Rcv channel. The action of this transition sets the new value of S to 2 and send the message $M2$ on Snd channel.

Composed Roles. A session of the protocol is represented as a composed role by parallel composition of the basic roles. This is specified using the $\wedge$ operator in *composition* section of the composed role.

Environment Role. A top-level role in which the protocol is analyzed is necessary. This environment role specifies the initial knowledge of the intruder and the protocol scenario to be verified. The protocol scenario is a composition of one or more protocol's sessions, where the intruder may play some protocol's roles as an honest agent.

Security Goals. The section *goal* is used to specify the security goals that are analyzed. In HLPSL, the only security goals that can be specified directly by *goal facts* are secrecy and authentication. A goal fact is specified in a basic role as an effect of a specific transition.

The confidentiality of an information E is modeled by using the *secret* goal fact in the form *secret(E,id,agents_set)* in the basic role where E is generated or communicated for the first time. The meaning of this fact is that E is a secret shared between the agents from *agents_set*. The label *id* of type *protocol_id* is used to identify the goal by including the statement *secrecy_of id* in the *goal* section. If the intruder learns E and he is not in the set *agents_set*, then the confidentiality of E is violated.

The strong authentication of an agent A to an agent B with agreement on an information E is modeled by *witness* and *request* goal facts, as follows:

- in the basic role of the authenticated agent A, the *witness(A,B,id,E)* fact is specified, meaning that A wants to authenticate itself to B agreeing on E;
- in the basic role of the agent B that does the authentication, the *request(B,A ,id,E)* fact is specified, meaning that B accepts the authentication of A and agrees with A on E;
- in the *goal* section, the statement *authentication_on id* is included to identify the goal.

Strong authentication is obtained if for an issued *request*, a corresponding *witness* was previously emitted. If in a protocol execution, a corresponding *witness* was not previously generated for a *request*, then the strong authentication is broken.

A more relaxed form of authentication can be also modeled, *weak authentication*. For this, in a similar manner with strong authentication, the *witness* and *wrequest* goal facts and the statement *weak_authentication_on id* are used. In weak authentication, a *witness* can be used for several *wrequest*.

4 Automated Verification of Chained Transaction Protocol

4.1 Agent's Basic Roles

In what follows, we will discuss the most significant parts of each basic role of *CTP* considering the scenario from Fig. 1. The complete HLPSL specification of *CTP* is available at [5].

The **customer role** in HLPSL is described in Table 4. The parameters of this role are the agents C, B1 and PG, C's card number CN0, the challenge code CC0, the product's identifier Pid0, the amount Am0, and the public keys of C, B1 and PG. The customer role has four transitions. The first transition corresponds to the message 1 of *CTP* from Fig. 1. This transition is triggered if the customer receives the *start* signal to begin the protocol's session. In this transition, the customer generates a new subtransaction identifier Id0 and a new symmetric session key Kcb1 to be used in the hybrid encryption. The customer's digital signature on his payment information PI0=C.CN0.CC0.Id0'.Am0.B1 is represented in HLPSL by encrypting hash of PI0 with the customer's corresponding private key inv(PKC). In this transition, the action is represented by customer sending the message {PM0'.OI0'}_Kcb1'.{Kcb1'}_PkB1 to the broker. Also, a *secret* goal fact and two *witness* facts are included in the transition's action. These goal facts will be detailed later in the Sect. 4.4. The second transition corresponds to the reception by C of two successful payment evidences in the message 8 of *CTP*: the current payment evidence CE01=1.C.B1.Id0.{H(1.C.B1.Id0.Am0)}_inv(PkPG). {H(1.Id0)}_inv(PkPG) in s_0, and the payment evidence E1=1.Id0.N1'.{H(1.Id0. N1')}_inv(PkPG) from s_1. The constant 1 contained in the payment evidences encodes the response YES, while 0 encodes ABORT.

The **broker role** has 12 transitions and is fully specified in [5]. A part of this specification is also in Table 5. The first transition of the broker's role is triggered if he receives from C the message 1 of *CTP* from Fig. 1 and the result is represented by broker sending to P the message 2 of *CTP*. The second transition corresponds to the reception from P of message 5 that contains the successful current payment evidence CE12=1.B1.P.Id0.N1.{H(1.B1.P.Id0.N1. Am1)}_inv(PkPG).

Table 4. Customer role.

---

role customer (C, B1, PG: agent,

        CN0, CC0, Pid0: text,

        Am0: nat,

        PkC, PkB1, PkPG: public_key,

        H: hash_func,

        Snd, Rcv: channel(dy)) played_by C def=

local S: nat,

Id0, N1: text,

Kcb1, Kcpg: symmetric_key,

PM0: {agent.text.text.text.nat.agent.{hash(agent.text.text.text.nat.agent)}

      _inv(public_key)}_public_key,

OI0: agent.agent.text.text.nat.{hash(agent.agent.text.text.nat)}_inv(public_key)

init S:=0

transition

1. S=0 ∧ Rcv(start) =|>

    S':=1 ∧ Id0':=new() ∧ Kcb1':=new() ∧ PM0':={C.CN0.CC0.Id0'.Am0.B1.

                            {H(C.CN0.CC0.Id0'.Am0.B1)}_inv(PkC)}_PkPG

    ∧ OI0':=C.B1.Pid0.Id0'.Am0.{H(C.B1.Pid0.Id0'.Am0)}_inv(PkC)

    ∧ Snd({PM0'.OI0'}_Kcb1.{Kcb1'}_PkB1) ∧ secret(CN0,scn,{C,PG})

    ∧ witness(C,PG,pg_c_pi0,C.CN0.CC0.Id0'.Am0.B1)

    ∧ witness(C,B1,b1_c_oi0,C.B1.Pid0.Id0'.Am0)

2. S=1 ∧ Rcv({1.C.B1.Id0.{H(1.C.B1.Id0.Am0)}_inv(PkPG).{H(1.Id0)}_inv(PkPG).

              1.Id0.N1'.{H(1.Id0.N1')}_inv(PkPG)}_Kcb1) =|>

    S':=2 ∧ request(C,PG,c_pg_ce01,1.C.B1.Id0.H(1.C.B1.Id0.Am0).H(1.Id0))

    ∧ request(C,PG,c_pg_e1,1.Id0.N1'.H(1.Id0.N1'))

    ∧ request(C,B1,c_b1_oi0,C.B1.Pid0.Id0.Am0)

3. S=1 ∧ Rcv({0.C.B1.Id0.{H(0.C.B1.Id0.Am0)}_inv(PkPG).{H(0.Id0)}_inv(PkPG)}

          _Kcb1) =|>

    S':= 3 ∧ request(C,PG,c_pg_ce01_0,0.C.B1.Id0.H(0.C.B1.Id0.Am0).H(0.Id0))

    ∧ request(C,B1,c_b1_oi0,C.B1.Pid0.Id0.Am0)

4. S=1 ∧ Rcv({0.C.B1.Id0.{H(0.C.B1.Id0.Am0)}_inv(PkPG).{H(0.Id0)}_inv(PkPG)}

          _Kcpg'.{Kcpg'}_PkC) =|>

    S':=4 ∧ request(C,PG,c_pg_ce01_0,0.C.B1.Id0.H(0.C.B1.Id0.Am0).H(0.Id0))

    ∧ request(C,B1,c_b1_oi0,C.B1.Pid0.Id0.Am0)

end role

Table 5. Part of broker role.

role broker1 (C, B1, P, PG: agent,

        CN1, CC1, Pid1: text,

        Am1: nat,

        PkC, PkB1, PkP, PkPG: public_key,

        H: hash_func,

        Snd, Rcv: channel(dy)) played_by B1 def=

local S, Am0: nat,

Pid0, Id0, N1: text,

Kcb1, Kb1p, Kb1pg: symmetric_key,

X: {agent.text.text.text.nat.agent.{hash(agent.text.text.text.nat.agent)}

    _inv(public_key)}_public_key,

PM1: {agent.text.text.text.text.nat.agent.{hash(agent.text.text.text.text.

        nat.agent)}_inv(public_key)}_public_key,

OI1: agent.agent.text.text.text.nat.{hash(agent.agent.text.text.text.nat)}

    _inv(public_key)

init S:=0

transition

1. S=0 ∧ Rcv({X'.C.B1.Pid0'.Id0'.Am0'.{H(C.B1.Pid0'.Id0'.Am0')}_inv(PkC)}_Kcb1'.

            {Kcb1'}_PkB1) =|>

    S':=1 ∧ Kb1p':=new() ∧ N1':=new() ∧ PM1':={B1.CN1.CC1.Id0'.N1'.Am1.P.

                      {H(B1.CN1.CC1.Id0'.N1'.Am1.P)}_inv(PkB1)}_PkPG

    ∧ OI1':=B1.P.Pid1.Id0'.N1'.Am1.{H(B1.P.Pid1.Id0'.N1'.Am1)}_inv(PkB1)

    ∧ Snd({PM1'.OI1'}_Kb1p'.{Kb1p'}_PkP) ∧ secret(CN1,scn1,{B1,PG})

    ∧ request(B1,C,b1_c_oi0,C.B1.Pid0'.Id0'.Am0')

    ∧ witness(B1,PG,pg_b1_pi1,B1.CN1.CC1.Id0'.N1'.Am1.P)

    ∧ witness(B1,P,p_b1_oi1,B1.P.Pid1.Id0'.N1'.Am1)

    ∧ witness(B1,C,c_b1_oi0,C.B1.Pid0'.Id0'.Am0')

2. S=1 ∧ Rcv({1.B1.P.Id0.N1.{H(1.B1.P.Id0.N1.Am1)}_inv(PkPG).{H(1.Id0.

            N1)}_inv(PkPG).certP}_Kb1p) =|> S':=2 ∧ Kb1pg':=new()

    ∧ Snd({X.{H(Id0.C.B1.Am0)}_inv(PkB1)}_Kb1pg'.{Kb1pg'}_PkPG)

    ∧ request(B1,P,b1_p_oi1,B1.P.Pid1.Id0.N1.Am1)

    ∧ witness(B1,PG,pg_b1_am0,Am0)

3. S=2 ∧ Rcv({1.C.B1.Id0.{H(1.C.B1.Id0.Am0)}_inv(PkPG).{H(1.Id0)}_inv(PkPG)}

      _Kb1pg) =|> S':=3

    ∧ Snd({1.C.B1.Id0.{H(1.C.B1.Id0.Am0)}_inv(PkPG).{H(1.Id0)}_inv(PkPG).

        1.Id0.N1.{H(1.Id0.N1)}_inv(PkPG)}_Kcb1)

    ∧ request(B1,PG,b1_pg_ce01,1.C.B1.Id0.H(1.C.B1.Id0.Am0).H(1.Id0))

    ∧ request(B1,PG,b1_pg_ce12,1.B1.P.Id0.N1.H(1.B1.P.Id0.N1.Am1).H(1.Id0.N1))

⋮

8. S=1 ∧ Rcv(t) =|> S':=8 ∧ Kb1pg':=new() ∧ Snd({PM1.OI1}_Kb1pg'.{Kb1pg'}_PkPG)

⋮

{H(1.Id0.N1)}_inv(PkPG) in s_1 and the sending to PG of the message 6. The third transition corresponds to the reception from PG of message 7 and the sending to C of message 8.

The **provider role**, specified in [5], includes as parameters two lists: OIL is the list of order information received by P, and PL is the list of pairs (Pid, Am) of products available at P. The order information received by P from B1 is B1.P.Pid1'.Id0'.N1'.Am1'. {H(B1.P.Pid1'.Id0'.N1'.Am1')}_inv(PkB1). The first transition of the provider's role is triggered if he receives the message 2, the order information from the message are not in OIL, and if the pair (Pid1', Am1') received is in PL. OIL list is necessary to protect P against replay attacks containing old information order. The effect of this transition is sending the message 3. The second/third transition corresponds to the reception of message 4 containing a successful/aborted current evidence CE12 in s_1 and sending of the corresponding message 5.

Table 6. Part of payment gateway role.

---

role paymentgateway (C, B1, P, PG: agent,
PkC, PkB1, PkP, PkPG: public_key,
CIL: (agent.text.text) set,
PRL: ({agent.text.text.text.text.nat.agent.{hash(agent.text.text.text.text.nat.agent)}
_inv(public_key)}_(public_key).{hash(text.text.agent.agent.nat)}_inv(public_key)) set,
H: hash_func, Snd, Rcv: channel(dy)) played_by PG def=
⋮

transition
1. S=0 ∧ Rcv({{B1.CN1'.CC1'.Id0'.N1'.Am1'.P.{H(B1.CN1'.CC1'.Id0'.N1'.Am1'.P)}
        _inv(PkB1)}_PkPG.{H(Id0'.N1'.B1.P.Am1')}_inv(PkP)}_Kppg'.{Kppg'}_PkPG)
    ∧ not(in({B1.CN1'.CC1'.Id0'.N1'.Am1'.P.{H(B1.CN1'.CC1'.Id0'.N1'.Am1'.P)}
            _inv(PkB1)}_PkPG.{H(Id0'.N1'.B1.P.Am1')}_inv(PkP) , PRL))
    ∧ in(B1.CN1'.CC1' , CIL) =|> S':=1
    ∧ PRL':=cons({B1.CN1'.CC1'.Id0'.N1'.Am1'.P.{H(B1.CN1'.CC1'.Id0'.N1'.Am1'.P)}
            _inv(PkB1)}_PkPG.{H(Id0'.N1'.B1.P.Am1')}_inv(PkP) , PRL)
    ∧ Snd({1.B1.P.Id0'.N1'.{H(1.B1.P.Id0'.N1'.Am1')}_inv(PkPG).{H(1.Id0'.N1')}
            _inv(PkPG)}_Kppg')
    ∧ witness(PG,P,p_pg_ce12,1.B1.P.Id0'.N1'.H(1.B1.P.Id0'.N1'.Am1').H(1.Id0'.N1'))
    ∧ witness(PG,B1,b1_pg_ce12,1.B1.P.Id0'.N1'.H(1.B1.P.Id0'.N1'.Am1').H(1.Id0'.N1'))
    ∧ request(PG,B1,pg_b1_pi1,B1.CN1'.CC1'.Id0'.N1'.Am1'.P)
    ∧ witness(PG,C,c_pg_e1,1.Id0'.N1'.H(1.Id0'.N1')) ∧ request(PG,P,pg_p_am1,Am1')
⋮

The **paymentgateway role** has 10 transitions and is fully specified in [5]. A part of this specification is described in Table 6. Two lists CIL and PRL are included as parameters in this role. CIL is the list of records of payment information for customer and broker. If the broker's payment information, $B1.CN1'.CC1'$, are in the list CIL, then this means that B1 is authorized to use the card. PRL is the list of payment requests received by PG, and this is necessary to protect PG against replay attacks containing already received payment requests. The payment request received from P is $\{B1.CN1'.CC1'.Id0'.N1'.Am1'.P.\{H(B1.CN1'.CC1'.Id0'.N1'.Am1'.P)\}\_inv(PkB1)\}\_PkPG.\{H(Id0'.N1'.B1.P.Am1')\}\_inv(PkP)$. The precondition of first transition is satisfied if PG receives the message 3, if the payment information of B1 are in CIL, and if the payment request received from P is not already in PRL. The action of this transition is represented by PG sending the successful CE12 to P in the message 4. In the second transition, if the payment information of B1 are not in CIL, then PG sends an aborted CE12 to P in the message 4. The third/fourth transition corresponds to the reception of message 6 from B1 containing the payment request in s_0 and sending to B1 the corresponding successful/aborted current evidence CE01 in message 7.

To model *Resolution 1* sub-protocol, two scenarios must taken into consideration. In first scenario, the subtransaction s_1 is successful and s_0 is aborted. The transition 4 from broker role models the reception in s_0 of aborted CE01, sending CE01 to C, and sending to PG the aborted CE01 and successful CE12 to abort s_1. The third transition from customer role corresponds to the reception of aborted CE01. PG receives the request from B1 in transition 6, aborts CE12 and sends it to B1 and P. The aborted CE12 is received by B1 in the transition 5 and received by P in the transition 4. So, both subtransactions are aborted.

In the second scenario, the subtransaction s_1 is aborted. The transition 6 from broker role models the reception in s_1 of aborted CE12 and sending to PG the aborted CE12 together with the request received from C in the message 1 to abort s_0. In transition 5, PG receives the request from B1, generates the aborted CE01 and sends it to B1 and C. C receives the aborted CE01 in the transition 4, while B1 receives it in the transition 7. As we can see, both subtransactions are now aborted.

In Fig. 2, we use the option *Intruder simulation* from SPAN (Security Protocol ANimator for AVISPA) [13] to show the Message Sequence Chart of *CTP* that highlights the scenario in that *Resolution 2* and *Resolution 1* sub-protocols are applied.

To model *Resolution 2* sub-protocol, we consider the scenario in that B1 sends the message 2 from Fig. 1 to P (Step2. in Fig. 2), but B1 does not receive the corresponding evidence CE12 from P and the timeout interval t expires. The transition 5 from the provider role models the scenario in that P receives from PG the successful CE12 in s_1 (Step4.), but P does not send it to B1. In the transition 8 from the broker role, B1 receives timeout t (from the intruder in Step5.) and he sends $\{PM1.OI1\}\_Kb1pg'$. $\{Kb1pg'\}\_PkPG$ to PG (in Step6.) to receive the corresponding CE12. PG receives the message above in transition 7, in which sends the successful CE12 and certP to B1 (Step7.). Reception by B1 of CE12 and certP in s_1 is modeled in transition 9, where he sends to PG the message 6 from Fig. 1 corresponding to s_0 (Step8.). If C is authorized to use the card, then PG responds to B1 with a successful CE01 in transition 8, otherwise PG responds with an aborted CE01 in transition 9 (Step9.). In the transition 10 from broker role, if B1 receives a successful CE01, then he sends the message 1 Fig. 1 to C. Otherwise, in transition 11, if B1 receive an aborted CE01, then he sends it to C (Step10.) and also sends CE01 and CE12 to PG to abort s_1 (Step11.). PG receives the request from B1 in transition 10, aborts CE12 and sends it to B1 and P (Step12. and Step13.). B1 receives the aborted CE12 in the transition 12 and P receives it in the transition 6. As a result, both subtransactions are aborted.

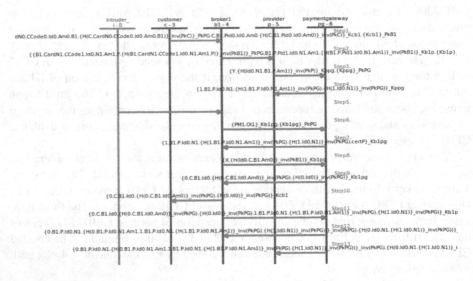

Fig. 2. Message Sequence Chart of *CTP* in *intruder simulation* from SPAN.

We model *CTP* in HLPSL considering the scenario with a customer C, a broker B1, a provider P and a payment gateway PG. This scenario required a total number of 32 transitions in all roles. We can extend the specification by adding a new broker B2 in the chain as in scenario in Fig. 1 from [4]. For this, a new broker2 role similar with broker1 role must be added in the specification. The paymentgateway role must be enlarged with the transitions corresponding with the communication between PG and B2, and the resolution sub-protocols must be accordingly updated. The customer role remains unchanged, and the broker1 and provider roles are changed only with respect to the entity they communicates with. In this manner, we can extend the specification to include any number of brokers.

4.2 Protocol's Sessions Composed Roles

Table 7 describes a session of *CTP* in HLPSL as a composed role that has no transitions. A session of *CTP* is specified by parallel composition of one instance of each basic role.

4.3   Environment Role

The environment role presented in Table 8 describes the global constants, the initial value of local variables, the initial knowledge of the intruder and the protocol scenario to be verified. The lists OIL and PRL are initially empty, P initially knows three pairs of products, and PG initially knows in CIL list the payment information of customer - c.cn0.cc0, of broker - b1.cn1.cc1 and of intruder - i.cn2.cc2. The intruder's initial knowledge includes the identities of customer, broker, provider and payment gateway, his payment information, all public keys, his own private key, a product identifier pid2, the amount am2, the public hash function h, and the timeout t. The constant i denotes the intruder. The scenario to be verified contains four protocol's concurrent sessions. First session is the protocol's session with an honest customer c, an honest broker b1, an honest provider p and the trusted party pg. The second, third and fourth sessions are one in which the intruder i is respectively customer, broker and provider.

4.4   Security Requirements

The security requirements analyzed for our protocol are specified in Table 9.

Table 7. CTP session.

---

role session(C, B1, P, PG: agent,
  CN0, CC0, Pid0, CN1, CC1, Pid1: text,
  Am0, Am1: nat,
  PkC, PkB1, PkP, PkPG: public_key,
  H: hash_func,
  OIL: (agent.agent.text.text.text.nat.{hash(agent.agent.text.text.text.nat)}
      _inv(public_key)) set,
  PL: (text.nat) set,
  CIL: (agent.text.text) set,
  PRL: ({agent.text.text.text.text.nat.agent.{hash(agent.text.text.text.text.nat.agent)}
  _inv(public_key)}_(public_key).{hash(text.text.agent.agent.nat)}_inv(public_key)) set,
  Snd, Rcv: channel(dy)) def=
composition
    customer (C,B1,PG,CN0,CC0,Pid0,Am0,PkC,PkB1,PkPG,H,Snd,Rcv)
    ∧ broker1 (C,B1,P,PG,CN1,CC1,Pid1,Am1,PkC,PkB1,PkP,PkPG,H,Snd,Rcv)
    ∧ provider (B1,P,PG,PkP,PkB1,PkPG,OIL,PL,H,Snd,Rcv)
    ∧ paymentgateway (C,B1,P,PG,PkC,PkB1,PkP,PkPG,CIL,PRL,H,Snd,Rcv)
end role

To obtain confidentiality of sensitive data communicated in *CTP*, we require that card number CN0 of customer to be known only by C and PG, and that card number CN1 of broker to be known only by B1 and PG. As a result, to specify first requirement in HLPSL, in the first transition of the customer role, the goal fact secret(CN0,scn,{C,PG}) is added. For the second requirement, a corresponding goal fact secret(CN1,scn1,{B1,PG}) is added in the first transition of the broker role.

To ensure strong authentication in *CTP*, we require a number of strong authentication security requirements that we will detail in what follows. To verify strong mutual authentication between C and B1 on order information OI0, we need to verify if B1 strong authenticates C on OI0 and if C strong authenticates B1 on OI0. For checking if B1 strong authenticates C on OI0, two goal facts are necessary:

- witness(C,B1,b1_c_oi0,C.B1.Pid0.Id0'.Am0) specifies that C wants to authenticate itself to B1 on OI0, in first transition of the customer role;
- request(B1,C,b1_c_oi0,C.B1.Pid0'.Id0'.Am0') specifies that B1 authenticates C on OI0, in first transition of the broker role.

Checking if C strong authenticates B1 on OI0 requires to add witness(B1,C, c_b1_oi0,C.B1.Pid0'.Id0'.Am0') in first transition of the broker role and request(C, B1,c_b1_oi0,C.B1.Pid0.Id0.Am0) in the second, third and fourth transition of the customer role. The request fact from the second transition of customer role is for the case when C receives from B1 a successful CE01, and the request from the third and fourth transition corresponds to the scenarios in which C receives an aborted CE01 in different cases in *Resolution 1* sub-protocol.

We also require (complete specification details are in [5]):

1. strong mutual authentication between B1 and P on the order information OI1 using the identifiers p_b1_oi1 and b1_p_oi1;
2. strong authentication of C at PG on PI0 using pg_c_pi0 identifier;
3. strong authentication of B1 to PG on the payment information PI1 using pg_b1_pi1;
4. strong authentication of P to PG on the amount Am1 using pg_p_am1;
5. strong authentication of B1 to PG on the amount Am0 using pg_b1_am0;
6. strong authentication of PG to P on successful CE12 using p_pg_ce12, on aborted CE12 using p_pg_ce12_0, and on aborted CE12 using p_pg_ace12 for the case in which CE12 was previously successful issued (the last requirement is necessary in the resolution sub-protocols);
7. strong authentication of PG to B1 on successful CE12 using b1_pg_ce12, on aborted CE12 using b1_pg_ce12_0, and on aborted CE12 using b1_pg_ace12 for the case in which CE12 was previously successful issued;
8. strong authentication of PG to B1 on successful CE01 using b1_pg_ce01, on aborted CE01 using b1_pg_ce01_0;
9. strong authentication of PG to C on successful CE01 using c_pg_ce01, on aborted CE01 using c_pg_ce01_0, and on successful E1 using c_pg_e1.

AVISPA can not directly verify fairness in *CTP* because this requirement is not explicitly modeled in HLPSL. Next, we explain how we use strong authentication to model fairness in HLPSL.

Table 8. Environment role.

---

role environment() def=
local OIL: (agent.agent.text.text.text.nat.{hash(agent.agent.text.text.text.nat)}
_inv(public_key)) set,
PL: (text.nat) set,
CIL: (agent.text.text) set,
PRL: ({agent.text.text.text.text.nat.agent.{hash(agent.text.text.text.text.nat.agent)}
_inv(public_key)}_(public_key).{hash(text.text.agent.agent.nat)}_inv(public_key)) set,
Snd, Rcv: channel(dy)

const c, b1, p, pg, i: agent,
cn0, cc0, cn1, cc1, cn2, cc2, pid0, pid1, pid2, t, certP: text,
am0, am1, am2: nat,
pkc, pkb1, pkp, pkpg, pki: public_key,
h: hash_func,
scn, scn1, b1_c_oi0, c_b1_oi0, p_b1_oi1, b1_p_oi1, pg_c_pi0, pg_b1_pi1, pg_p_am1,
pg_b1_am0, p_pg_ce12, p_pg_ce12_0, p_pg_ace12, b1_pg_ce12, b1_pg_ce12_0,
b1_pg_ace12, b1_pg_ce01, b1_pg_ce01_0, c_pg_ce01, c_pg_ce01_0, c_pg_e1: protocol_id,

init OIL:= {}
∧ PL:={pid0.am0, pid1.am1, pid2.am2}
∧ CIL:={c.cn0.cc0, b1.cn1.cc1, i.cn2.cc2}
∧ PRL:={}

intruder_knowledge={c,b1,p,pg,cn2,cc2,pkc,pkb1,pkpg,pki,inv(pki),pid2,am2,h,t}

composition
    session(c, b1, p, pg, cn0, cc0, pid0, cn1, cc1, pid1, am0, am1, pkc, pkb1, pkp, pkpg,
            h, OIL, PL, CIL, PRL, Snd, Rcv) ∧
    session(i, b1, p, pg, cn2, cc2, pid2, cn1, cc1, pid1, am2, am1, pki, pkb1, pkp, pkpg,
            h, OIL, PL, CIL, PRL, Snd, Rcv) ∧
    session(c, i, p, pg, cn0, cc0, pid0, cn2, cc2, pid2, am0, am2, pkc, pki, pkp, pkpg,
            h, OIL, PL, CIL, PRL, Snd, Rcv) ∧
    session(c, b1, i, pg, cn0, cc0, pid0, cn1, cc1, pid1, am0, am1, pkc, pkb1, pki, pkpg,
            h, OIL, PL, CIL, PRL, Snd, Rcv)
end role

Table 9. Security requirements.

---

goal

secrecy_of scn, scn1

authentication_on b1_c_oi0, c_b1_oi0, p_b1_oi1, b1_p_oi1

authentication_on pg_c_pi0, pg_b1_pi1

authentication_on pg_p_am1, pg_b1_am0

authentication_on p_pg_ce12, p_pg_ce12_0, p_pg_ace12

authentication_on b1_pg_ce12, b1_pg_ce12_0, b1_pg_ace12

authentication_on b1_pg_ce01, b1_pg_ce01_0

authentication_on c_pg_ce01, c_pg_ce01_0, c_pg_e1

end goal

CTP ensures fairness if either both subtransactions s_0 and s_1 from the chained transaction successfully complete *CTP*, or both are aborted. s_1 is successful/aborted if both B1 and P receive the successful/aborted CE12, while s_0 is successful/aborted if both C and B1 receive the successful/aborted CE01. So, to obtain fairness in *CTP*, either all agents C, B1 and P receive from PG successful evidences in s_0 and s_1, or all receive from PG aborted evidences in s_0 and s_1. As a result, we require strong authentication of PG to P on CE12, strong authentication of PG to B1 on CE12, strong authentication of PG to B1 on CE01, strong authentication of PG to C on CE01 and E1, all these being mentioned in the items 6-9 from strong authentication requirements above. Besides these, we remark how B1 authenticates PG on evidences CE12 and CE01. So, only after B1 receives successful evidences in s_1 and afterward in s_0, he simultaneous authenticates PG on successful CE12 and CE01 in the transition 3 from Table 5 using two request goals: request(B1,PG,b1_pg_ce01,1.C.B1.Id0.H(1.C.B1.Id0.Am0).H(1.Id0)) and request(B1,PG,b1_pg_ce12,1.B1.P.Id0.N1.H(1.B1.P.Id0.N1.Am1).H(1.Id0.N1)).

Similar, B1 simultaneous authenticates PG on successful CE12 and CE01 in the transition 10 from broker role in the case *Resolution 2* sub-protocol is applied. Also, B1 simultaneous authenticates PG on aborted CE12 and CE01 in the transition 7 in the case *Resolution 1* sub-protocol is applied. In the same manner, B1 simultaneous authenticates PG on aborted CE12 (when CE12 was previously successful issued) and aborted CE01 in the transitions 5 and 12 in the case resolution sub-protocols are applied.

In conclusion, we model fairness in *CTP* by strong authentication requirements using *witness* and *request* goal facts, combined with simultaneous strong authentication performed by B1 regarding the payment evidences.

4.5 Verification Results

We use SPAN to perform verification of *CTP* by CL-AtSe. Cl-AtSe back-end applies constraint solving to find any protocol attack for a bounded number of protocol's sessions. This bound makes the search of attacks to be correct and complete. The verification is done using both options: typed and untyped model. In the *typed model* option, all variables and constants are typed, and this option is set by default. The *untyped model* option is used for detection of type-flaw attacks by ignoring all type information and considering all variables to be of generic type *message*.

In Fig. 3 is shown the output of Cl-AtSe verification on CTP specification using typed model option. The verification results prove that Cl-AtSe did not find any attack and all specified security requirements are ensured. Also, using untyped model option, Cl-AtSe verification does not find any attack.

```
SUMMARY
  SAFE

DETAILS
  BOUNDED_NUMBER_OF_SESSIONS
  TYPED_MODEL

PROTOCOL
  /home/span/span/testsuite/results/CTP.if

GOAL
  As Specified

BACKEND
  CL-AtSe

STATISTICS
|
  Analysed   : 181214918 states
  Reachable  : 2414377 states
  Translation: 3.62 seconds
  Computation: 8701.23 seconds
```

Fig. 3. Cl-AtSe verification results.

The verification results demonstrate that *CTP* ensures the confidentiality of the card number CN0 between C and PG, and of the card number CN1 between B1 and PG.

Also, all strong authentication requirements for *CTP* specified in Sect. 4.4 are satisfied. The verification results prove that fairness in *CTP* is achieved because P strong authenticates PG on CE12, B1 strong authenticates PG on CE12 and CE01, C strong authenticates PG on CE01, and also, both CE012 and CE01 are either successful or both aborted.

CTP ensures non-repudiation requirements by checking strong authentication requirements. As we can see in the verification results, C can not deny its involvement in *CTP* as initiator because PG strong authenticates C on PI0, and B1 can not deny its involvement in *CTP* as initiator because PG strong authenticates B1 on PI1. Also, B1 can not deny its involvement in *CTP* as receiver because PG strong authenticates B1 on Am0, and P can not deny its involvement in *CTP* as receiver because PG strong authenticates P on Am1.

5   Conclusions

In this paper, we formally prove the correctness of the chained transaction protocol using Cl-AtSe. This turned out to be a challenging task due to the complexity of specification that leads to a high number of states that were analyzed. Despite this, we formally proved that the chained transaction protocol ensures all required security properties.

References

1. AVISPA team: AVISPA v1.1 user manual. Version: 1.1 (2006). http://www.avispa-project. org/
2. AVISPA team: HLPSL tutorial: a beginner's guide to modelling and analysing internet security protocols. Version: 1.1 (2006). http://www.avispa-project.org/
3. Bîrjoveanu, C.V., Bîrjoveanu, M.: An optimistic fair exchange e-Commerce protocol for complex transactions. In: 15th International Joint Conference on e-Business and Telecommunications, ICETE 2018 - vol. 2. SECRYPT, pp. 277–288. SCITEPRESS (2018). https://doi.org/10.5220/0006853502770288
4. Bîrjoveanu, C.V., Bîrjoveanu, M.: Fair exchange E-commerce protocol for multi-chained complex transactions. In: 17th International Joint Conference on e-Business and Telecommunications. vol. 2. ICE-B, pp. 49–60. SCITEPRESS (2020). https://doi.org/10.5220/0009824000490060
5. Bîrjoveanu, C.V., Bîrjoveanu, M.: HLPSL specification of chained transaction protocol. https://profs.info.uaic.ro/~cbirjoveanu/CTP.pdf (2021)
6. Chevalier, Y., et al.: A high level protocol specification language for industrial security-sensitive protocols. In: Workshop on Specification and Automated Processing of Security Requirements, pp. 193–205. Austrian Computer Society (2004)
7. Dolev, D., Yao, A.: On the security of public-key protocols. IEEE Trans. Inf. Theory. **2**, 29 (1983)
8. Draper-Gil, G., Ferrer-Gomila, J.L., Hinarejos, M.F., Zhou, J.: An asynchronous optimistic protocol for atomic multi-two-party contract signing. Comput. J. **56**(10), 1258–1267 (2013)
9. Draper-Gil, G., Zhou, J., Ferrer-Gomila, J.L., Hinarejos, M.F.: An optimistic fair exchange protocol with active intermediaries. Int. J. Inf. Secur. **12**, 299–318 (2013). https://doi.org/10.1007/s10207-013-0194-9
10. Khill, I., Kim, J., Han, I., Ryou, J.: Multi-party fair exchange protocol using ring architecture model. Comput. Secur. **20**(5), 422–439 (2001)
11. Liu, Y.: An optimistic fair protocol for aggregate exchange. In: 2nd International Conference on Future Information Technology and Management Engineering. IEEE (2009). https://doi.org/10.1109/FITME.2009.145
12. Onieva, J.A., Zhou, J., Lopez, J.: Agent-mediated non-repudiation protocols. Electr. Commerce Res. Appl. **3**(2), 152–162 (2004)
13. SPAN, a security protocol animator for AVISPA, http://people.irisa.fr/Thomas.Genet/span/. Accessed 9 Oct 2021
14. Turuani, M.: The CL-Atse protocol analyser. In: 17th International Conference on Rewriting Techniques and Applications, LNCS, vol. 4098, pp. 277–286, Springer (2006). https://doi.org/10.1007/11805618_21
15. Vigano, L.: Automated security protocol analysis with the AVISPA tool. Electr. Notes Theor. Comput. Sci. **155**, 61–86 (2006). https://doi.org/10.1016/j.entcs.2005.11.052
16. Zhang, N., Shi, Q., Merabti, M.: A unified approach to a fair document exchange system. J. Syst. Softw. **72**(1), 83–96 (2004). https://doi.org/10.1016/S0164-1212(03)00088-8
17. Zhou, J., Onieva, J.A., Lopez, J.: Optimised multi-party certified email protocols. Inf. Manage. Comput. Secur. J. **13**(5), 350–366 (2005). https://doi.org/10.1108/09685220510627250

Overall Feasibility of RF Energy Harvesting for IoT

Florian Grante$^{(\boxtimes)}$, Ghalid Abib$^{(\boxtimes)}$, Muriel Muller$^{(\boxtimes)}$, and Nel Samama$^{(\boxtimes)}$

Département Electronique et Physique (EPh) - Télécom SudParis,
Institut Polytechnique de Paris, 19, rue Marguerite Perey, 91120 Palaiseau, France
{florian.grante,ghalid.abib,muriel.muller,
nel.samama}@telecom-sudparis.eu

Abstract. This paper presents a global vision of the study of an IoT sensor node entirely powered by ambient Radio Frequency (RF) waves in the WiFi 2.45 GHz ISM band. The node includes a temperature sensor and an RF microcontroller to send the measurements through Bluetooth Low Energy signal. After characterizing the energy consumption of the sensor node and measuring the available WiFi surrounding power, we were able to size the RF to DC converter and the associated optimal capacitor capable of storing the converted WiFi energy necessary to supply the node. The result was a study of the energetically viable nature of such a system. According to the node's supply voltage, varying from 1.8 V to 3.3 V, it is possible to perform a measurement and a transmission of the sensor data several times a day from a WiFi signal as low as −20 dBm.

Keywords: Energy harvesting · RF electromagnetic energy · WiFi · Autonomous sensor · Schottky diode · RF/DC rectifier · Boost · Energy budget analysis

1 Introduction

Nowadays, the Smart City is no longer a concept. A connected, agile and innovative city, relies on information and digital technologies to meet the challenge of improving the quality of life for citizens, and to develop the economic and tourist appeal of communities and businesses.

One of the biggest objectives of the advent of Smart Cities is to manage and optimize our energy consumption and to enable an increase in the share of renewable energy. For example, this involves measuring and optimizing road and rail flows, managing the distribution of power on the electrical network, but also measuring the temperature of a company's offices, since heating is one of the main pillars of our energy consumption.

However, billions of connected objects are needed worldwide to sufficiently monitor the various infrastructures. This raises the question of how we power these connected objects. For the moment, a large part of the connected objects already in the market are powered by batteries, which raises the issue of autonomy, the maintenance required for recharging and the cost in resources represented by batteries considered as a consumable. This need for energy and resources pushes us to propose alternative power solutions, leading to a green internet of things (IoT).

M. S. Obaidat and J. Ben-Othman (Eds.): ICETE 2020, CCIS 1484, pp. 215–227, 2021.
https://doi.org/10.1007/978-3-030-90428-9_10

It is on this basis that solutions are developed under the term Energy Harvesting. Here we find common energy recovery processes such as photovoltaics [11], which is however differentiated by the possibility of installing organic solar panels, which are therefore, by essence, free of rare earths. Other sources are the subject of research work such as thermal [3], mechanical [2] or electromagnetic energy [4].

During the last 10 years, Radio Frequency (RF) energy harvesting state of the art has evolved from a converter system using TV signals [9], which was commonly used and powerful in the early 2010's, to more research in the Industrial, Scientific and Medical (ISM) 2.45 GHz and GSM 900/1800 bands [6] because of the emergence of WiFi, 3G, 4G and 5G systems.

To our knowledge, few works take into account the sizing of the harvester system for a dedicated application or a sensor node according to its energy requirements. A well-optimized "wake-up" principle allows the sensor to be powered for a short period to measure and send data, then turned off to allow the converter to charge a capacitor for energy storage. But we would like to go further and propose a new approach in the study of RF/DC (Direct Current) converters by concretely characterizing the energy requirement of an application such as powering an IoT sensor node and thus discuss the feasibility of such a system.

The purpose of this paper is to study the global feasibility of a system capable of measuring and transmitting sensor data and powered by ambient WiFi electromagnetic waves in the 2.45 GHz ISM band. This paper is an extended version of "Autonomous sensor node powered over WiFi: A use case study", carried out within the framework of the WINSYS 2020 conference [5]. It aims to provide details and measurements on some parts of the complete system such as the study of the energy consumption of a platform and then the choice of the associated storage capacitor. We have also added measurements of the RF/DC converter which was carried out following a scheme similar to the one presented in simulation in the conference paper.

We will therefore study WiFi energy harvesting in the ISM band on a system represented in Fig. 1 and detailed it further. We will first see in Sect. 2 the different constraints that will allow us to size our RF/DC converter, i.e. the RF ambient power that we can expect to receive and the amount of energy required for the proper functioning of our application. The study of the antenna is not considered in this work, we can refer to studies such as [7,8] or [10]. Then, we will characterize the energy storage capacitor in Sect. 3. Sect. 4 describes the simulation and the realization of the RF/DC converter which will justify the need for a voltage boost. Finally, in Sect. 5 we will determine the overall feasibility of the system by estimating the time between two data transmissions by incorporating the conclusions of the previous sections.

2 Constraints

Before taking an in-depth look at our RF/DC converter on which we will base our work, we need to put some context by defining the different requirements for the proper functioning of an IoT sensor node and an inventory of our electromagnetic environment in the 2.45 GHz ISM band.

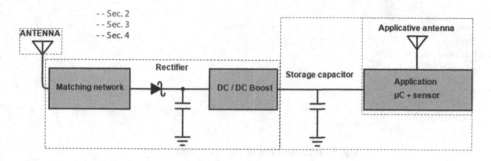

Fig. 1. Global schematic of the system.

2.1 Ambient Energy

In France, the legislation limits the transmission power on all channels in the 2.45 GHz ISM band to 100 mW (20 dBm) [1]. We want to define here the ambient energy that we can hope to harvest, i.e. the amount of energy that passes through the antenna. We have done a measurement campaign on a WiFi router in a normal use in order to get an idea of the ambient RF powers that can be expected to be received.

The measurements were performed using the Aaronia Spectran HF-2025E spectrum analyzer with the OmniLOG30800 antenna in two different situations. The analyzer scanned all the WiFi channels and Fig. 2 shows the maximum power measured at each scan over a period of 7 h for situation 1 and over 8 h for situation 2.

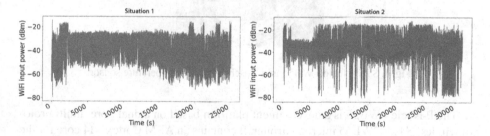

Fig. 2. Received WiFi power.

We notice for both situations a very heterogeneous results. Our power in reception pivot being −30 dBm (1 μW), a value below which we consider the energy received to be negligible, nearly 25% of the measurements show a power greater than or equal to −30 dBm for both situations. By time integration, we can plot the energy accumulation as a function of time at reception as displayed by Fig. 3.

So, our spectrum analyzer received respectively almost 25 mJ in 7 h and over 60 mJ in 8 h in the ISM band, for situation 1 and 2. However, this energy is the one received by the antenna before conversion and is therefore not usable as it is by the connected object's microcontroller. We will see Sect. 5 the study of the amount of converted energy.

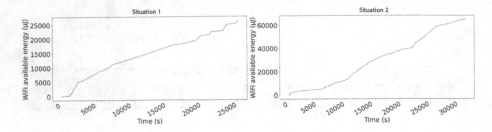

Fig. 3. Accumulation of received WiFi energy.

2.2 Energy Consumption

The other constraint of our platform is its consumption. We must indeed characterize the energy requirement of our application in order to size the energy harvesting unit afterwards. While we had based our study on the ON Semiconductor RSL10-Solarsens platform using one of their white paper for the conference work [5], we decided for practical reasons to perform measurements on an ST Microelectronics P-Nucleo-WB55 platform presented on Fig. 4.

Fig. 4. ST P-Nucleo-WB55 and Bosch BME280 temperature sensor.

The P-Nucleo-WB55 is a development platform based on a dual-core, multi proto-col wireless STM32WB55 microcontroller. It contains an ARM Cortex-M4 core for the application as well as a Cortex M0+ managing the radio layer which differs according to the RF protocol used like Bluetooth Low Energy (BLE), Thread and Zigbee. For the rest of the study, we will use BLE. As the P-Nucleo-WB55 platform does not have an embedded temperature sensor, we added it through a development board, making sure it was the same reference as the one used by ON Semiconductor, i.e. the BME280 from Bosch Sensortec.

The ST microcontroller's datasheet indicates an operating voltage range between 1.71 V and 3.6 V. The same applies to the sensor. The ON Semiconductor platform was based on an operating voltage of 2.63 V, so it is possible to use the new platform without having to modify our system from a voltage point of view.

Now, what about the energy required for its proper functioning? To determine the energy consumption of the ST Microelectronics platform, we have developed an application that:

1. Starts and initializes peripherals (Boot)
2. Measures the temperature (Measurement)
3. Sends the measured value via BLE (Transmission)

This power consumption is determined using the measurement board proposed by ST Microelectronics (X-Nucleo-LPM01A). It allows the power consumption of a device to be determined by measuring current variations. The result is a current versus time curve shown in Fig. 5. The measurement board allows, in order to ensure the most accurate current measurement possible, to connect platforms like ours in such a way that only the microcontroller's consumption is taken into account. Indeed, the debugger and programmer interface between the microncontroller and a PC is not powered and therefore, does not influence the consumption. The measurement board also allows to choose the supply voltage between 1.8 V and 3.3 V. We then have access to the associated energy consumption, knowing the voltage and the current consumed as a function of time, thanks to the software.

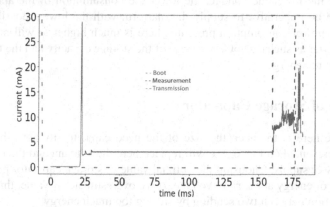

Fig. 5. Evolution of application current consumption on the ST Microelectronics platform.

We can distinguish three phases on the curve:

1. A first grouping of peaks and a 3 mA plateau, associated with the start-up and initialization of the platform.
2. A second phase which corresponds to the execution of the application, which consists in the communication between the sensor and the microcontroller and the preparation to send this measurement.
3. A third phase which corresponds to the sending of the temperature measurement with BLE.

By taking each part of the curve independently on our software, we can determine the energy consumption of each of these phases for a voltage of 3.3 V which are respectively 1436, 450 and 174 µJ.

We obtain a total consumption of 2060 µJ. This difference from ON Semiconductor's platform, which was 200 µJ and can be explained by the fact that ST Microelectronics platform is not optimized to reduce power consumption at software level. However, we can see that most of the power consumption is done during the boot, which gives us a clue on where the work needs to be done on the software part. The other difference with ON Semiconductor's platform is the supply voltage. In the case of the curve shown Fig. 5, we have a voltage of 3.3 V. Table 1 shows the start, measurement and transmission energy consumption for a supply voltage of 3.3 V and 1.8 V.

Table 1. Consumption of the different phases of the application according to the supply voltage.

Supply voltage (V)	3.3	1.8
Boot (μJ)	1436	430
Measurement (μJ)	450	210
Transmission (μJ)	174	110
Total (μJ)	2060	750

So we notice a factor close to 3 between the consumption at 3.3 V and 1.8 V. So obviously the lower the voltage, the lower the consumption of the application. It will therefore be imperative to supply the platform with the lowest possible voltage. Although the power consumption presented here is much higher, it will not affect the RF/DC converter as such except for the size of the storage capacity and the time it takes to accumulate the energy.

3   Choice of Storage Capacitor

The objective here is to check the size of the need capacitor to store the harvested energy as represented on Fig. 6. We will replace here the antenna and the rectifier by a stabilized power supply. Choosing the optimal value of storage capacitor providing the right amount of energy at the right voltage. If we overestimate its value, this will cause a longer duration between two sending by storing too much energy.

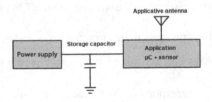

Fig. 6. Capacitor to store the harvested RF energy.

While we have seen different possible consumptions of the platform according to the supply voltage in Sect. 2.2, we can determine the corresponding needed storage capacitor using the Equ. 1 where C is the capacitance, U the capacitor voltage and E_u the capacitor energy associated to the voltage U.

$$E_U = \frac{1}{2}.C.U^2 \qquad (1)$$

However, we also noticed that the minimum operating voltage of the platform was 1.8 V. We must therefore ensure that the voltage at the capacitor is always higher than 1.8 V when it discharges. If we use a supply voltage of 3.3 V, we have to be sure that between 3.3 V and 1.8 V, the capacitor will provide at least an energy (noted $E_{App_{3.3V}}$) of 2060 µJ during the discharge. We can then use the Equ. 2 to determine the corresponding C.

$$E_{App_{3.3V}} = 2060\,\mu J = E_{3.3V} - E_{1.8V} \qquad (2)$$

So:

$$C = \frac{2.E_{App_{3.3V}}}{3.3^2 - 1.8^2} = 534\,\mu F \qquad (3)$$

We thus obtain a capacitor value of 534 µF for a starting supply voltage of 3.3 V. We can see different capacitor values depending on the supply voltage on Table 2.

Table 2. Optimized capacitor value for different supply voltages and associated total energy.

Voltage (V)	App consumption (µJ)	C (µF)	Total storage capacity (µJ)
3.3	2060	534	2905
3	1761	611	2752
2.7	1431	707	2576
2.4	1265	1004	2891
2.1	970	1658	3656
2.0	845	3485	6491

The lower the voltage, the less energy the application consumes. However, the lower the voltage, the higher the value of the capacitor must be in order to contain the right amount of energy over a reduced voltage range. This will therefore have a consequence on the amount of energy unusable by our application but which is necessary during the first charge to reach 1.8 V. But if we plot the total energy curve needed to charge the capacitor to the right supply voltage, we can see that a minimum can be obtained for 2.7 V as shown in Fig. 7 and Table 2.

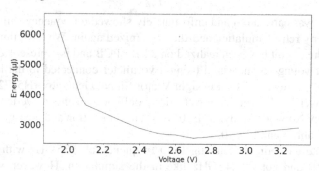

Fig. 7. Energy needed in the storage capacitor to reach the associated voltage.

A compromise must then be made between the consumption of the application, i.e. the amount of energy to be stored between the operating voltage and 1.8 V, and the amount of energy needed to reach 1.8 V during the first charge. Let's assume that we will now use an operating voltage of 2.7 V for our platform which seems to be the best compromise in the light of Fig. 7. So the application will need an energy (E) equal to 1431 µJ to be powered properly.

4 Rectifier

In order to harvest the WiFi energy, we will use the simplest RF/DC converter (known as rectifier) which is a basic crest detector, based on a single Skyworks SMS7630 Schottky diode as presented on Fig. 8.

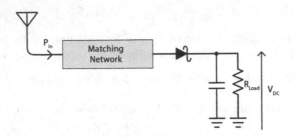

Fig. 8. RF/DC converter.

Matching network includes transmission lines and inductors and are determined thanks to simulations performed with Keysight Advanced Design System software, as explicited in the conference paper [5]. The impedance matching is performed for maximum power transfer by minimizing signal reflection between the antenna and the converter and also harmonics created by the Schottky diode due to its non linearities.

We will also optimize the circuit parameters to maximize the DC output voltage for our load which here is a $1000\,\Omega$ resistor. Since the WiFi input power (P_{in}) will be converted into DC power (P_{DC}), we can then look at the evolution of the efficiency (η) (Eq. 4).

$$\eta = \frac{P_{DC}}{P_{in}} \tag{4}$$

The circuit was carried out and unfortunately showed a frequency shift. This offset was corrected by retro simulation and then optimized again. We have thus obtained a new design. The circuit has been realized on a FR4 PCB and is represented by Fig. 9.

The output voltage is measured using a voltmeter connected to the load resistor. The RF signal is generated by a Keysight Vector Signal Generator (N5172B) allowing to vary the power levels. The input reflection coefficient of the converter is measured using a Keysight Network Analyzer (E5071C). The simulation and measurement results are presented Table 3 and Fig. 10.

We can note an optimal matching for a frequency of 2.35 GHz with an $|S(1,1)|$ around -20 dB and not at 2.45GHz like in the simulation. However, we still have a coefficient of around -10 dB for 2.45 GHz. Given the bandwidth of WiFi which ranges from 2.4 GHz to 2.5 GHz, it would have been preferable to obtain a similar curve centered on 2.45 GHz but our current circuit still allows us to cover a large part of the WiFi band with results close to the simulation that suits us as it stands. In view of the measured voltage levels obtained at the output of the RF/DC converter, the use of a DC boost is mandatory to have the necessary 2.7 V. We chose a boost (LTC3108) which allows us to have a boost from a 20 mV input voltage.

Now that we have an idea on how the different blocks that make up our system work, whether it is the conversion of WiFi signals to DC voltage, the energy consumption of our application or the choice of storage element, we can assess the overall feasibility of the system to verify its energy viability.

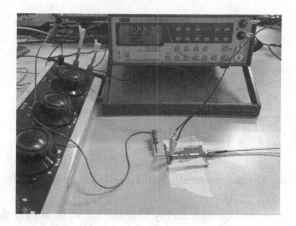

Fig. 9. RF/DC converter measuring bench.

Table 3. Simulated and measured DC output voltage V_{out} and efficiency η for different P_{in}.

P_{in} (dBm)	$V_{out_{Sim}}$ (mV)	out_{Meas} (mV)	η_{Sim} (%)	η_{Meas} (%)
−30	1.4	1.2	0.2	0.17
−25	4.5	3.8	0.6	0.51
−20	14.8	12.1	2.2	1.8
−18	23.4	19.7	3.4	2.7
−15	44.3	36.6	6.2	5.1
−10	112.8	94.2	12.7	10.6
−5	250.4	213.7	19.8	16.9
0	510.1	444	26	22.6

5 Overall System Feasibility

For this last part, we will assume that we can connect our RF/DC converter to the boost without any constraint or loss related to this connection. How often can we expect to measure and send our data, i.e. store the 1431 µJ needed to operate the sensor node with an operating voltage of 2.7 V? The objective here is to check if our system is energetically viable and if not, where the system should have better performance to minimize the time between two sendings.

5.1 Theoretical Model

Firstly, we will start with an ideal converter with 100% efficiency ($\eta = 1$), what would be the duty cycle (T), i.e. how long would it take the converter to store the required energy (E) 1431 µJ in the capacitor in order to power the sensor node. We will consider

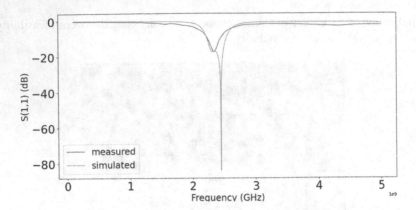

Fig. 10. Simulated and measured reflection coefficient for different frequency.

here that we already stored enough energy to reach 1.8 V. To answer this, we will use the Eq. 5

$$T = \frac{E}{P_{DC}} = \frac{E}{\eta . P_{in}} \tag{5}$$

Table 4 presents the duty cycle T for different P_{in}. So, for P_{in} equal to -30 dBm, T will be equal to 1431 s. Consequently, we won't manage to get better than 1431 s (23 min and 51 s) between two transmissions with a permanent harvested RF power of -30 dBm.

Table 4. Duty cycle (T) for different P_{in} with an ideal converter.

P_{in} (dBm)	T (s)
-30	1431
-20	143.1
-10	14.31
0	1.431

When considering our real converter, whose efficiency is given in Table 3, the estimated duty cycle (T) is presented in Table 5.

Table 5. Duty cycle (T) for different P_{in} with a real converter.

P_{in} (dBm)	η (%)	T (s)
-30	0.17	841 765 (over 9 days)
-20	1.8	7950 (2 h 13 min)
-10	10.6	135
0	22.6	6.3

We therefore notice a drastic drop in performance with a system that is no more sustainable at −30 dBm with more than 9 days between two sending. This is mainly due to the converter efficiency of 0.17%.

To get to the end of our approach, we also have to take into account the DC boost efficiency, the LTC3108. The component datasheet specifies an efficiency (η') around 40%. Then, let us compute the full efficiency ($\eta.\eta'$) to estimate the duty cycle (T) of our global system in Table 6.

Table 6. Duty cycle (T) when taking into account the boost efficiency.

P_{in} (dBm)	$\eta.\eta'$ (%)	T (s)
−30	0.07	2 104 412 (over 24 days)
−20	0.72	19 875 (5 h 31 min)
−10	4.24	337
0	9.04	16

For a constant RF input power of −20 dBm, the result indicates a duty cycle of 19875 s (around 5 h and 31 min) between two transmissions when using our RF converter associated to the DC boost. So next step will be to consider a non-constant harvested RF power to have a closer approach for real conditions use case.

5.2 Application of the Model

In order to determine the obtained amount of DC energy harvested from a real WiFi signal, like one displayed on Fig. 2, we have first to model the efficiency $\eta = F(P_{in})$ of our converter. We can apply a polynomial fitting on the data given in Table 3 and then, use the obtained model to determine the converter efficiency associated to the measured WiFi input powers. The available DC energy could be obtained after time integration of P_{DC}, determined using Eq. 4 and displayed on Fig. 11 for both situations.

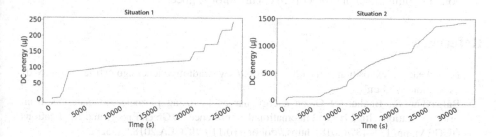

Fig. 11. Amount of DC energy available to power the sensor node.

We end up with 244 μJ for situation 1 and 1423 μJ for situation 2. While it is not possible to transmit the data in situation 1, we can expect a transmission with a 2.7 V operating voltage considering that we start the system with the capacitor charged at $t = 0s$ in situation 2. It results to 1 transmission in 8 h in situation 2. We can almost reach 2 transmissions if we supply with 2 V by supposing the capacitor charged at $t = 0s$. For comparison purpose, situation 2 would result in at least 7 transmissions in 8 h with the ON Semiconductor platform presented in the conference paper [5], so one transmission every 70 min in average.

6   Conclusion

The objective of this study was to carry out a work of reflection, design and measurement of a sensor node communicating via BLE and exclusively powered by ambient radio waves in the 2.45 GHz ISM band. For that, a classical crest detector base on a Schottky diode is choosen as a RF/DC converter. Based on the complete diagram of our system, we were able to detail each of the parts independently of the others before trying to group them all together to verify the overall functioning.

We therefore started studied the various constraints that would be imposed on our RF/DC converter, starting with the measurement of the available and recoverable ambient energy in the 2.45 GHz ISM band. Then we measured the energy requirements of the ST Microelectronics platform, which allowed us to study the sizing of the storage capacity. It leads to a compromise between the time required during its first charge and the time between two charges allowing transmission. It differs according to the supply voltage and the platform's voltage operating range.

We then had all the data necessary to develop and realize our RF/DC converter. However, the performances of our converter led us to revise upwards the minimum power level to be received in order to hope to store enough energy from -30 dBm to -20 dBm. Since the majority of the measured incident power presented Sect. 2.2 are between this two values, the amount of stored energy is lower than expected. But the last part showed us that we can still get ST Microelectronics platform up and running with one transmission in 8 h in one of the two ambient WiFi power measurement situations. While the ON Semiconductor's platform would give us better performance because it consumes less power, ST Microelectronics microcontroller will allow us to transmit with other communication protocols like Thread or Zigbee.

References

1. Les niveaux d'exposition WiFi (2018). http://www.radiofrequences.gouv.fr/les-niveaux-d-exposition-a73.html
2. Balguvhar, S., Bhalla, S.: Green energy harvesting using piezoelectric materials from bridge vibrations. In: 2018 2nd International Conference on Green Energy and Applications (ICGEA), pp. 134–137 (2018). https://doi.org/10.1109/ICGEA.2018.8356282
3. Correa-Betanzo, C., Lopez-Perez, C., Rodriguez, A., Lopez-Nuñez, A.: Isolated DC-DC converter for thermoelectric energy harvesting based on a piezoelectric transformer. In: 2019 IEEE Applied Power Electronics Conference and Exposition (APEC), pp. 3443–3447 (2019). https://doi.org/10.1109/APEC.2019.8721959

4. Franciscatto, B.R., Freitas, V., Duchamp, J.M., Defay, C., Vuong, T.P.: High-efficiency rectifier circuit at 2.45 GHz for low-input-power RF energy harvesting. In: 2013 European Microwave Conference, pp. 507–510, October 2013. https://doi.org/10.23919/EuMC.2013.6686703
5. Grante, F., Abib, G., Muller, M., Samama, N.: Autonomous sensor node powered over WiFi: a use case study. In: Proceedings of the 17th International Joint Conference on e-Business and Telecommunications - Volume 1: WINSYS, pp. 127–132. INSTICC, SciTePress (2020). https://doi.org/10.5220/0009804101270132
6. Ho, D.K., Kharrat, I., Ngo, V.D., Vuong, T.P., Nguyen, Q.C., Le, M.T.: Dual-band rectenna for ambient RF energy harvesting at GSM 900 MHz and 1800 MHz. In: 2016 IEEE International Conference on Sustainable Energy Technologies (ICSET), pp. 306–310, November 2016. https://doi.org/10.1109/ICSET.2016.7811800
7. Krakauskas, M., Sabaawi, A.M., Tsimenidis, C.C.: Suspended patch microstrip antenna with cut rectangular slots for RF energy harvesting. In: 2014 Loughborough Antennas and Propagation Conference (LAPC), pp. 304–307. https://doi.org/10.1109/LAPC.2014.6996382
8. Kurvey, M., Kunte, A.: Design and optimization of stepped rectangular antenna for RF energy harvesting. In: 2018 International Conference on Communication information and Computing Technology (ICCICT), pp. 1–4. https://doi.org/10.1109/ICCICT.2018.8325885
9. Parks, A.N., Sample, A.P., Zhao, Y., Smith, J.R.: A wireless sensing platform utilizing ambient RF energy. In: 2013 IEEE Topical Conference on Biomedical Wireless Technologies, Networks, and Sensing Systems, pp. 154–156, January 2013. https://doi.org/10.1109/BioWireleSS.2013.6613706
10. Shaker, M.F., Ghali, H.A., Elsheakh, D.M.N., Elsadek, H.A.E.: Multiband coplanar monopole antenna for energy harvesting. In: 2018 IEEE International Symposium on Radio-Frequency Integration Technology (RFIT), pp. 1–3. https://doi.org/10.1109/RFIT.2018.8524049
11. Wu, T., Arefin, M.S., Redouté, J., Yuce, M.R.: Flexible wearable sensor nodes with solar energy harvesting. In: 2017 39th Annual International Conference of the IEEE Engineering in Medicine and Biology Society (EMBC), pp. 3273–3276 (2017). https://doi.org/10.1109/EMBC.2017.8037555

Author Index

Printed in the United States
by Baker & Taylor Publisher Services